HISTORIC PHOTOS OF
INDIANAPOLIS

TEXT AND CAPTIONS BY GEORGE HANLIN

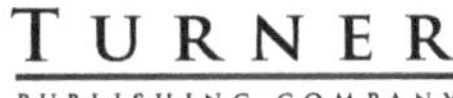
TURNER
PUBLISHING COMPANY

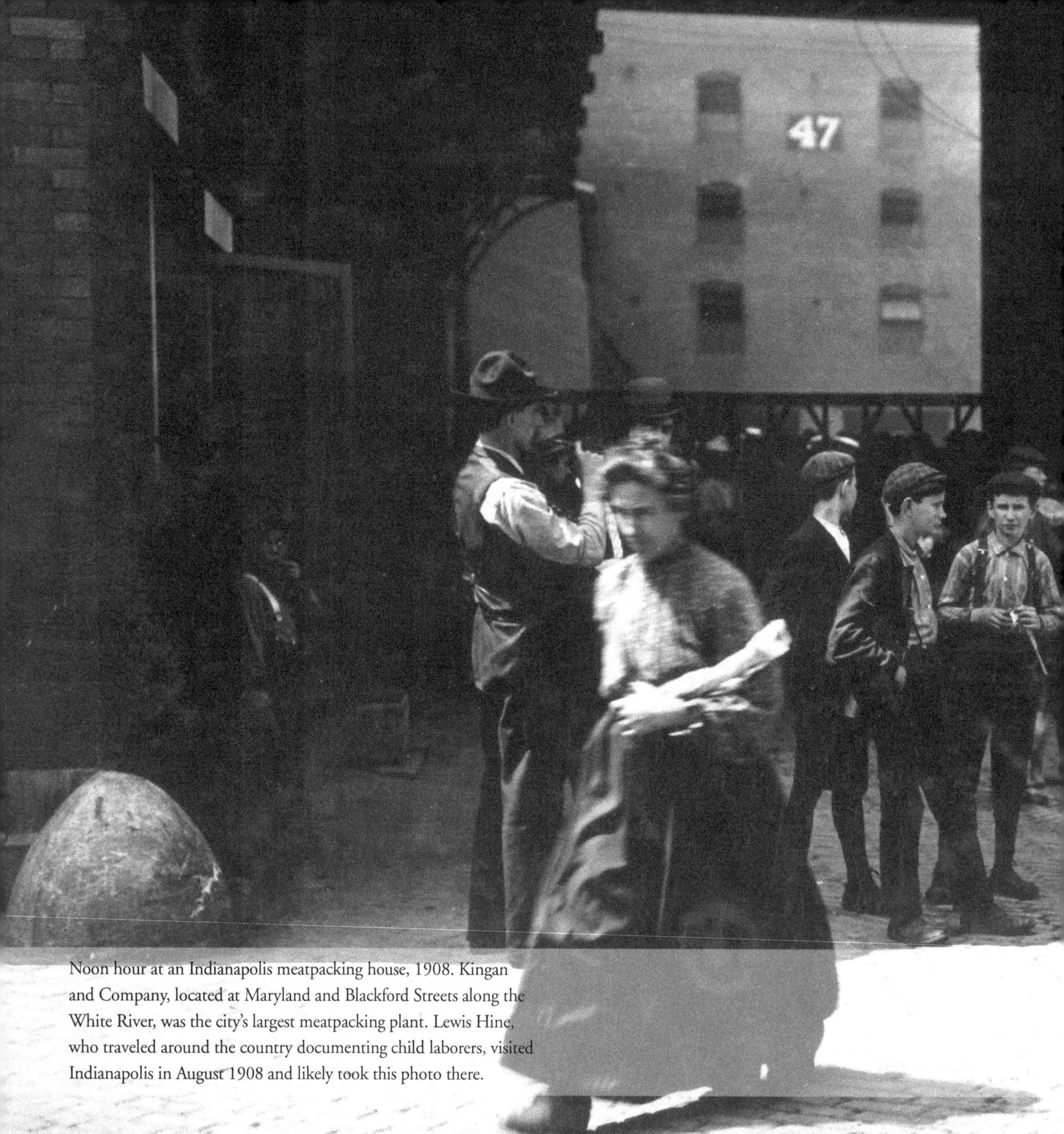

Noon hour at an Indianapolis meatpacking house, 1908. Kingan and Company, located at Maryland and Blackford Streets along the White River, was the city's largest meatpacking plant. Lewis Hine, who traveled around the country documenting child laborers, visited Indianapolis in August 1908 and likely took this photo there.

HISTORIC PHOTOS OF
INDIANAPOLIS

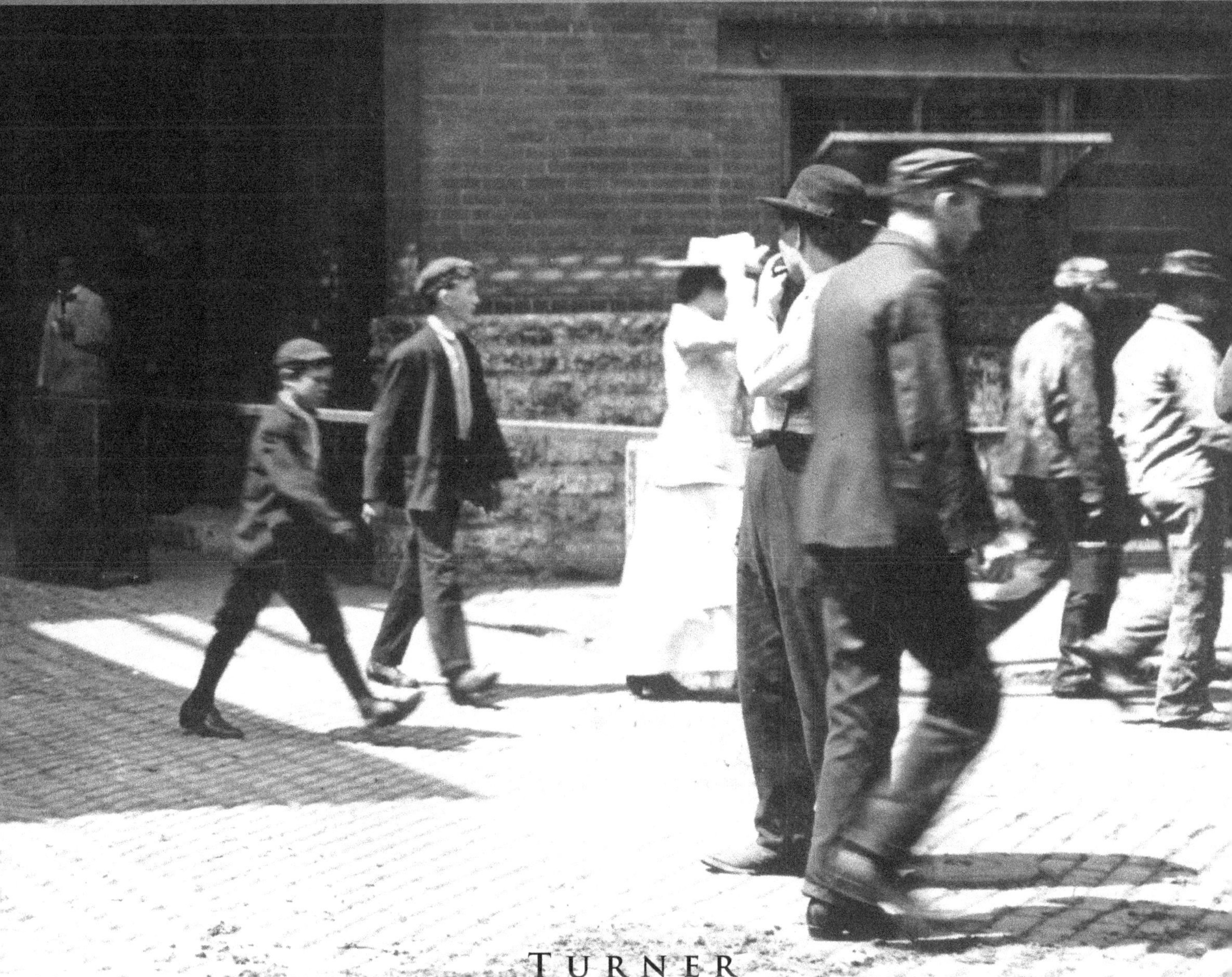

TURNER
PUBLISHING COMPANY

Turner Publishing Company
www.turnerpublishing.com

Library of Congress Control Number: 2006905290

ISBN: 1-59652-253-4

Printed in the United States of America

ISBN 978-1-68336-910-3 (hc)

Contents

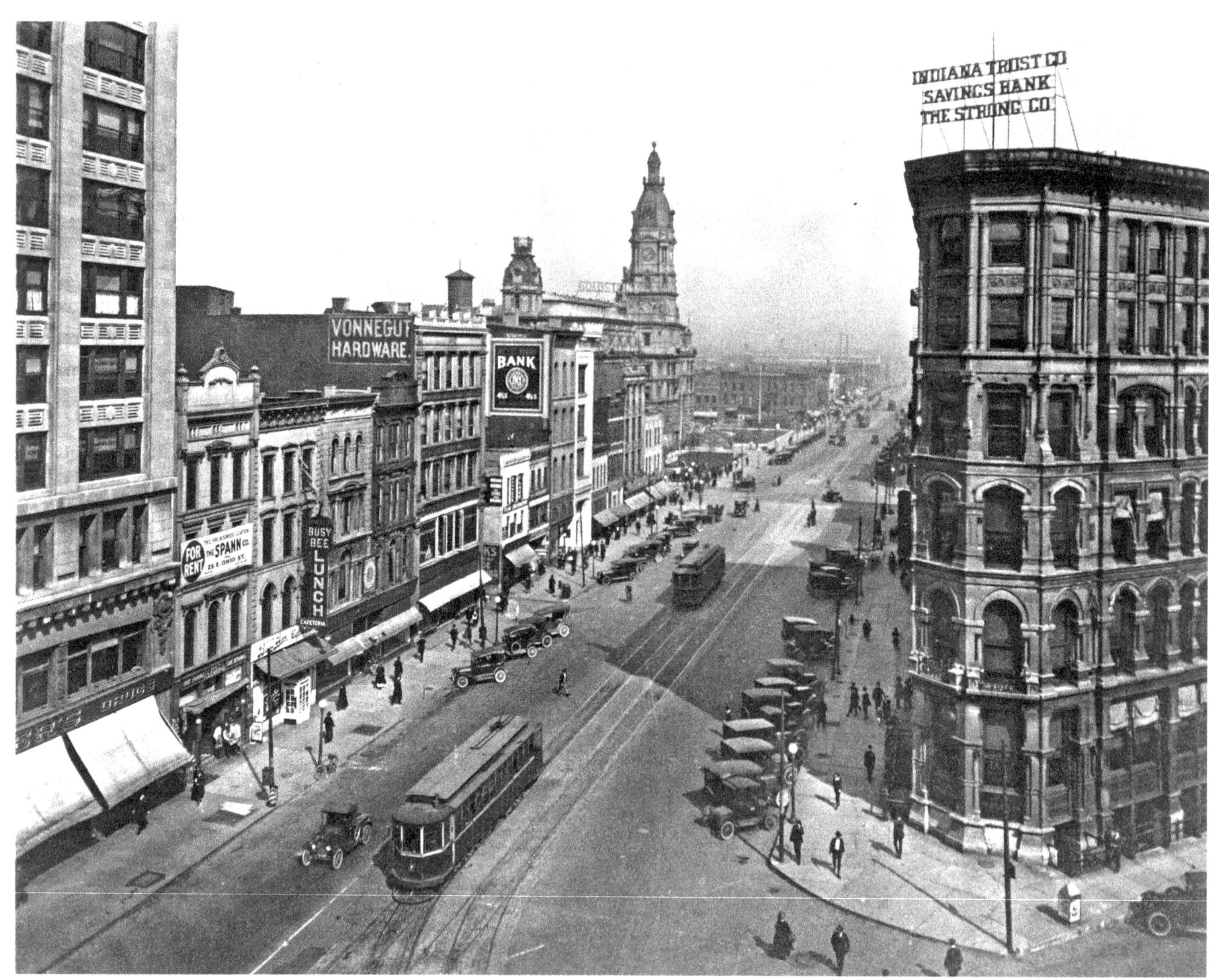

Washington Street, looking east from the intersection of Pennsylvania Street and Virginia Avenue, circa 1920

ACKNOWLEDGMENTS

This volume, Historic Photos of Indianapolis, is the result of the cooperation and efforts of several individuals, organizations, institutions, and corporations. It is with great thanks that we acknowledge the valuable contribution of the following for their generous support.

Buchanan Group
Indiana State Library
Indiana Historical Society
Indiana Power and Light
Library of Congress

We would also like to express our gratitude to Marcia Caudell, Joan Hostetler, Susan Sutton, and Elizabeth Wilkinson for providing research and assisting the author.

Preface

Indianapolis has thousands of historic photographs that reside in archives, both locally and nationally. This book began with the observation that, while those photographs are of great interest to many, often they are not easily accessible. During a time when Indianapolis is looking ahead and evaluating its future course, many people are asking, "How do we treat the past?" These decisions affect every aspect of the city–architecture, public spaces, commerce, tourism, recreation, and infrastructure—and these, in turn, affect the way that people live their lives. This book seeks to provide easy access to a valuable, objective look into the history of this great city.

The power of photographic images is that they are less subjective in their treatment of history. Although the photographer can make decisions regarding what subject matter to capture and some limited variation in its presentation, photographs do not provide the breadth of interpretation that text does. For this reason, they offer an original, untainted perspective that allows the viewer to interpret and observe.

This project represents countless hours of research and review. The researchers and author have reviewed thousands of photographs in numerous archives. We greatly appreciate the generous assistance of the archivists listed in the acknowledgments of this work, without whom this project could not have been completed.

The goal in publishing this work is to provide broader access to a set of extraordinary photographs that seek to inspire, provide perspective, and evoke insight that might assist people who are responsible for determining Indianapolis's future. In addition, the book seeks to preserve the past with adequate respect and reverence.

The photographs selected have been reproduced in dramatic black-and-white tones to provide depth to the images. With the exception of touching up imperfections caused by the damage of time, no other changes have been made. The focus and clarity of many images is limited to the technology and the ability of the photographer at the time they were taken.

The work is divided into eras. Beginning with some of the earliest known photographs of Indianapolis, the first section records photographs from the Civil War through the end of the nineteenth century. The second section spans the beginning of the twentieth century to the end of World War I. Section three moves from the 1920's to the 1930's. And finally, section four covers the 1940's to the 1960's.

In each of these sections we have made an effort to capture various aspects of life through our selection of photographs. People, commerce, transportation, infrastructure, religious institutions, educational institutions, and scenes of natural beauty have been included to provide a broad perspective.

We encourage readers to reflect as they traverse the streets of downtown, stroll along Monument Circle, or peer into the city's many shops and venues. Electric streetcars once traveled throughout the city, farms were in abundance, and many buildings, long since demolished, stood where newer buildings of the late twentieth century stand today. It is my hope that in utilizing this work, longtime residents will learn something new and that new residents will gain a perspective on where Indianapolis has been, so that each can contribute to its future.

Todd Bottorff, Publisher

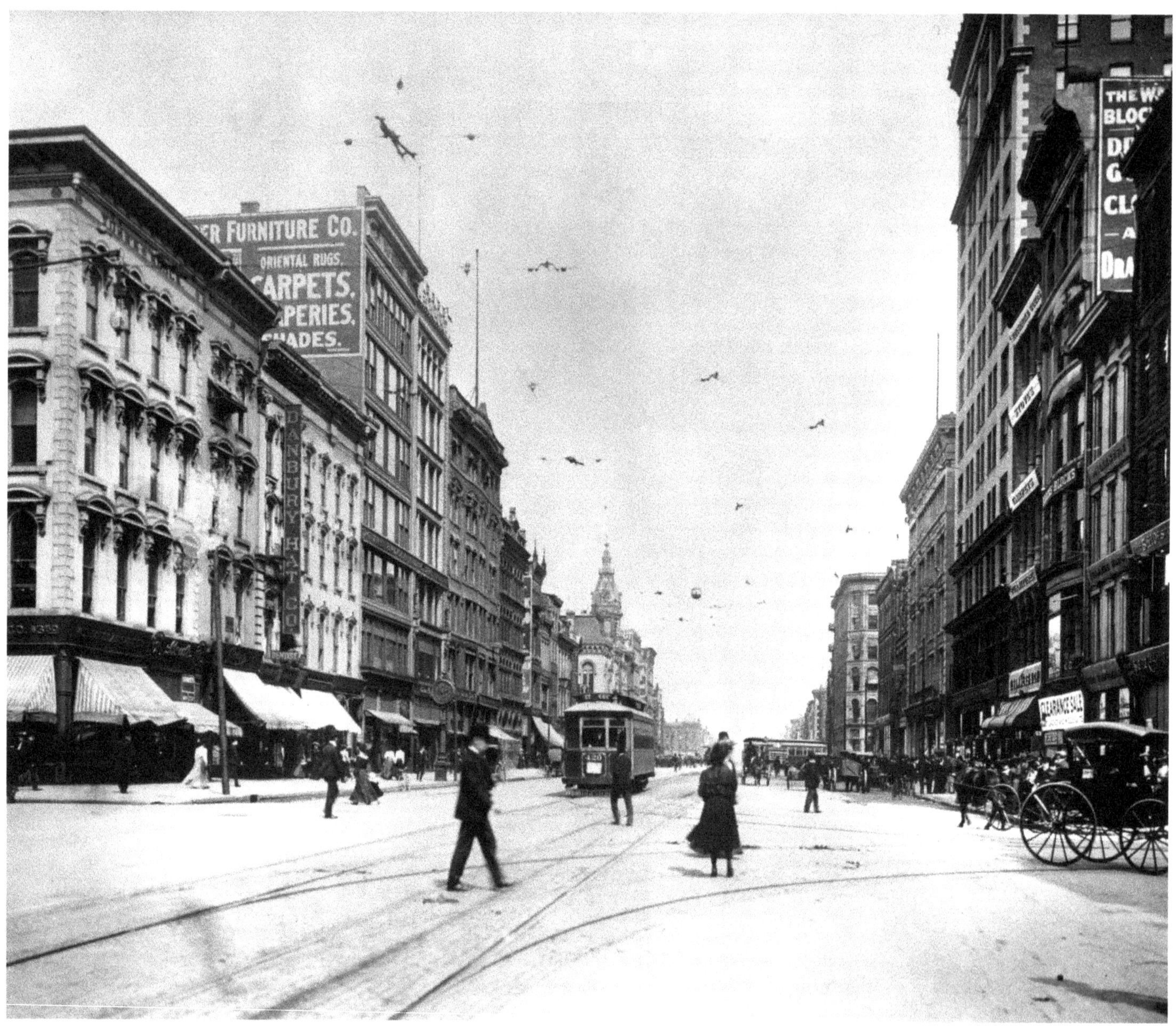

Looking east on Washington Street from Meridian Street, circa 1890's.
The tower of the Marion County courthouse is seen in the distance.

Out of the Wilderness
1860–1899

If the early residents of Indianapolis had hopes for their town—and no doubt they did—then surely those visions were modest. After all, the village was nothing but a forest in 1820 when a state commission selected the site as the new location for Indiana's capital. Certainly Alexander Ralston and Elias Fordham, the town's surveyors, weren't dreaming big. Although they created an attractive design for Indianapolis, establishing a circle in the center of town with avenues angling toward it, they kept it small, platting only a square mile.

For the first decades after its founding, Indianapolis met expectations, but within twenty years it was on solid ground. A boom came with the construction of the National Road through the town in the 1830's, but the biggest boom came after the first railroad arrived in 1847. Suddenly Indianapolis was no longer so isolated. Buyers and sellers had greater access to East Coast markets, and because of that the town grew dramatically in the next decade.

While the Civil War brought much heartache, it also afforded many opportunities. Soldiers flocked to Indianapolis, swelling its population and providing an economic influx. Manufacturers, the numbers of which had increased tremendously in the 1850's, supplied Union troops with munitions and provisions and benefited greatly from the war effort. As the population grew, it began spreading farther and farther beyond the Mile Square, putting Ralston and Fordham's limited vision to rest.

The next few decades saw the transition of Indianapolis from town to city. Industry continued to grow at breakneck speed, and with the tax revenues came many improvements in services and infrastructure. Streetcars, introduced in 1864, allowed residents to build homes farther from the city center, and beginning in 1889 many of these new homes had access to an incredible new convenience—electricity. Meanwhile, Indianapolis residents could point with pride to new civic structures, including an impressive county courthouse (opened in 1876) and a new statehouse and train station (both completed in 1888).

Amid all this growth, Hoosier culture began to flourish. Art and music schools opened, and a number of theaters began promoting the dramatic arts. The city's literary scene thrived, with authors such as James Whitcomb Riley and Lew Wallace gaining national attention. Indianapolis also influenced national politics during the 1880's and 1890's, most notably with the election of president Benjamin Harrison to the White House in 1888.

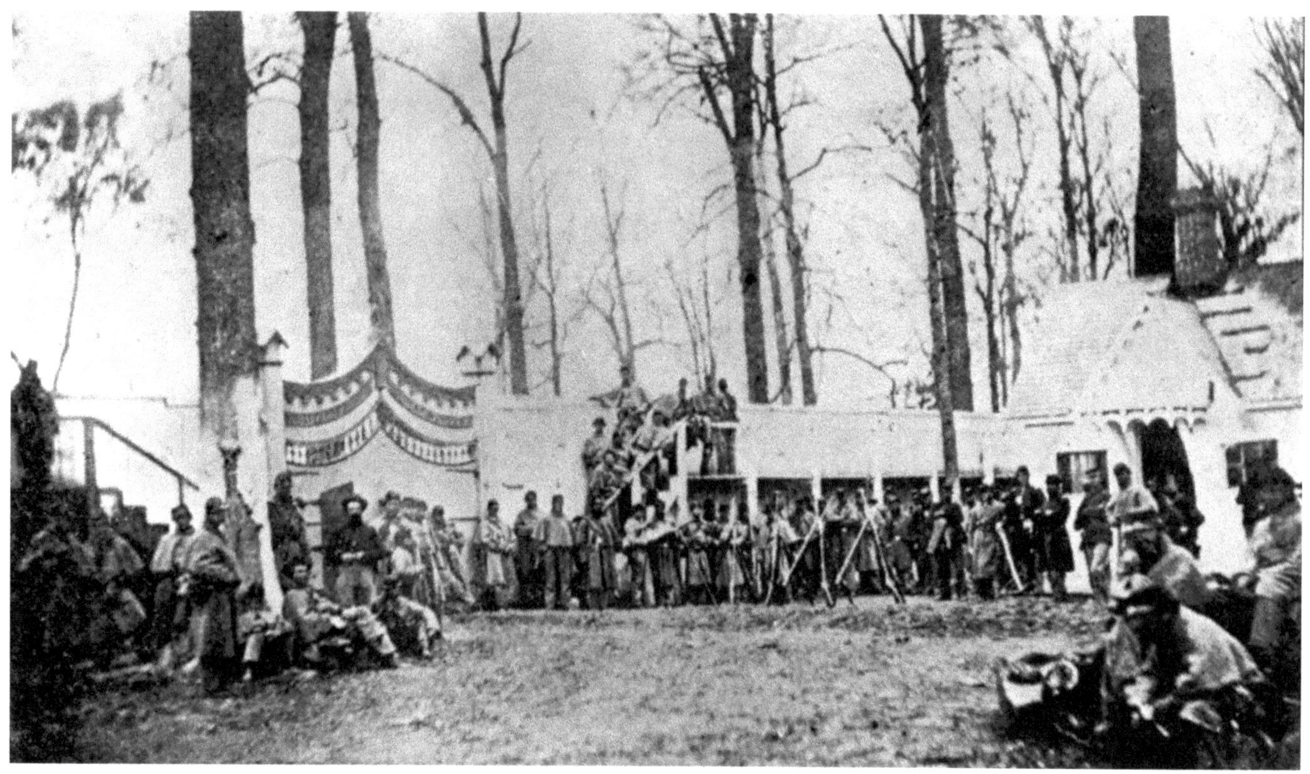

The entrance to Camp Morton during the Civil War. The camp opened in 1861 at the new state fairgrounds on the north side of Indianapolis, roughly bounded today by Nineteenth, Twenty-second, Delaware, and Talbott Streets. It first served exclusively as a training facility for recruits, but by late winter 1862 it began housing Confederate prisoners. According to one city history, as many as 15,000 prisoners were interned at the camp during the course of the war.

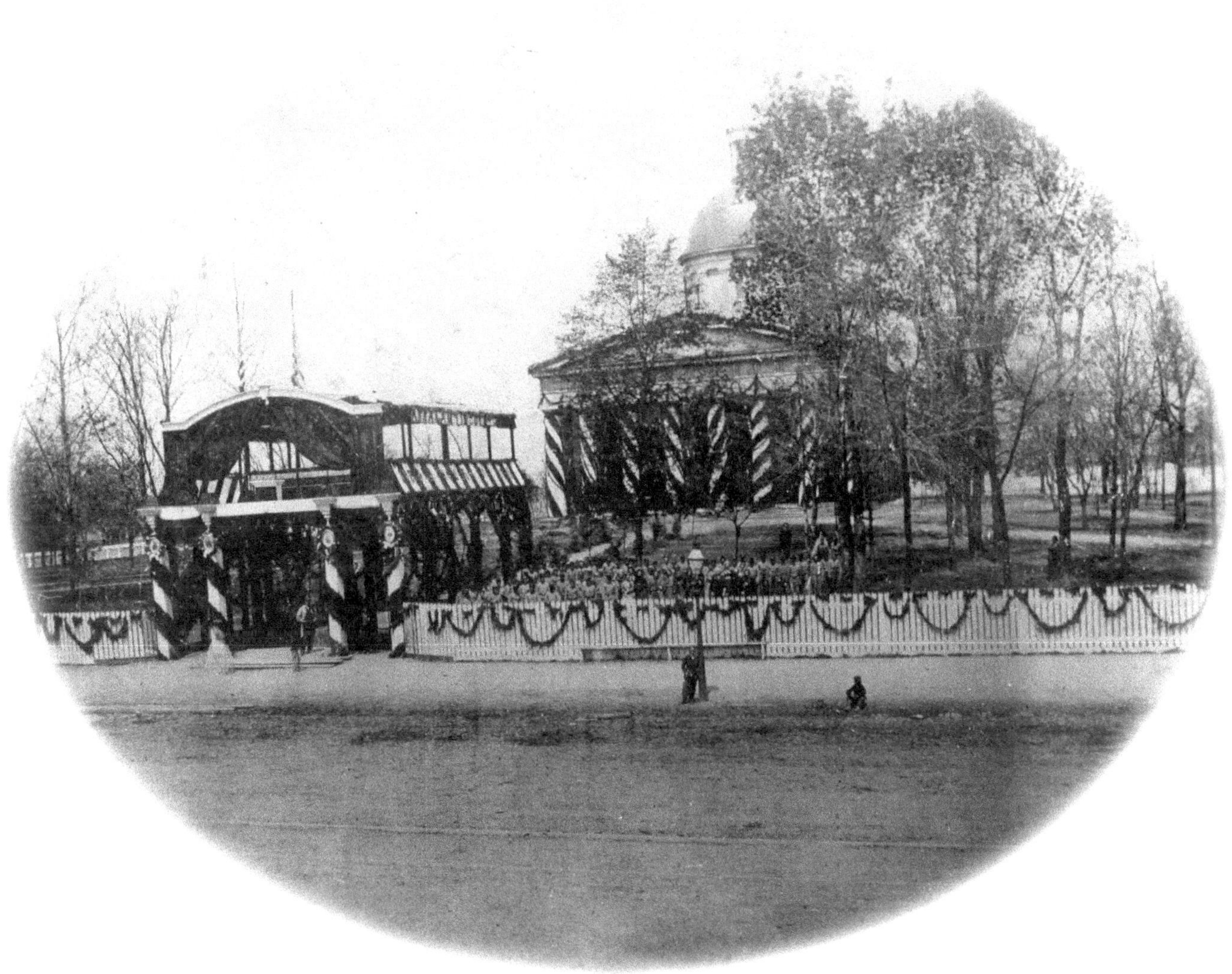

The old Indiana state capitol draped for Abraham Lincoln's funeral. On Sunday, April 30, 1865, Lincoln's funeral train arrived in Indianapolis. Heavy rains prevented a procession through city streets, but tens of thousands of mourners passed by the president's body as it lay in state in the capitol rotunda from 8:00 a.m. to 10:00 p.m. This photograph was taken the following day, after the rains subsided.

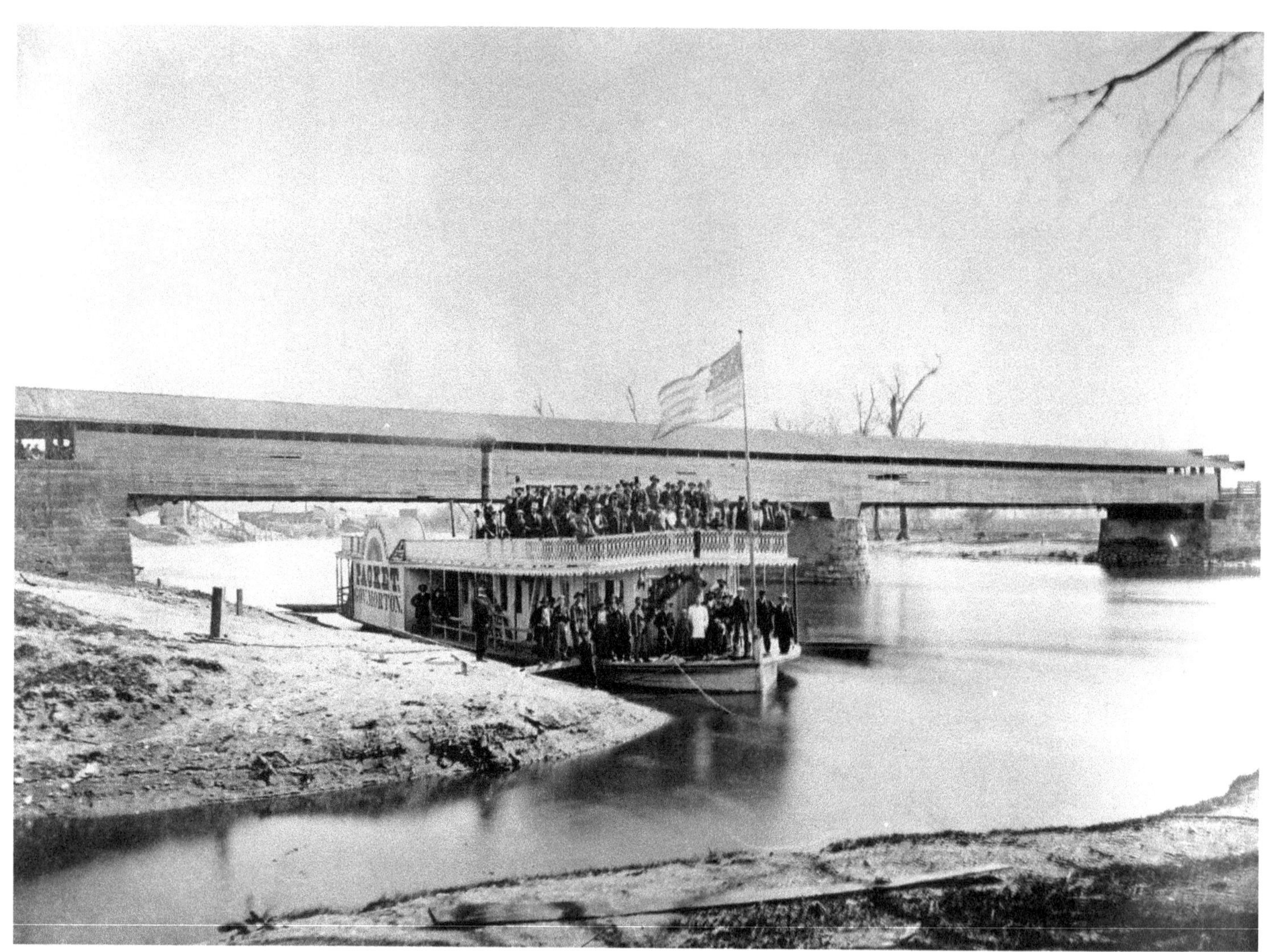

Indianapolis residents enjoy a trip on the packet *Governor Morton* in 1866. The small boat, which began offering excursions on the White River at the end of the Civil War, sank not long after this photograph was taken. In the background is the old National Road (Washington Street) covered bridge, which carried travelers across the river from 1834 until 1902.

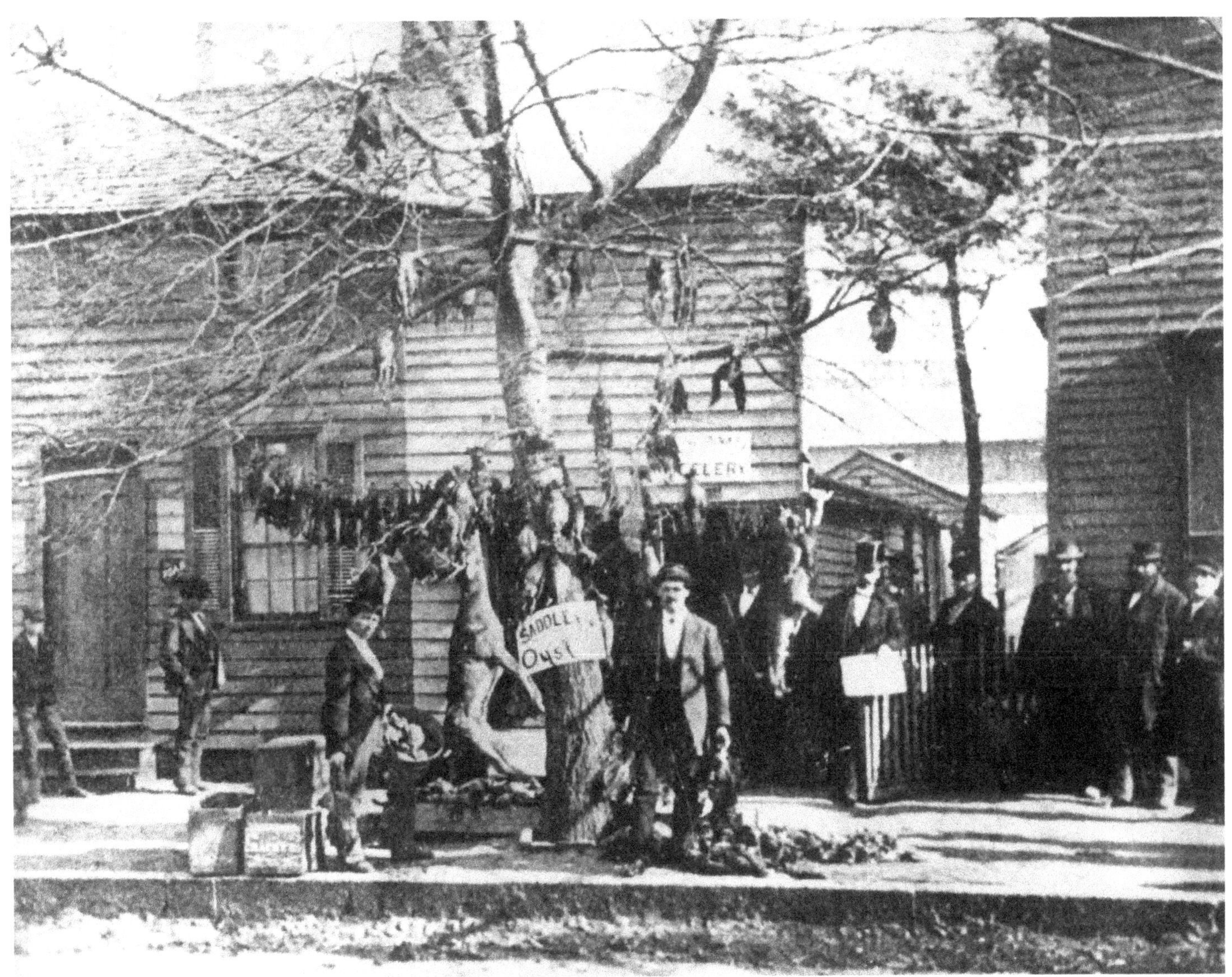

An outdoor fish and game market. The caption on this photograph indicates that it was taken in 1872 and that the market was on the site where the Grand Opera House was later built (on the east side of Pennsylvania Street, north of Market Street).

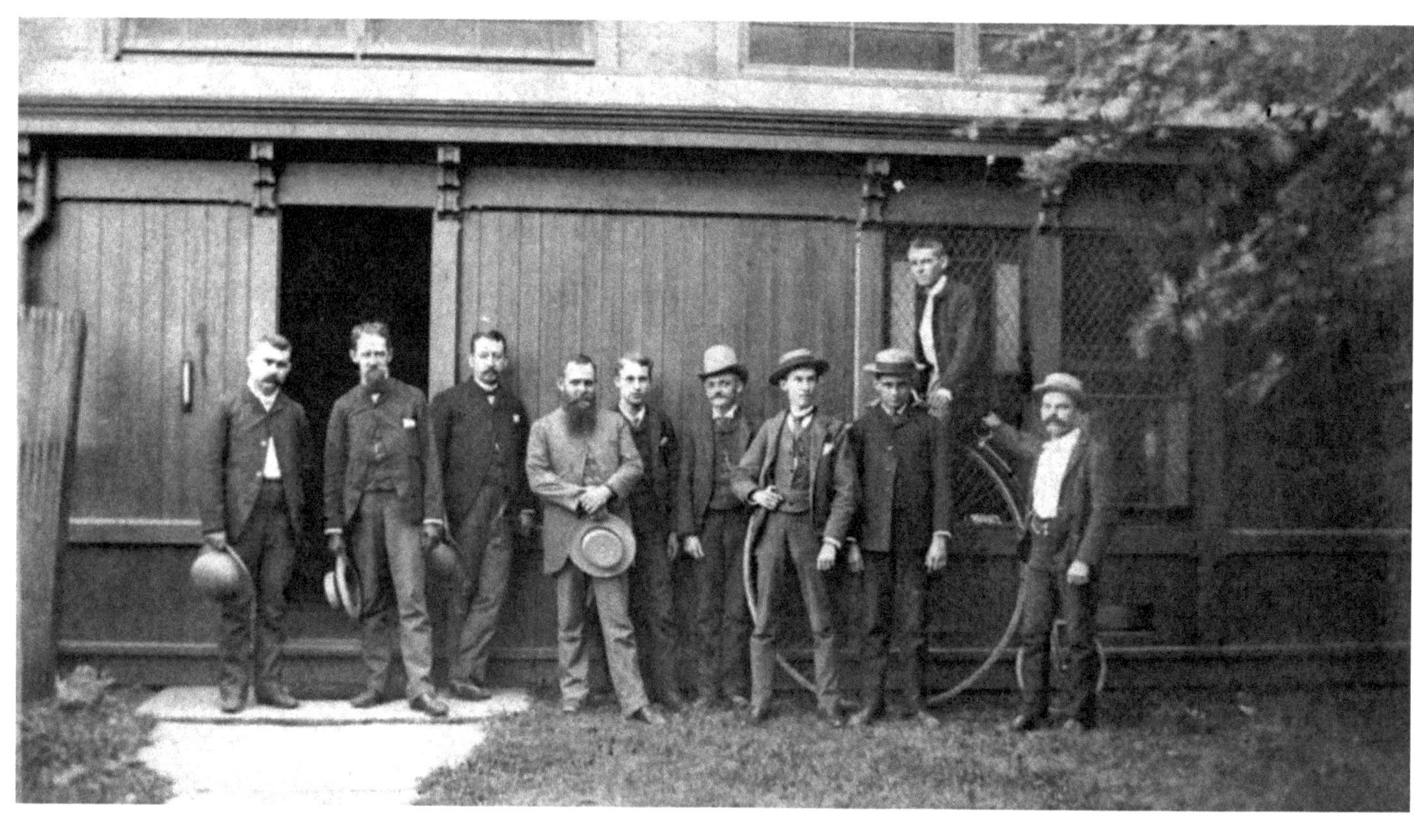

Workers at the Nordyke and Marmon Company, circa 1886. Ellis Nordyke founded the company in Richmond, Indiana, in 1851, and his son relocated it to an area called West Indianapolis in 1876. The company manufactured mill equipment and later automobiles. The Marmon Wasp won the first Indianapolis 500 in 1911.

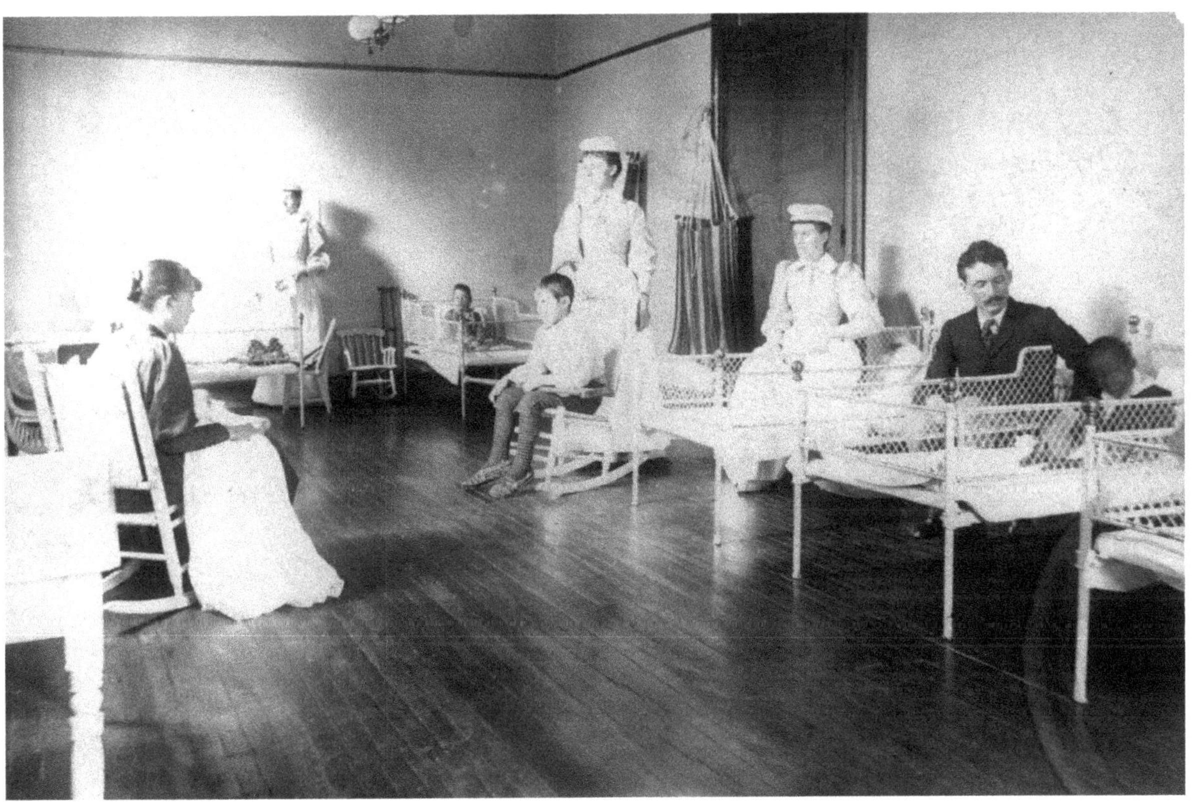

The children's ward of the Indianapolis City Hospital, 1887. The city built the charity hospital in the mid-1850's but did not take responsibility for operating it until after the Civil War. While services were lacking in the early years, conditions improved greatly under the leadership of William Niles Wishard, Sr., the hospital's administrator from 1879 to 1886. Today the hospital carries Wishard's name and is managed by the Indiana University School of Medicine.

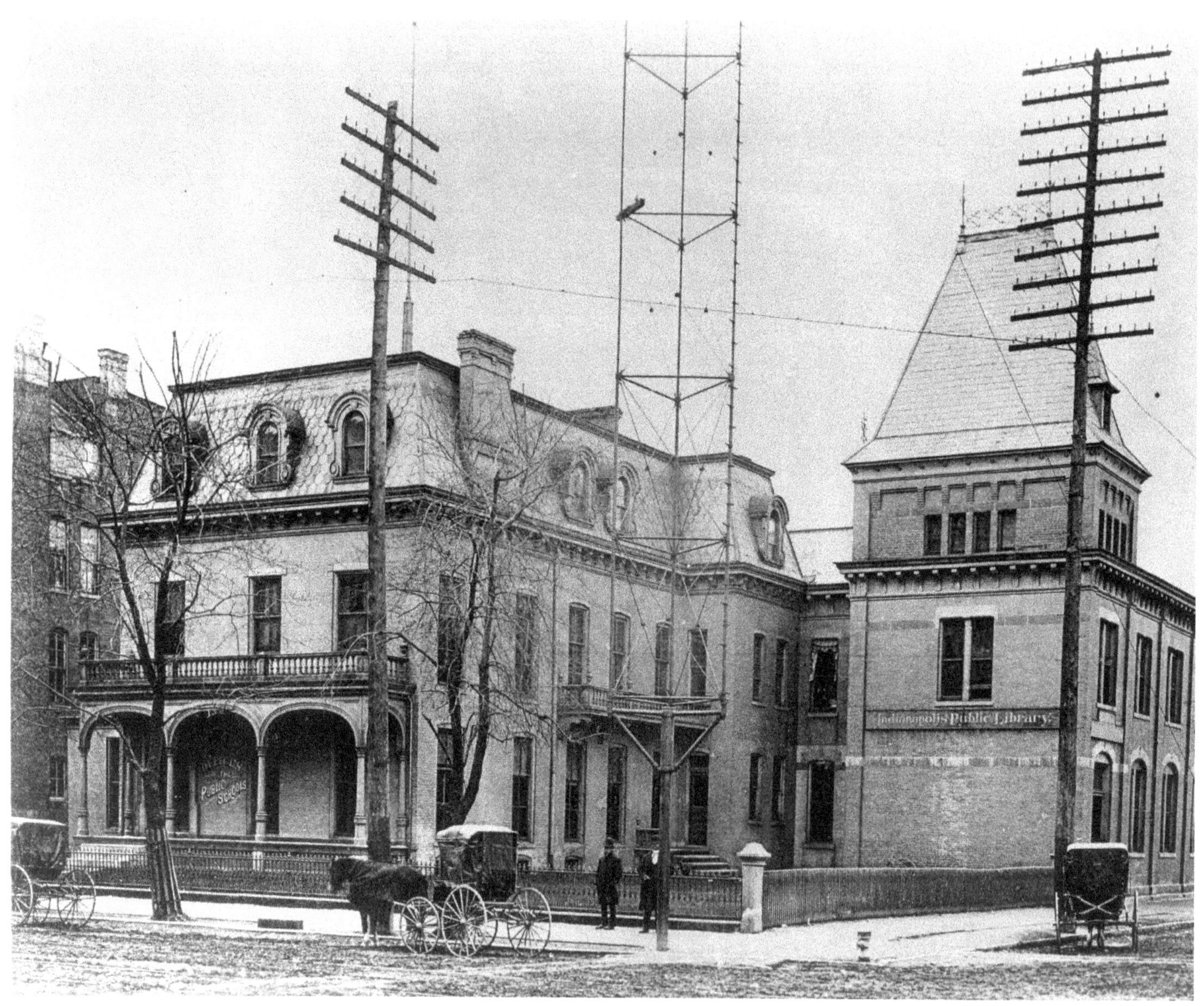

Offices of the Indianapolis School Board and Indianapolis Public Library, circa 1880's. Indianapolis's library opened in 1873. In 1880 it moved to this site, the former Alvord House on the corner of Pennsylvania and Ohio Streets, and remained there until 1893. Today the central library's permanent home, a 1917 Greek Doric structure on St. Clair Street, is undergoing renovation and expansion. The library is also served by twenty-two branch locations.

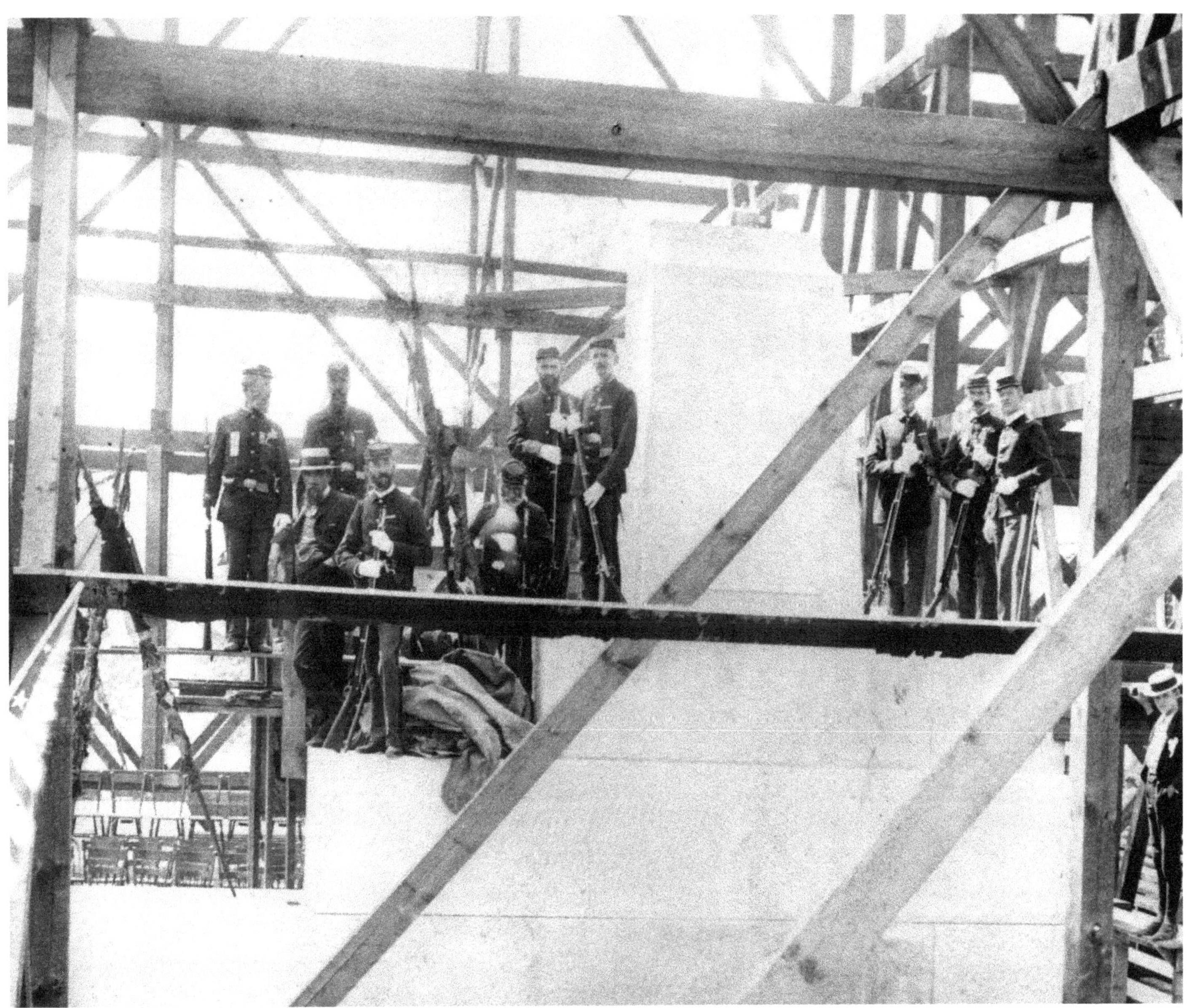

Laying the cornerstone for the Soldiers and Sailors Monument, August 22, 1889. After more than two decades of lobbying and debate, the Indiana General Assembly voted in 1887 to build a memorial to Indiana's Civil War veterans. Construction began the following year at Circle Park, in the heart of Indianapolis, and finished with the monument's dedication fourteen years later.

The L.G. Twente Upholstering Shop, circa 1880. Louis G. Twente ran this business on Central Avenue, just north of today's Tenth Street.

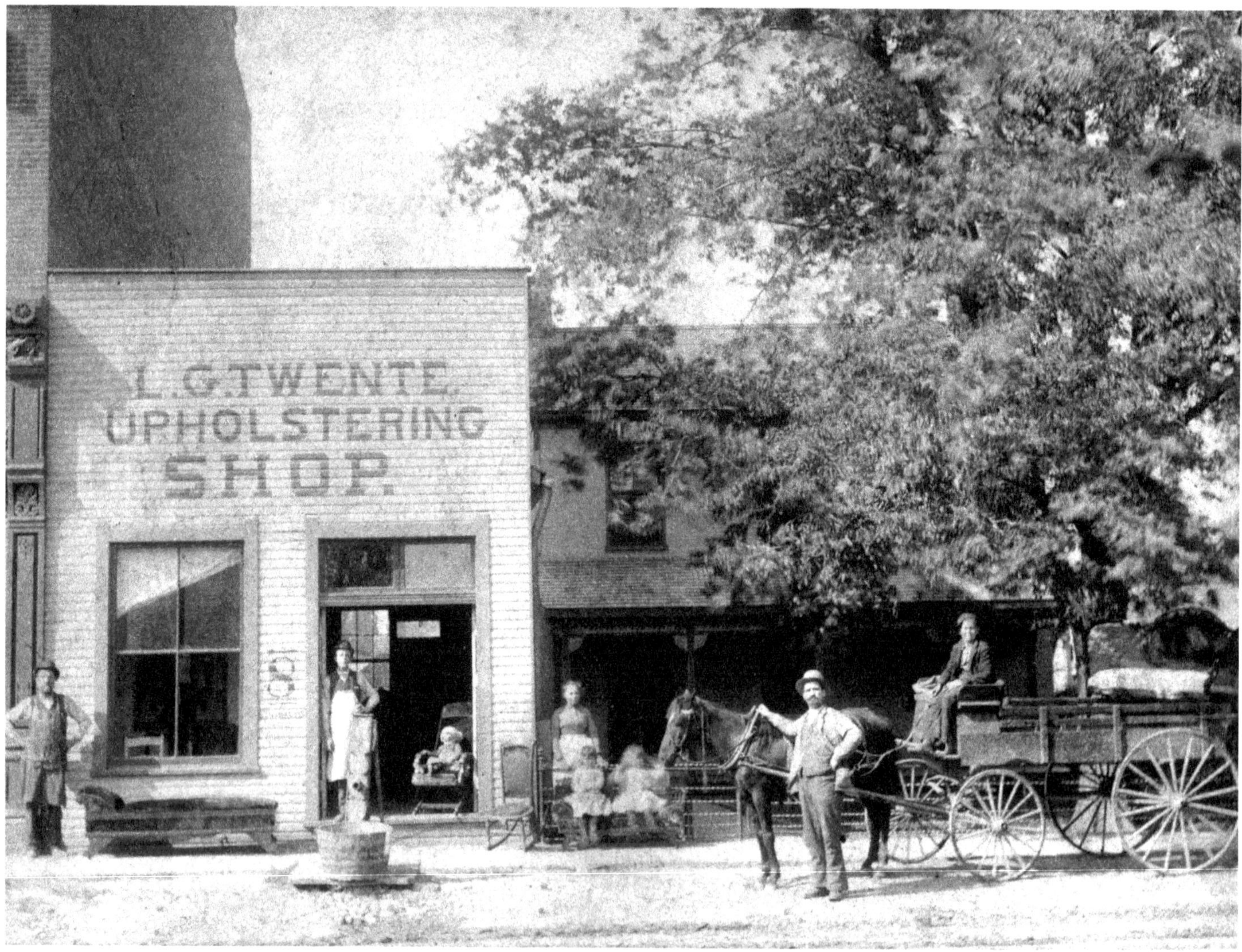

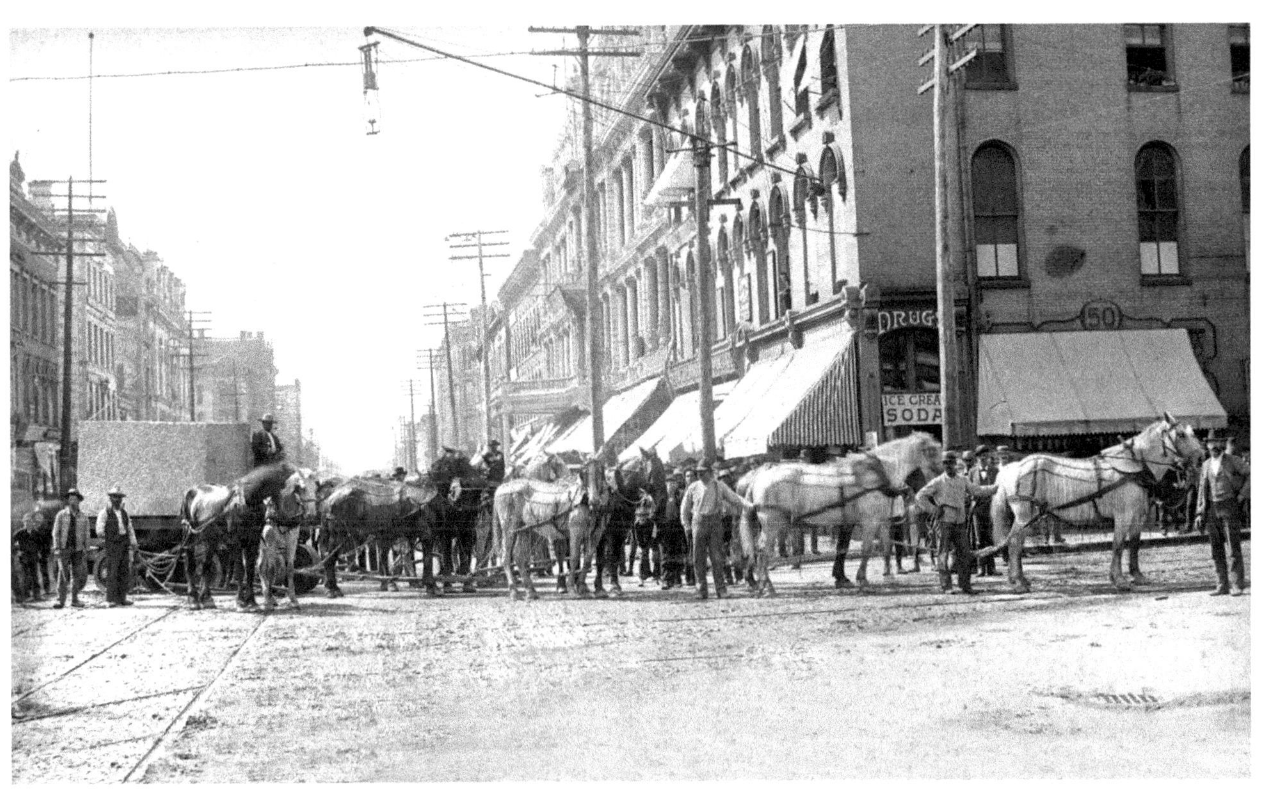

Teams of horses pull stone to the Soldiers and Sailors Monument construction site, circa 1890.

A mule-drawn streetcar on McCarty Street, circa 1890. Behind the reins is Ira Bartholomew, one of the first streetcar drivers in Indianapolis.Mules pulled cars along the city's streets from 1864 until 1894, when electric cars finally phased them out.

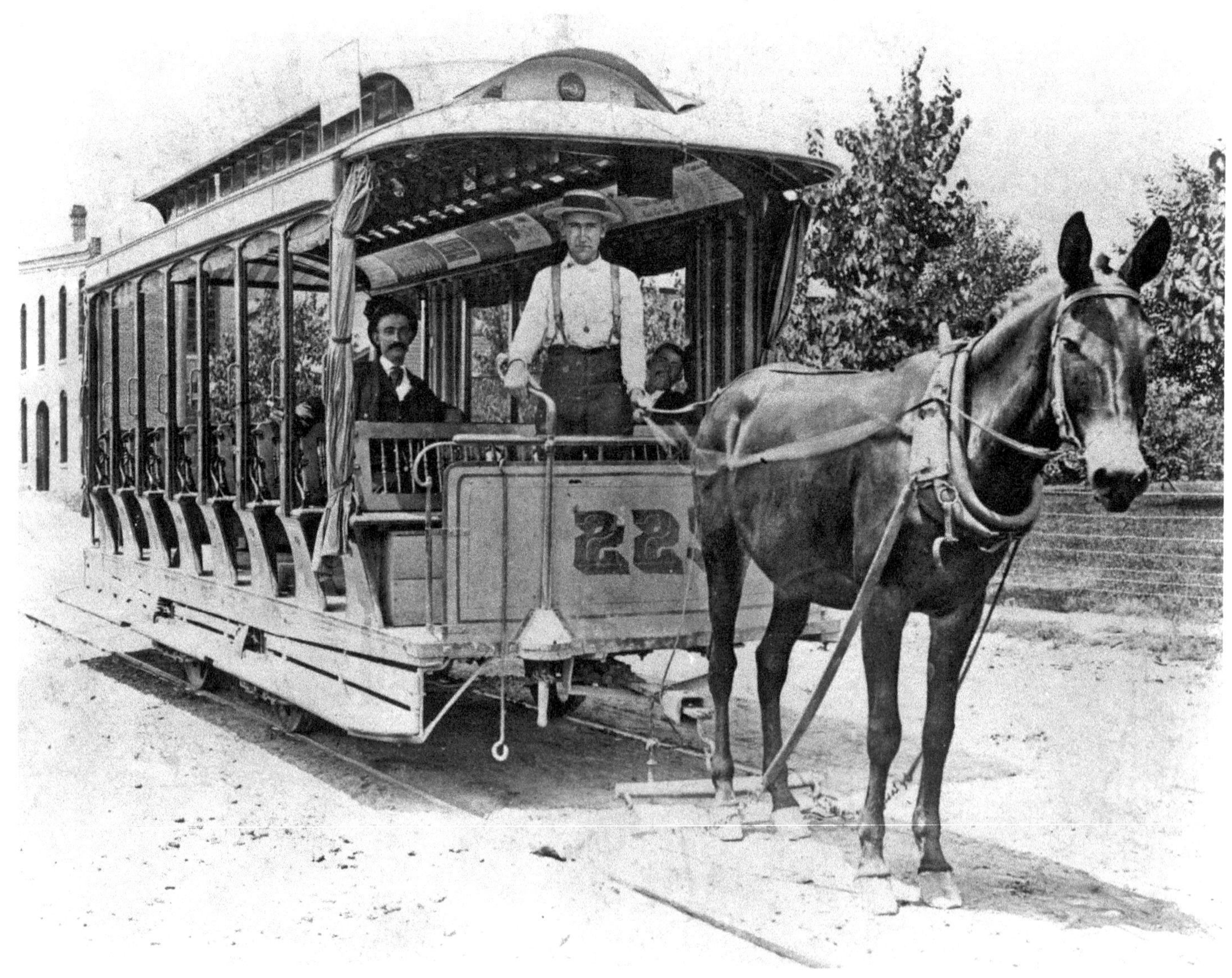

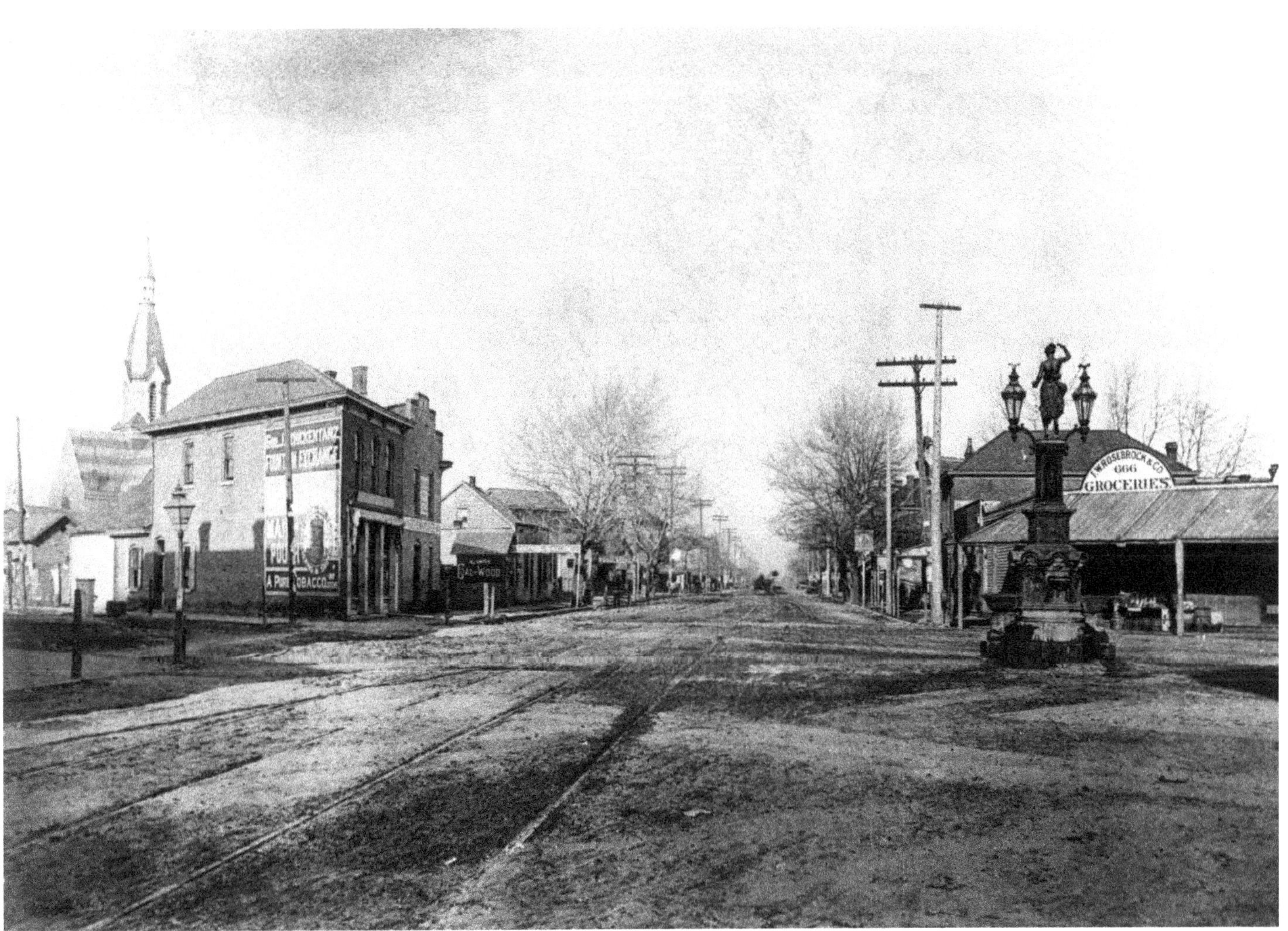

Fountain Square, circa 1890. This view looks northwest along Virginia Avenue, from where it intersects with Prospect and Shelby Streets. The fountain to the right was built in 1889 and is the namesake for the surrounding neighborhood. It stood for about 30 years until, legend states, wind caught an advertising banner attached to it and toppled it. A new fountain took its place in 1924.

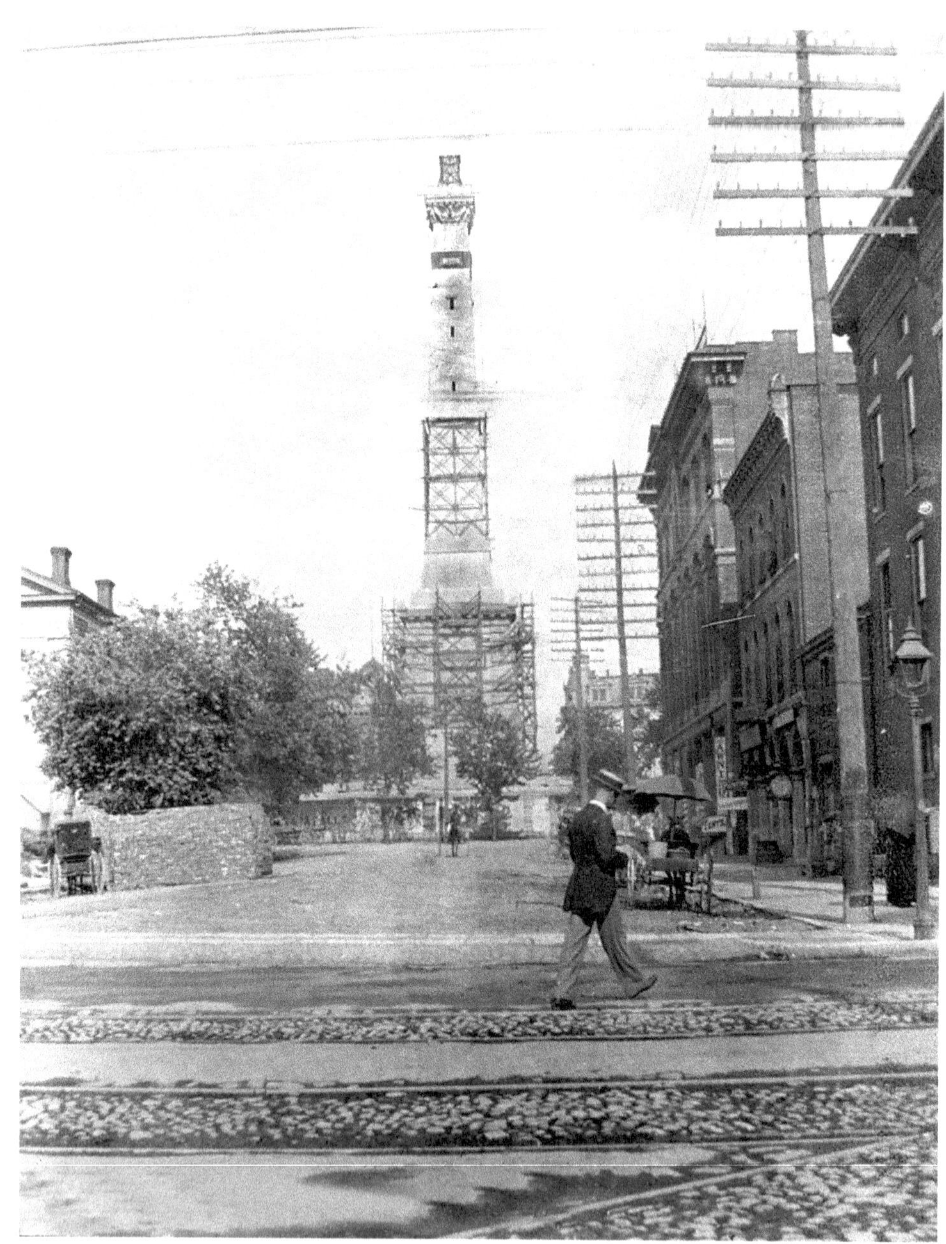

The Soldiers and Sailors Monument during construction. The photo was taken after workers added the date astragal in 1892 but before they crowned the top with the sculpture of *Victory* (known more popularly as *Miss Indiana*) in 1893. This view looks east from Market Street.

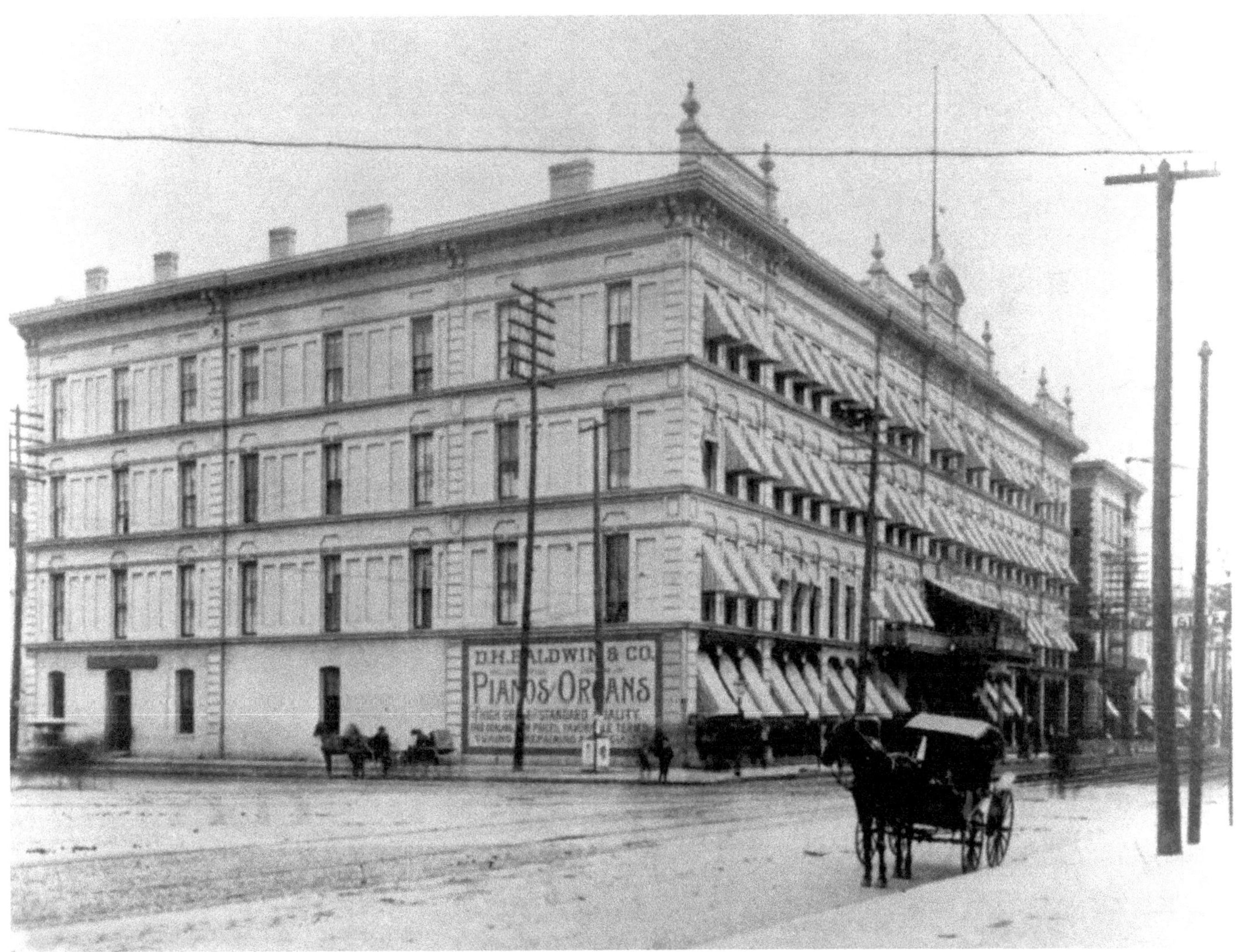

The Denison Hotel, circa 1890. The Denison opened in 1880 on the southeast corner of Pennsylvania and Ohio Streets. In the early 1890's (after this photograph was taken), a new owner added more floors and a mansard roof. In its heyday the Denison housed the offices of both political parties and saw much behind-the-scenes maneuvering. The hotel declined by the 1920s and was eventually torn down. In 1934 the city's first modern parking facility opened on the site, and today Denison Parking operates several garages in the city. First Indiana Bank's office tower now rises on this corner.

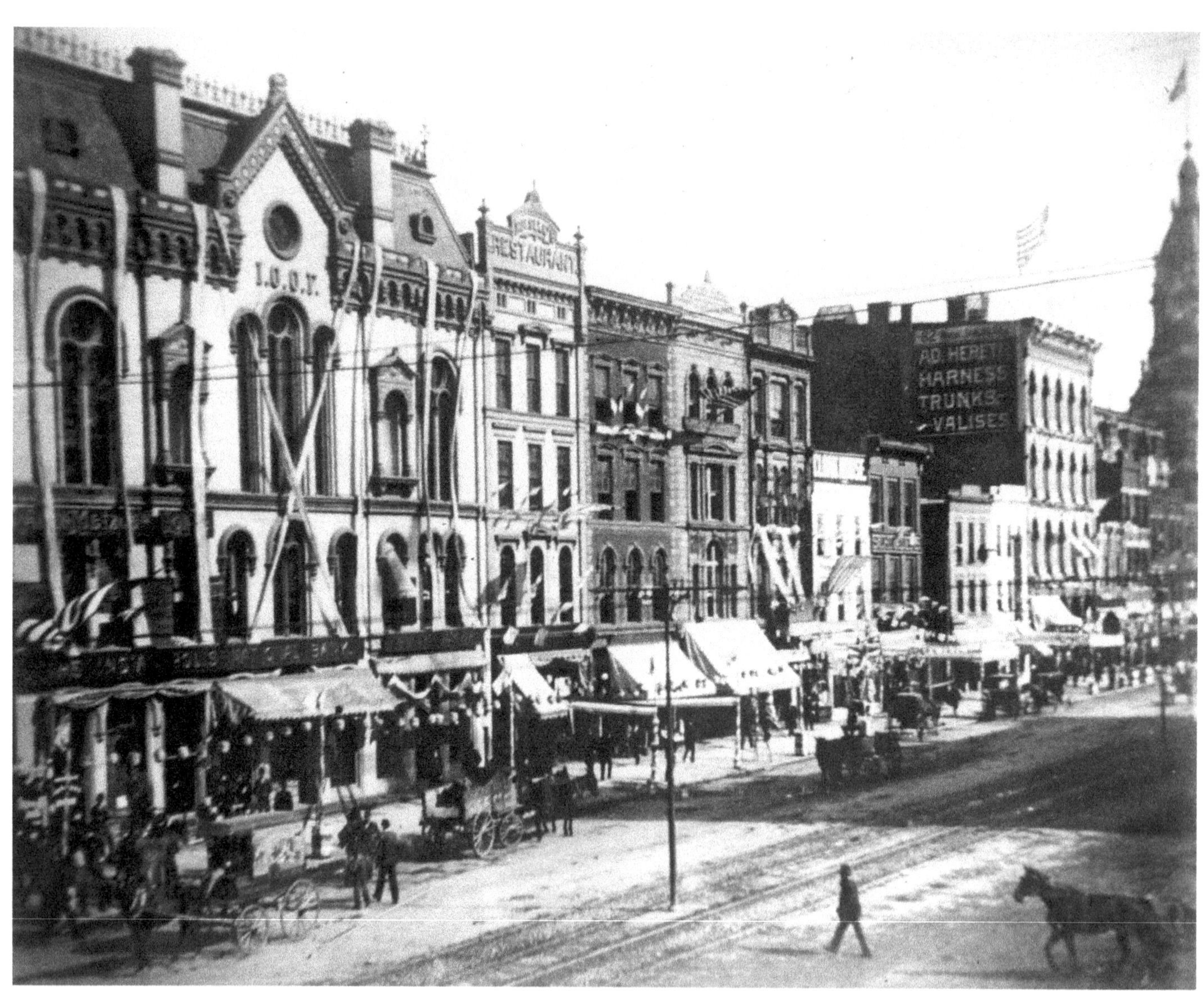

Washington Street, looking east from Pennsylvania Street, circa 1890. To the left of the photo is the old Independent Order of Odd Fellows building. In the early 1900's the IOOF built a new thirteen-story headquarters on the site, and it still dominates the intersection today.

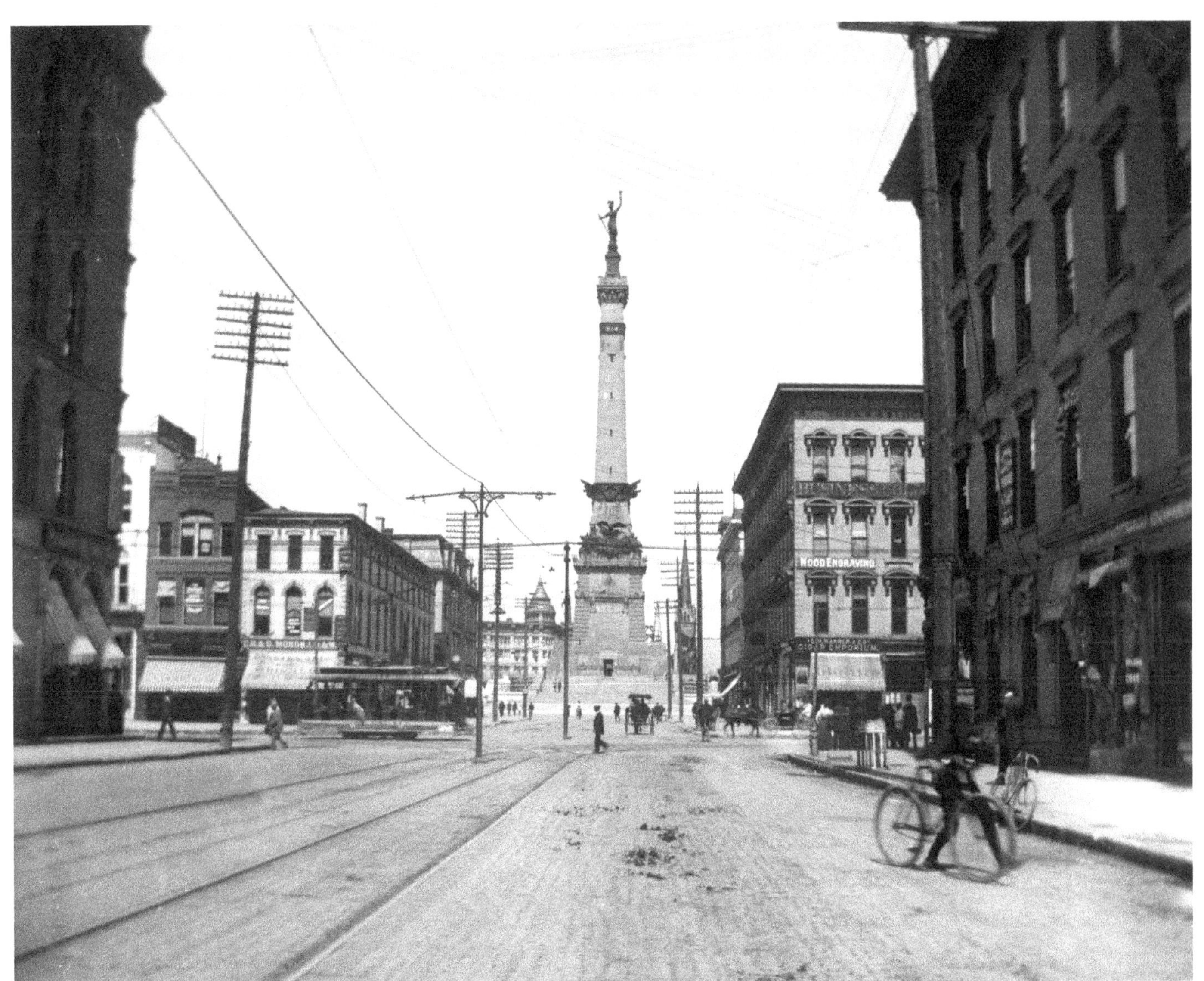

A view of the Soldiers and Sailors Monument from South Meridian Street in the mid-1890's. Note the bicyclists to the right. Indianapolis saw its first safety bicycles in 1889, and according to the *Encyclopedia of Indianapolis*, by the early 1890's "so many bicycles clogged the streets that in 1893 the City Council passed an ordinance requiring a $1 license fee."

M. P. Grady's saloon, circa early 1890's. City directories from this period indicate that Martin P. Grady operated his drinking establishment on West Washington Street.

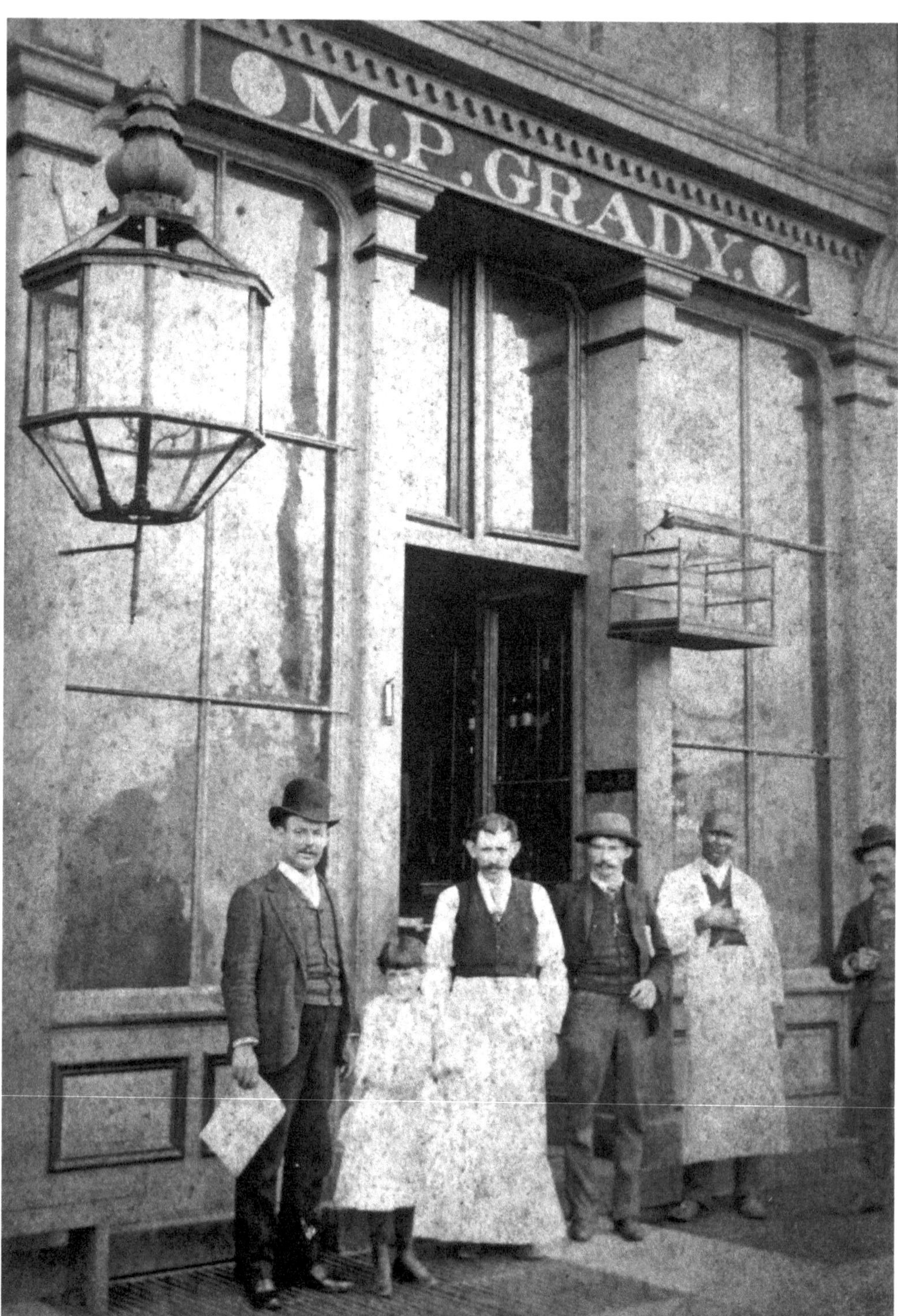

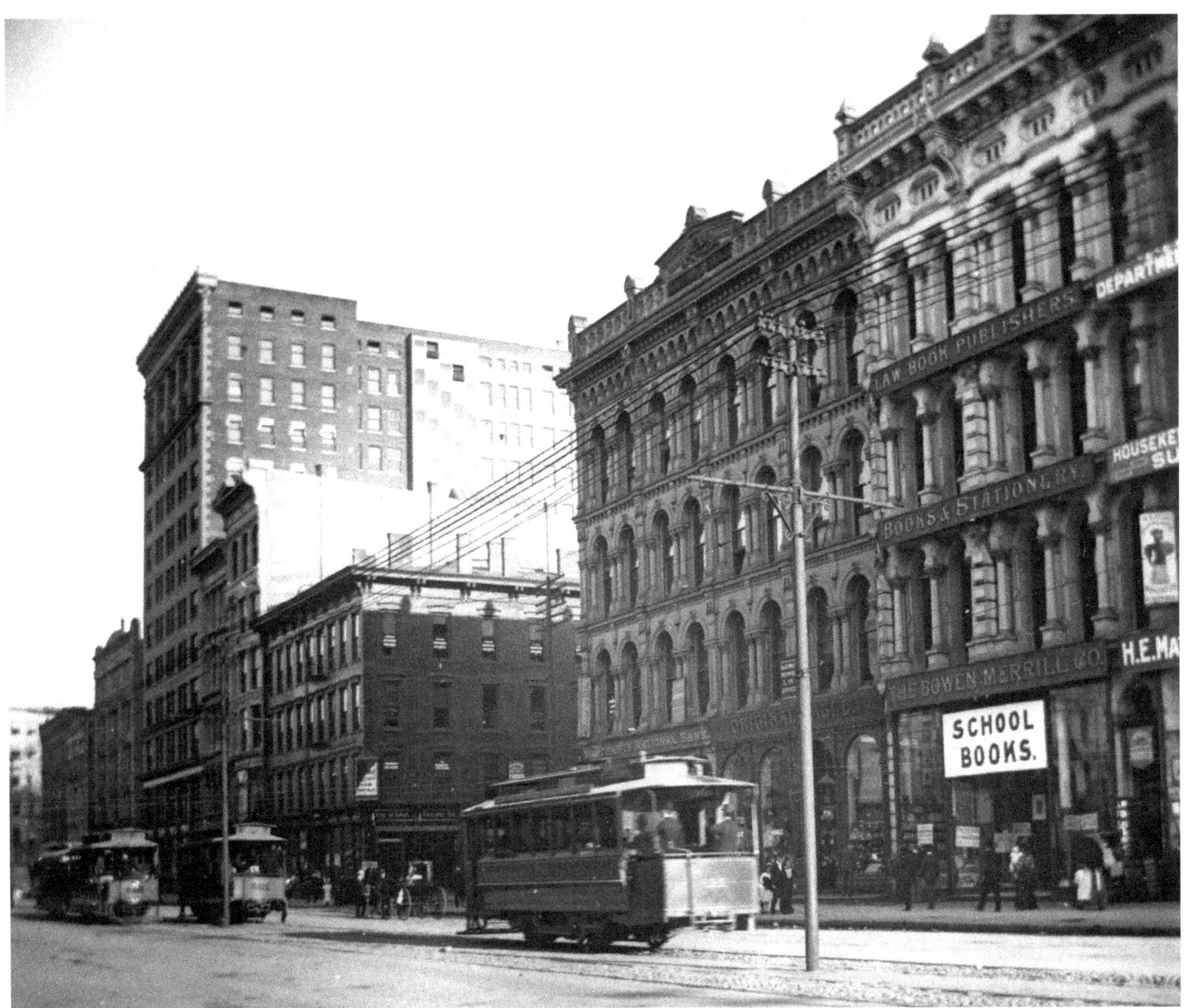

A streetcar passes by the Bowen-Merrill Company on West Washington Street, circa 1898. Bowen-Merrill was a publishing company with Indianapolis roots dating to the 1850's. In 1903 it became known as Bobbs-Merrill and was noted for publishing the work of Indiana authors such as James Whitcomb Riley and Meredith Nicholson. By the 1940's it was the largest general publisher west of the Alleghenies. Among the noted works it introduced were Irma Rombauer's *Joy of Cooking*, Ayn Rand's *The Fountainhead*, and William Stryon's *Lie Down in Darkness*. After various company buyouts over the years, the Bobbs-Merrill imprint disappeared by the mid-1980's.

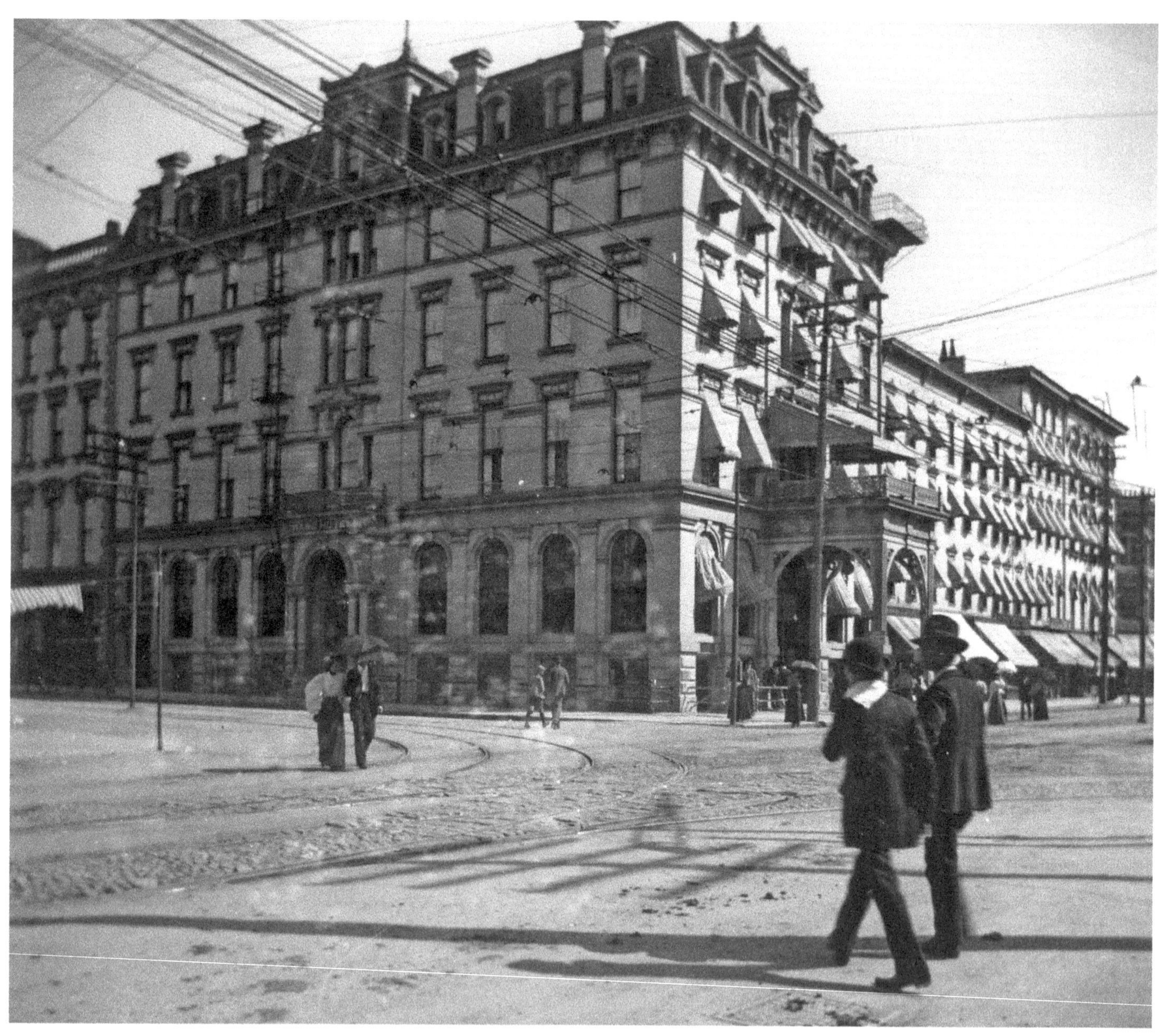

The Grand Hotel, circa 1890's. The hotel stood on the southeast corner of Illinois and Maryland Streets. When it opened in 1875 it was one of the finest in the city.

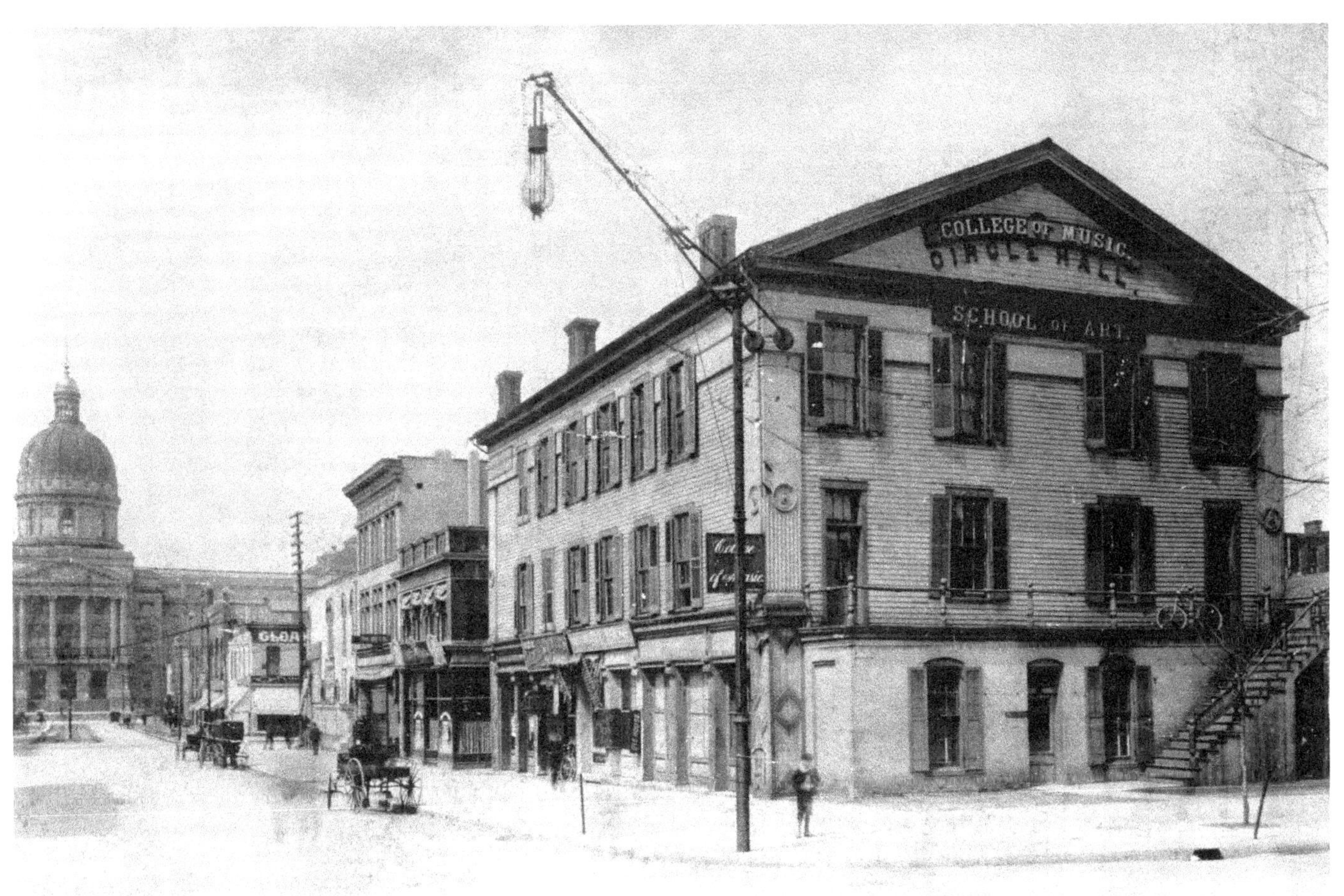

Circle Hall, circa mid-1890s. This structure, built in 1840, originally served as the home of Henry Ward Beecher's Second Presbyterian Church. When the church moved after the Civil War, the building was used as a school. By the 1890's it was known as Circle Hall and housed the city's College of Music and the second Indiana School of Art. It was torn down to make way for the expansion of the English Hotel in 1896.

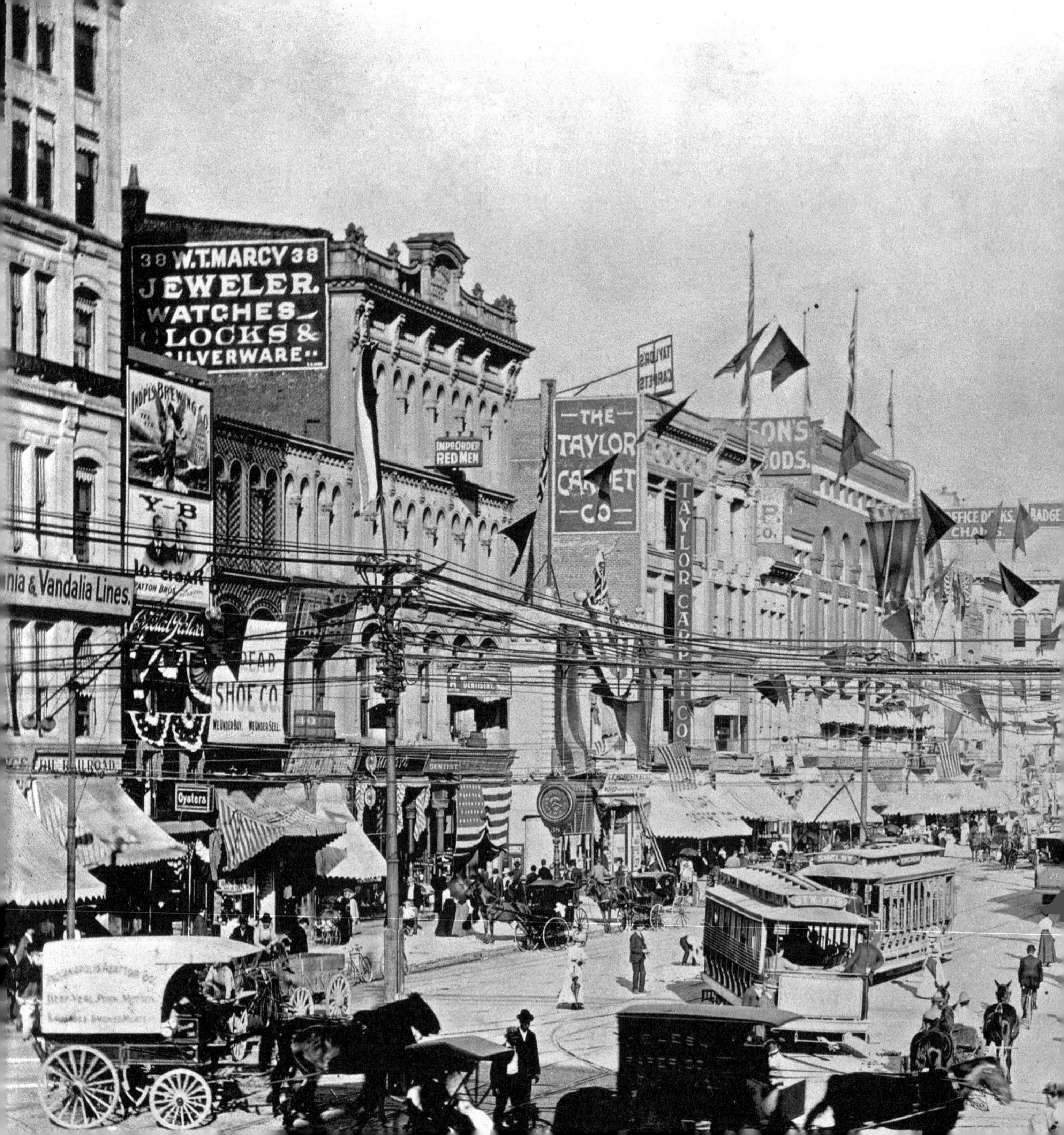
38 W.T.MARCY 38
JEWELER.
WATCHES
LOCKS &
ILVERWARE
INDPL'S BREWING CO
Y-B
10¢ CIGAR
PATTON BROS
nia & Vandalia Lines.
SHOE CO.
WE UNDER BUY. WE UNDER SELL.
Oysters
IMP. ORDER RED MEN
THE TAYLOR CARPET CO
TAYLOR CARPET CO
DENTIST
SHELBY
OFFICE DESKS
CHAIRS
BADGE

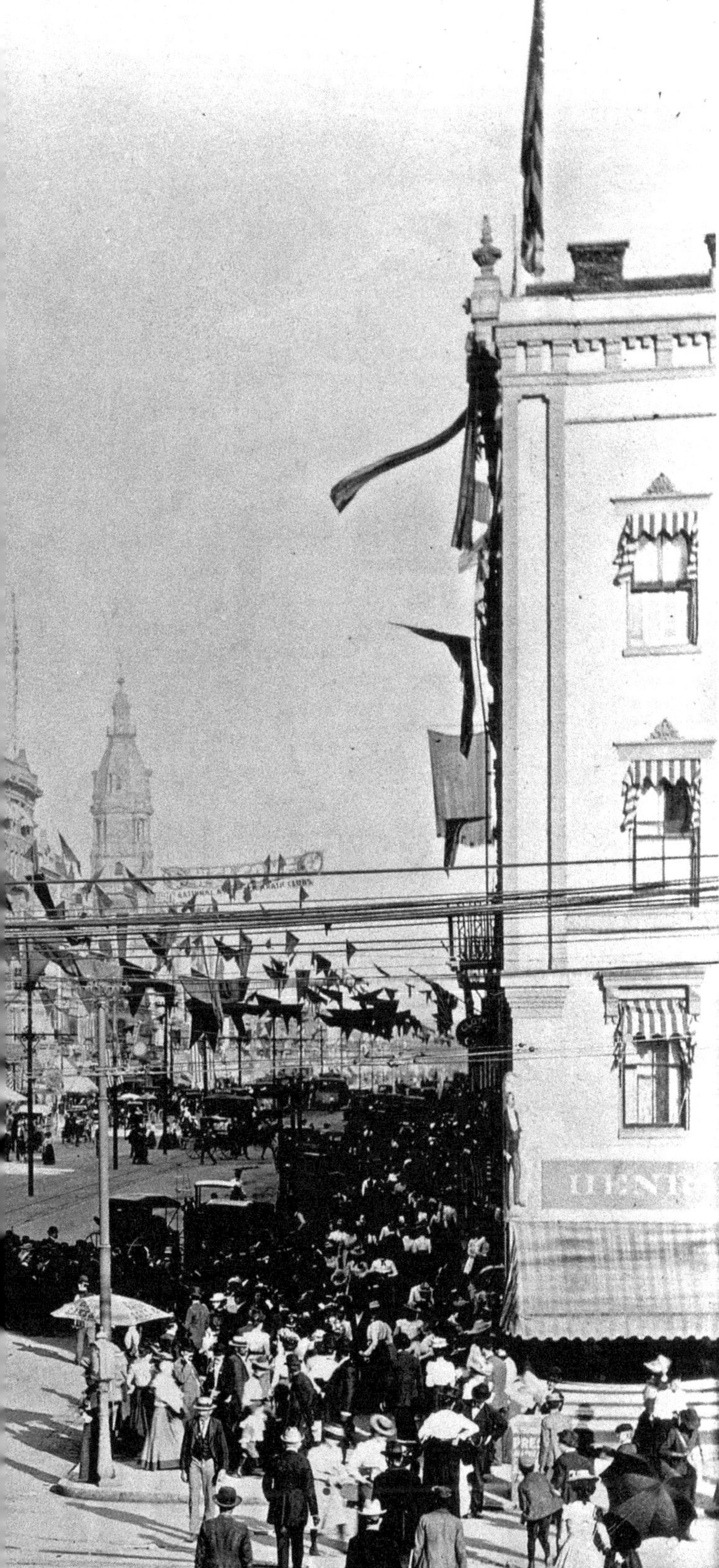

Washington Street, looking east from Illinois Street. Indianapolis historian Jerry Marlette dates the photo the summer of 1891 and indicates that the flags and bunting are hung to celebrate a convention of the National Association for Democratic Clubs.

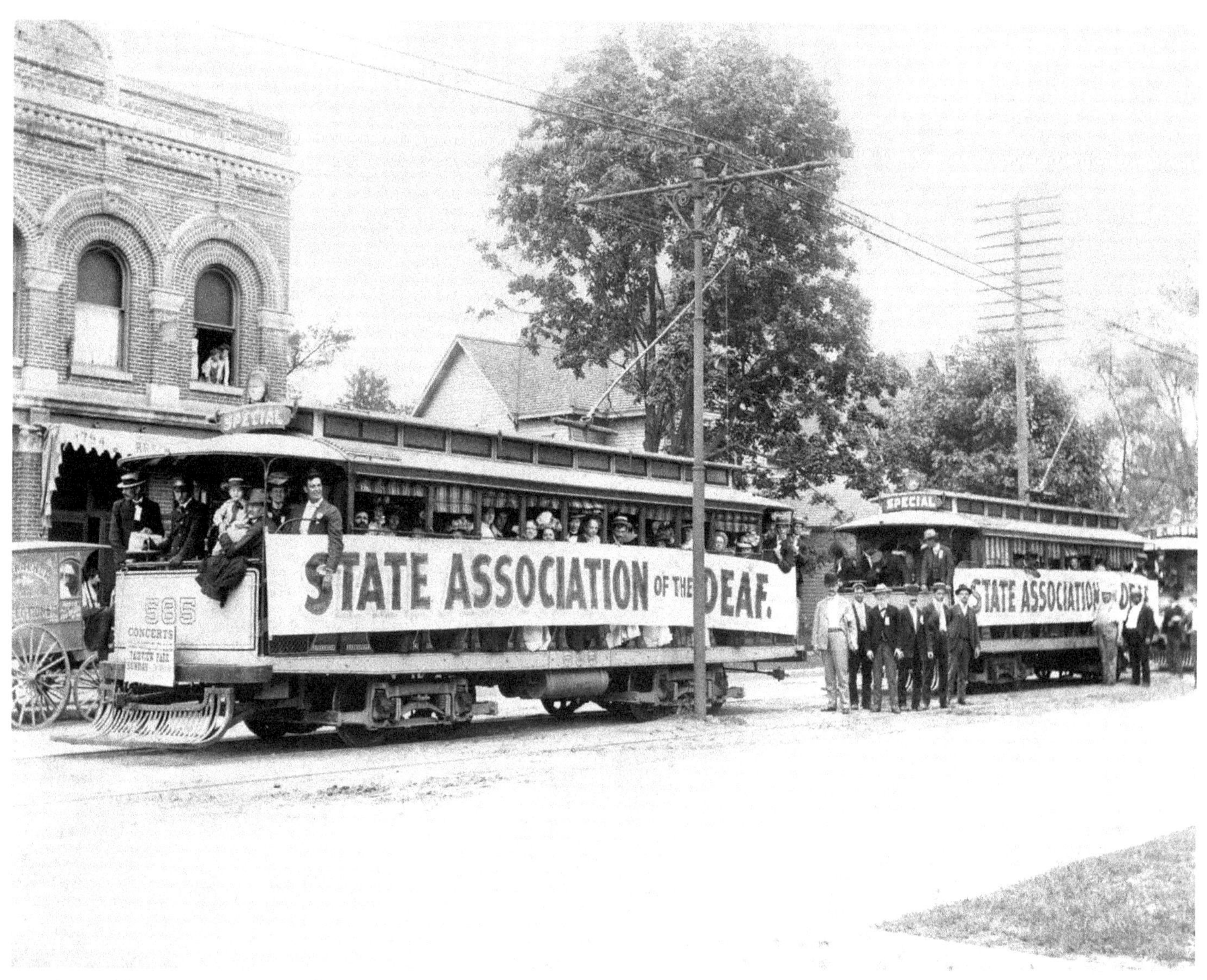

Members of the State Association of the Deaf participate in a streetcar parade, circa 1890's. In 1843 the Indiana General Assembly passed legislation allowing for the establishment of a state-run deaf school, and in 1850 the first permanent campus opened on Indianapolis's east side, near Washington Street and State Avenue. In 1905 the school moved to its current location on Forty-second Street, north of the state fairgrounds.

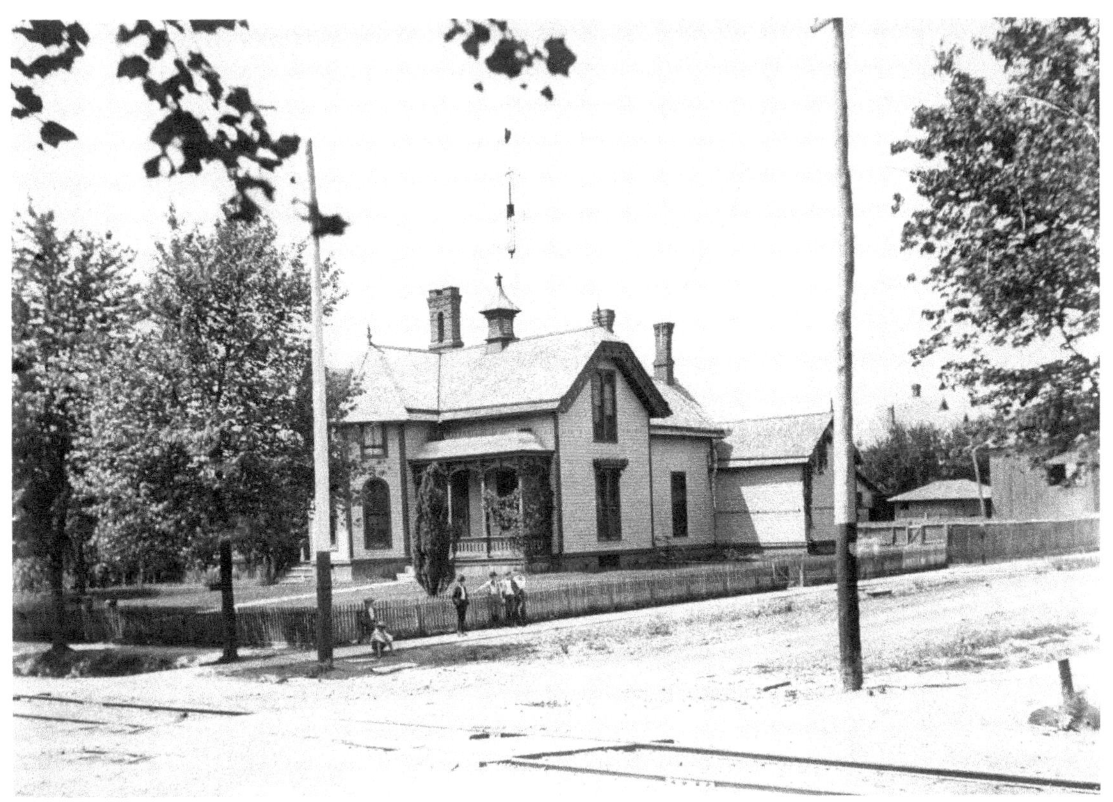

An example of an Indianapolis home around the late nineteenth century. After the Civil War many middle-class and wealthy residents built new houses on the outskirts of the growing city, and Indianapolis adopted the moniker "City of Homes."

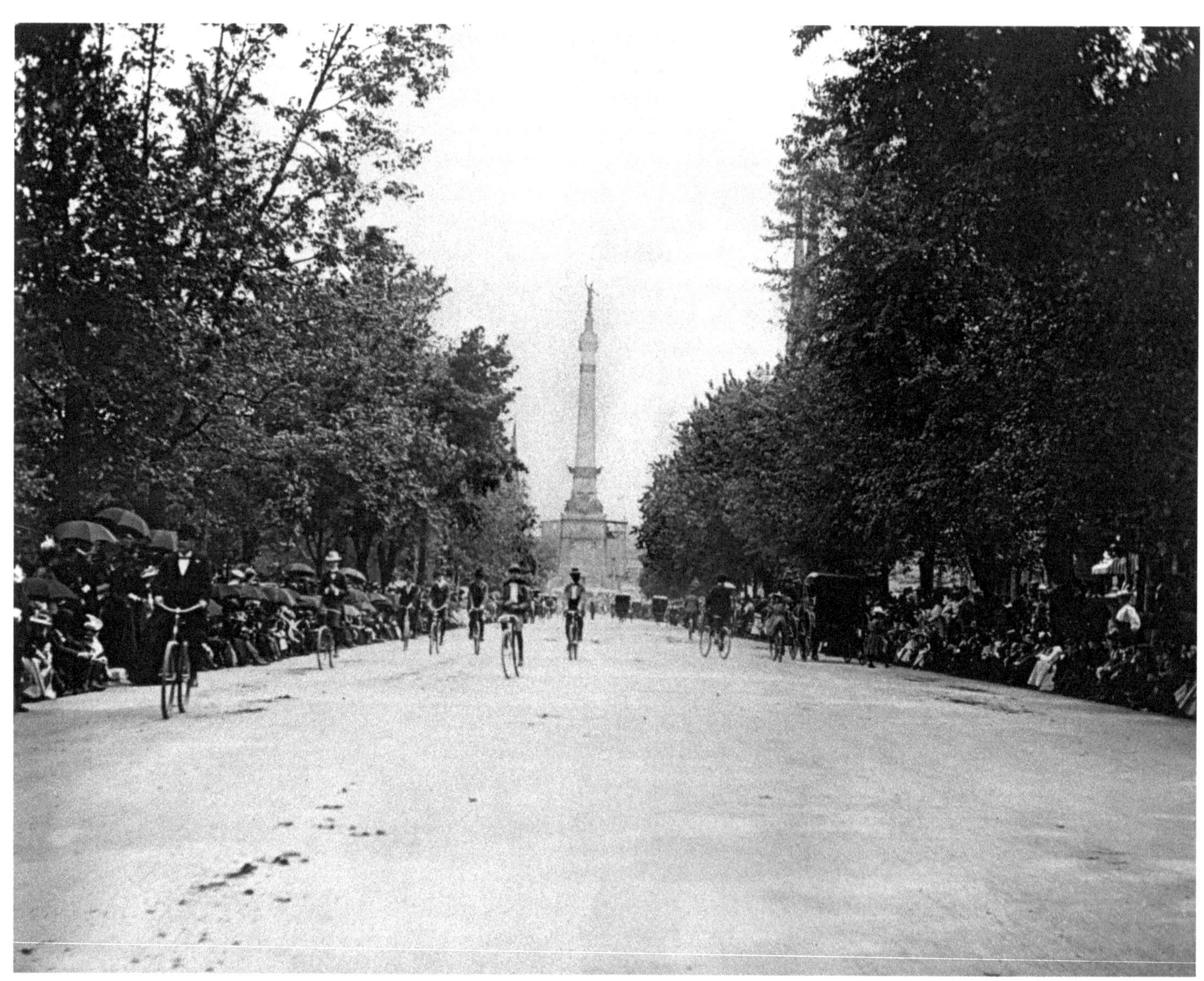

Meridian Street looking south toward the Soldiers and Sailors Monument. The caption on the photo says it was taken about May 1898 and that the people lining the street were waiting for men to march by to leave for service in the Spanish-American War.

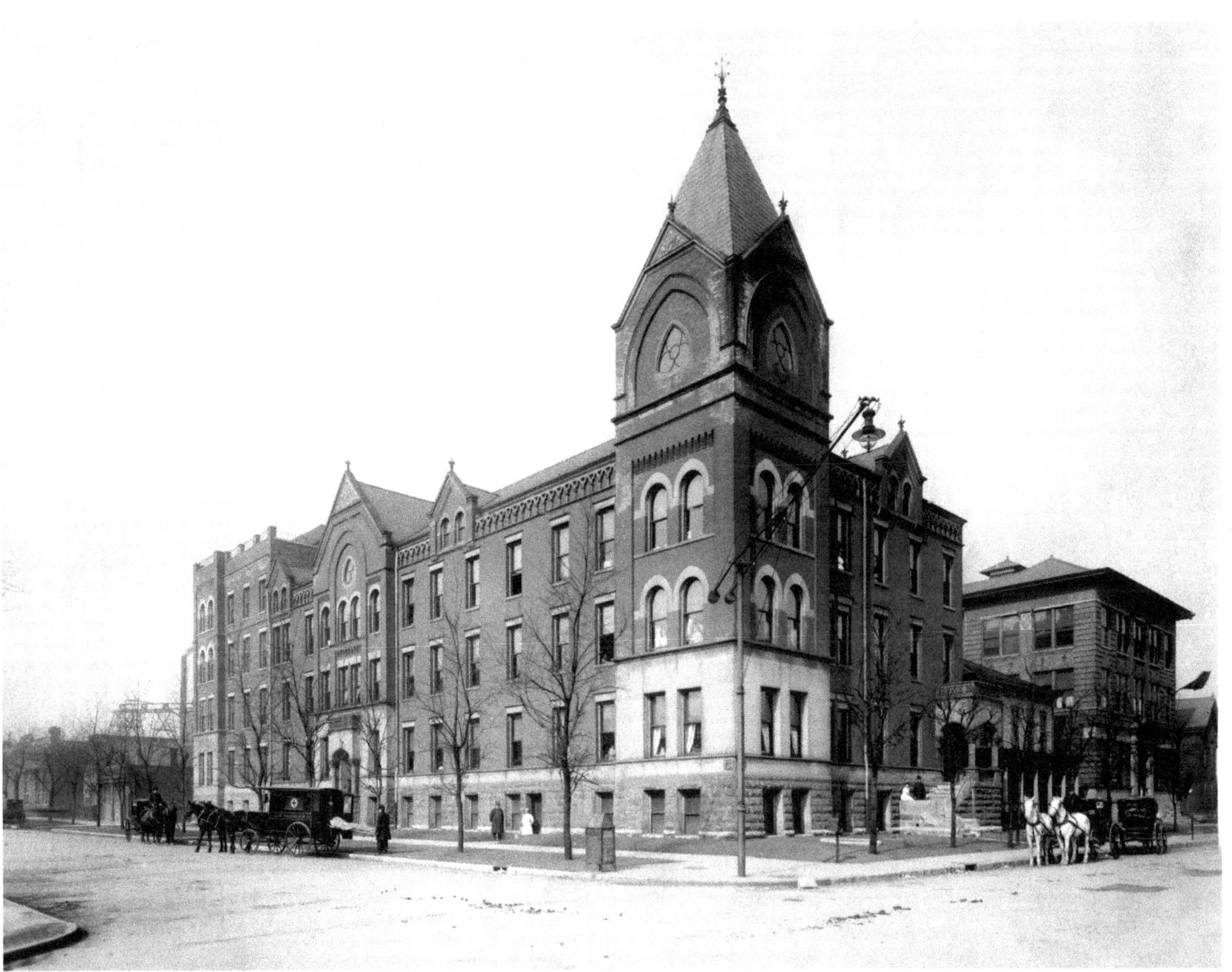

Deaconess Hospital around the time it opened in 1899. Deaconess stood on the northwest corner of Ohio Street and Senate Avenue. It closed in 1935 because of financial difficulties.

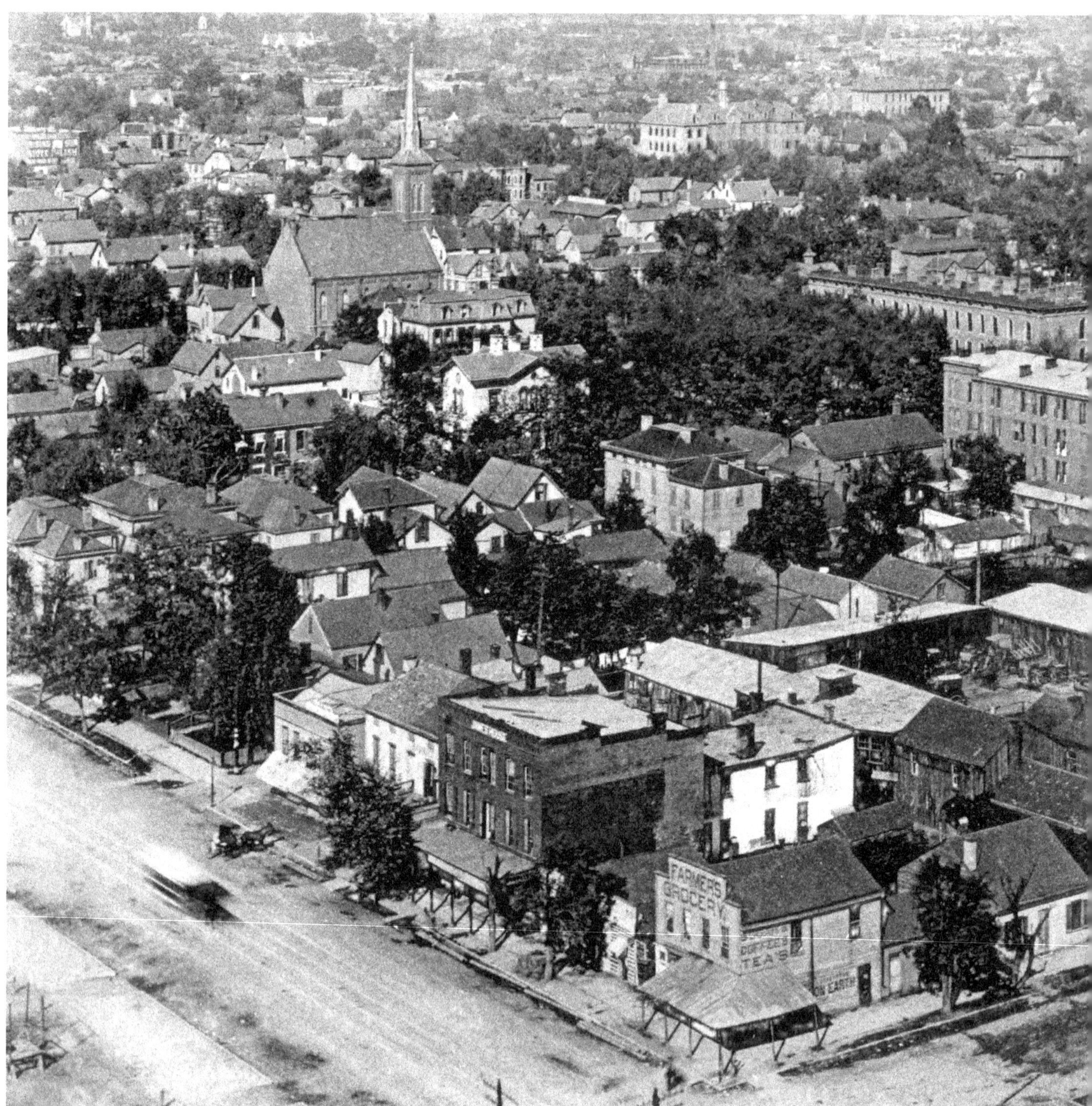
FARMERS
GROCERY
COFFEES
TEA'S
ON EARTH

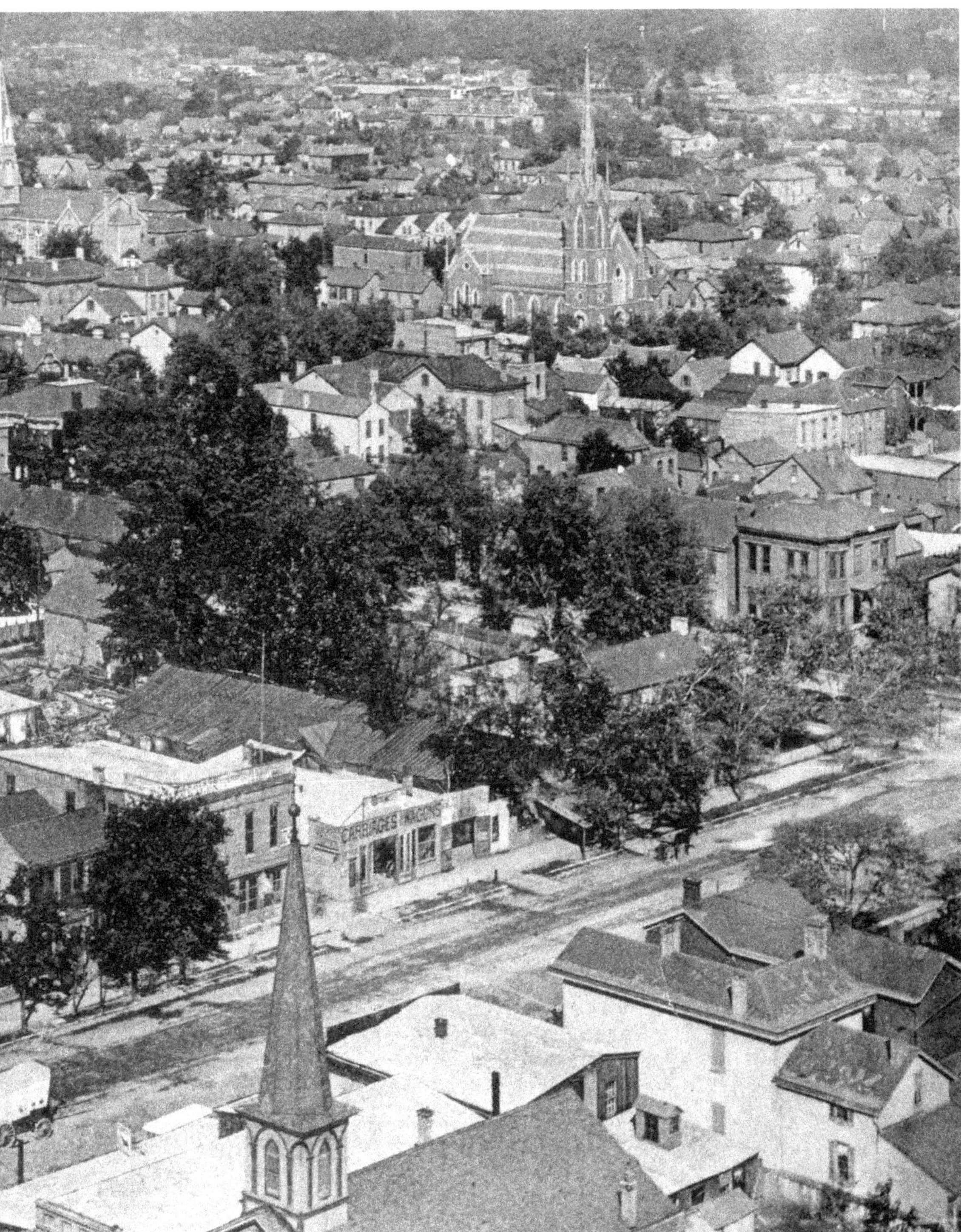

Looking northeast from the Marion County courthouse, late 1880's. This image appeared in a book titled *Indianapolis Illustrated*, published in 1889.

A city carnival, October 1903. According to historian Edward Leary, downtown merchants sponsored the weeklong festivities, which took place in the shadows of these arches spanning Meridian Street. The carnival included daily parades, a midway on New Jersey Street, and, Leary writes, "Galarno, the Human Fly, who climbed the Soldiers and Sailors Monument and took bows on the arm of Miss Indiana."

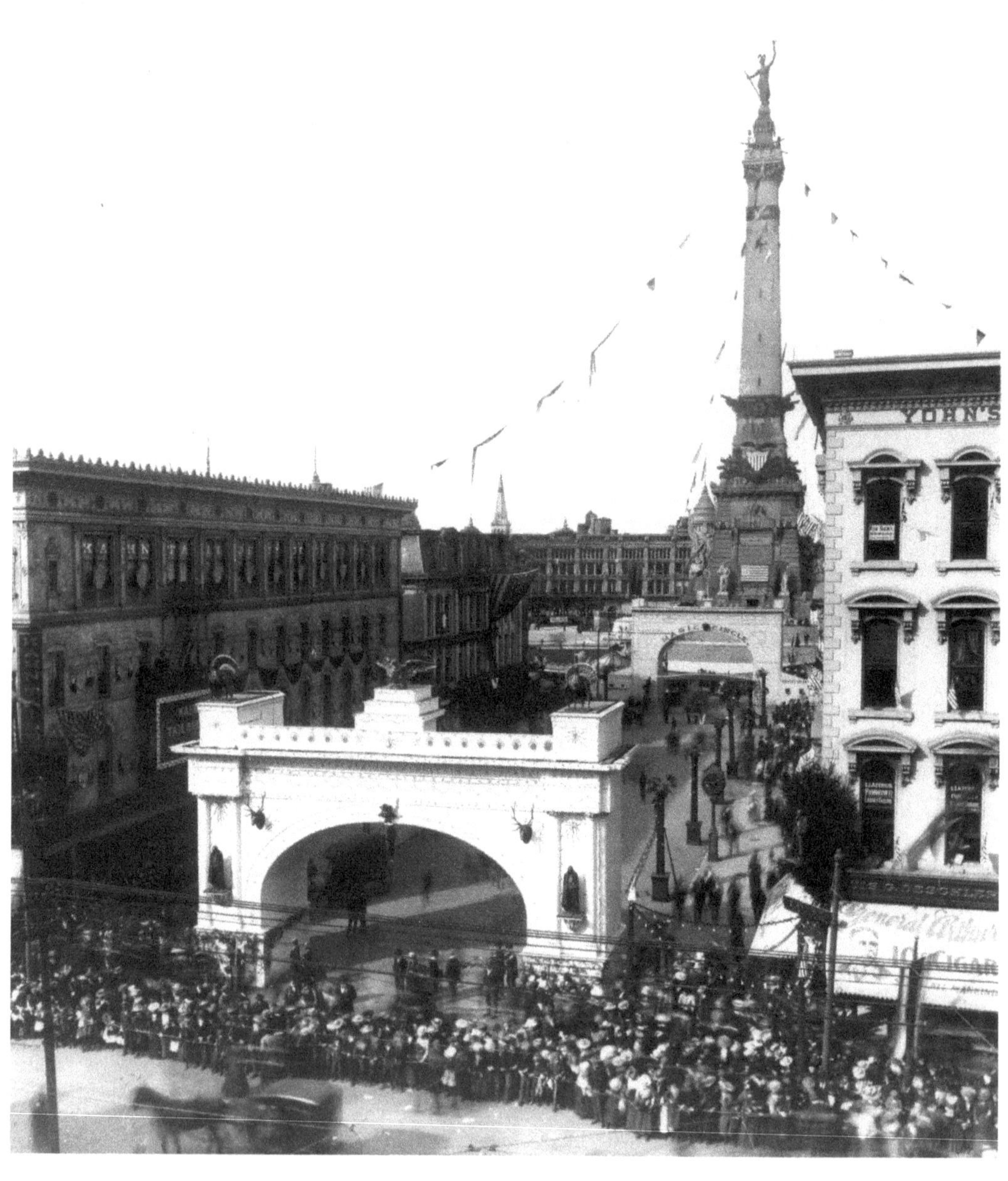

Monumental Celebrations 1900–1919

The 1880's and 1890's had brought prosperity to Indianapolis, and residents welcomed the arrival of the twentieth century with much fanfare and hope. The city was in its golden age, and the good fortune was to last through the next two decades. The early 1900's saw continued growth for Indianapolis, and during this time many of its most cherished icons and institutions were established.

Soldiers and Sailors Monument was one of those icons, and in many ways it symbolized the city's struggles and successes. Conceived by Governor Oliver P. Morton in the 1860's as a way to honor the state's Civil War veterans, it languished for twenty years before the state legislature authorized its construction. Even with the state's approval the project was fraught with delay, and progress came slowly. But after fourteen long years, workers finally completed the monument, and in 1902 thousands of Hoosiers turned out to see its dedication. At 284 feet, it soared above the cityscape, exclaiming to all that Indianapolis had arrived. Today it remains the city's signature landmark.

Other successes were cause for celebration as well. In 1900 the first interurbans arrived in Indianapolis, connecting residents to towns across the state via a quick electric train ride. Residents welcomed their first modern department store in 1905 when L. S. Ayres and Company moved into a new building on the southwest corner of Washington and Meridian streets. Methodist Hospital brought the latest medical advance to the city when it opened in 1908. And Indianapolis continued to rise, with architects designing taller and taller buildings every year, culminating in the completion of the seventeen-story Merchants National Bank in 1913.

Then there was the automobile. Introduced to the city in the late 1890's, cars began taking over the roadways in the early twentieth century. While they would ultimately have an adverse impact (adding to pollution and congestion, promoting sprawl and the decline of the city center, and curbing public transportation by streetcar and interurban), they offered residents increased mobility and allowed the city to continue growing. At one time Indianapolis was home to some ninety automobile manufacturers and produced such luxury cars as Marmon, Stutz, and Duesenberg. In 1909 developers opened Indianapolis Motor Speedway as a testing track for some of these manufacturers, and two years later the speedway hosted the first Indianapolis 500, the race that would put the city on the map.

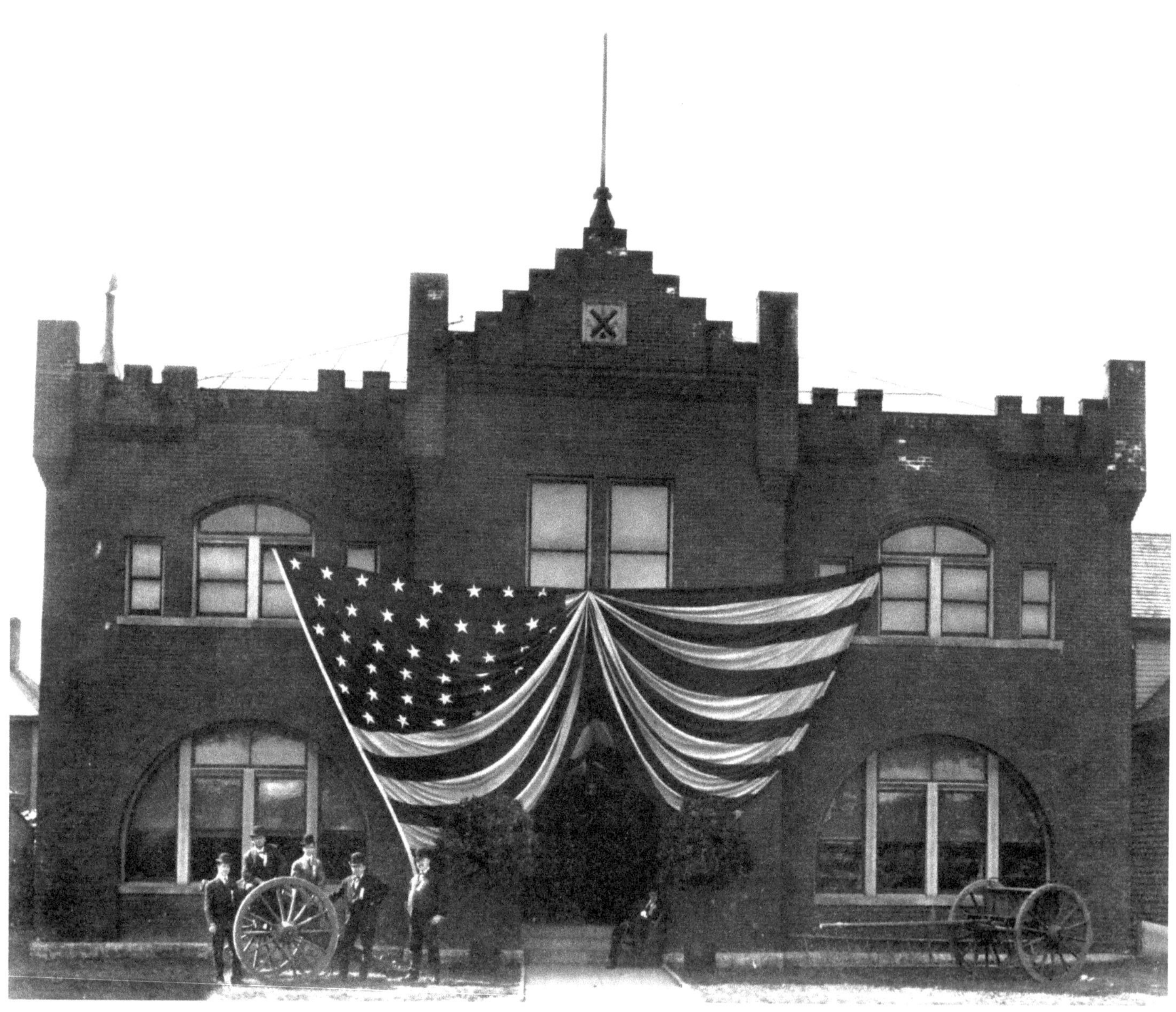

The Battery A Armory around the turn of the century. Battery A of the Indiana National Guard's First Regiment of Light Artillery was mustered into the Spanish-American War in May 1898 and became the 27th Battery of Light Artillery, Indiana Volunteers. The battery served in Puerto Rico and was on the line when peace was declared. This armory was located on the west side of Senate Avenue just north of Sixteenth Street; across the street was a vacant lot on which the troops trained (now the site of Methodist Hospital). In later years the building was named Curtis Armory, and eventually it was remodeled into a church.

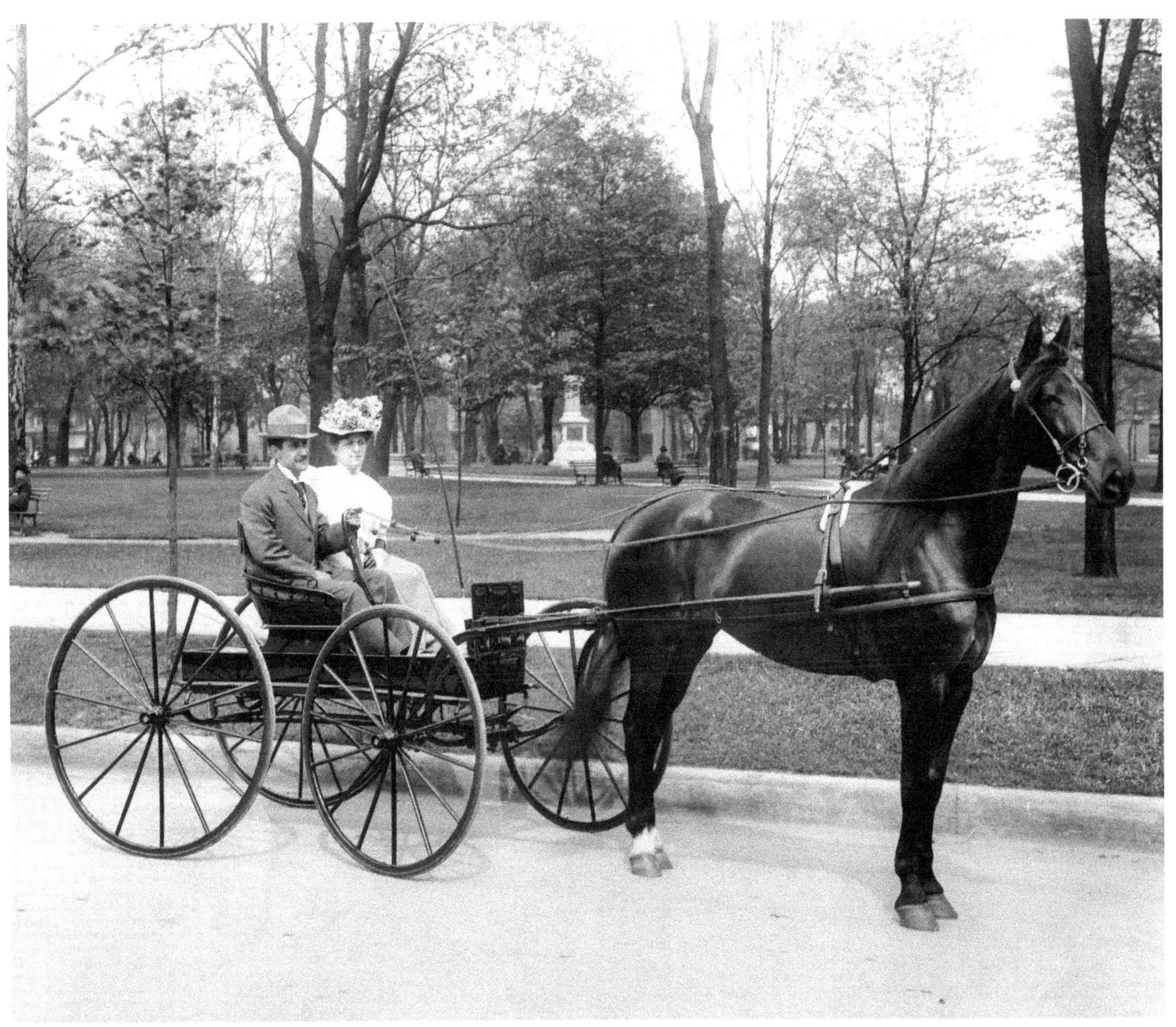

A couple enjoys a carriage ride, early 1900's. The two are passing by University Park downtown.

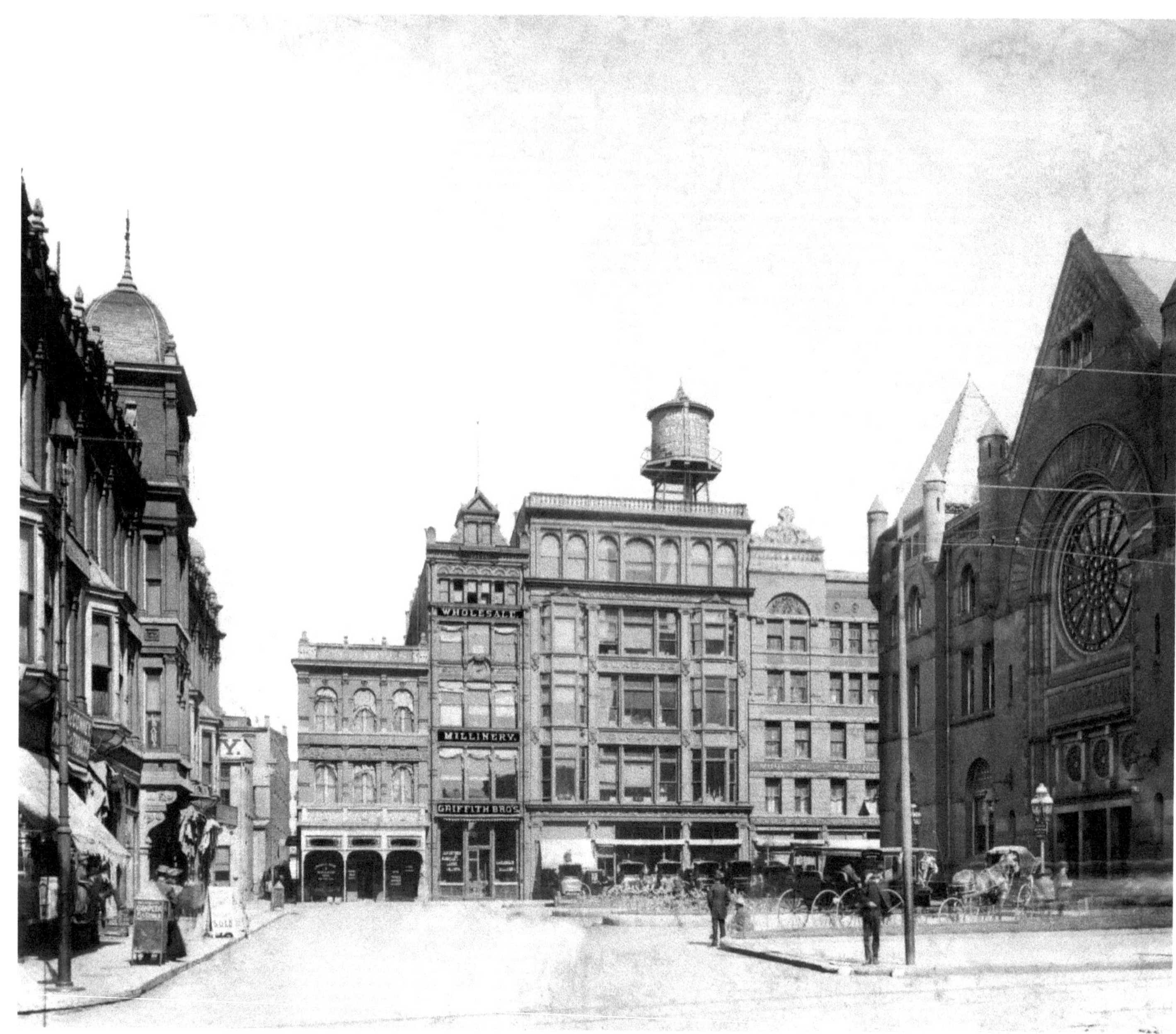

Jackson Place and Union Station, circa early 1900's. Union Station, seen on the right, replaced the old Union Depot, which was the first station in the country to serve multiple independent rail lines. In the early twentieth century some two hundred passenger trains arrived and departed daily from the station.

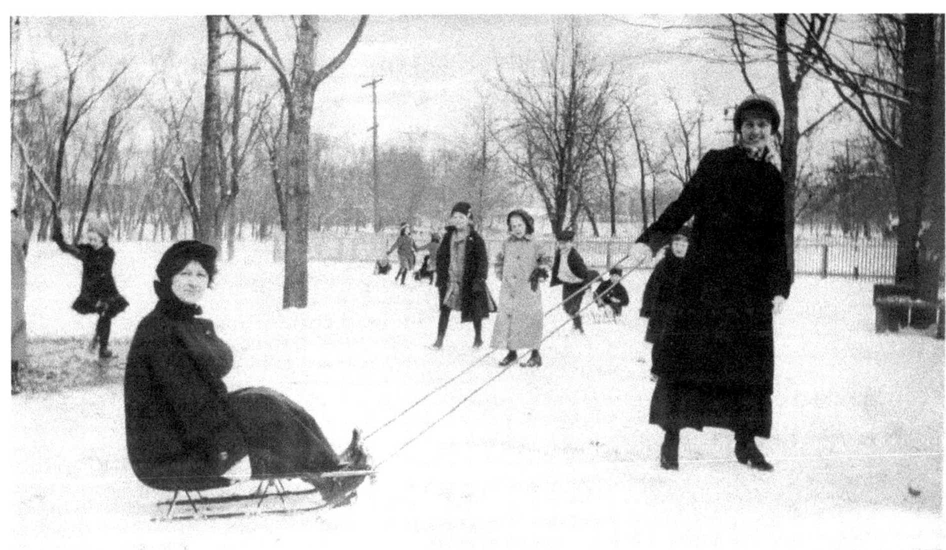

Women and children sledding in Broad Ripple Park, circa 1910's. The park, located on the city's north side, featured popular amusement attractions from 1906 until the mid-1940's.

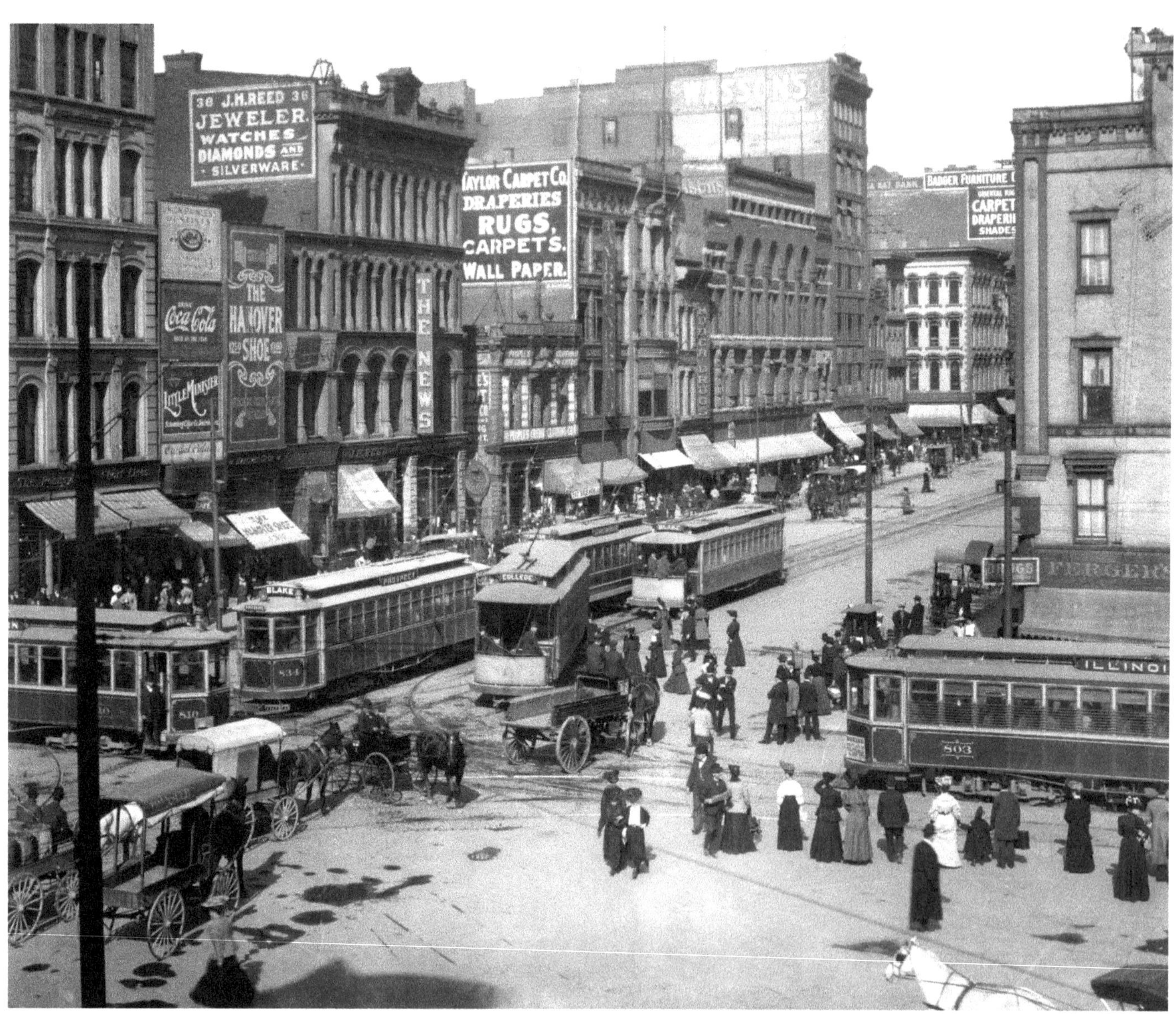

Washington and Illinois Streets, circa 1905. In the days before stoplights, busy Indianapolis intersections such as this were a jumble of streetcars and horse-drawn wagons and carriages.

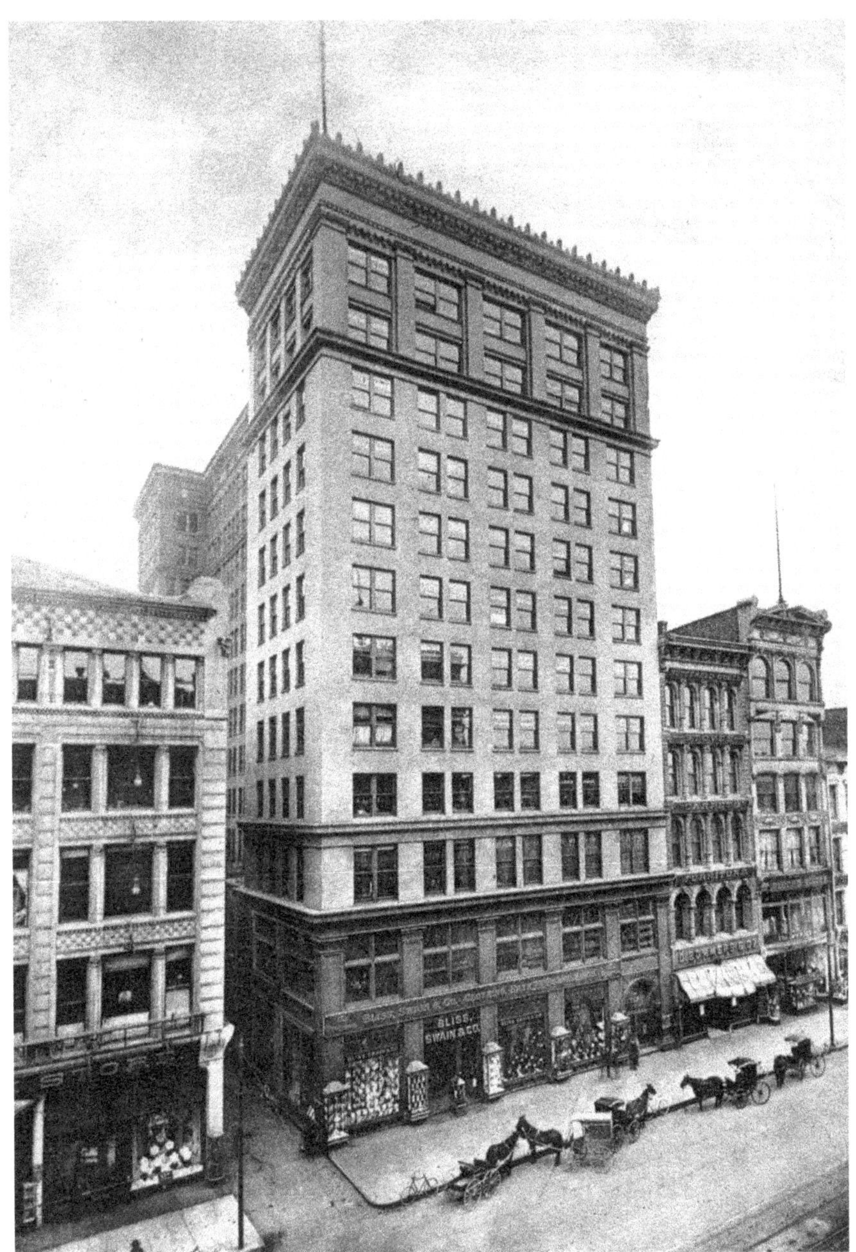

The State Life building, early 1900's. This building stood on the south side of Washington Street between Meridian and Pennsylvania Streets. A large fire destroyed it and a neighboring structure in 1973.

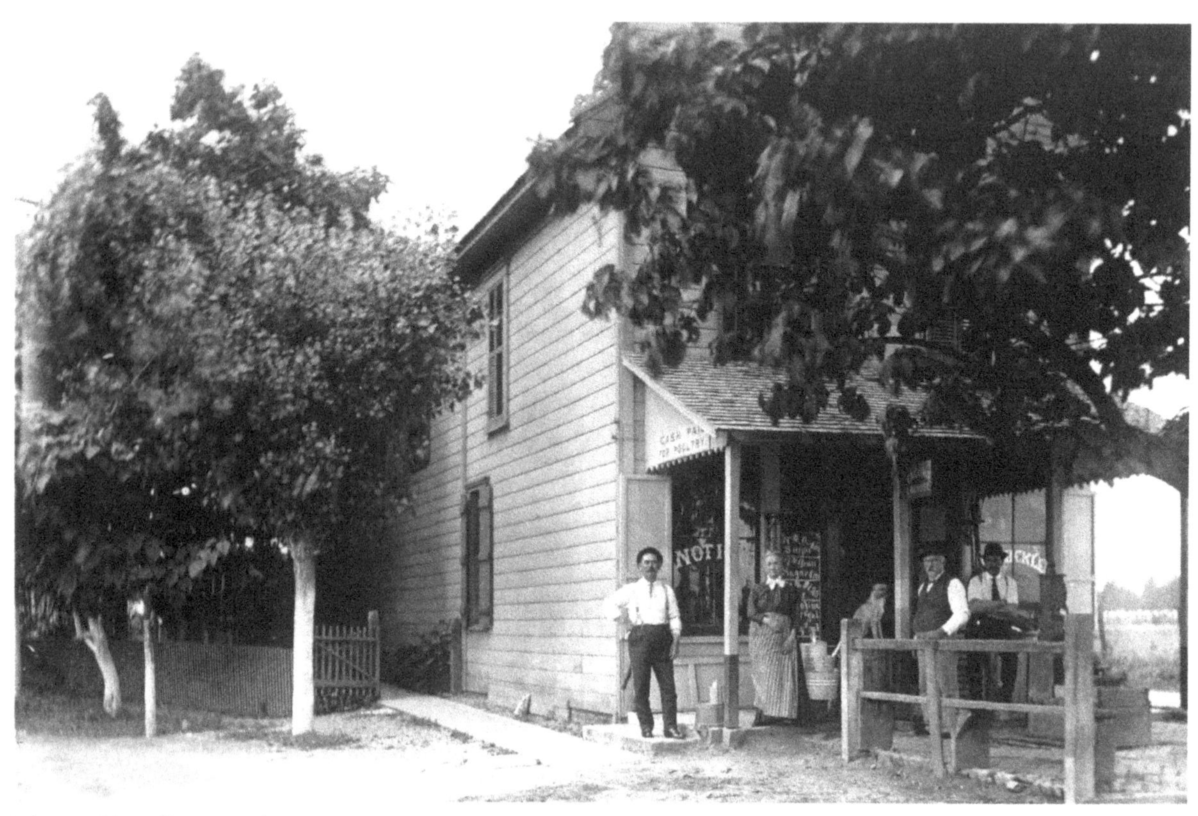

The Mickleyville General Store, circa 1905. Mickleyville was located west of Indianapolis, off the National Road (near the I-465/ Washington Street interchange today).

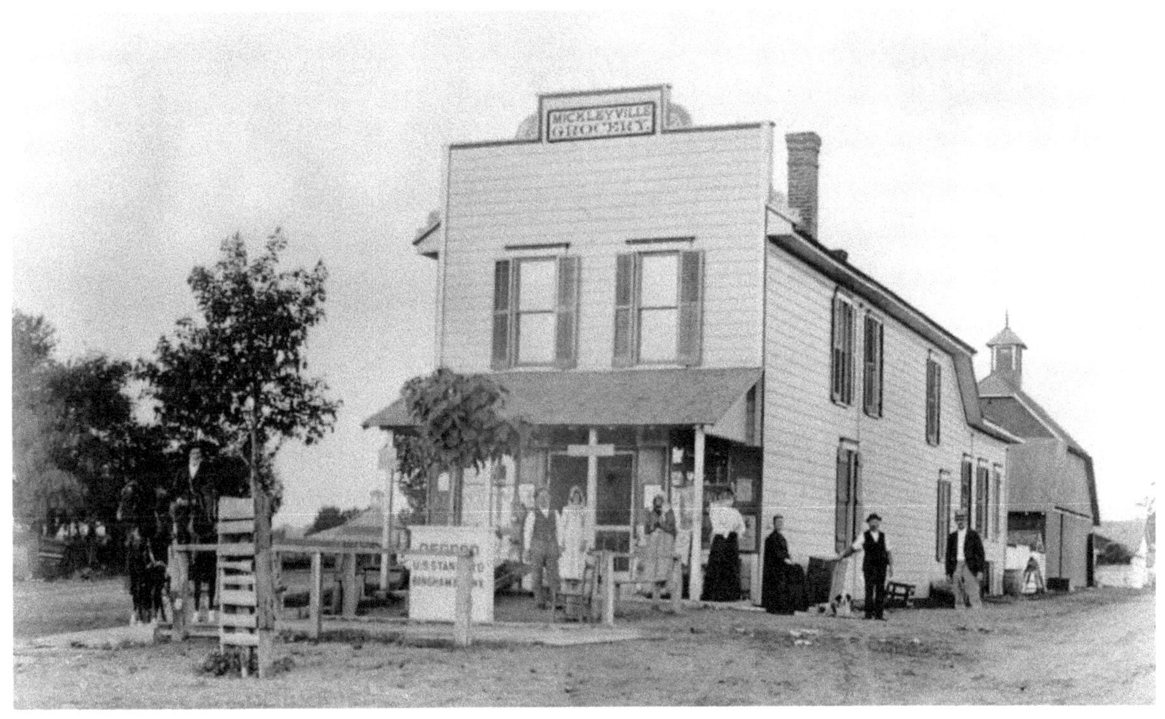

Joseph A. Mickley and family outside the Mickleyville Grocery, circa 1905.

The Commercial Club building, early 1900's. Col. Eli Lilly, founder of the pharmaceutical giant that bears his name, helped establish the Commercial Club in 1890. Its purpose was to promote economic development and improve the city. In 1893 members built this structure to house the club's offices. It was located on the southwest corner of Meridian and Pearl Streets, just east of where Lilly opened his first lab.

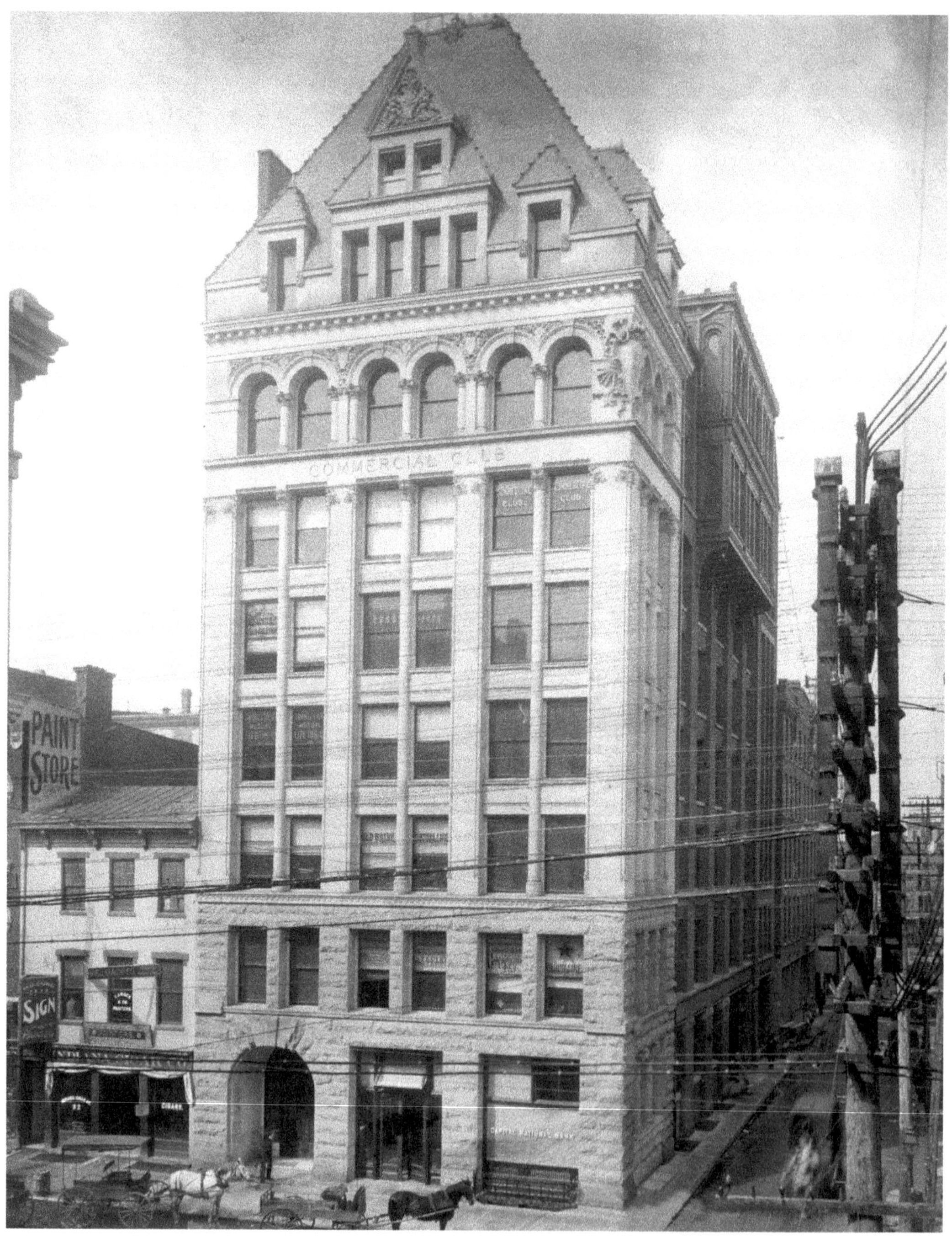

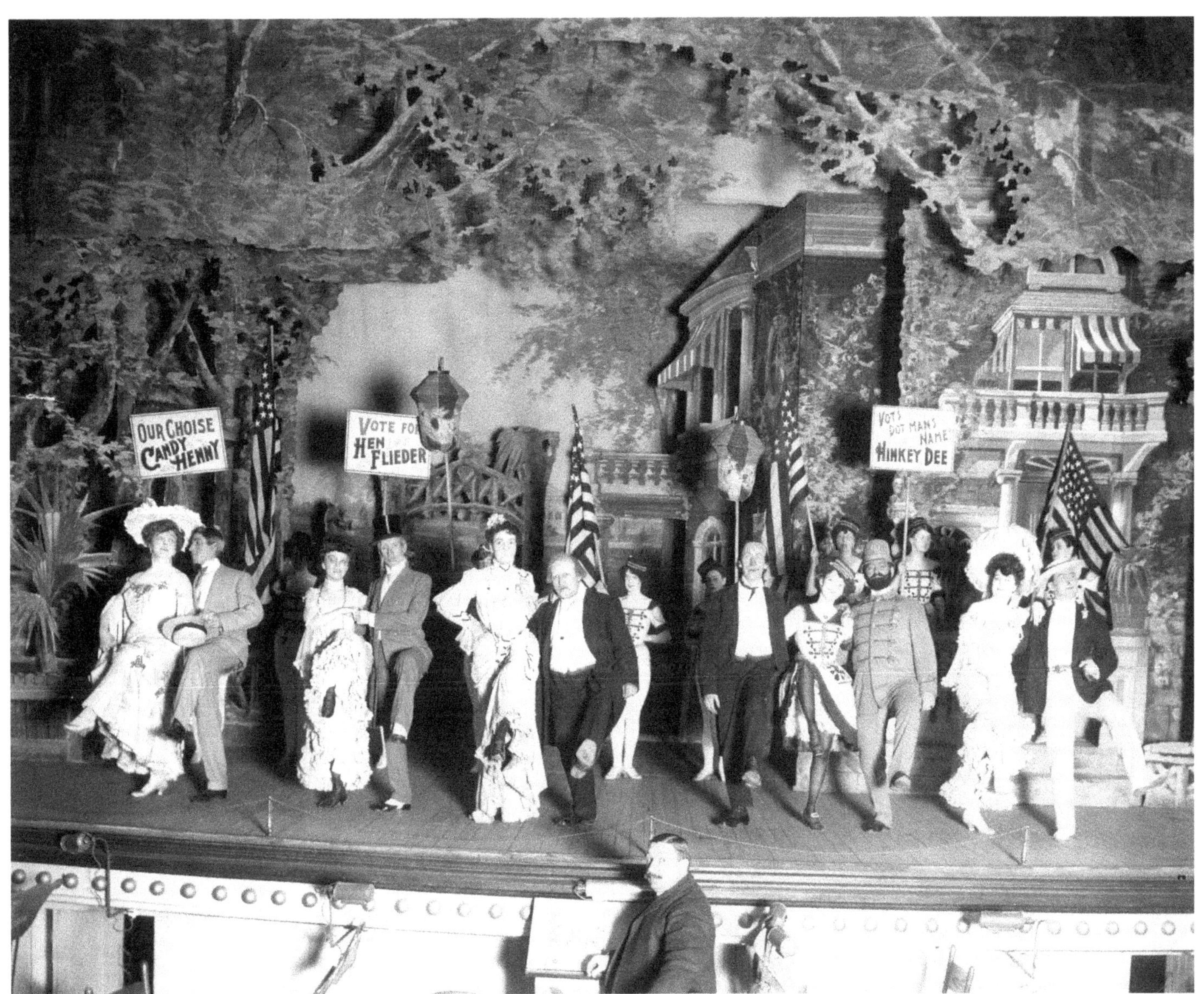

An early-twentieth-century production at the Empire Theater. The Empire was located on the east side of Delaware Street north of Market Street. It opened in 1892 and was renamed the Columbia Theater in 1913.

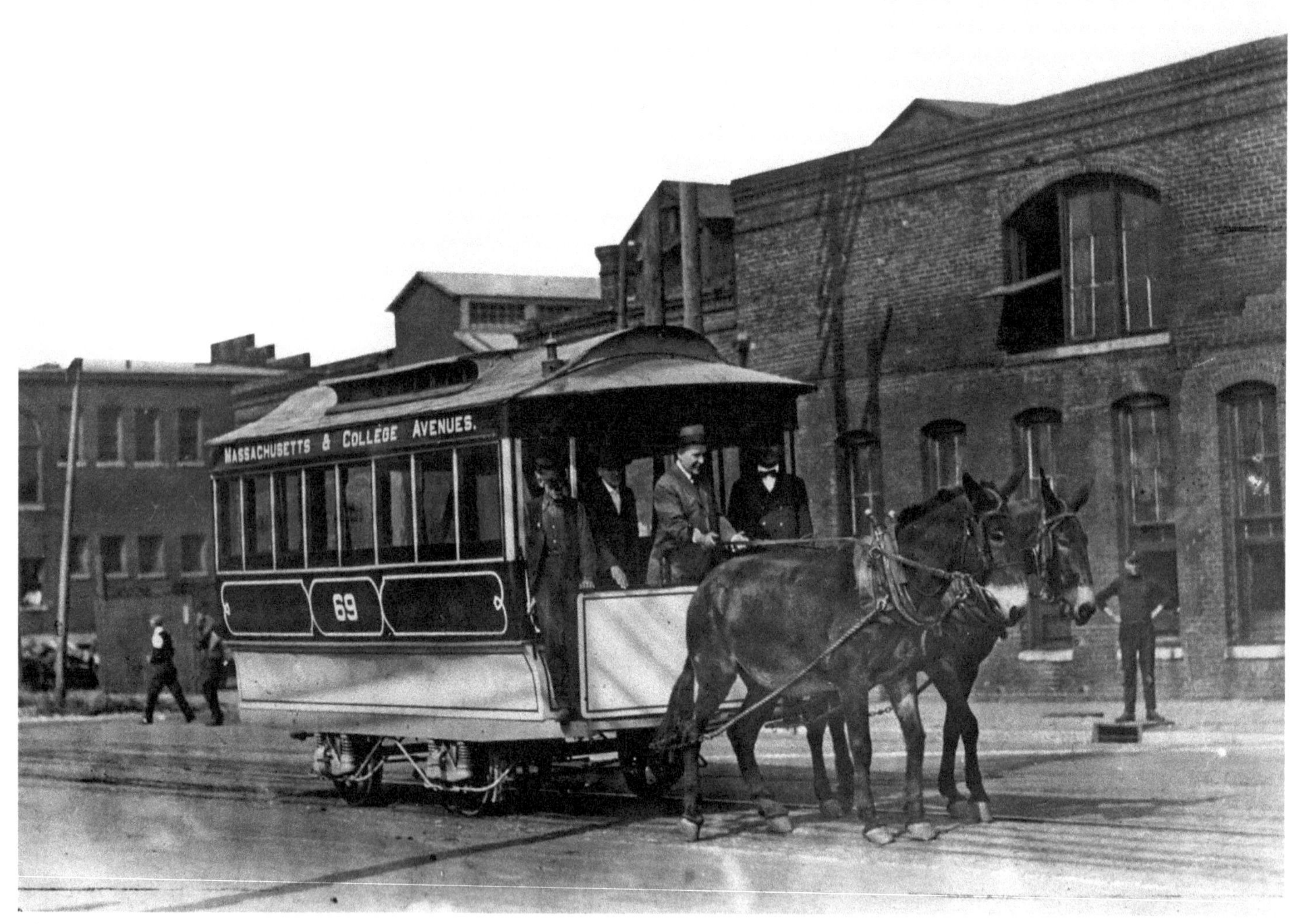

The old Massachusetts and College Avenues streetcar, circa late 1910's. Indianapolis's street railway company kept its prized No. 69 car and displayed it frequently. Here officials give it an "airing" on West Washington Street. The old car shops are seen in the background. The era of the mule-drawn streetcar ended in 1894.

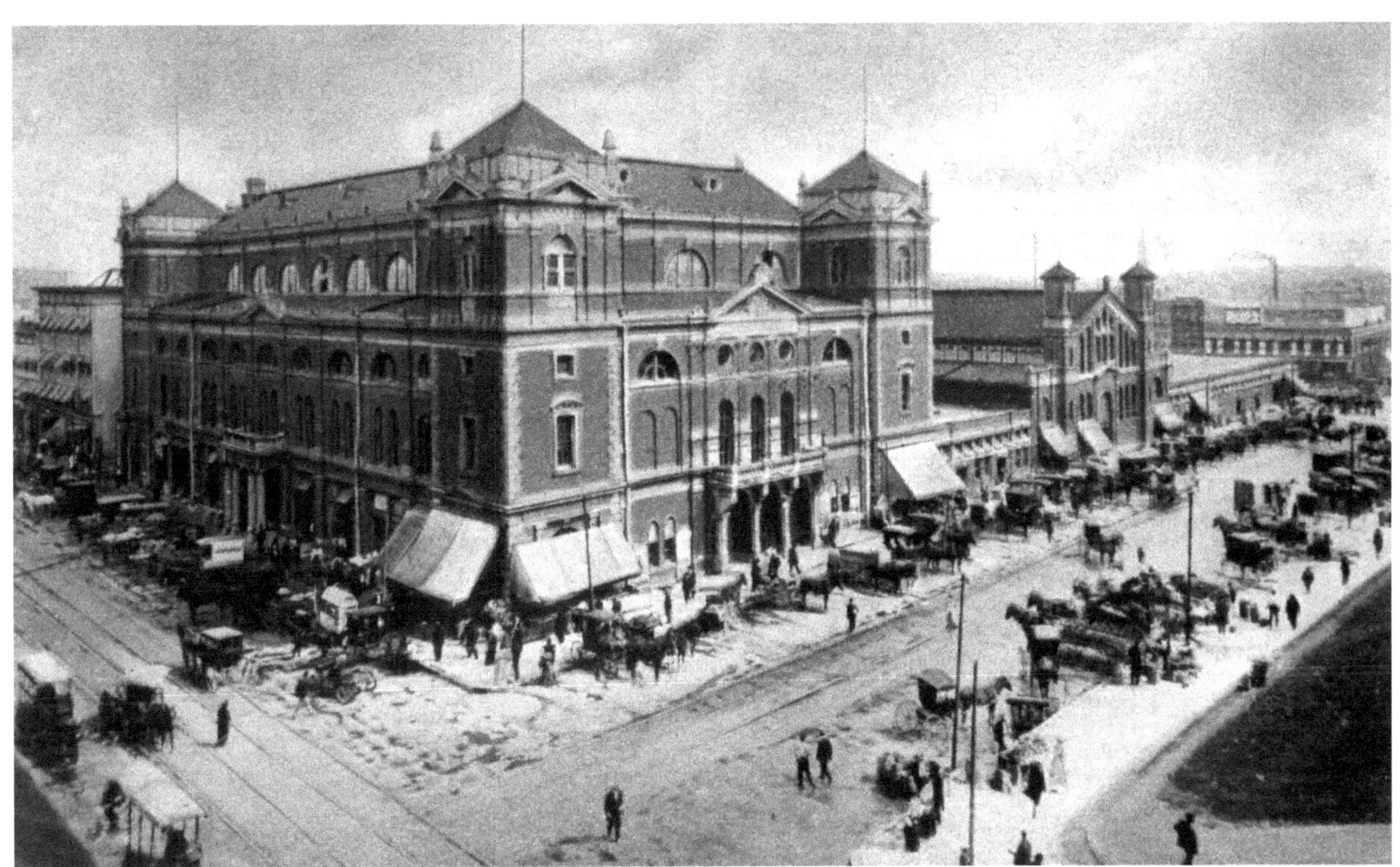

Tomlinson Hall and the city market. These buildings, both completed in 1886, were two of Indianapolis's important civic spaces in the late 1800's and early 1900's. Tomlinson Hall served as a convention hall and could seat more than four thousand people. It burned in 1958, and all that remains is a side-door arch. The city market still stands, and while it is now primarily home to lunch stands, it does host a farmers' market each Wednesday from spring through fall. This early-twentieth-century postcard view looks east from the corner of Delaware and Market Streets.

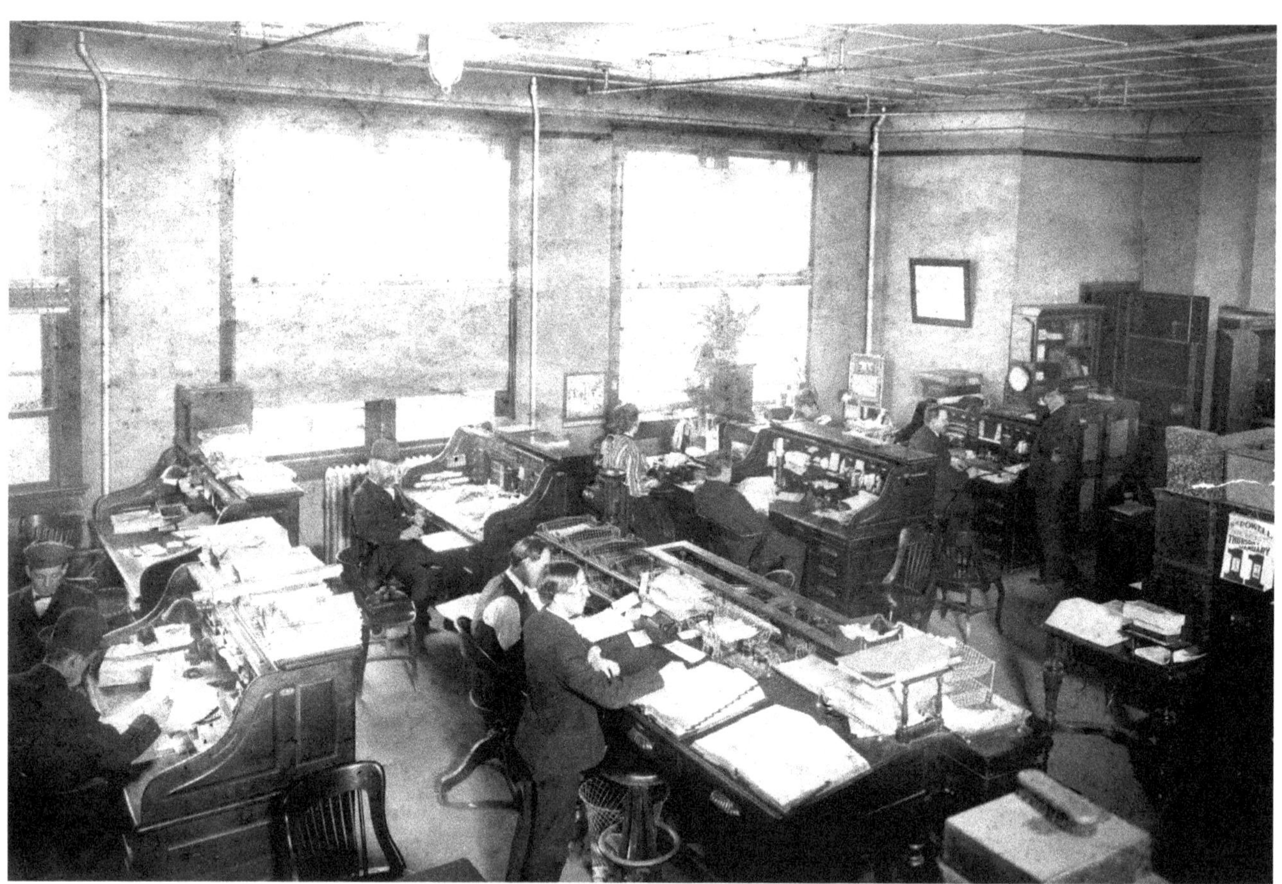

Workers in the Nordyke and Marmon Company offices. Male employees dominate in this early-twentieth-century view, with a lone woman working along the windows.

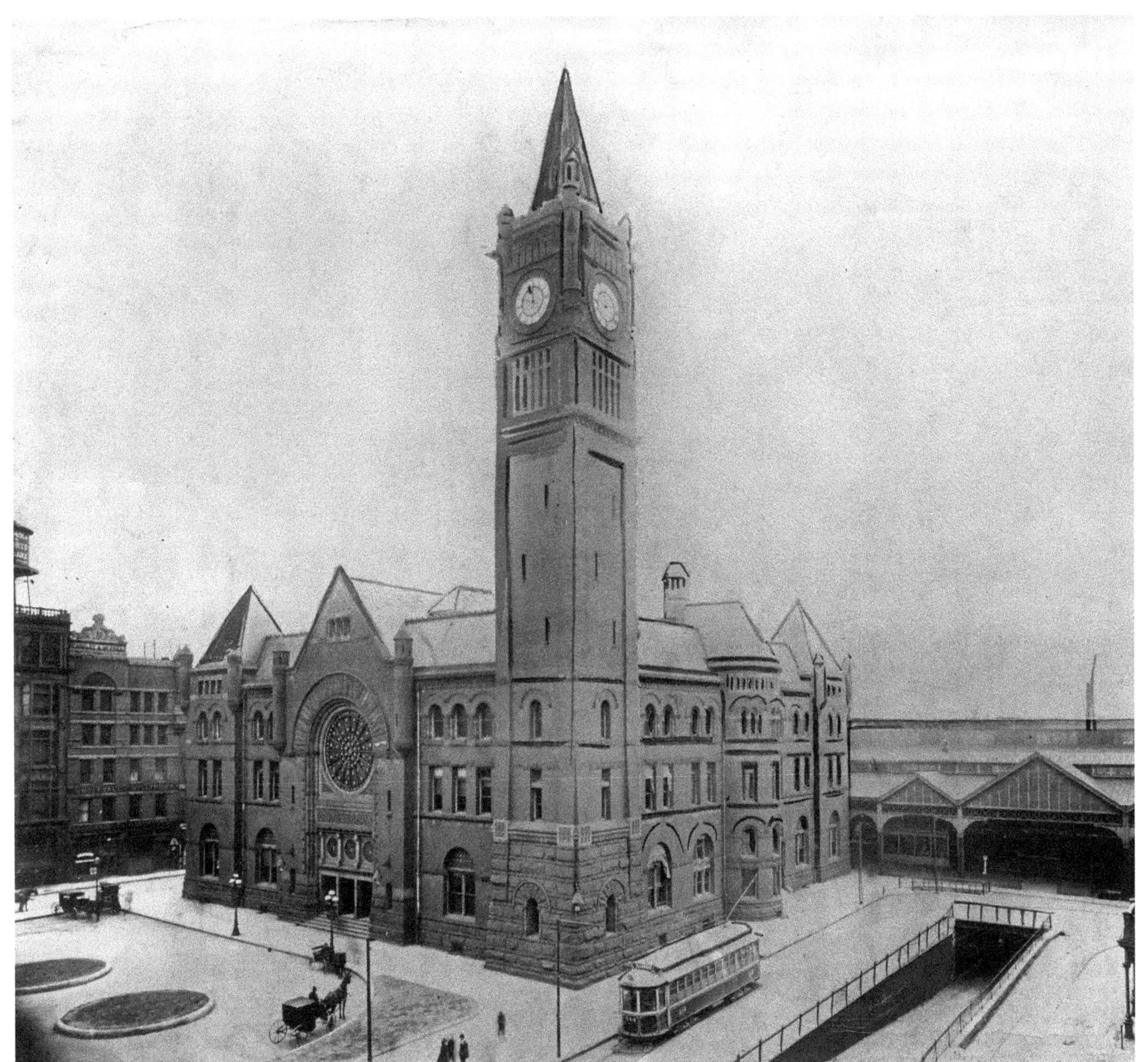

Union Station, 1903. The station, designed by Philadelphia architect Thomas Rodd and completed in 1888, serves as an excellent example of Romanesque Revival architecture. In the early twentieth century it was one of the nation's busiest rail hubs, but traffic was barely trickling through by the 1970's. In 1986 it reopened as a "festival marketplace," and today its magnificent headhouse serves as a banquet hall. This photo was taken before the tracks were elevated in 1915-18.

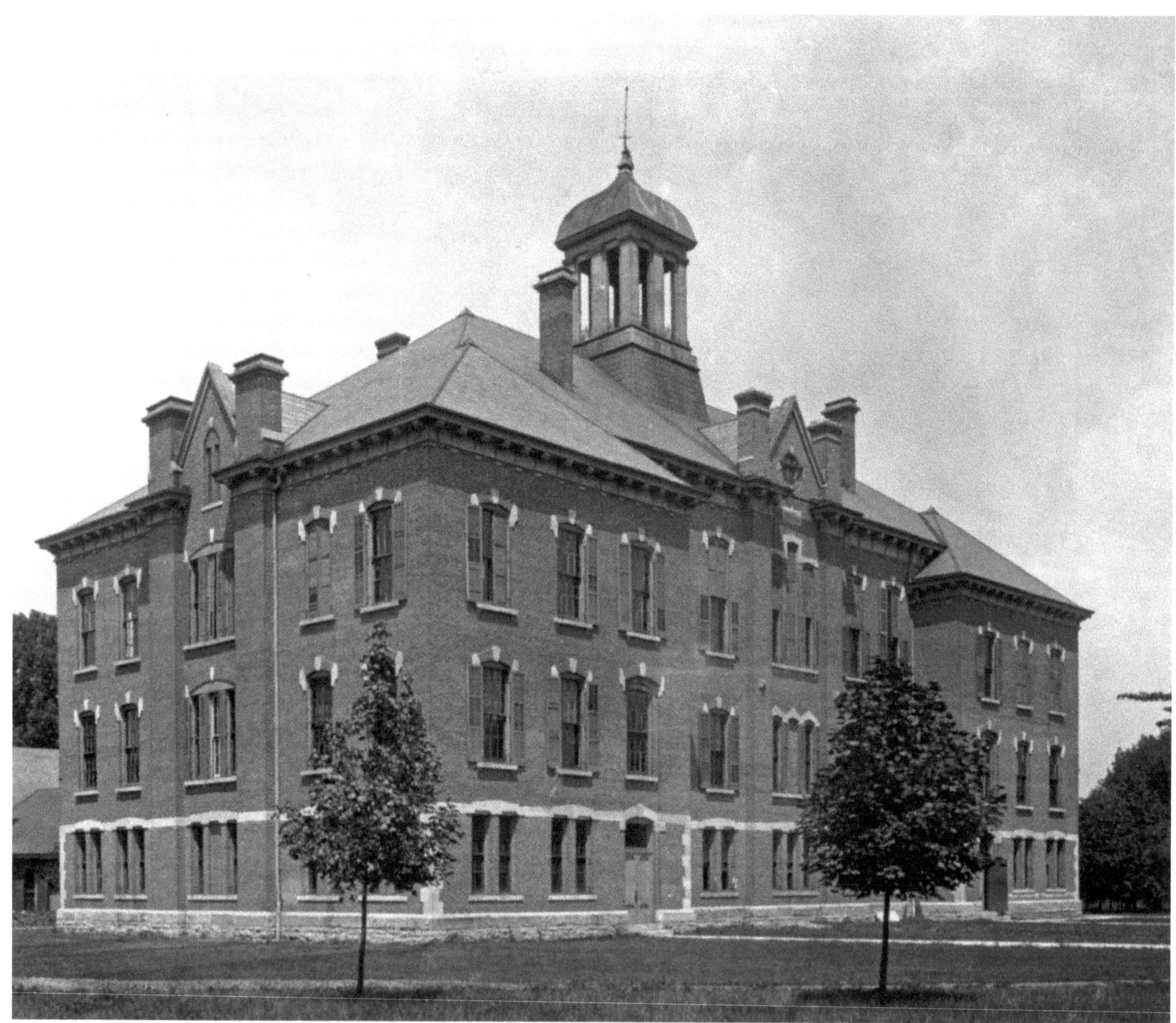

The administration building at Butler University, 1904. The Christian Church (Disciples of Christ) opened the school as North Western Christian University in 1855 at what is now College Avenue and Thirteenth Street. In 1875 the trustees moved the campus to the east-side suburb of Irvington, where this photograph was taken, and two years later they renamed it to honor longtime leader and benefactor Ovid Butler. In 1928 the university moved to its current location on the city's north side, where it has become one of the Midwest's leading private liberal-arts schools.

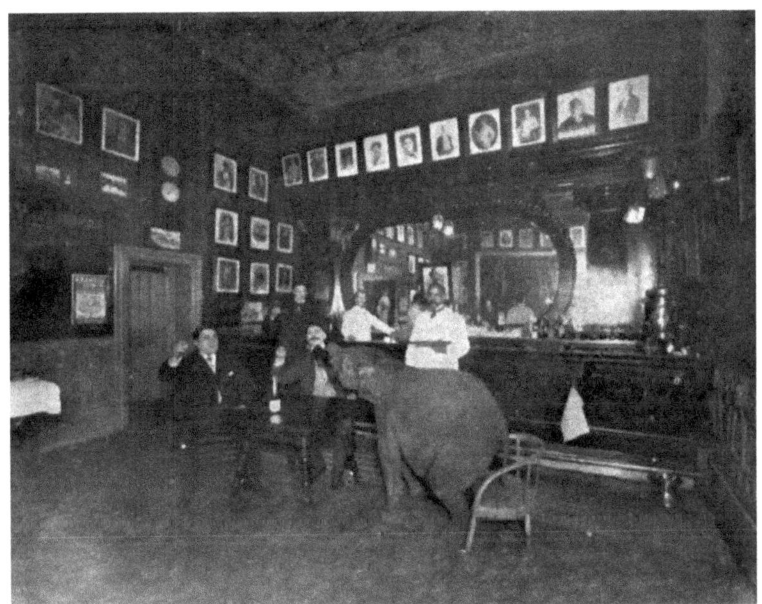

Little Hip, the "smallest elephant in the world," hosts a wine party at Indianapolis's Cozy Buffet, January 5, 1907. Little Hip was somewhat of a celebrity, making stops around the country and even appearing in a Broadway show.

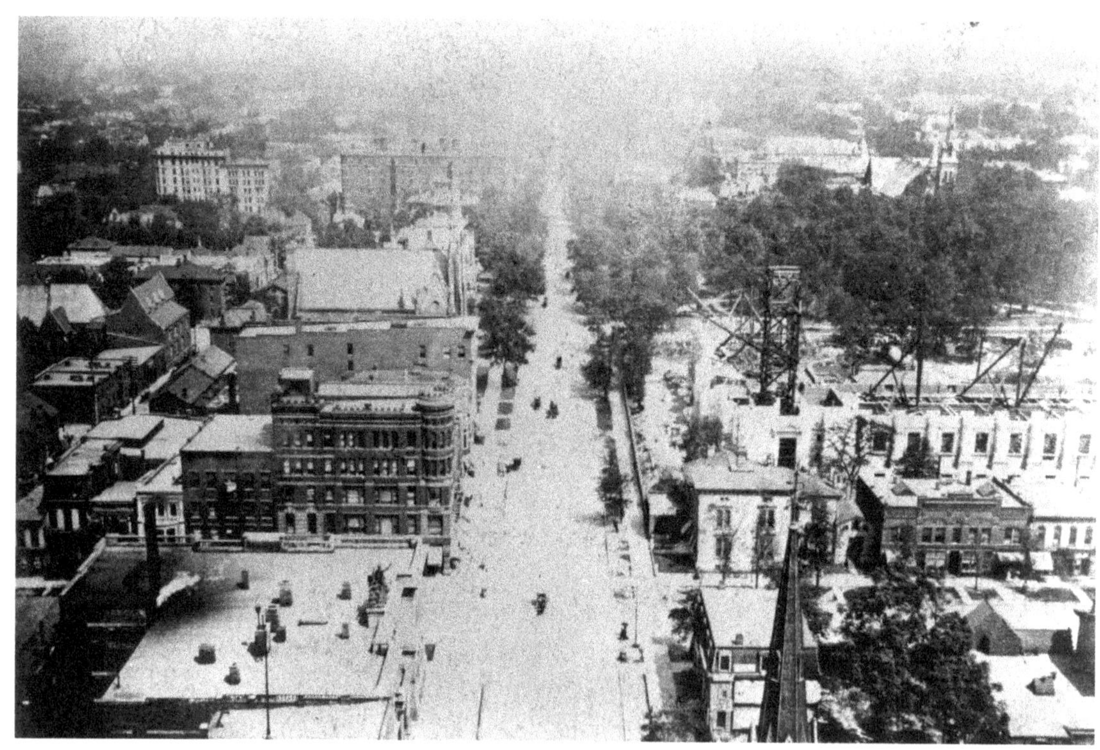

A view of North Meridian Street from the top of the Soldiers and Sailors Monument, 1903. Under construction at right center is the United States courthouse and post office on Ohio Street. Workers broke ground on it in 1902 and completed it in 1905.

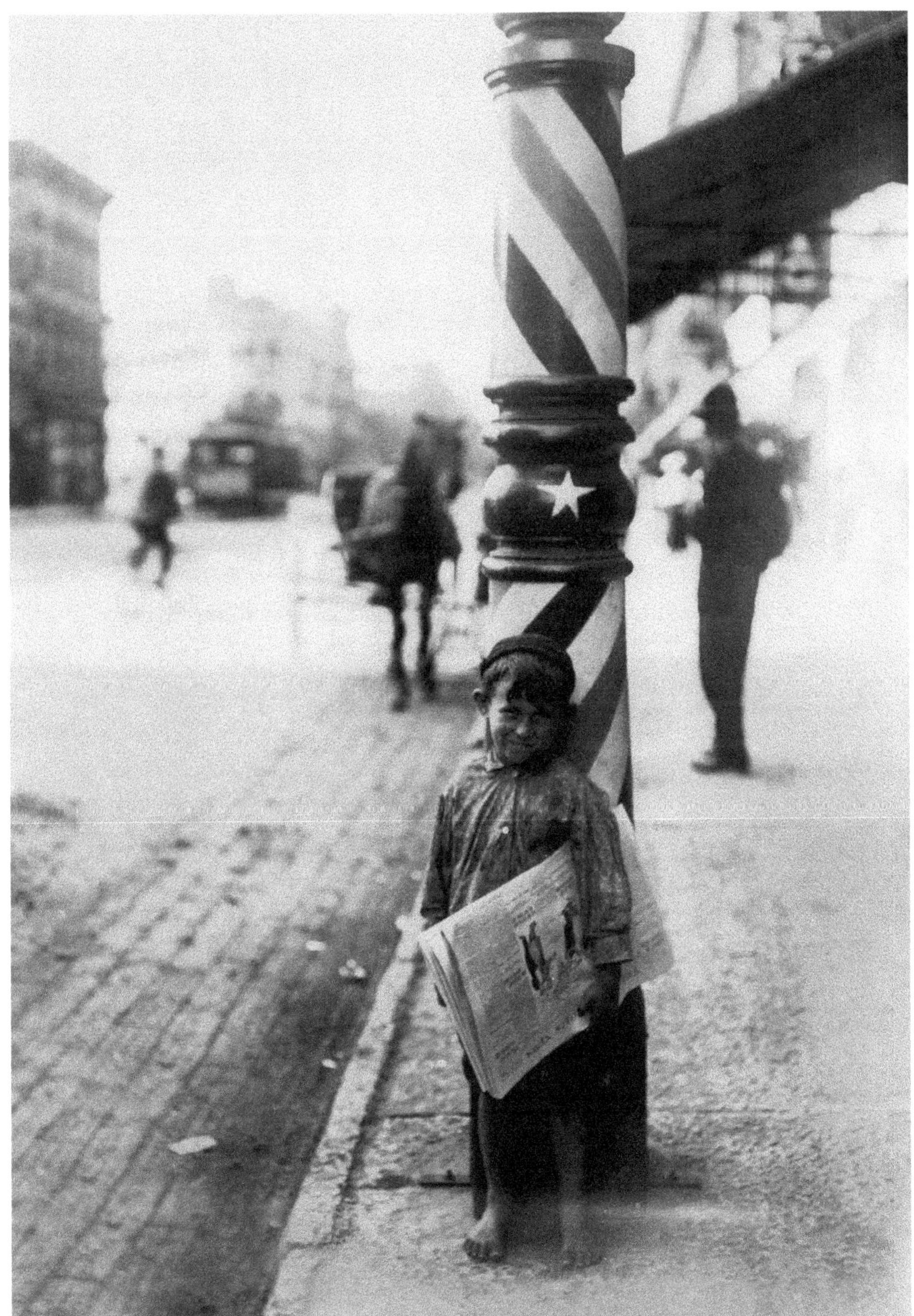

An Indianapolis newsboy, 1908. Noted photographer Lewis Hine took this picture as well as many other images of child laborers in this volume. According to Hine this child was only six years old and just forty-one inches high.

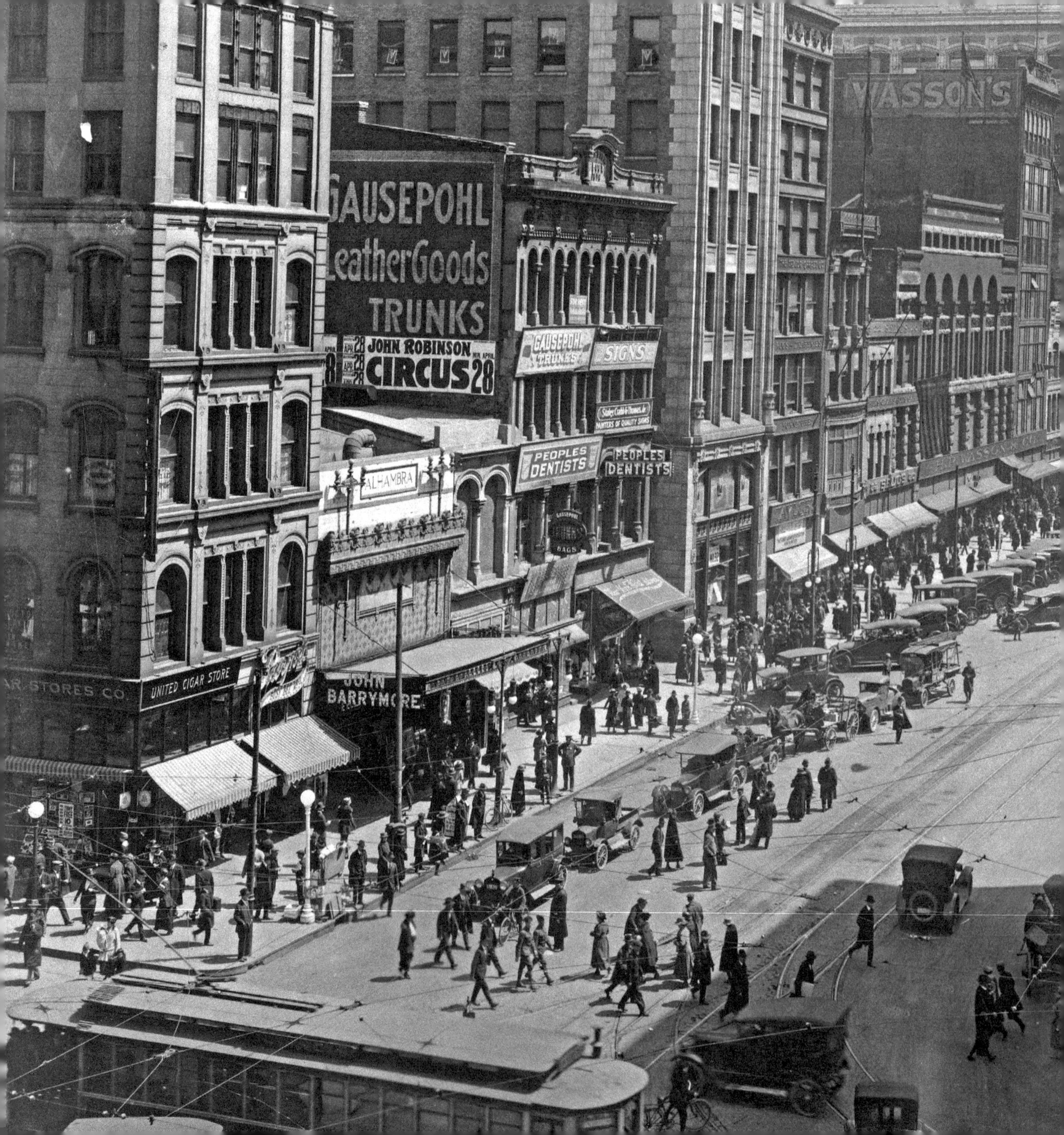
WASSON'S
GAUSEPOHL
Leather Goods
TRUNKS
JOHN ROBINSON
CIRCUS
APRIL 28
GAUSEPOHL
TRUNKS
SIGNS
PEOPLES
DENTISTS
PEOPLES
DENTISTS
ALHAMBRA
GAUSEPOHL
BAGS
UNITED CIGAR STORE
AR STORES CO.
JOHN
BARRYMORE

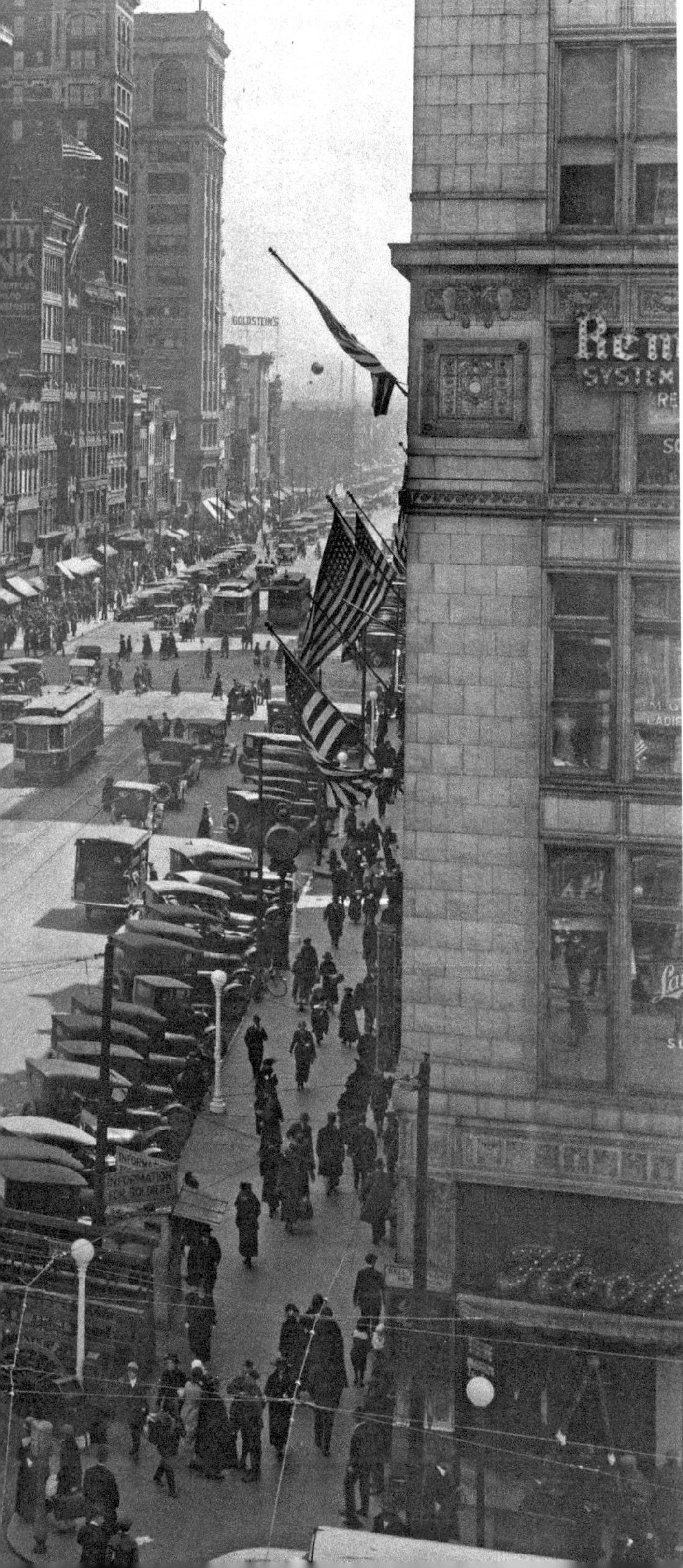

Washington Street looking east from Illinois Street, 1919. Washington Street served as Indianapolis's retail center from the time of the city's founding until suburban shopping malls began drawing away business in the late 1950's. This early-twentieth-century photograph shows the crowds that used to flock to its department stores, shops, hotels, and theaters.

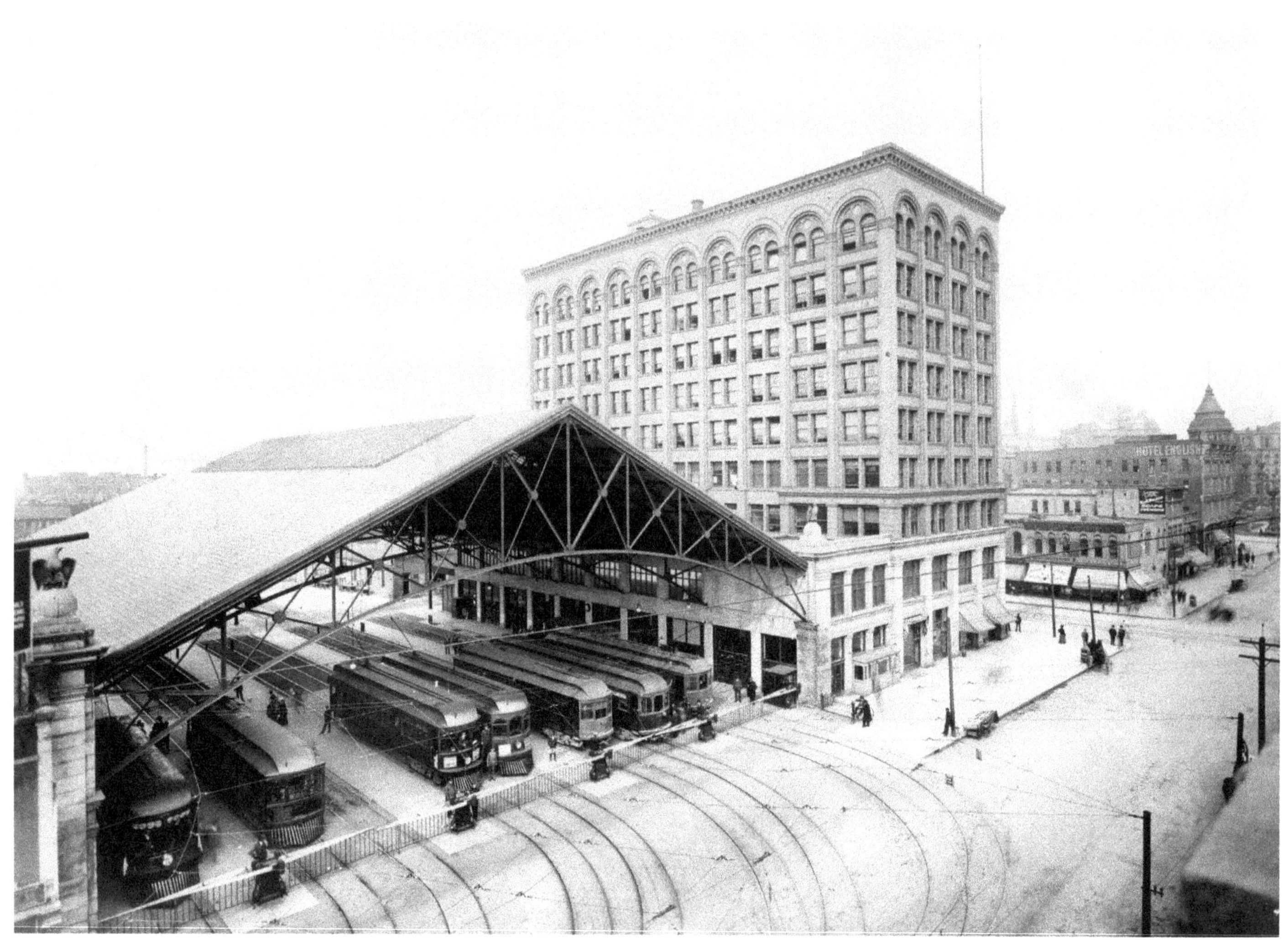

The Indianapolis Traction Terminal. The traction terminal opened in 1904 on the northwest corner of Illinois and Market Streets, just east of the state capitol. It served as a station for the numerous interurban trains that traveled across the state in the first three decades of the twentieth century. The shed covered nine tracks and the terminal building held 250 offices, making the complex the largest of its kind in the world. The shed was torn down in 1968 and the terminal building in 1972. Two stone eagles that graced the south side of the shed still remain, relocated to the former city hall on Alabama Street.

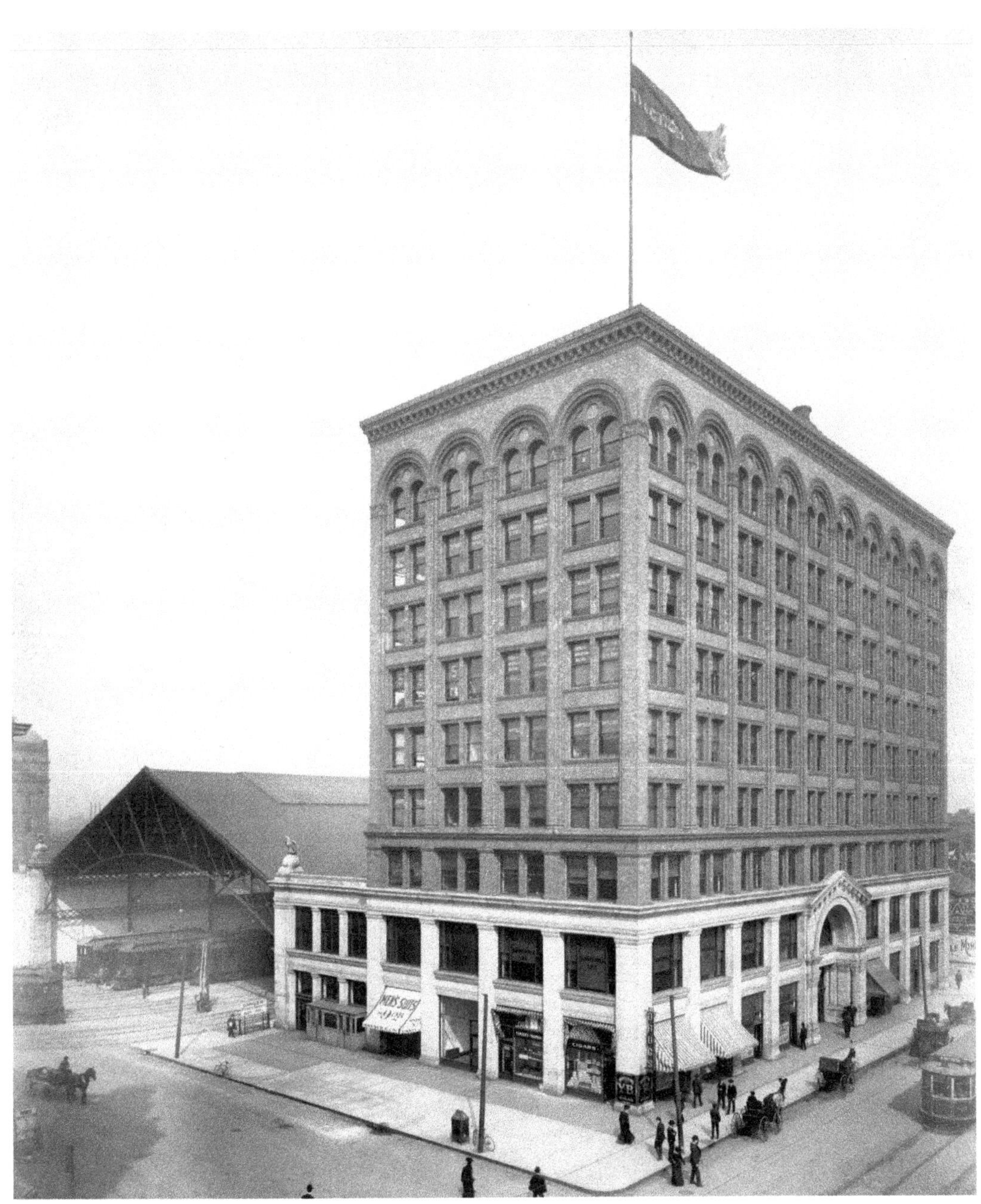

A view of the traction terminal from the east. The firm of Chicago architect Daniel Burnham designed the nine-story building.

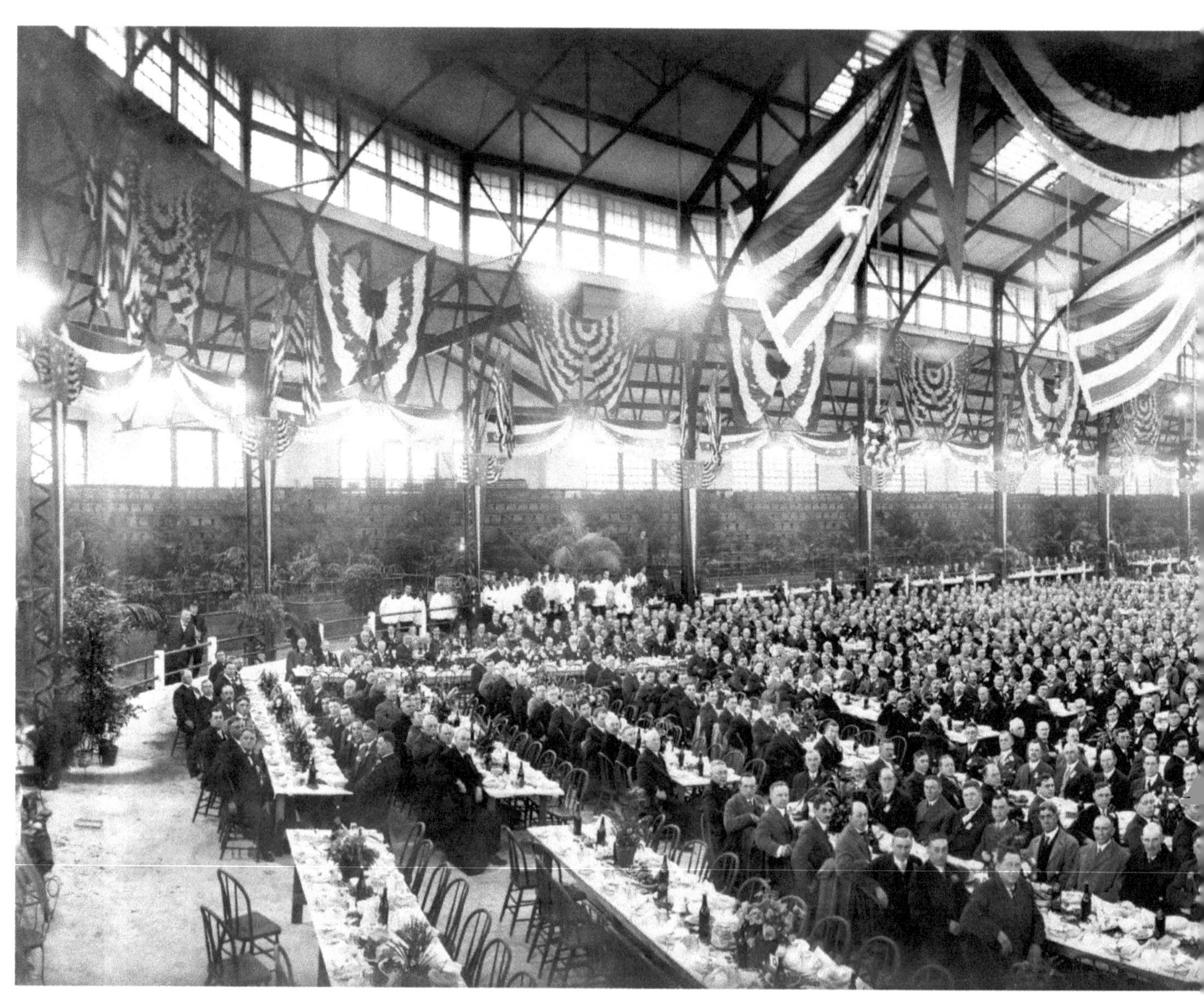

Members of the Ancient Accepted Scottish Rite celebrate the organization's golden jubilee, May 19, 1915. The celebration took place at the Indiana state fairgrounds coliseum.

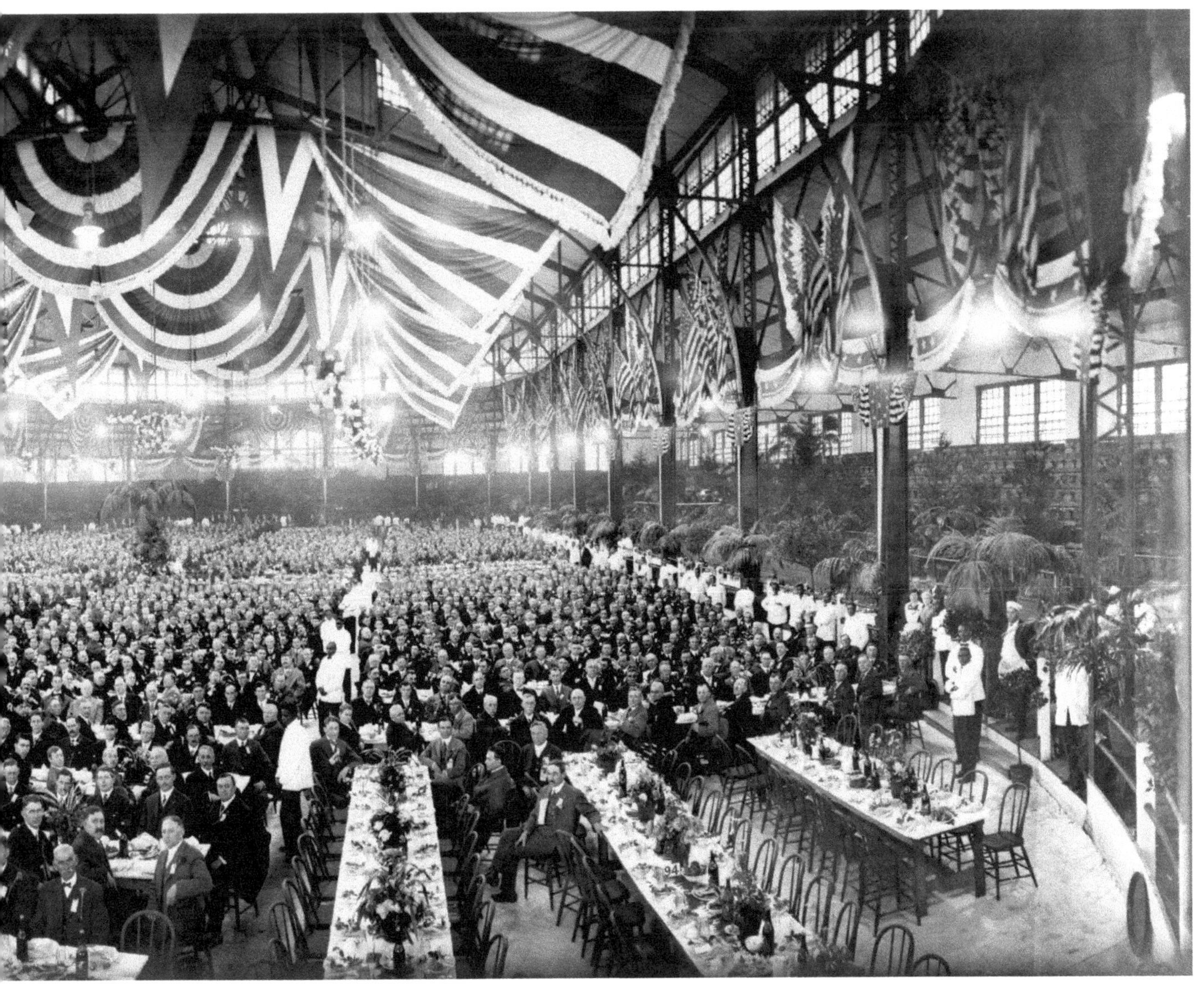

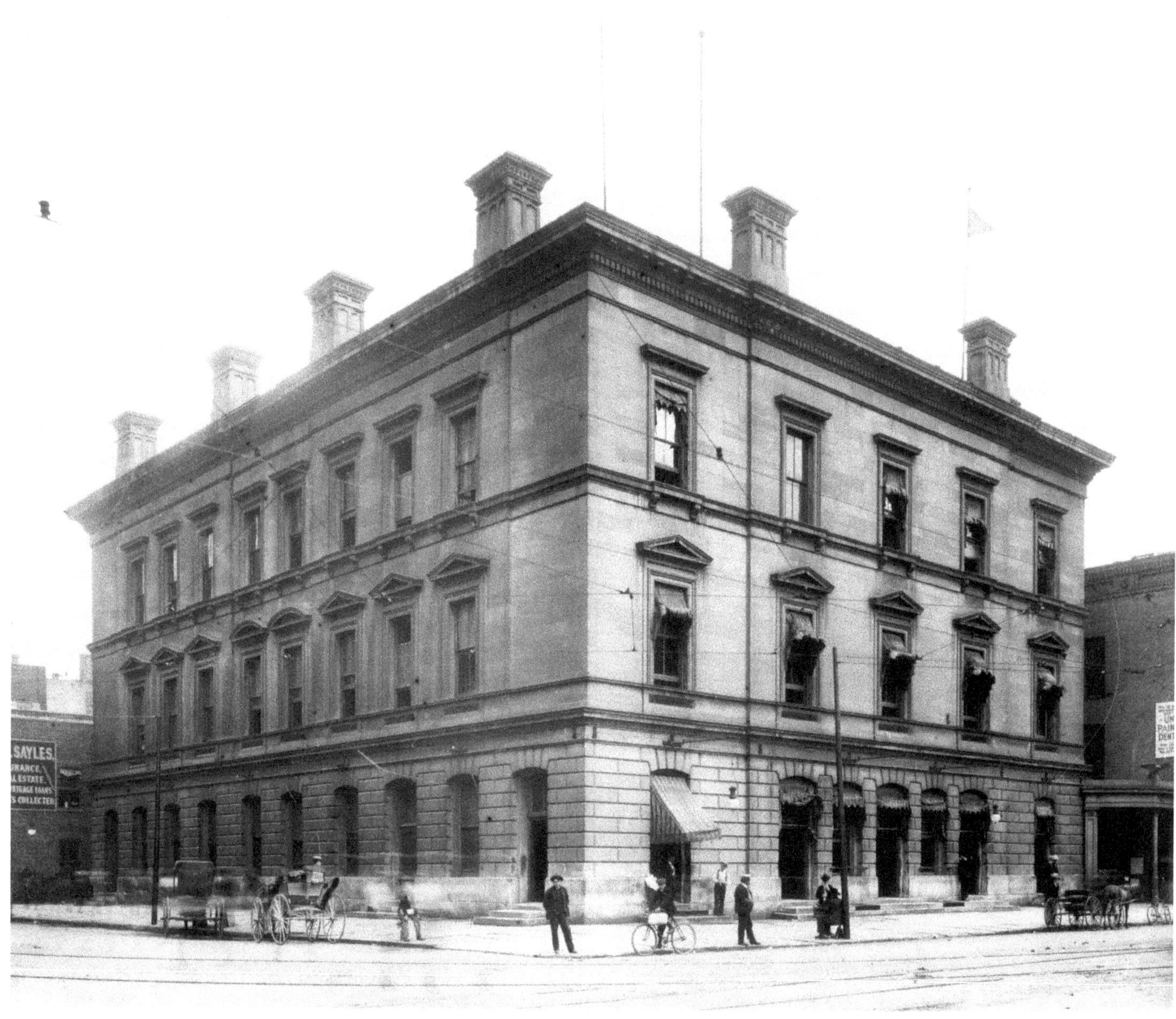

The old federal building, 1905. Completed in 1860, this was the first federal building in Indianapolis. It stood on the southeast corner of Pennsylvania and Market Streets and housed the post office and federal courtrooms. Though it was expanded in the mid-1870s, it quickly ran out of space, so the government constructed a new federal building at Meridian and Ohio Streets in the early 1900's. Afterward this structure served as a bank.

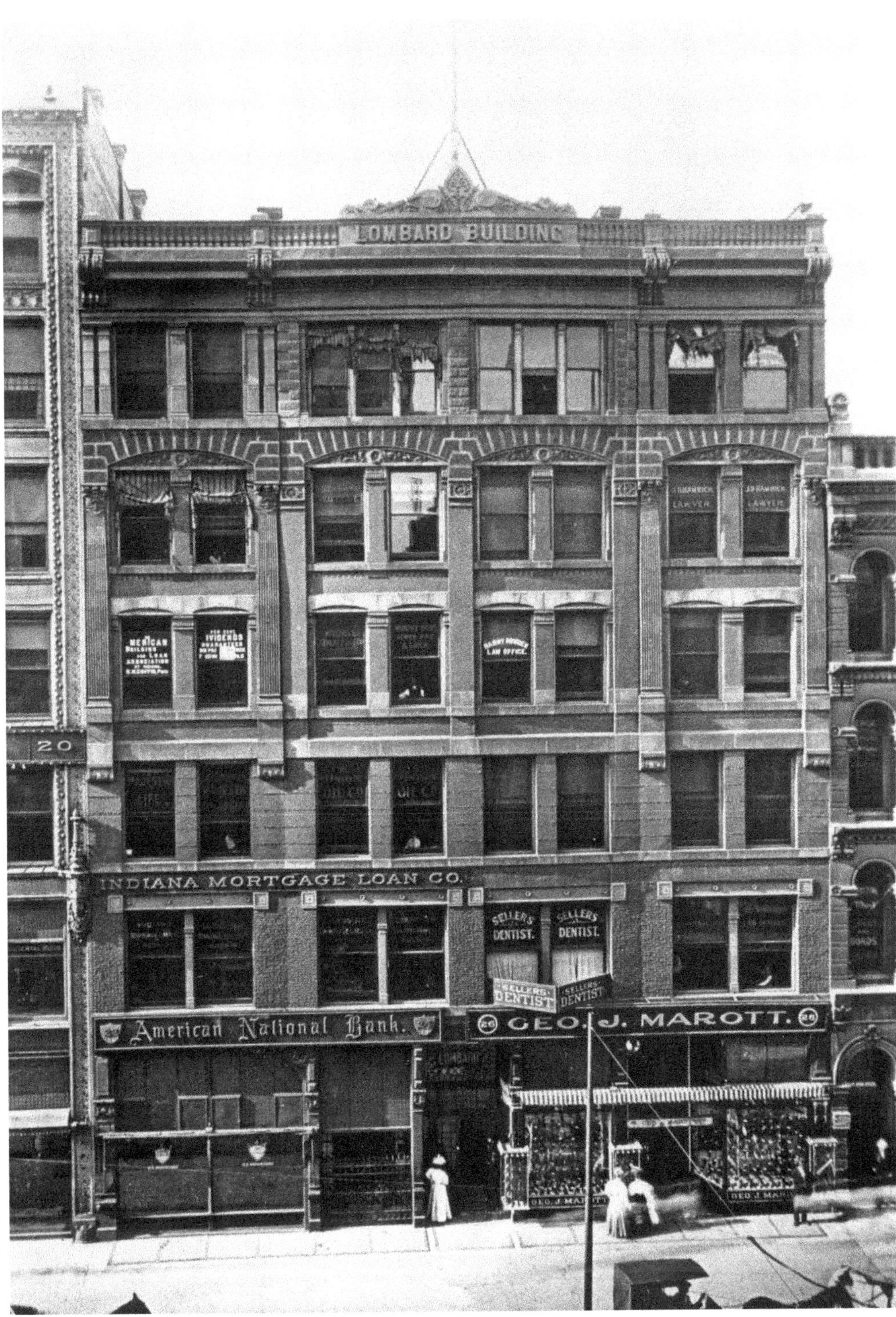

The Lombard building, circa 1905. Architect Robert Platt Daggett designed this building, which was constructed in 1893 on the north side of Washington Street between Meridian and Pennsylvania Streets. Now renamed the Victoria Centre, it is listed on the National Register of Historic Places.

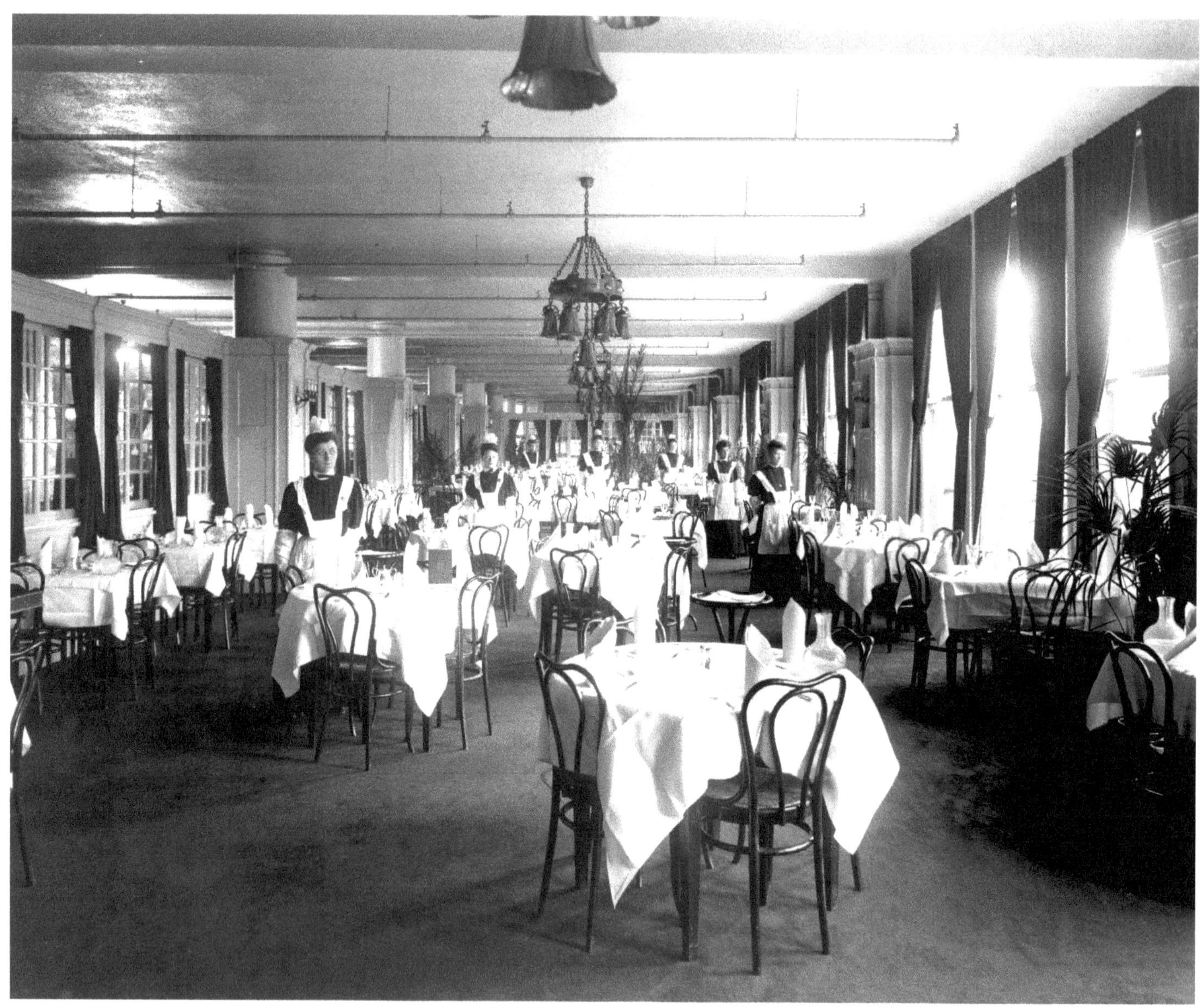

The L. S. Ayres tea room, circa 1905. When L. S. Ayres and Company opened its new department store at Washington and Meridian Streets in 1905, it included a tea room on the fifth floor, where shoppers could rest and have a meal. Years later the tea room relocated to the top floor, the eighth. Many Hoosiers still recall with fondness its chicken velvet soup and children's toy chest. Though Ayres is now gone, the Indiana State Museum has re-created the tea room, giving visitors the chance to once again enjoy its recipes and relive a bit of the Ayres experience.

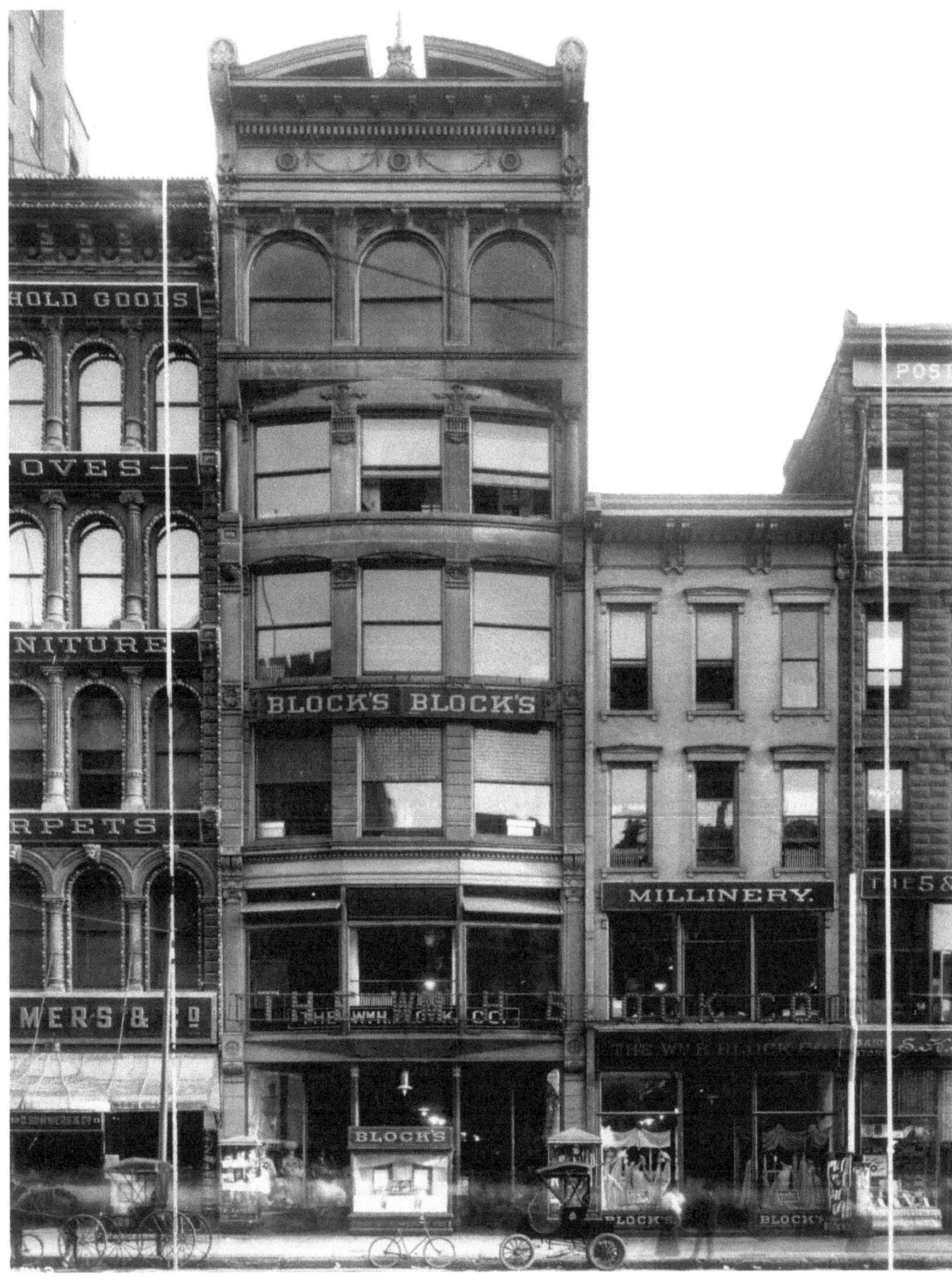

The William H. Block Company, circa 1906. William Block moved to Indianapolis in 1896 and opened his first retail shop on Washington Street, seen here. Business grew quickly, and in 1911 he built a large eight-story department store on the southwest corner of Illinois and Market Streets. Block's fiercely competed with rival L. S. Ayres and Company until 1988, when its corporate owners sold it and it became part of the Lazarus department store chain.

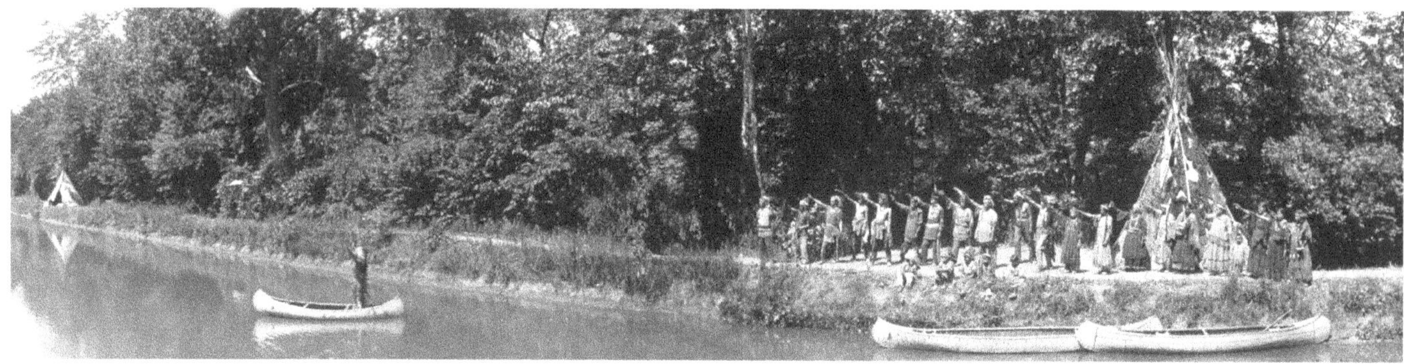

Members of the Ojibway tribe perform a dramatization of Henry Wadsworth Longfellow's "Song of Hiawatha," 1913. Performances ran from July 4 through July 9 and took place along the old Central Canal at Fairview Park, today the site of Butler University. According to the *Indianapolis Star*, proceeds from the show were to benefit the Summer Mission for Sick Children, a "fresh air" mission that worked to improve the health and general well-being of impoverished youth.

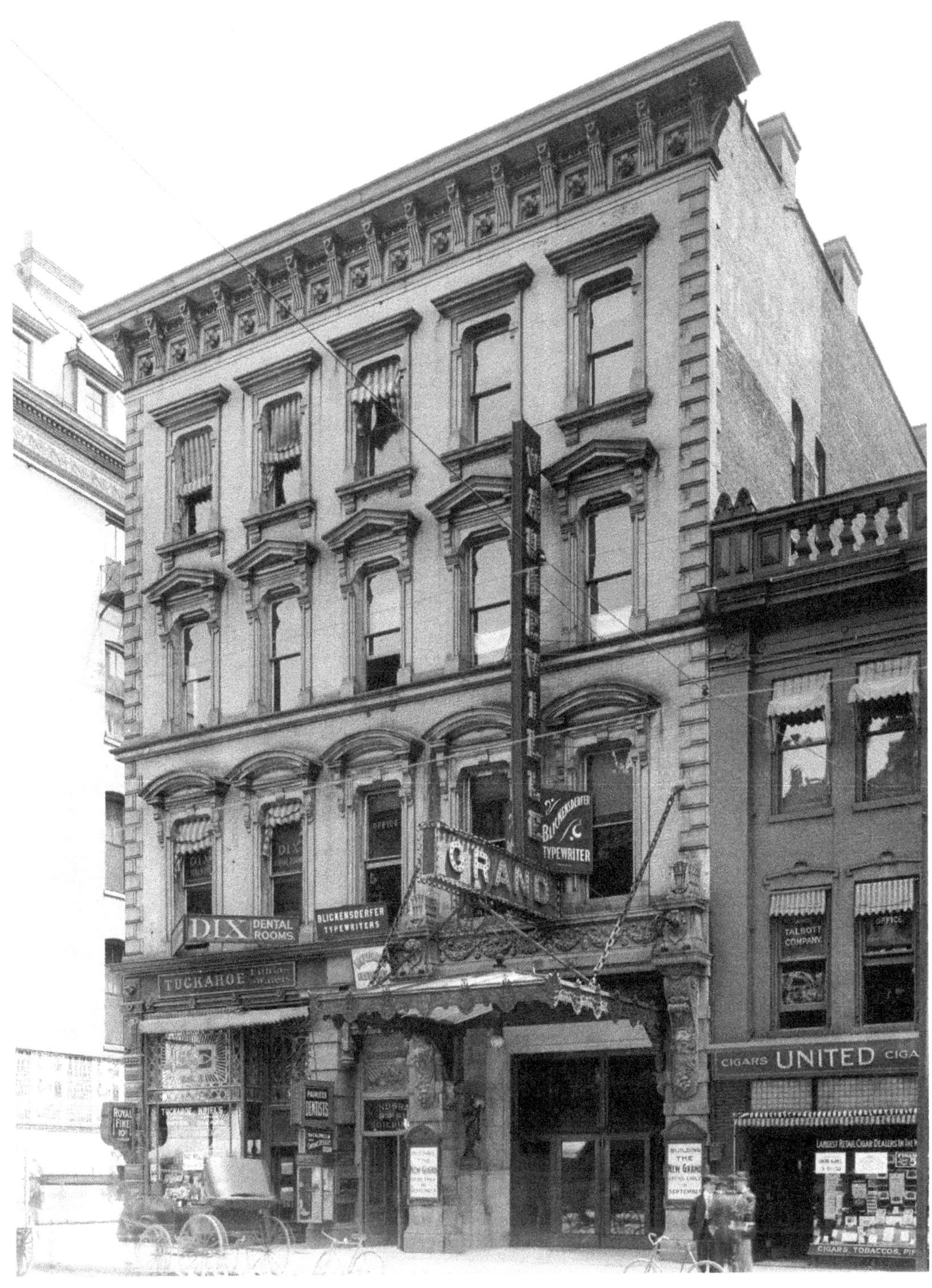

The Grand Opera House, circa 1907. The opera house opened in 1875 on Pennsylvania Street north of Market, and the caption on this photo describes it as the "original of the Pennsylvania Street amusement center." One history claims that it was the first American theater to be electrically lit. In 1910 it was renamed B. F. Keith's.

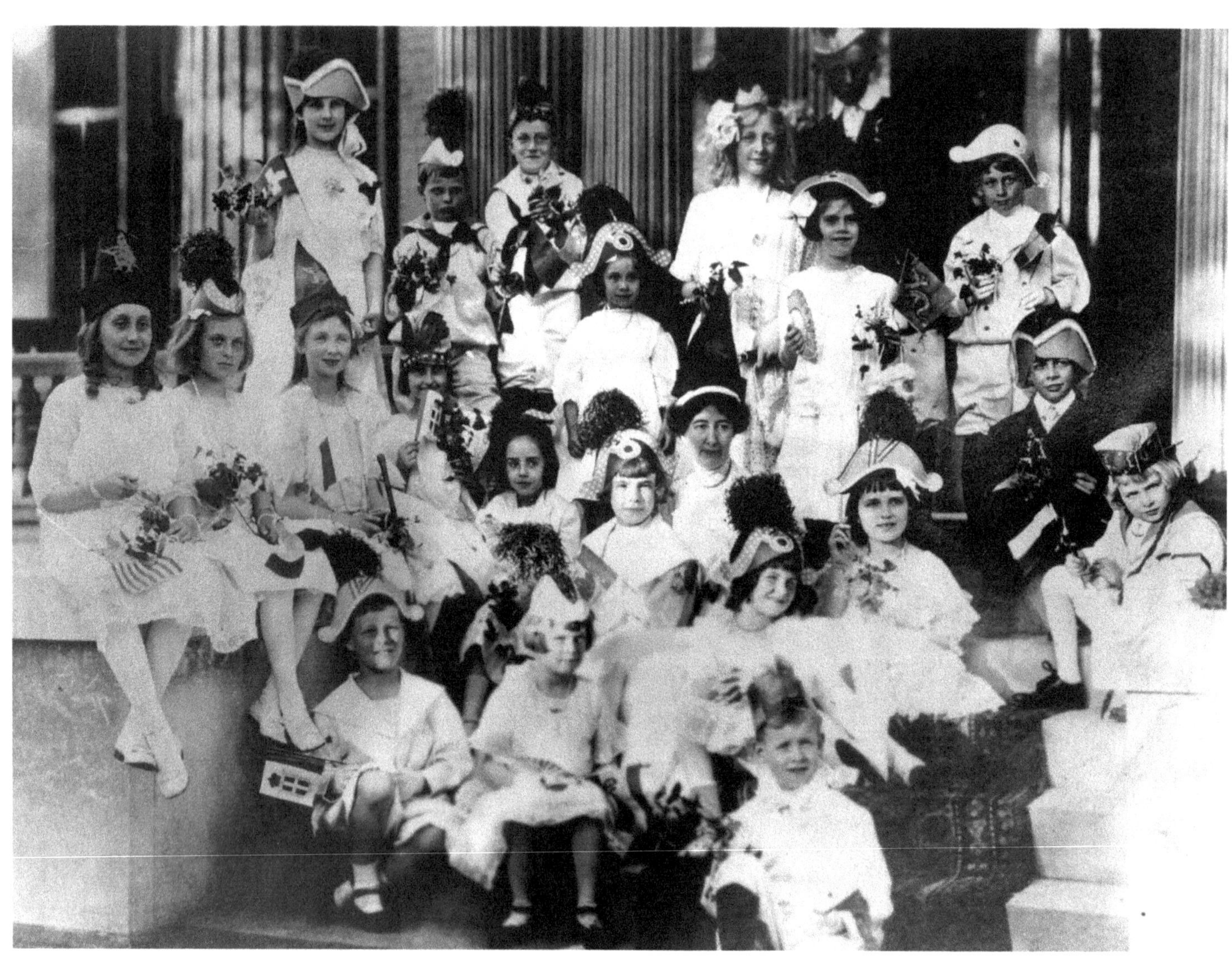

A children's dance class, circa 1907. The students appear ready to give a performance.

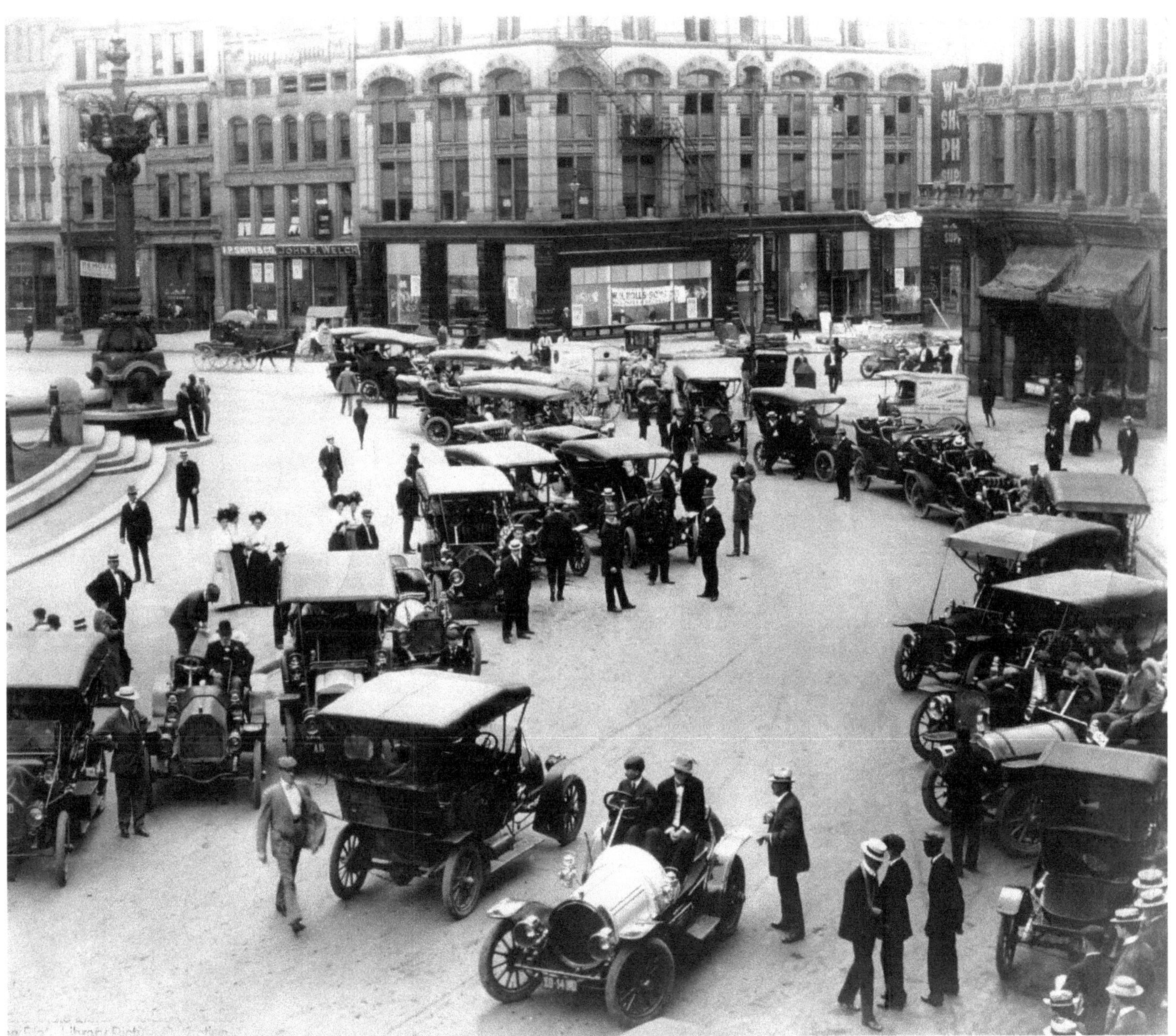

The west side of Monument Circle, 1908. Automobiles began appearing in Indianapolis in the 1890's, and they were starting to dominate the streets by the time this photograph was taken. In Indianapolis author Booth Tarkington's Pulitzer Prize-winning novel *The Magnificent Ambersons*, character Eugene Morgan predicts the effect: "This town's already spreading; bicycles and trolleys have been doing their share, but the automobile is going to carry city streets clear out to the county line."

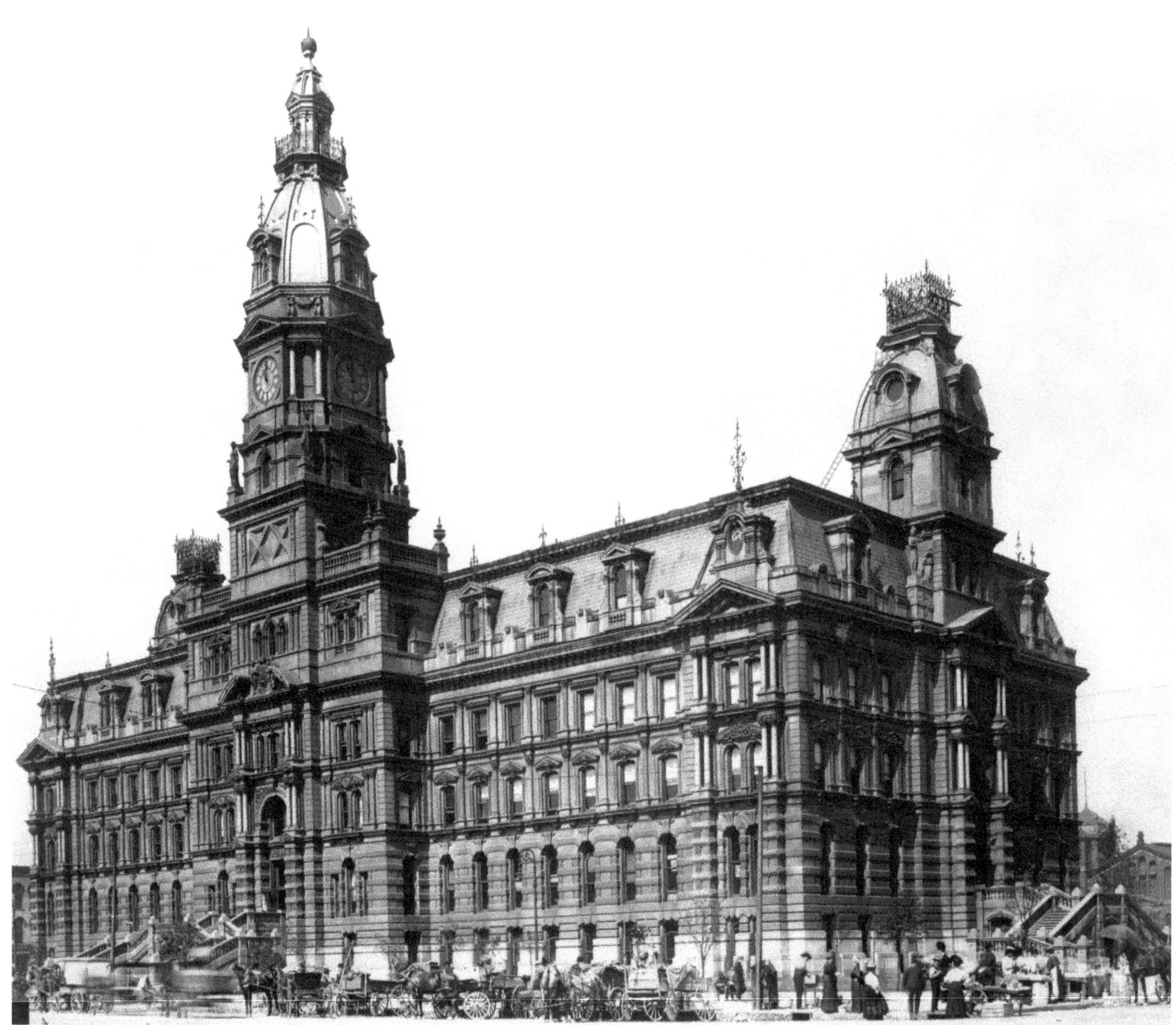

The Marion County courthouse, 1908. This structure, located on the north side of Washington Street between Delaware and Alabama Streets, served as Marion County's second seat of government. Designed by Isaac M. Hodgson and dedicated in 1876, it epitomized Second Empire-style architecture. By the 1950's it had fallen into disrepair, and because both it and the city hall had run out of space, community leaders decided to build a new structure that would combine the offices of both the city and the county. After the new city-county building opened in 1962, wrecking crews demolished the courthouse. Over the years Indianapolis has suffered many architectural losses, but the courthouse is one of the greatest.

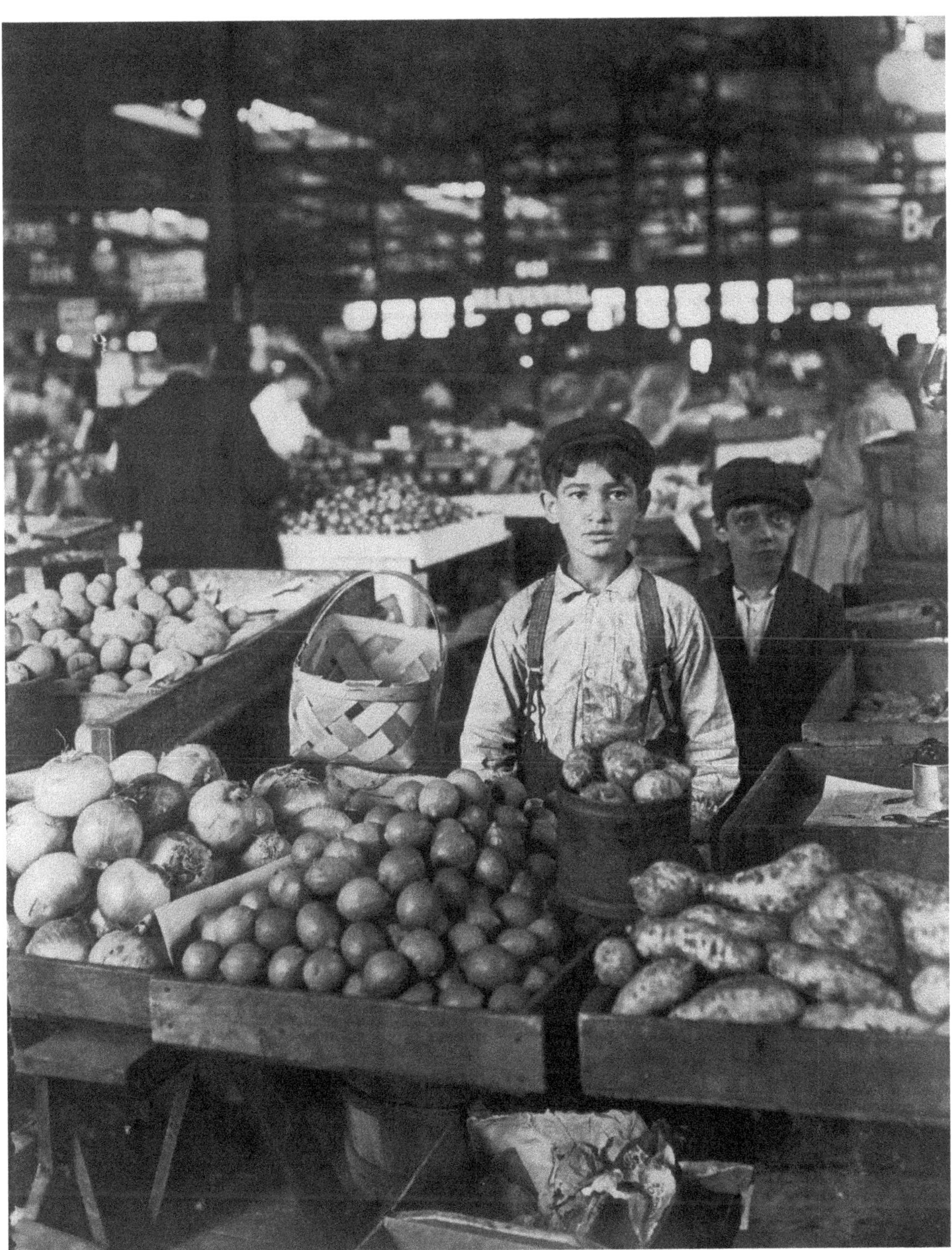

A young boy sells fruit at the Indianapolis city market, 1908.

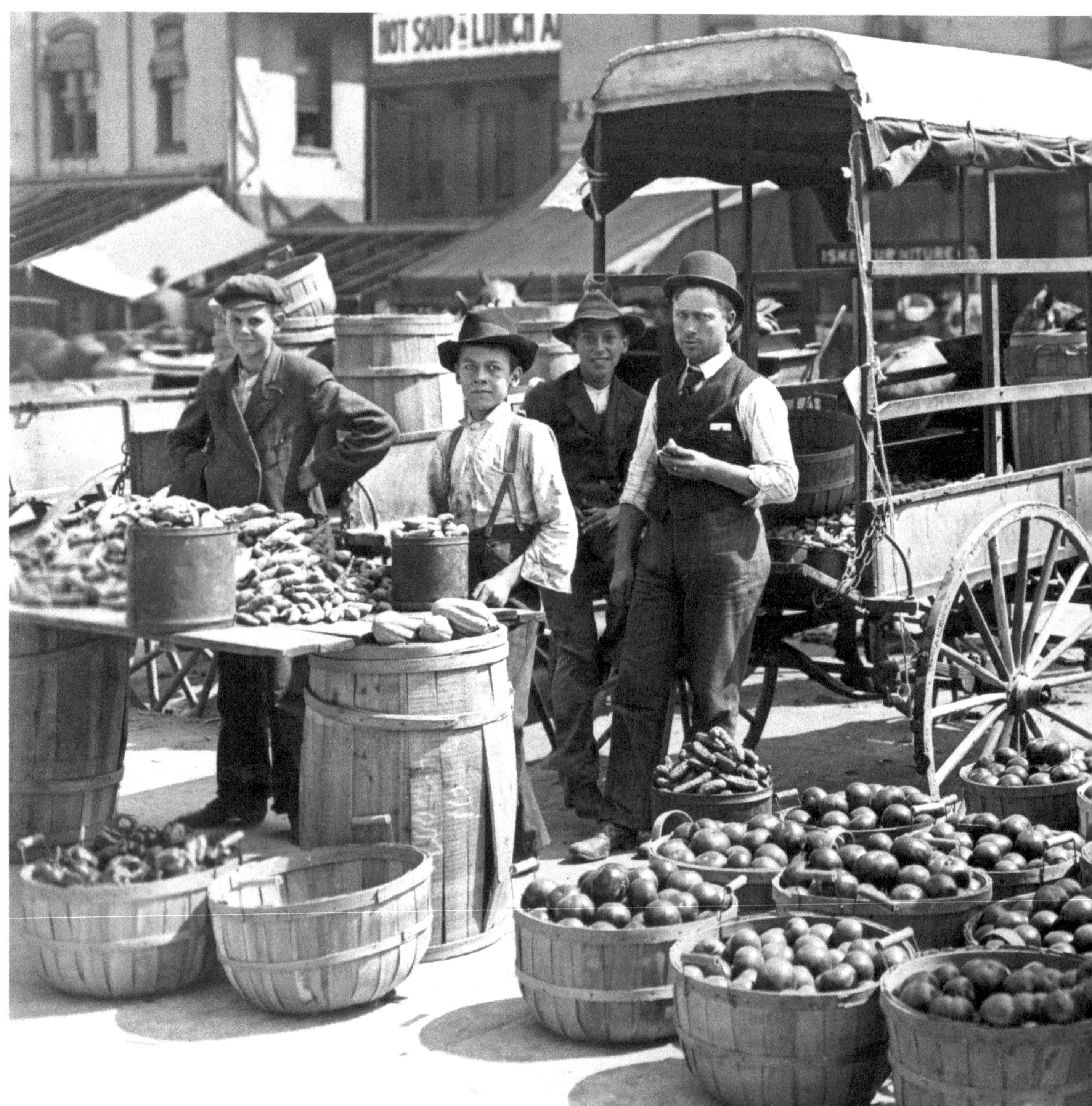
HOT SOUP & LUNCH

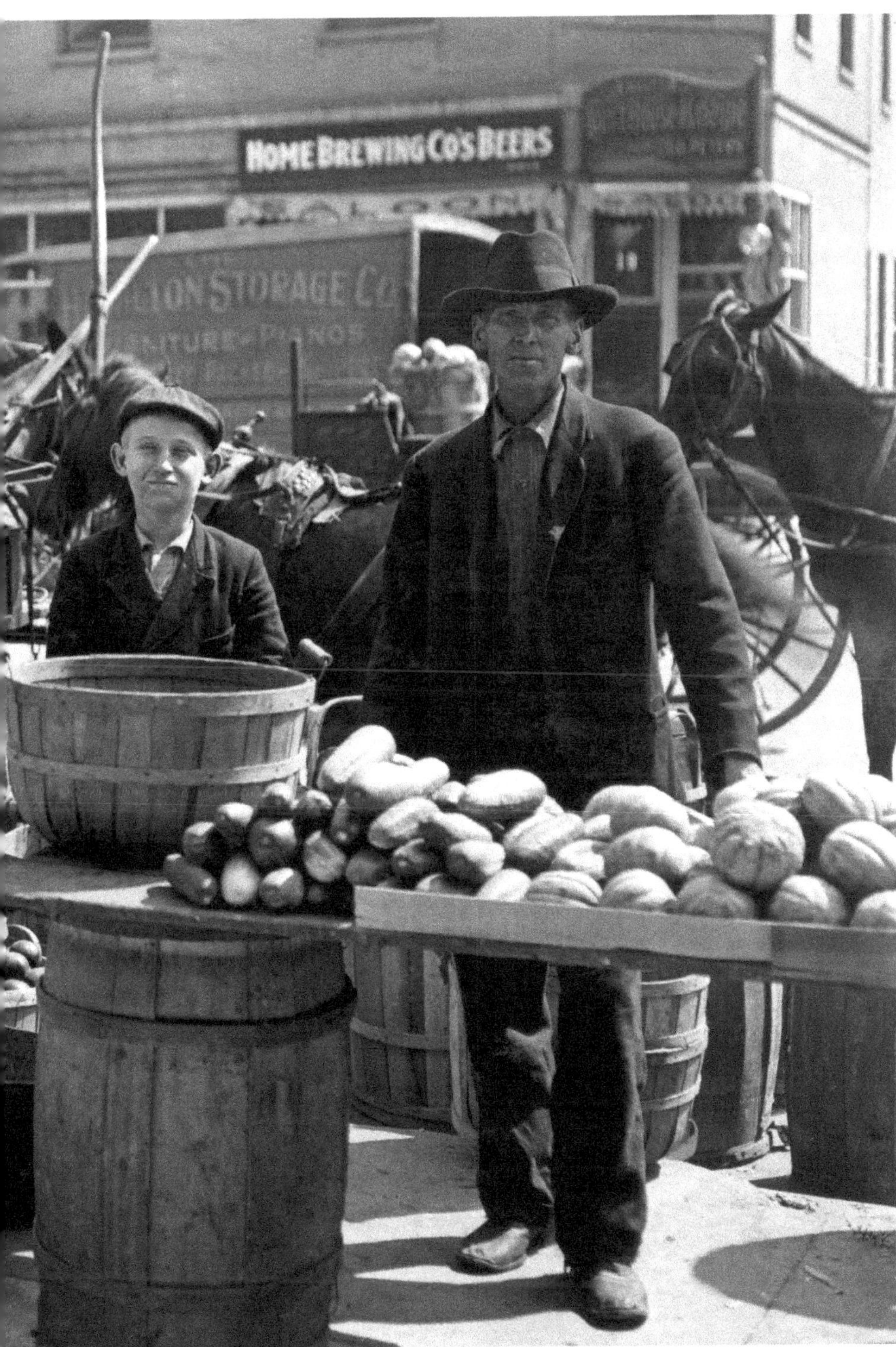

Vendors sell produce outside the city market, 1908.

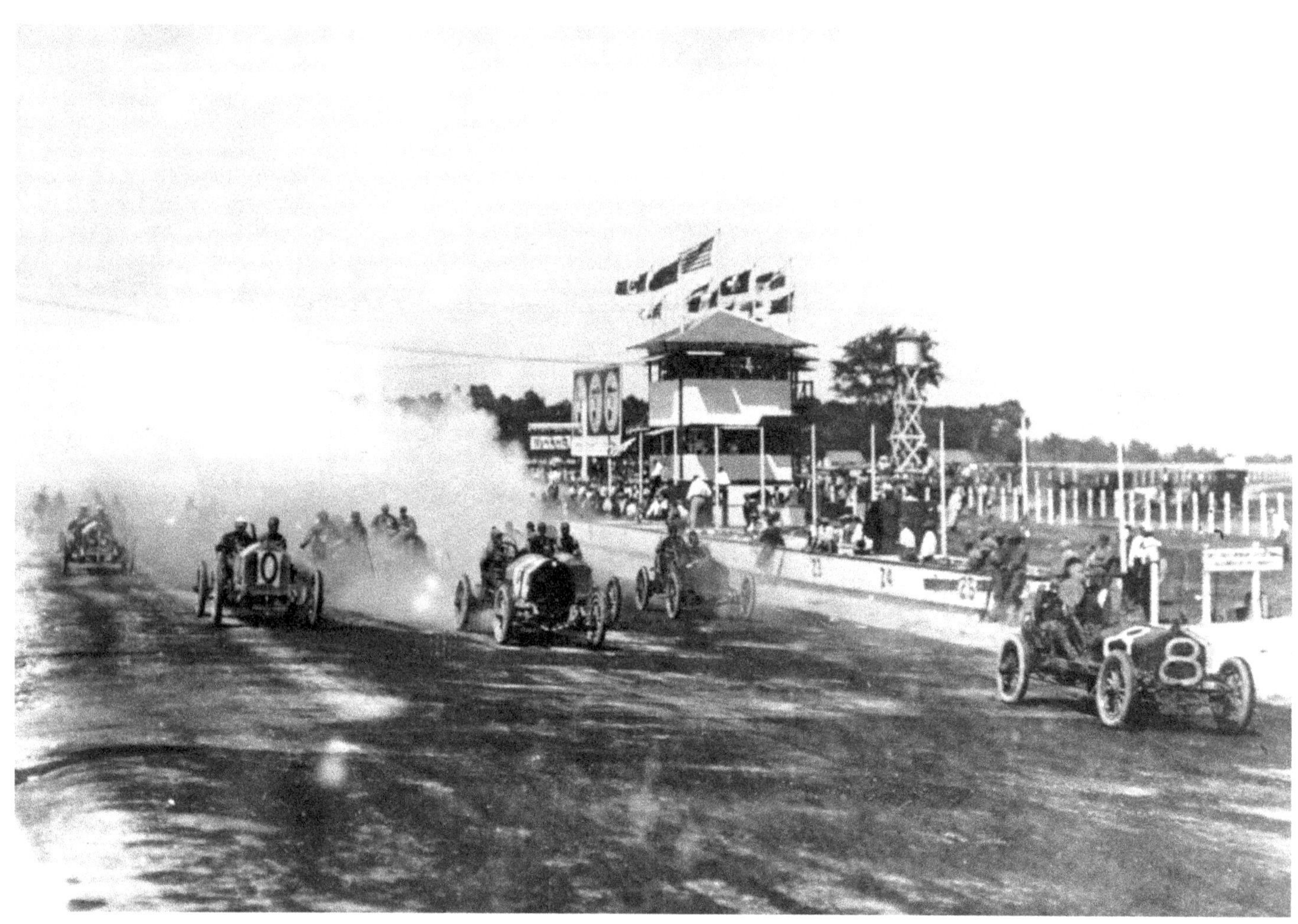

The start of an automobile race at the Indianapolis Motor Speedway, 1909. The speedway was built as a testing ground for the numerous Indianapolis-based auto manufacturers, and the first motorcycle and auto races were held there in August 1909. The track of crushed rock and tar was rough and resulted in many accidents, so in September the owners paved it with 3,200,000 bricks. The track hosted the first 500-mile race on May 30, 1911.

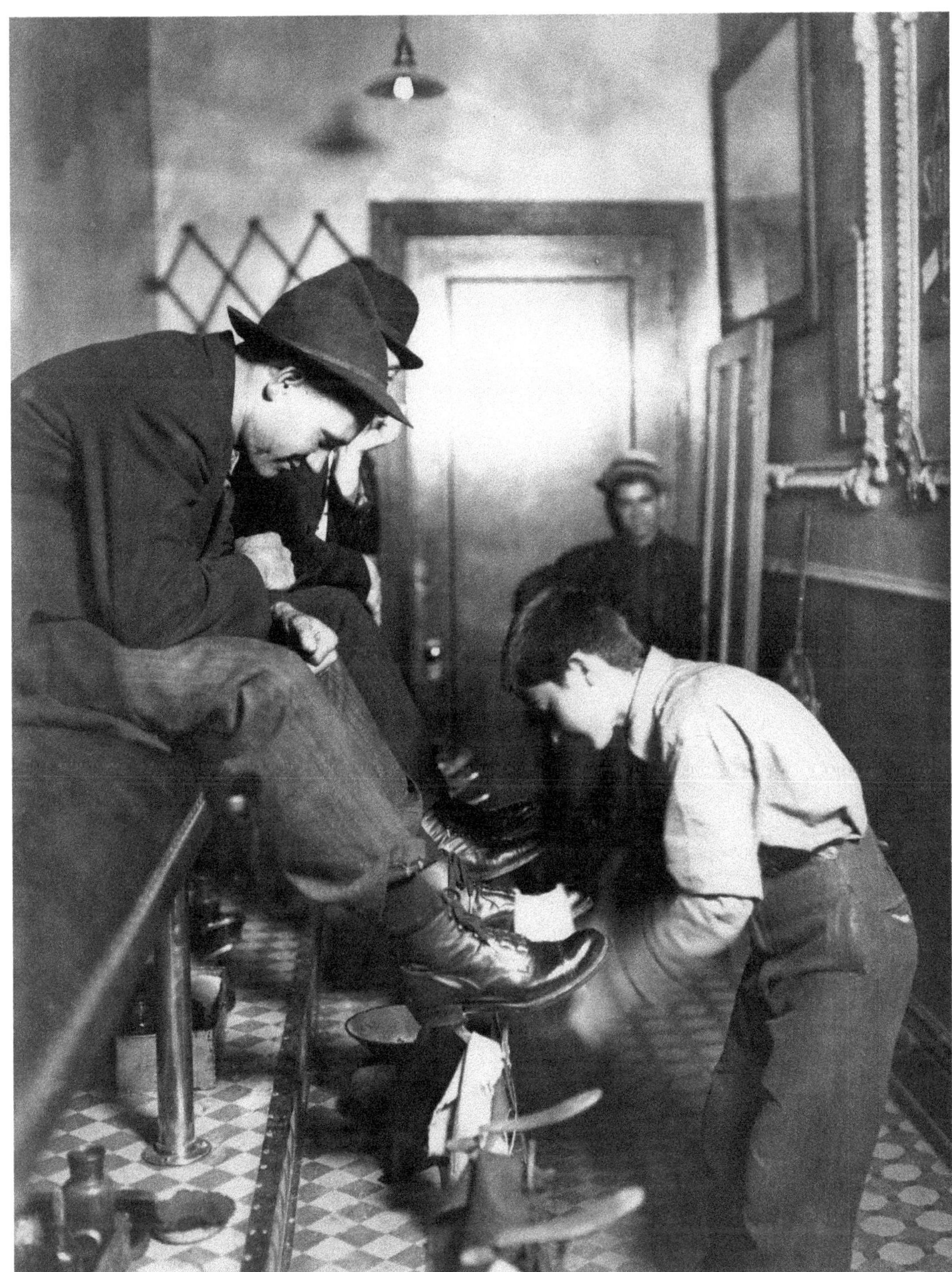

A fifteen-year-old boy works at Greel's shoe-shining parlor, 1908. According to notes on the photo, the boy sometimes stayed until 11 p.m.

Indianapolis newsboys wait for the baseball edition in the offices of a local paper, 1908.

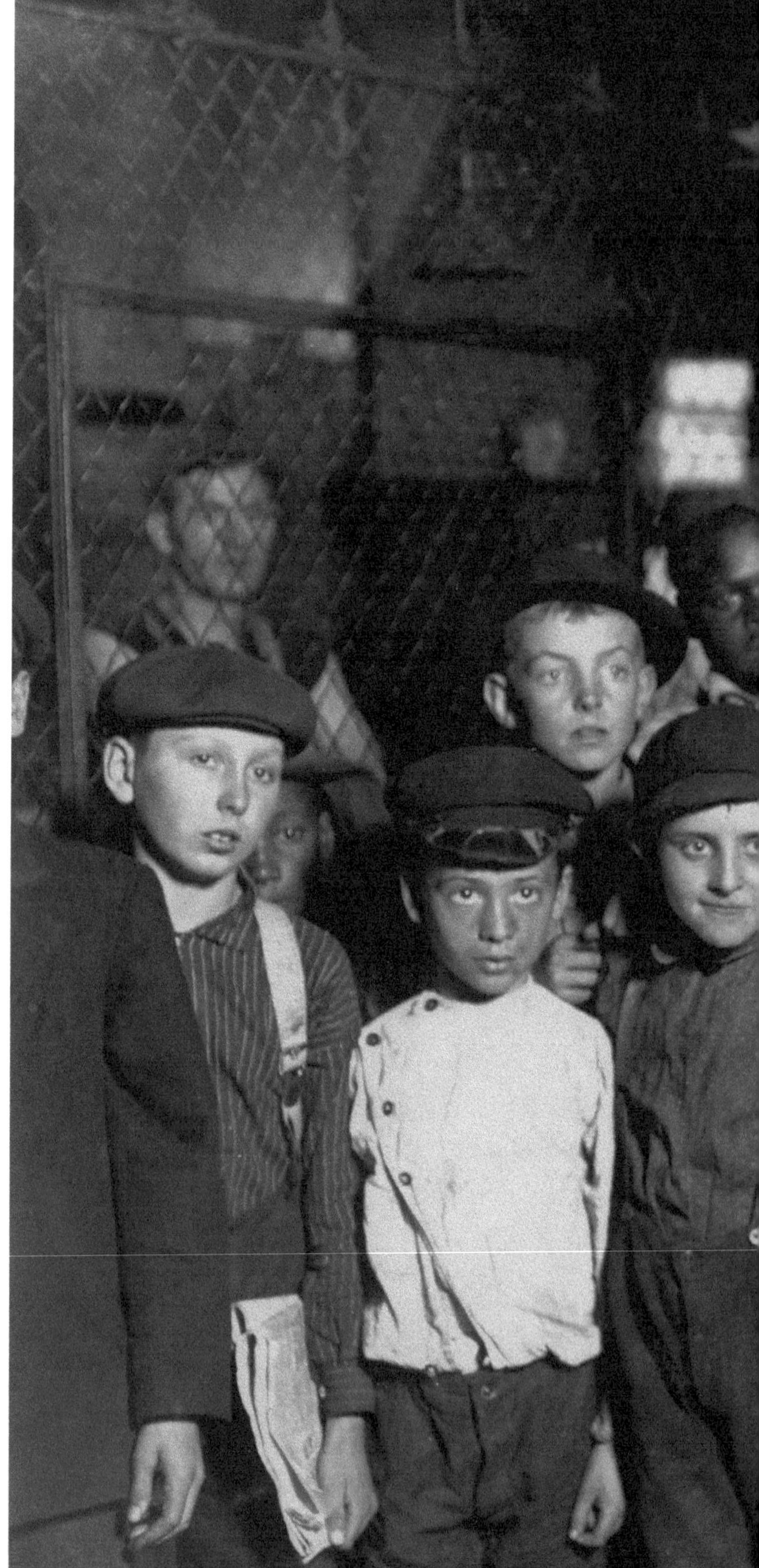

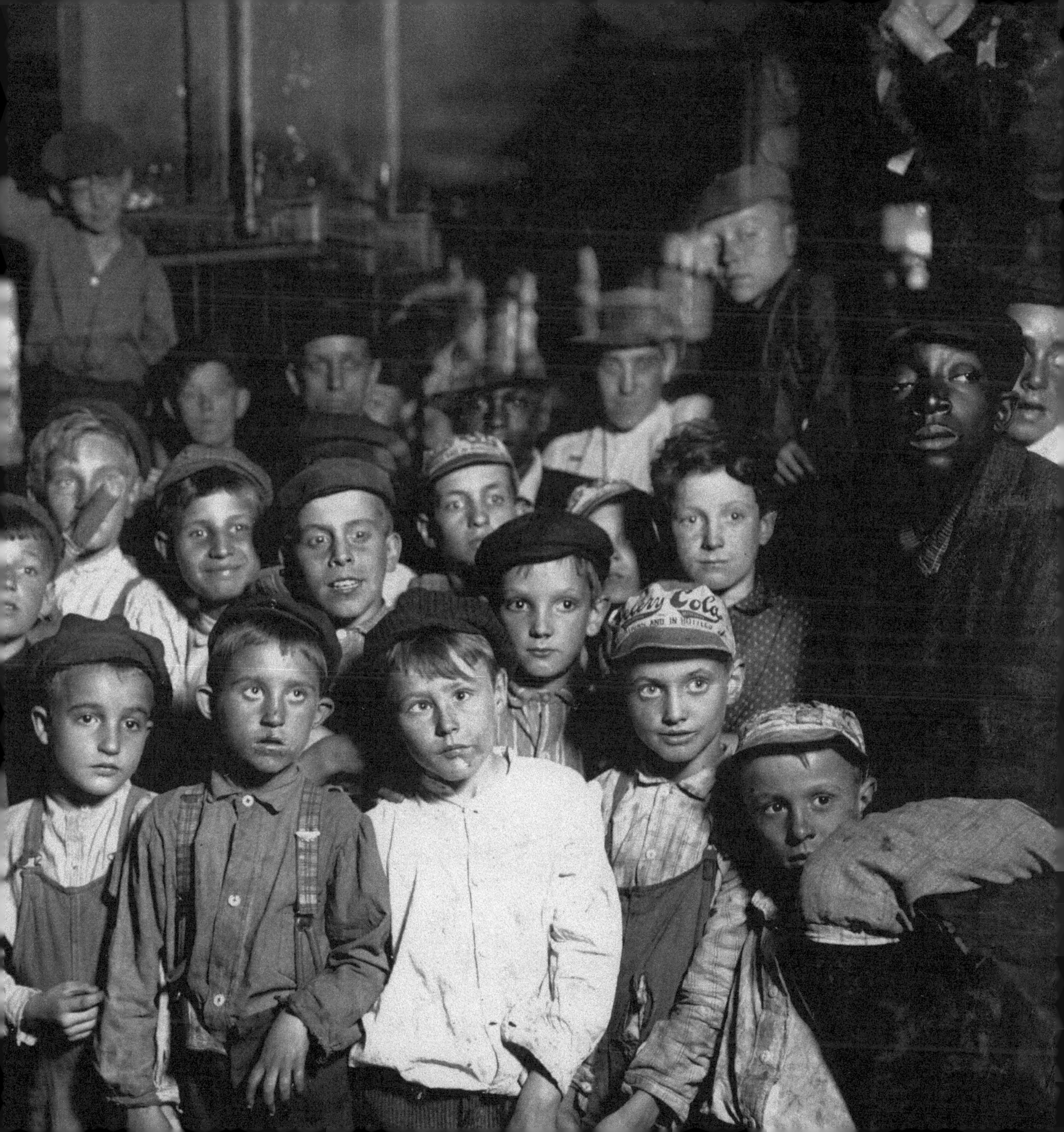

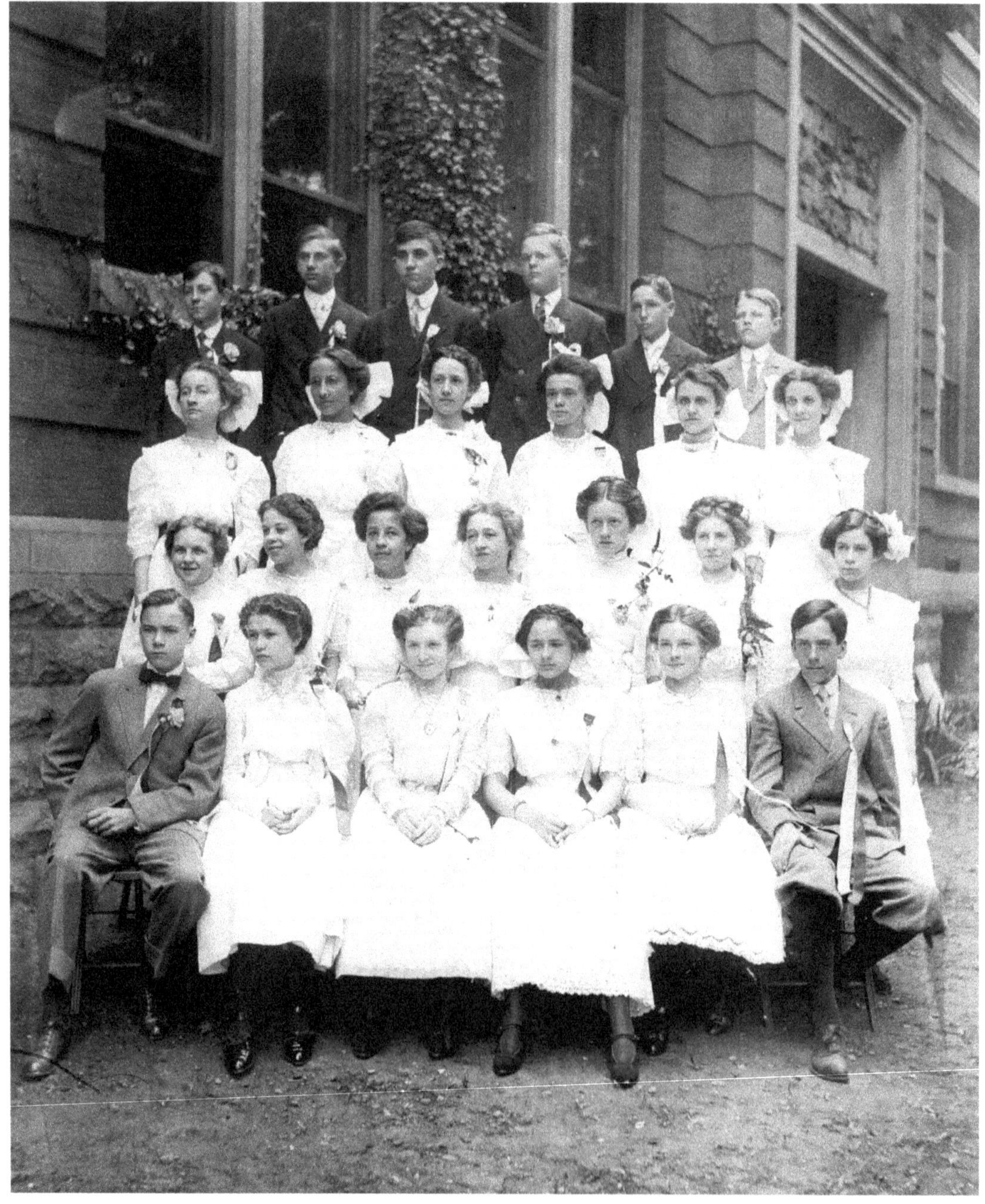

Eighth-grade graduates of School No. 10, 1910. The school was located on the southeast corner of Thirteenth Street and Carrollton Avenue. Today the entire intersection is gone, paved over by ramps connecting I-65 and I-70.

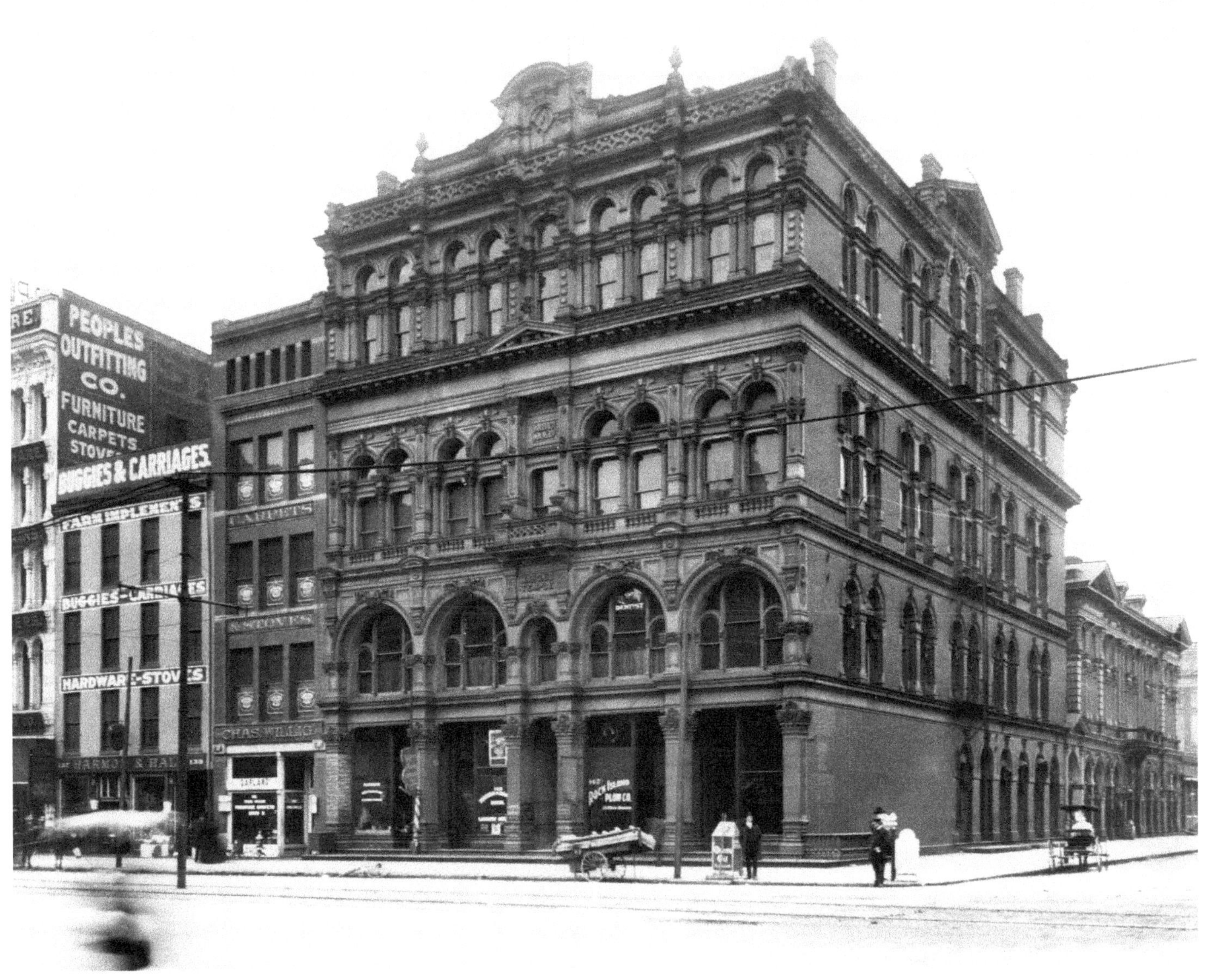

The Masonic Temple at Washington Street and Capitol Avenue, ca. 1910. This photo was taken about the time the Masons moved to a new lodge at Illinois and North Streets.

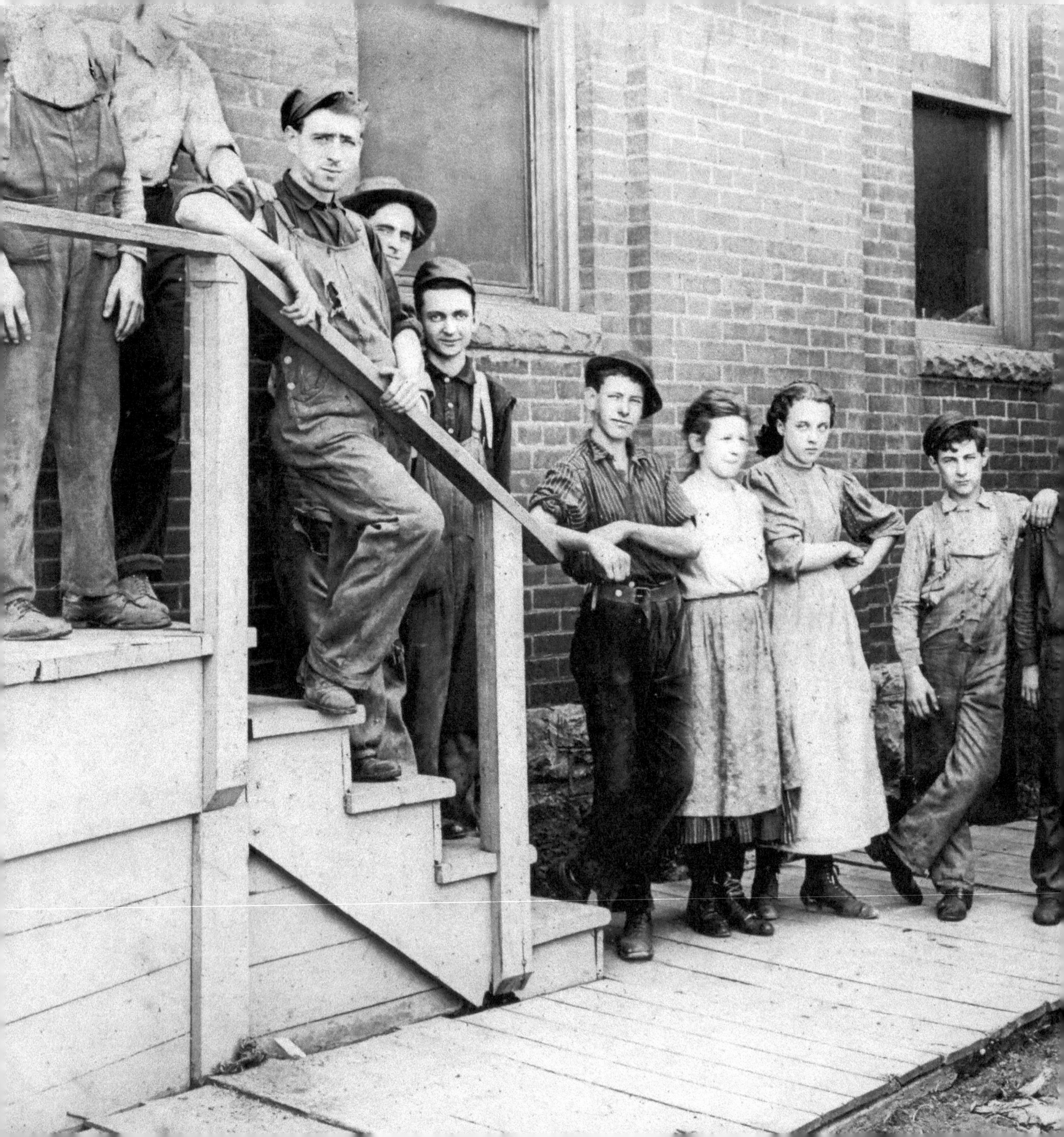

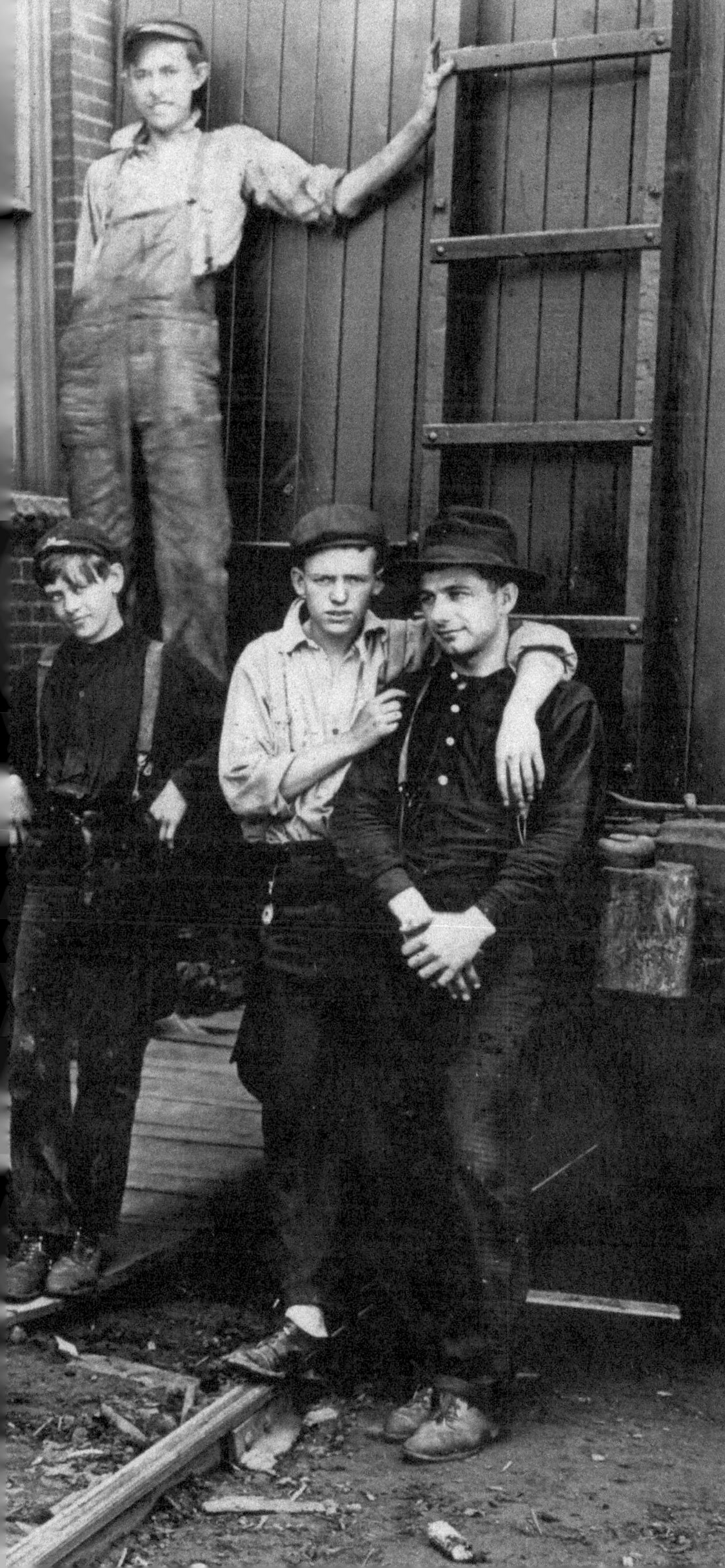

Noon hour at an Indianapolis cannery, 1908.

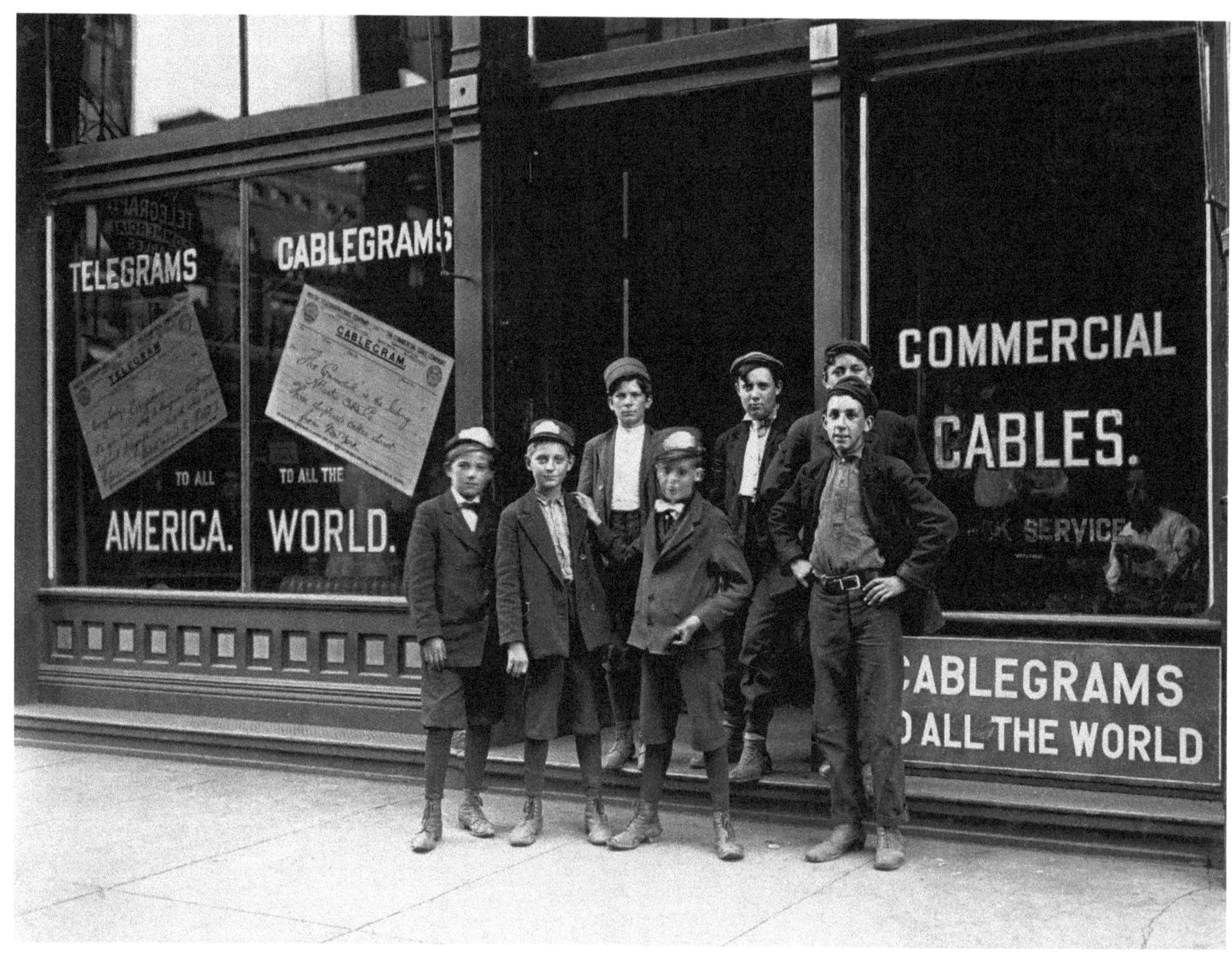

American District Telegraph Company messengers outside the company office, 1908. The office was located on Monument Circle.

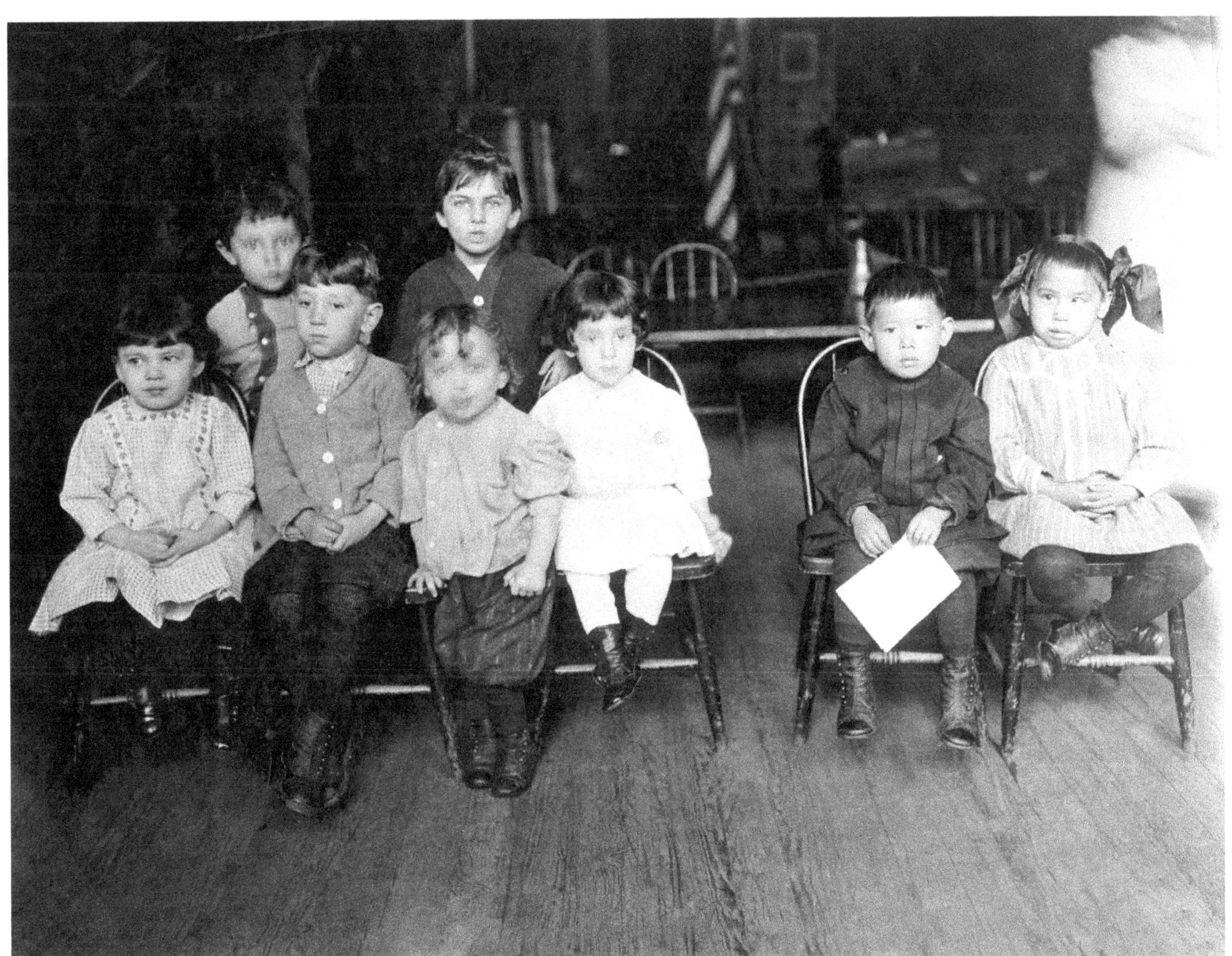

A kindergarten class, circa 1910's. This class may have gathered at the Foreign House, an immigrant settlement located on West Pearl Street. Although Indianapolis had a relatively small foreign-born population compared to other cities, the number of immigrants was high in certain sections of town, so in 1911 the Commercial Club started an immigrants' aid association. The association promoted Americanization and operated the Foreign House, which offered classes for both children and adults.

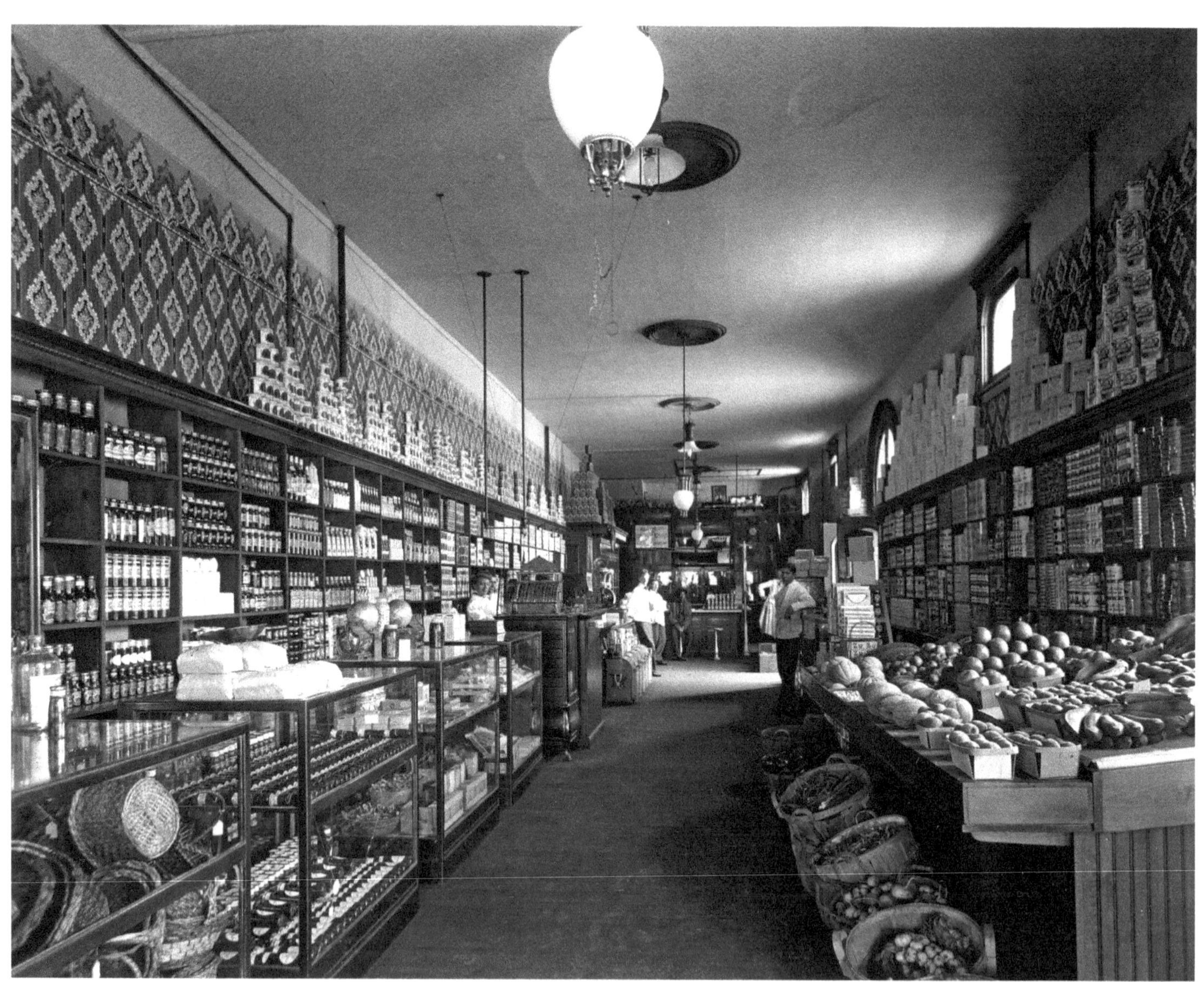

The Moore Grocery Company, circa 1910. The grocery was located on the east side of Illinois Street near Ohio Street.

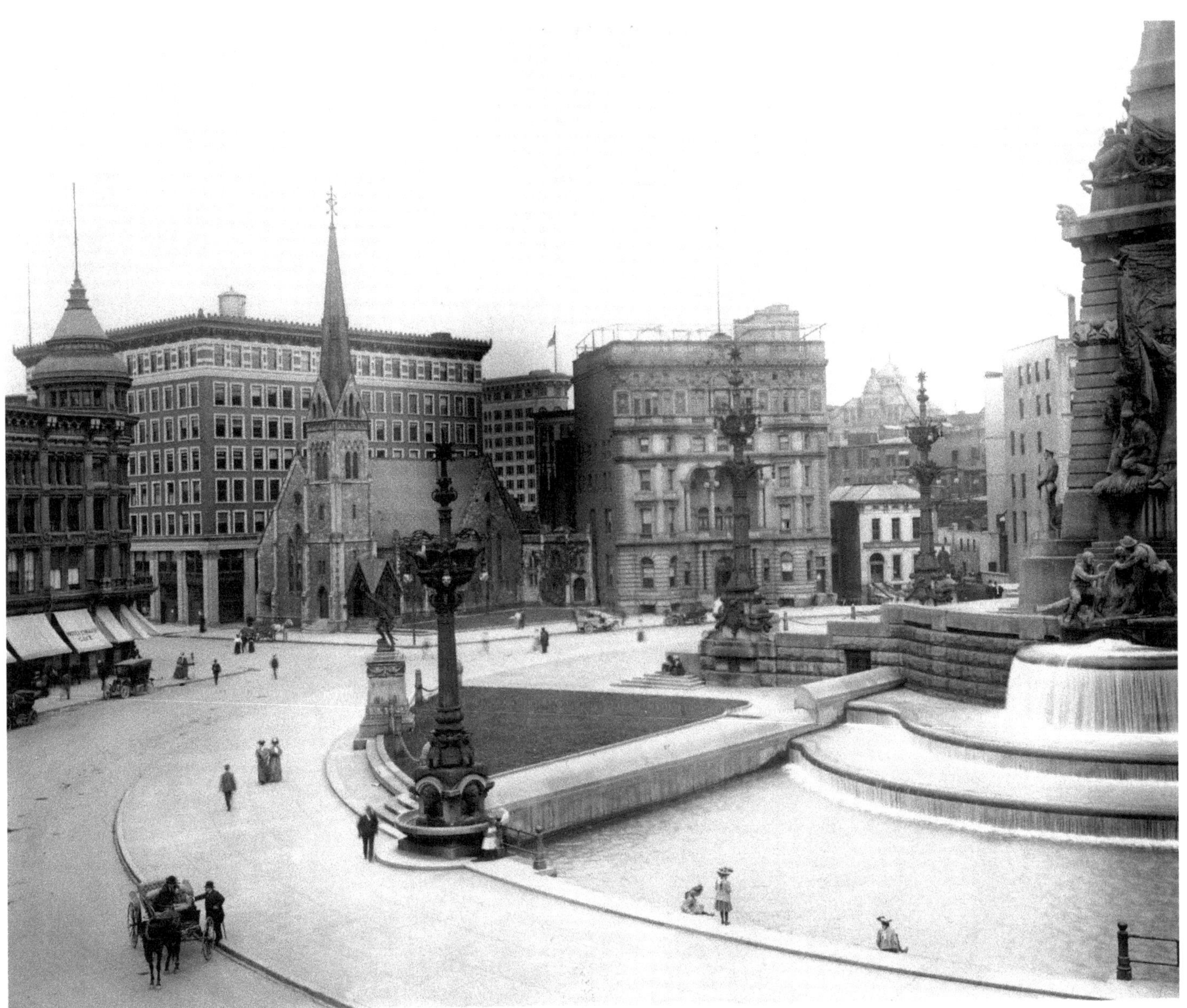

A view from the northwest quadrant of Monument Circle, circa 1910's. The buildings shown here include (from left) the English Hotel, the Board of Trade building, Christ Church, the old Columbia Club, and the Indianapolis Water Company office (located in the house). Christ Church, completed in 1859, is the only one of these structures still standing.

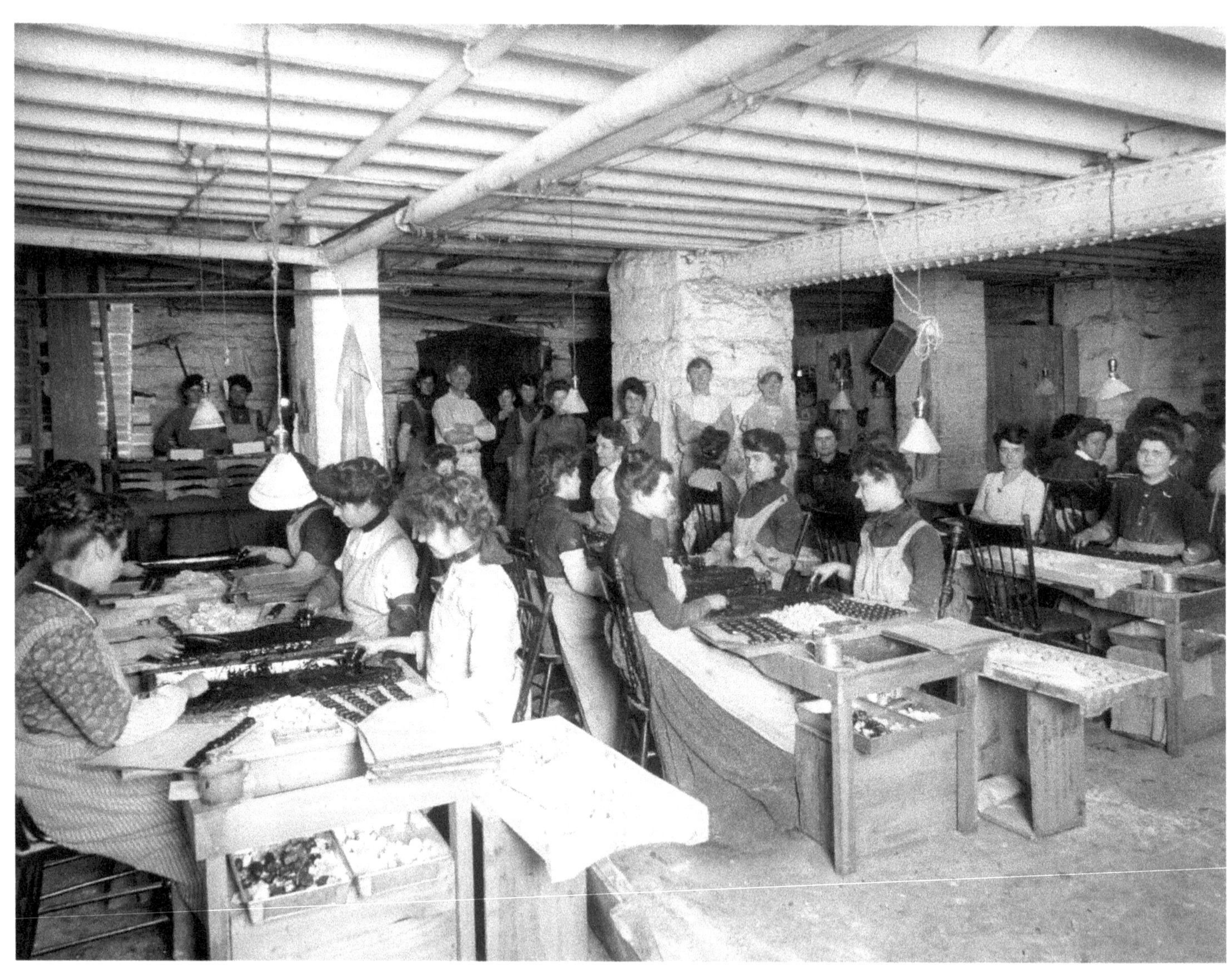

Workers at an Indianapolis candy factory, circa 1910. This photo may have been taken at the National Candy Company on South Meridian Street.

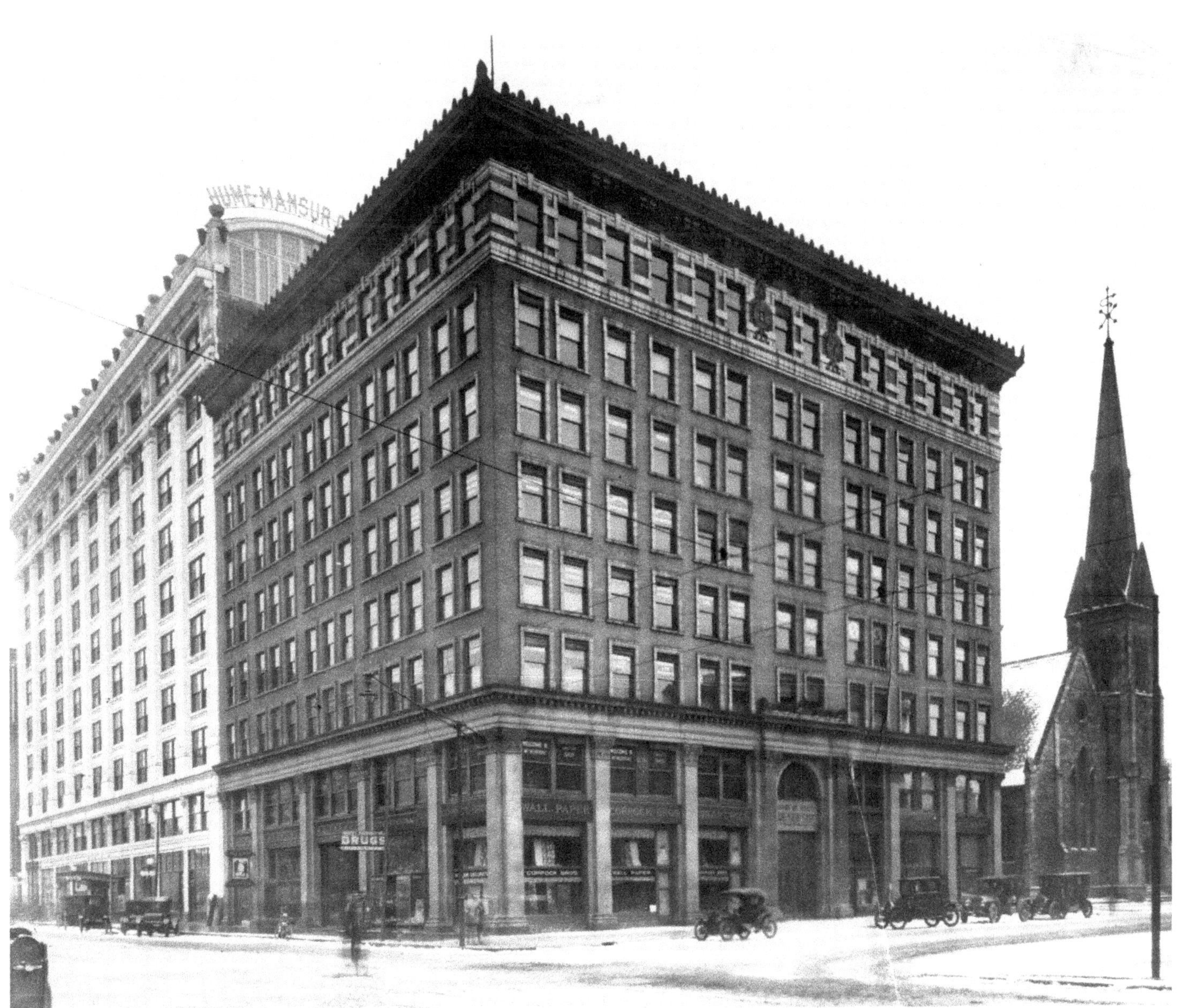

The Board of Trade building, 1912. Founded in 1853, the Board of Trade was an early promoter of Indianapolis's business community. In later years it helped establish uniformity in commercial practices, advance business ethics, and settle trade disputes. This building on the southeast corner of Meridian and Ohio Streets served as the board's home from 1907 until it ceased operations in 1977. The Chase Tower, Indianapolis's tallest skyscraper, now stands on the site.

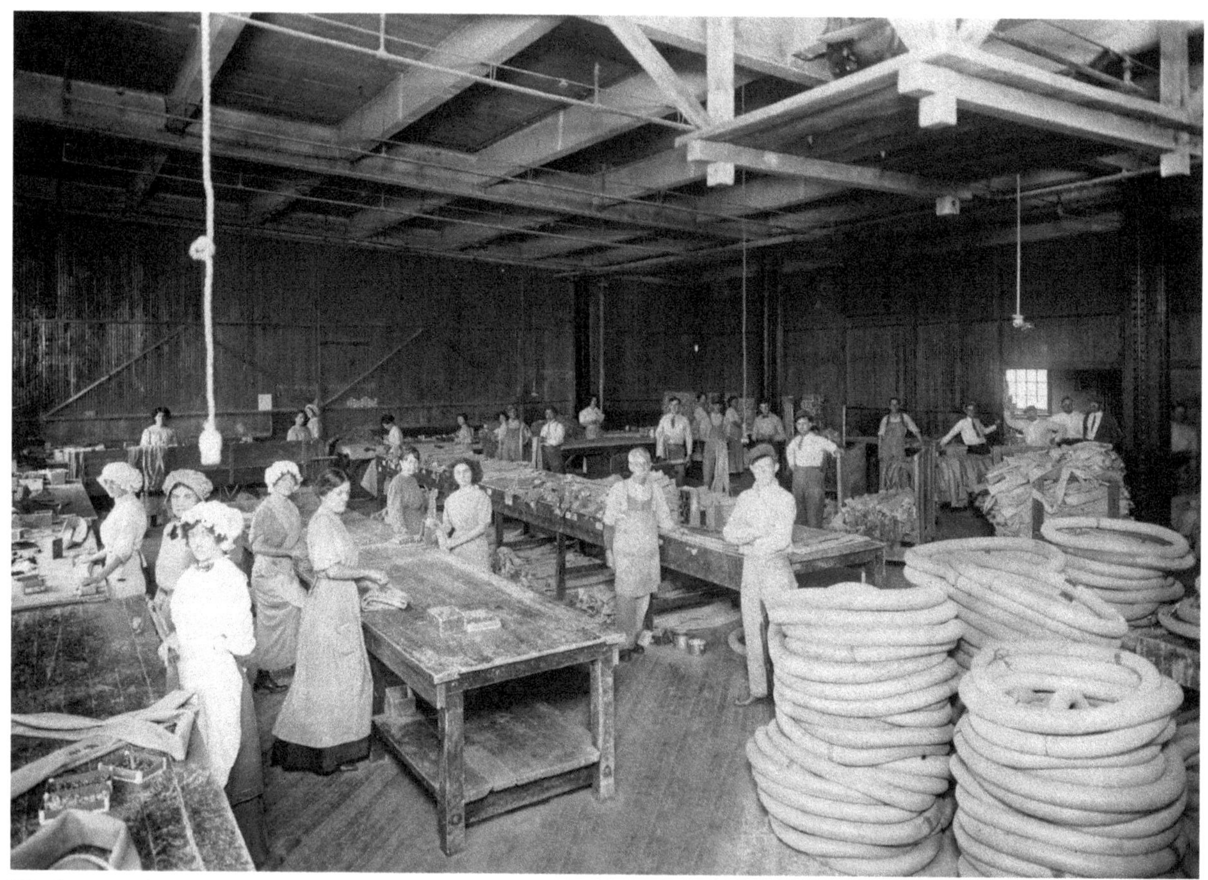

Workers at the G and J Tire Company, circa 1910. The company was located on East Georgia Street.

Vendors sell their wares along Alabama and Market Streets, circa 1912. For decades farmers peddled meats and produce on these streets near the city market (which is partially seen in the background, obscured by the tree).

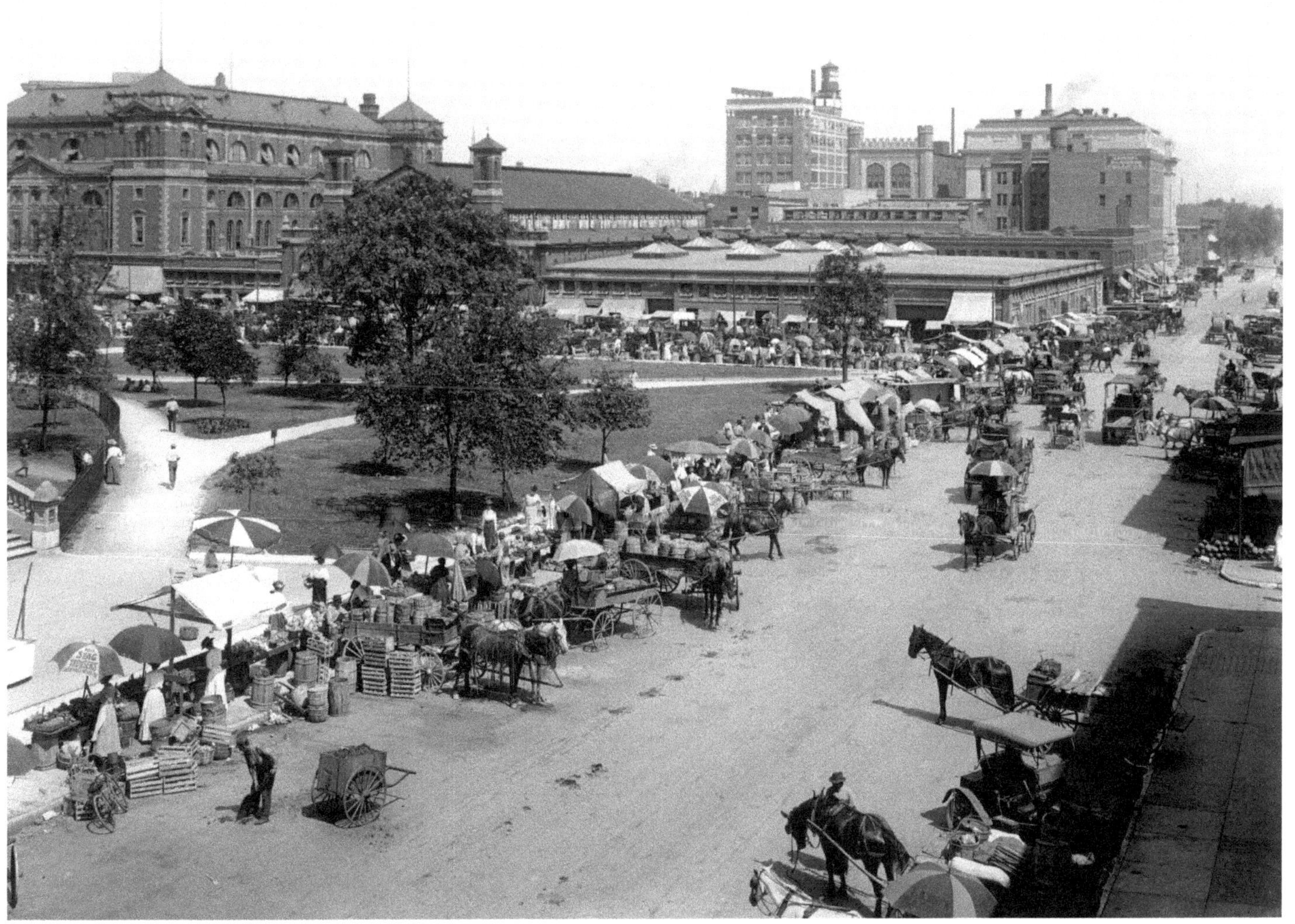

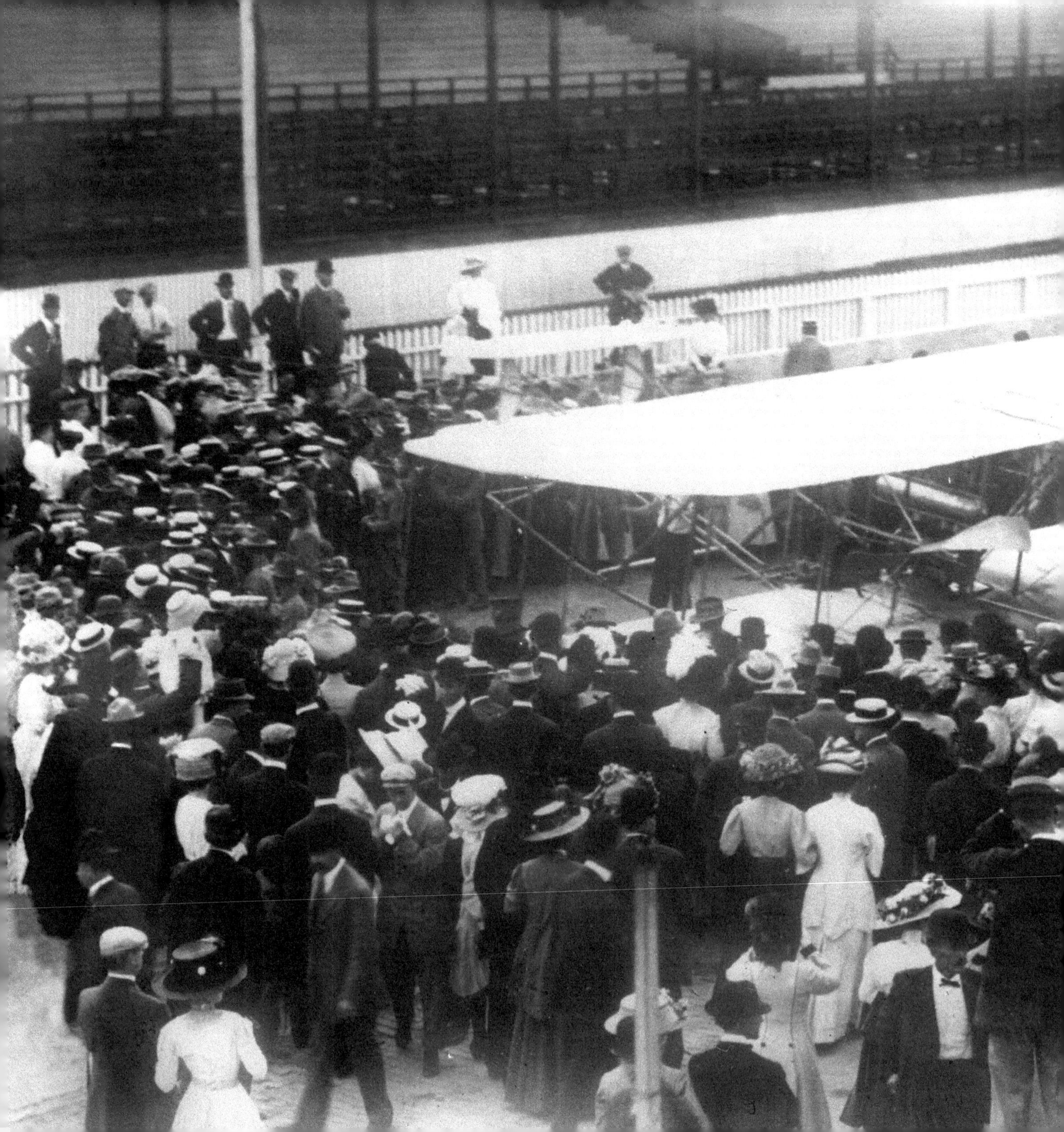

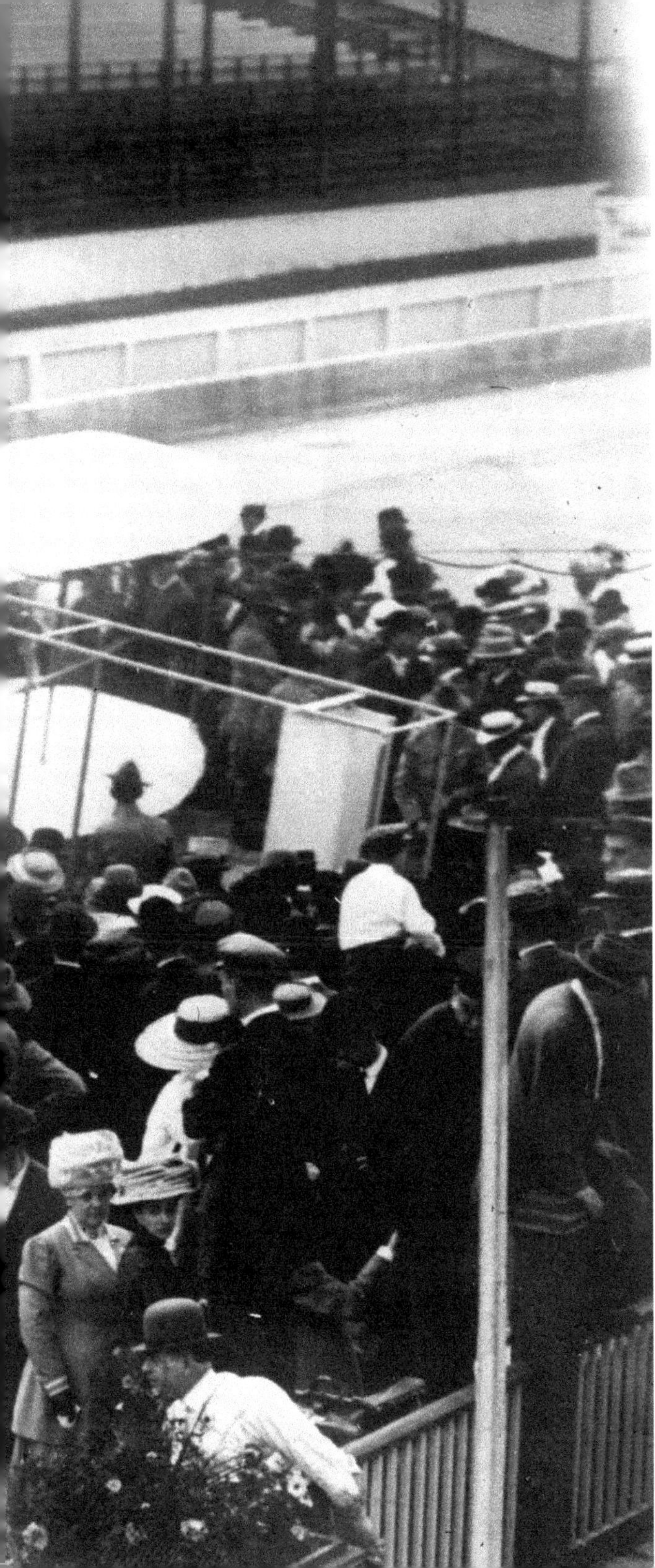

Crowds gather around an airplane at the Indianapolis Motor Speedway, circa 1910's. This photograph may have been taken during a June 1910 aviation meet featuring the Wright brothers and six of their planes. The Speedway played an important role in the city's early aviation history, hosting many airplane races, serving as home to the Aero Club of Indianapolis, and housing hangars during World War I.

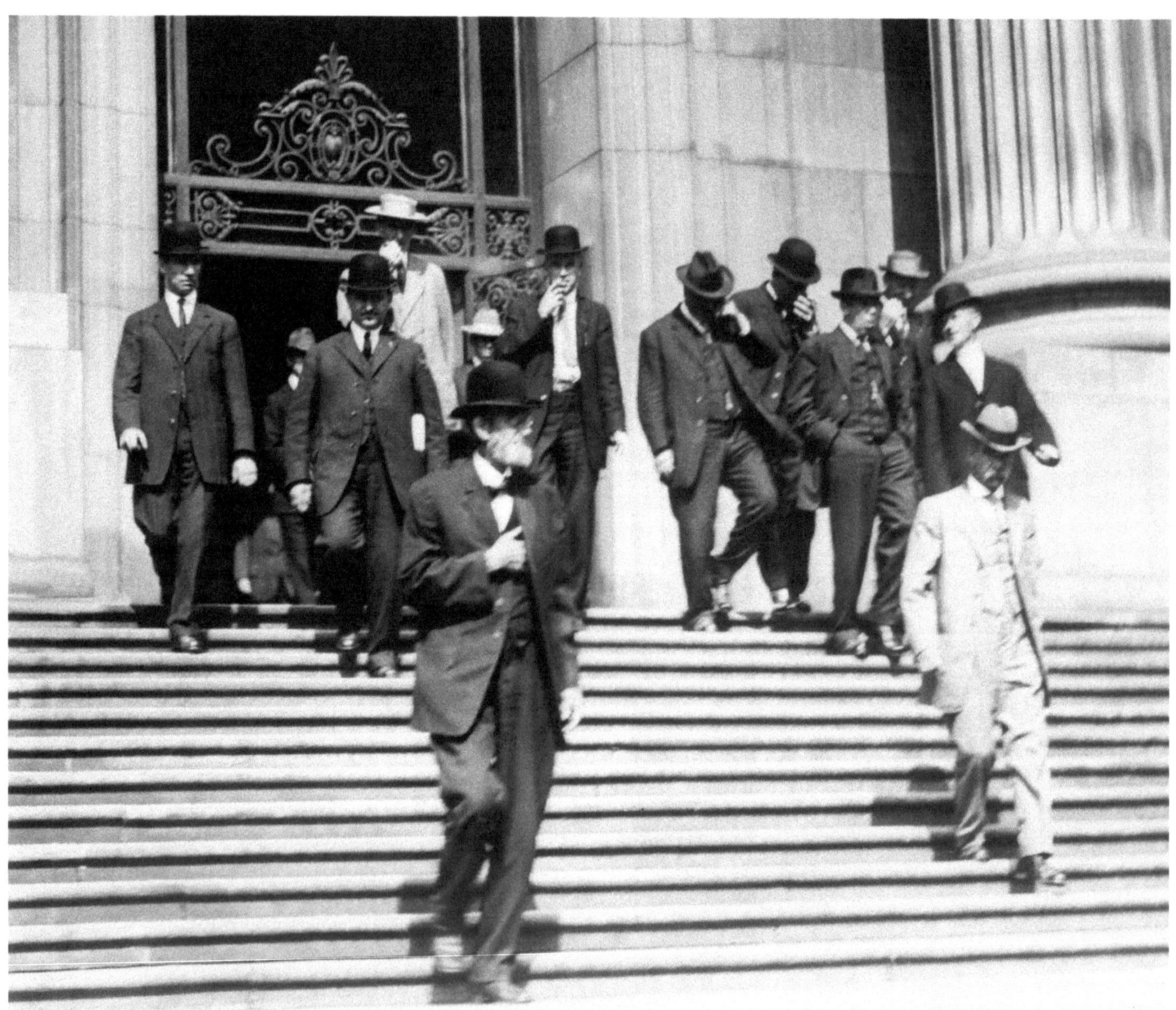

Defendants leave the federal building, 1912. Two years earlier labor unrest had led to the bombing of the Los Angeles Times building and the deaths of twenty-one people. These men and several others (more than fifty total) were implicated in the crime, charged with conspiracy to violate the laws of the United States and with illegally transporting dynamite on passenger trains. Prosecutors tried the case in Indianapolis's federal court, and a jury convicted thirty-eight of the defendants.

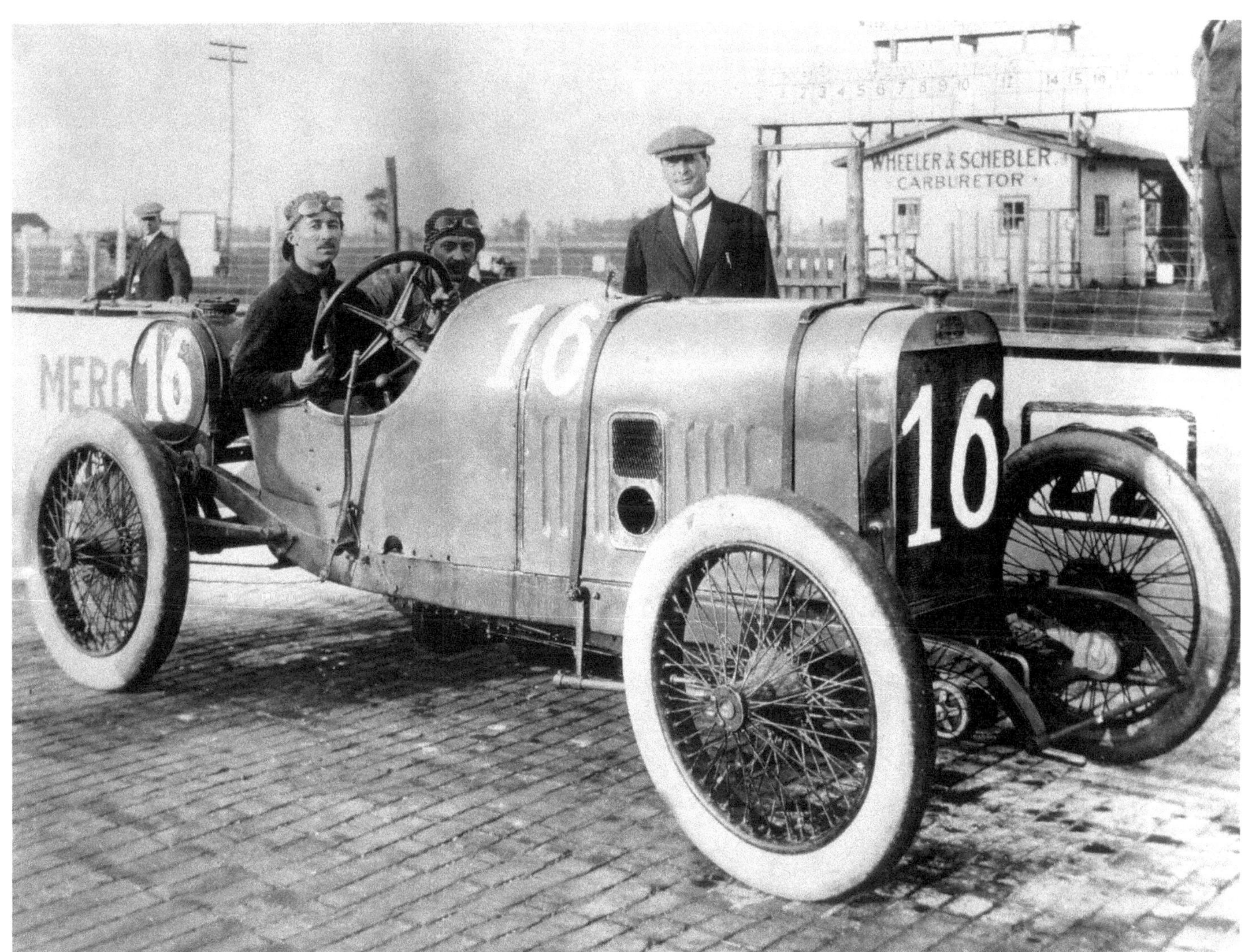

Jules Goux poses in his No. 16 Puegeot after victory at the 1913 Indianapolis 500. Goux, a Frenchman, was the first European to win the famed race.

Judge Alton B. Parker speaks at Thomas R. Marshall's vice-presidential notification, August 20, 1912. Marshall ran on the Democratic ticket with Woodrow Wilson and was elected vice president that fall. The notification ceremony took place at Meridian and Vermont Streets. Thousands turned out to celebrate, but the festivities were dampened when a viewing stand collapsed during Parker's speech, injuring dozens.

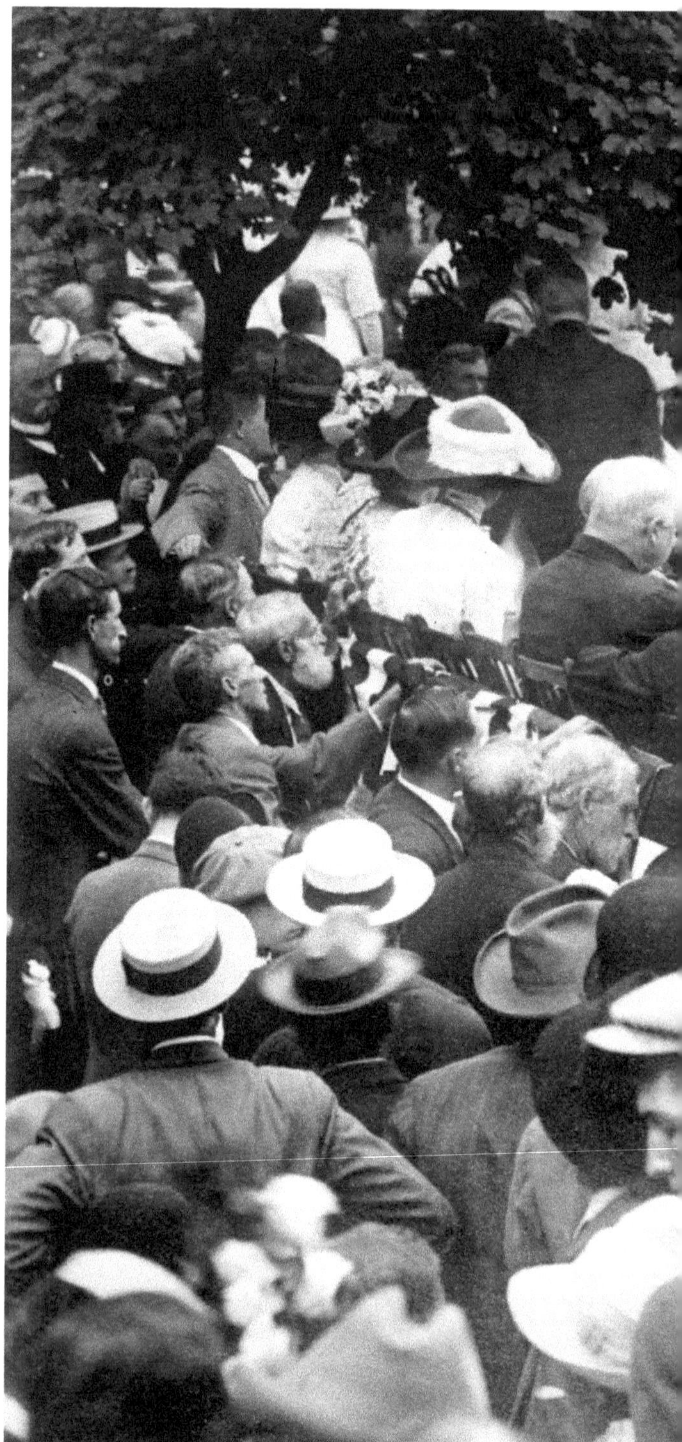

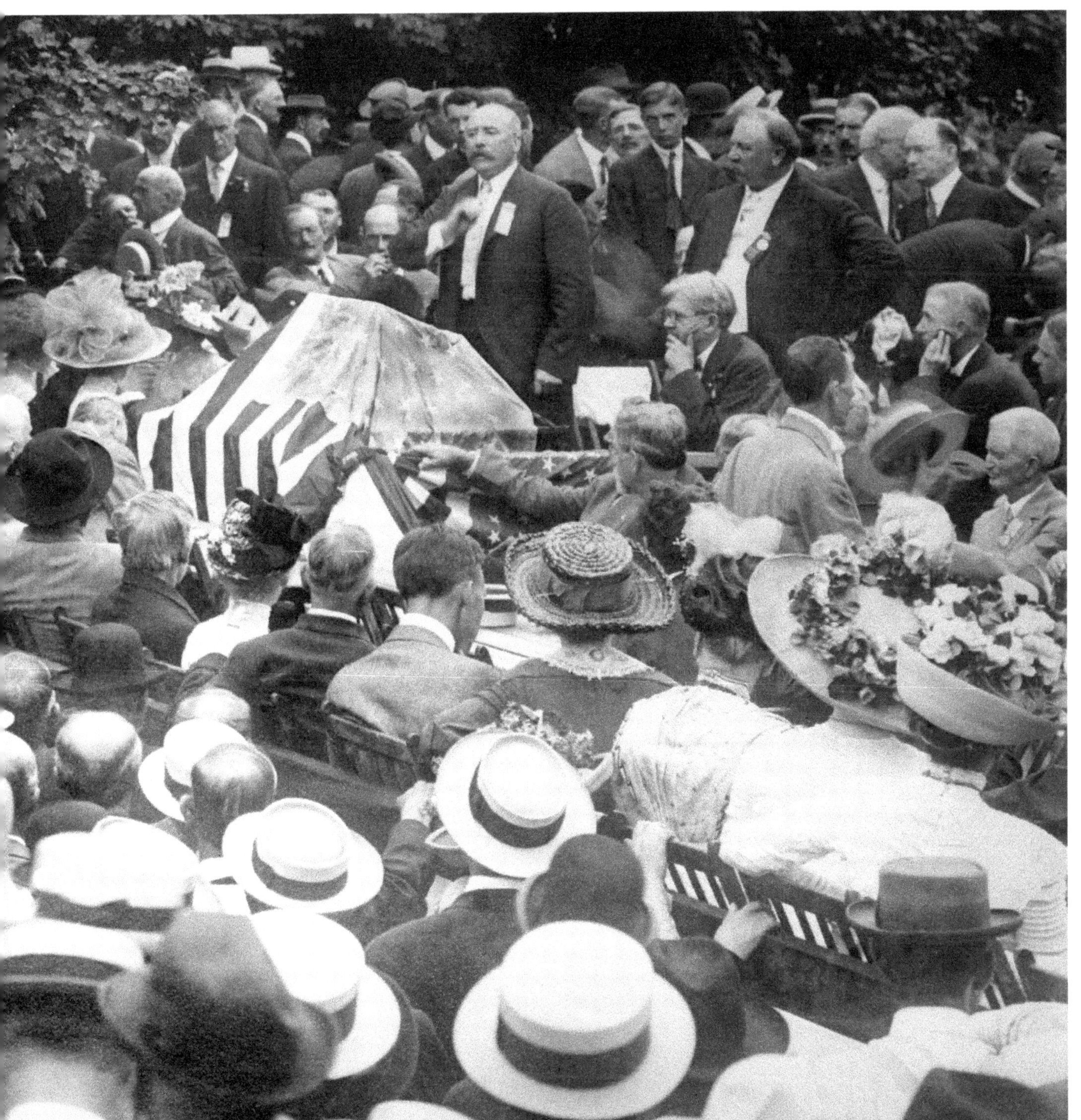

Joe Dawson receives the checkered flag, signaling victory at the 1912 Indianapolis 500. Dawson's No. 8 National averaged just over 78.7 miles per hour during the course of the race.

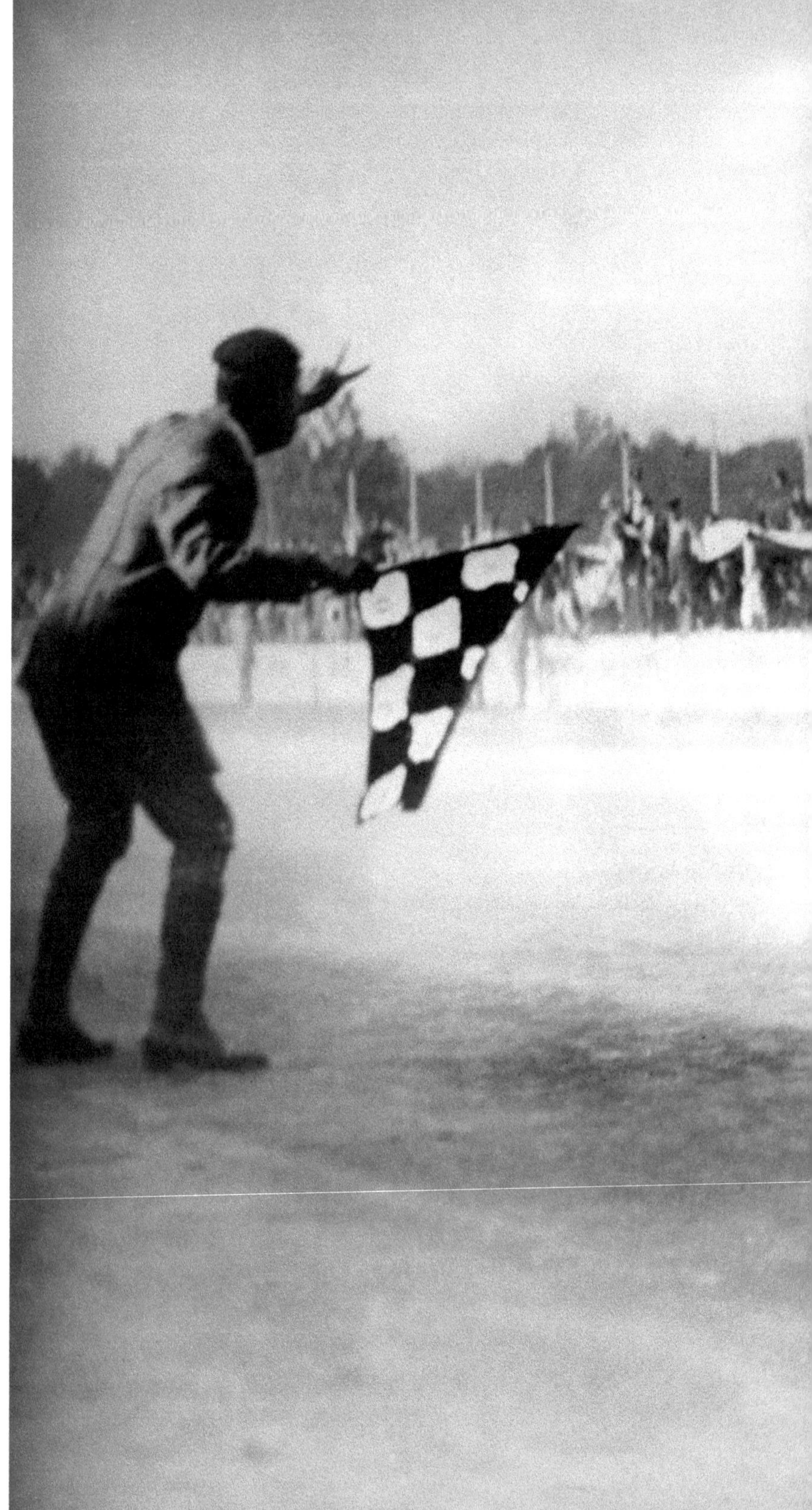

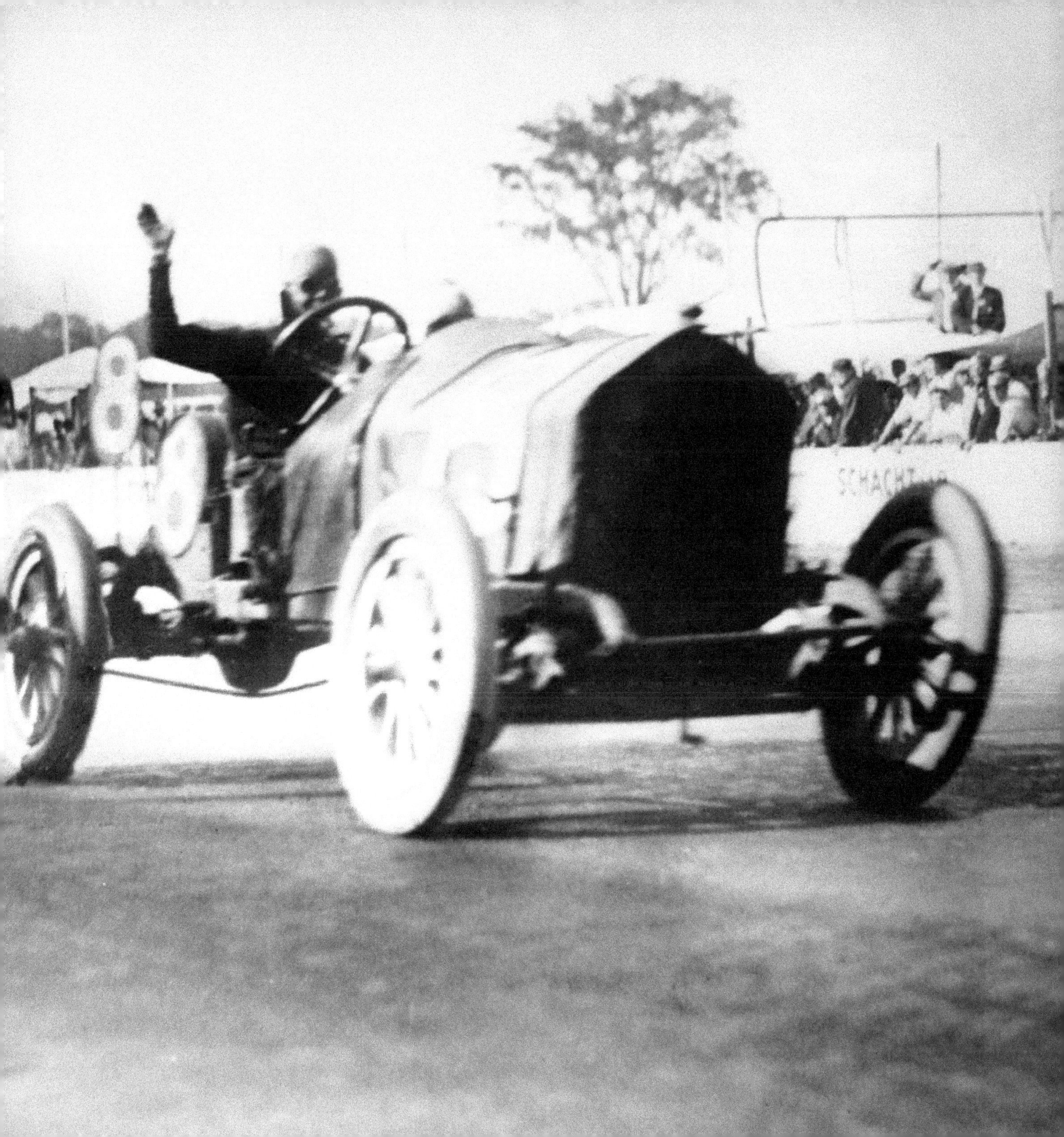
SCHACHT

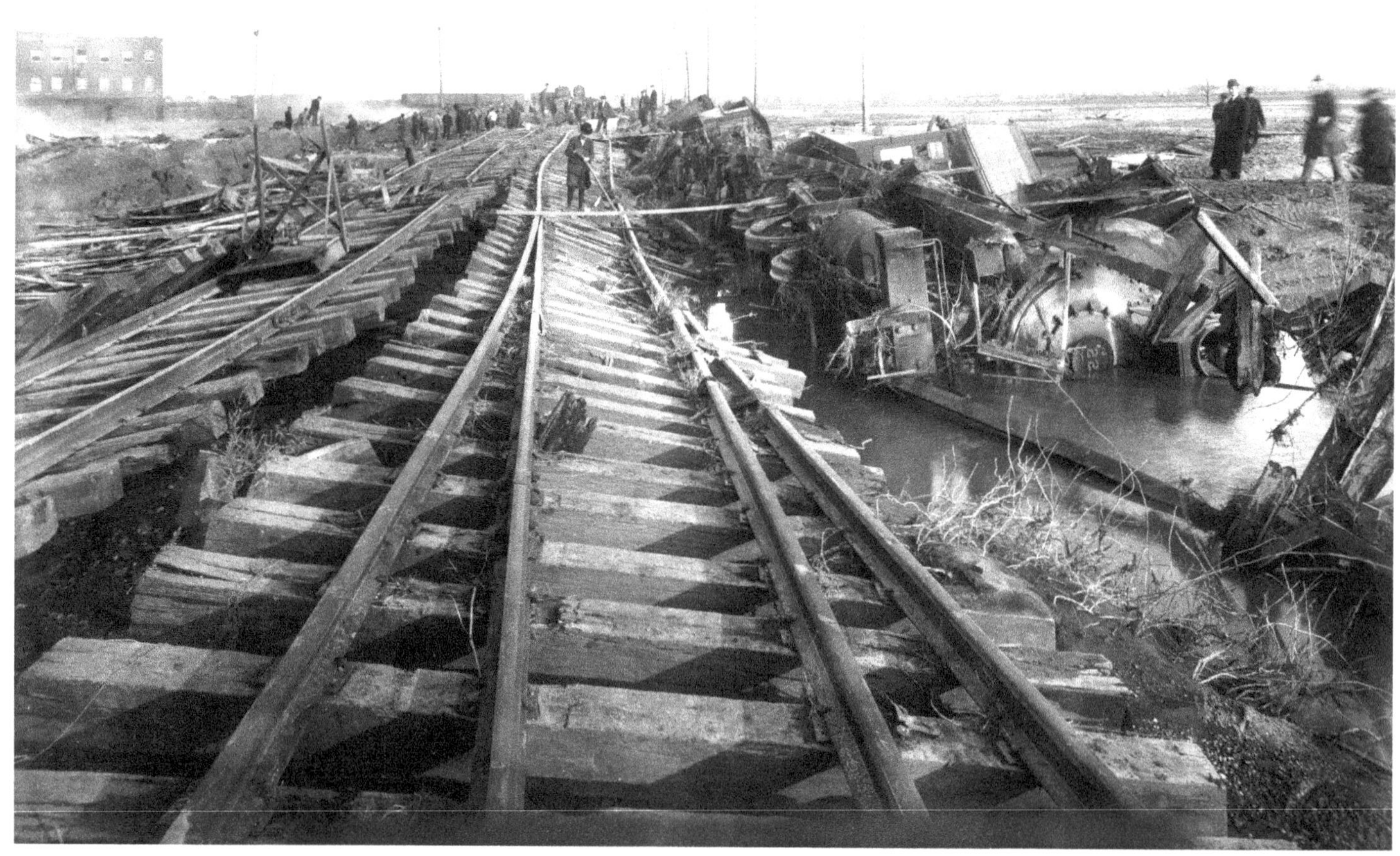

Flood damage to trains and rails, 1913. In March 1913, heavy rains fell on Indiana and other parts of the Midwest, causing extensive flooding. In Indianapolis the White River crested at an estimated 19.5 feet above flood level, bursting levees and sending water rushing through the city, especially the western sections. The flood was the worst in the city's history, causing about two dozen deaths and leaving some 7,000 families homeless.

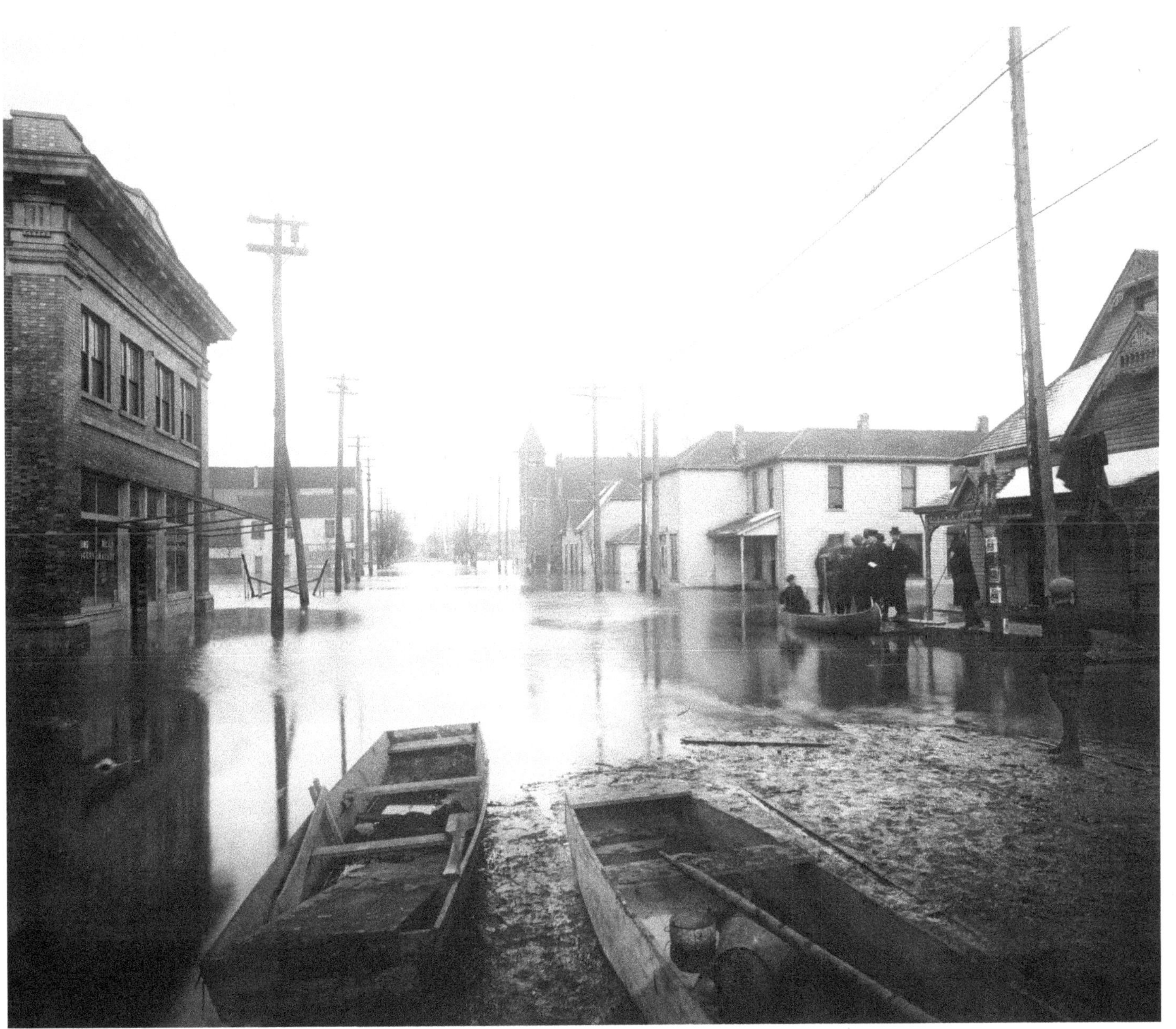

Morris Street during the 1913 flood. At the time of the flood, Morris Street was in the heart of an early suburb known as West Indianapolis (bounded by today's Washington Street, White River Parkway, Raymond Street, and Belmont Avenue). The area was especially hard hit by the deluge.

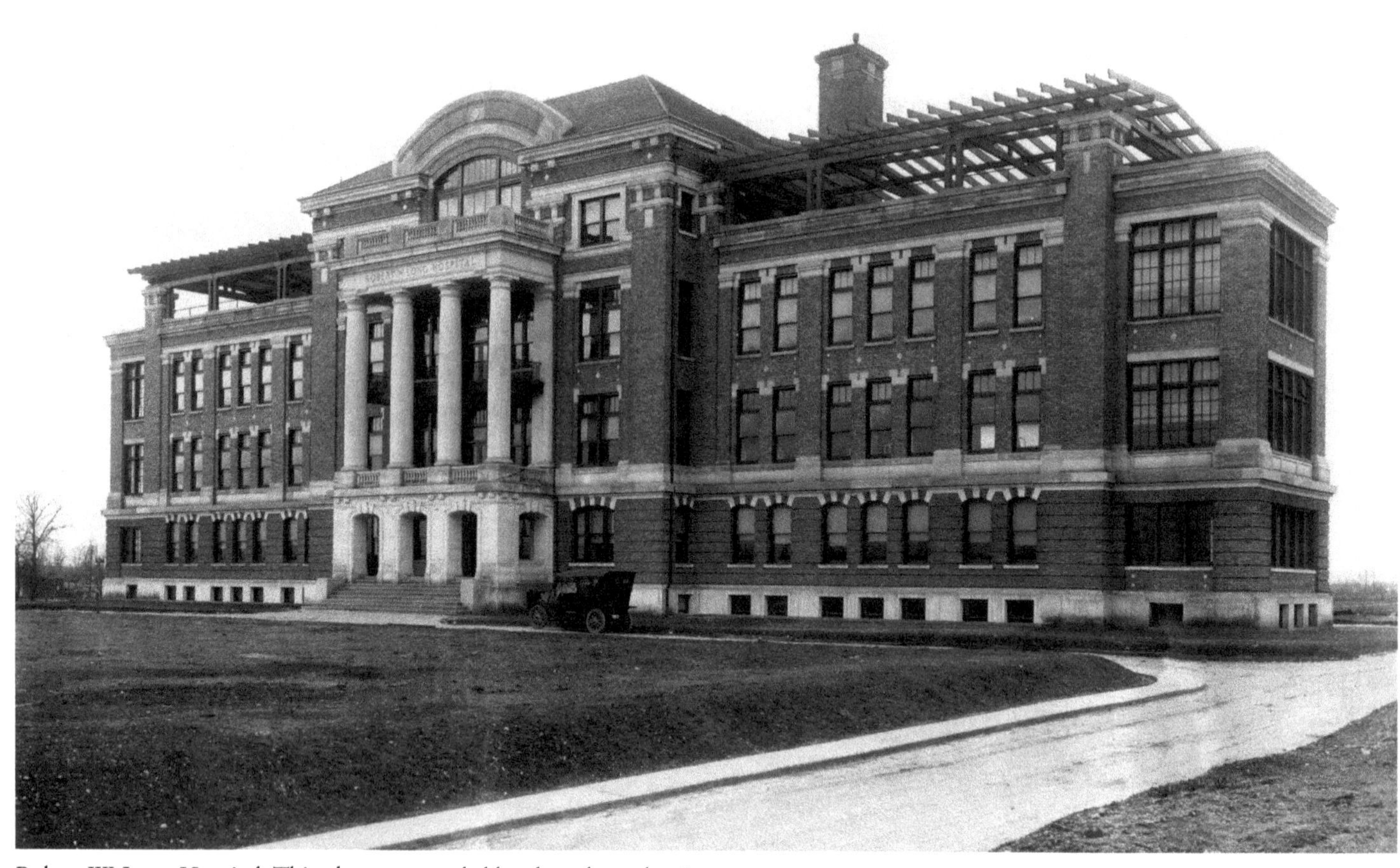

Robert W. Long Hospital. This photo was probably taken about the time the hospital opened in 1914. It was established as the teaching center for the Indiana University School of Medicine and still stands on West Michigan Street.

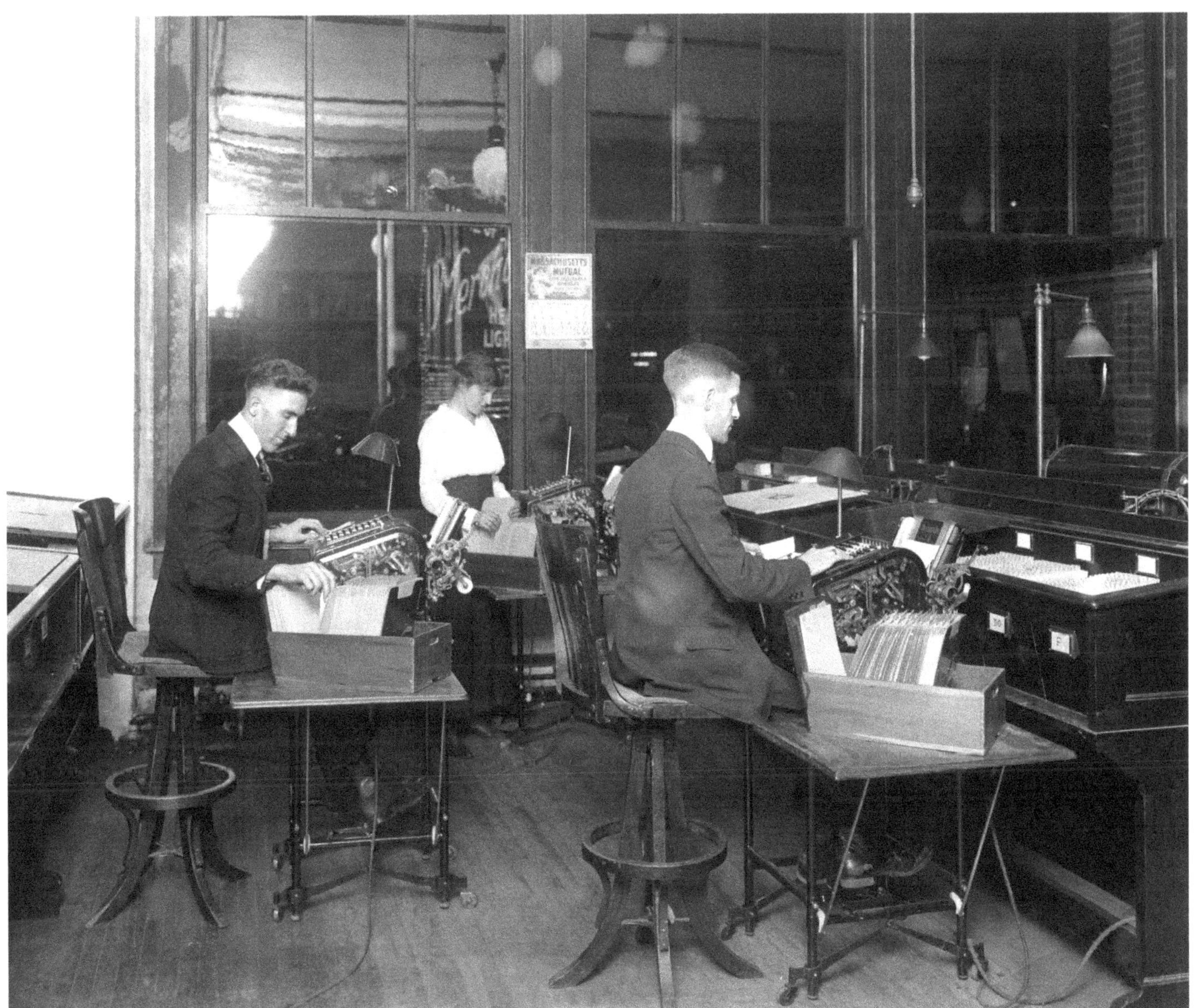

Clerks at L. S. Ayres and Company, 1916. In 1872 Lyman S. Ayres bought a controlling interest in the Trade Palace, an Indianapolis dry-goods store. Two years later he moved to the city from New York state and changed the name of the establishment to L. S. Ayres and Company. As Indianapolis grew, business at Ayres prospered, and in 1905 Lyman Ayres's son Frederic moved operations to a new eight-story building on the southwest corner of Washington and Meridian Streets. It was the city's first modern department store. Over the years Ayres became the city's premier retail establishment and a beloved fixture of Indianapolis life.

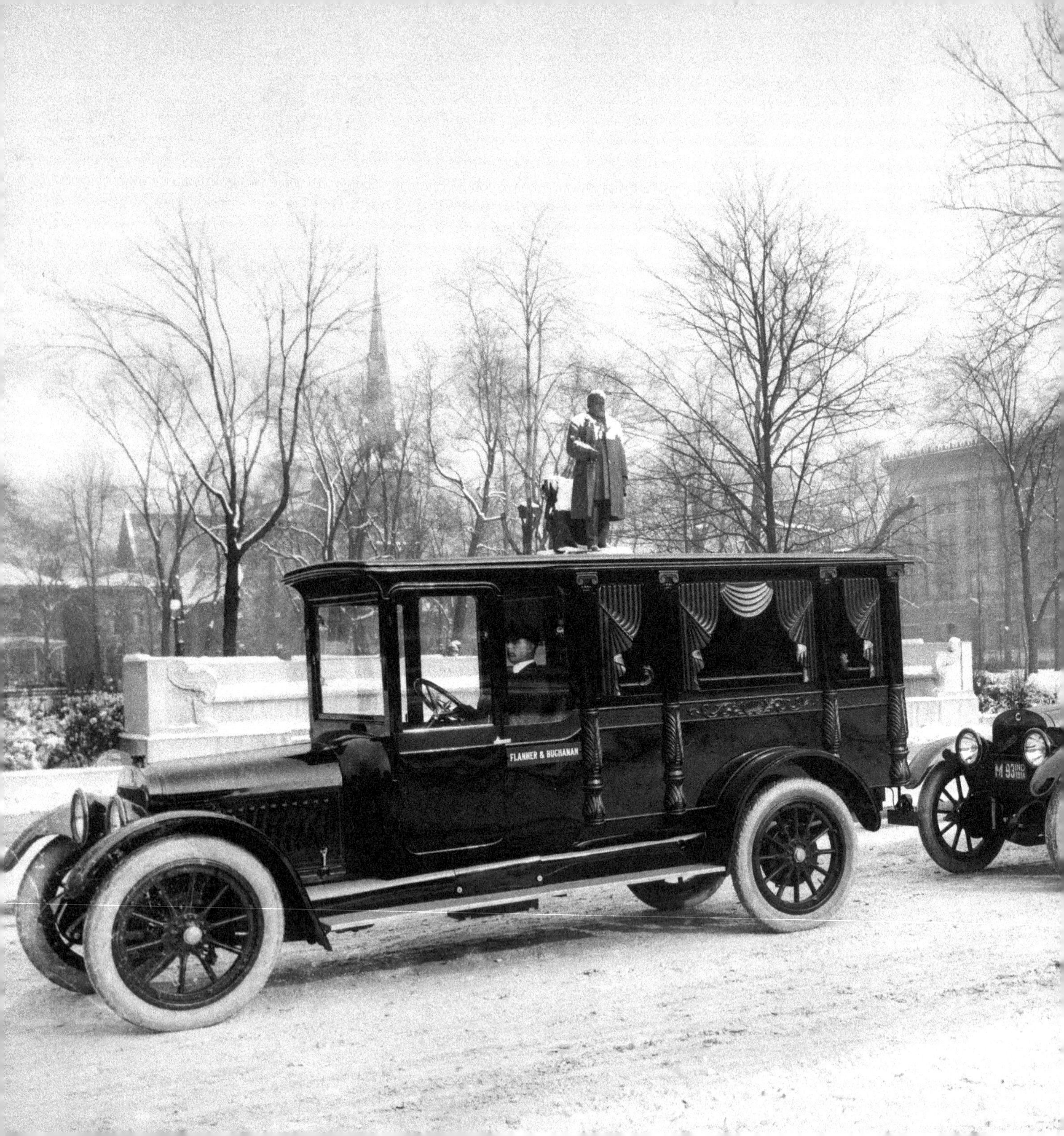
FLANNER & BUCHANAN

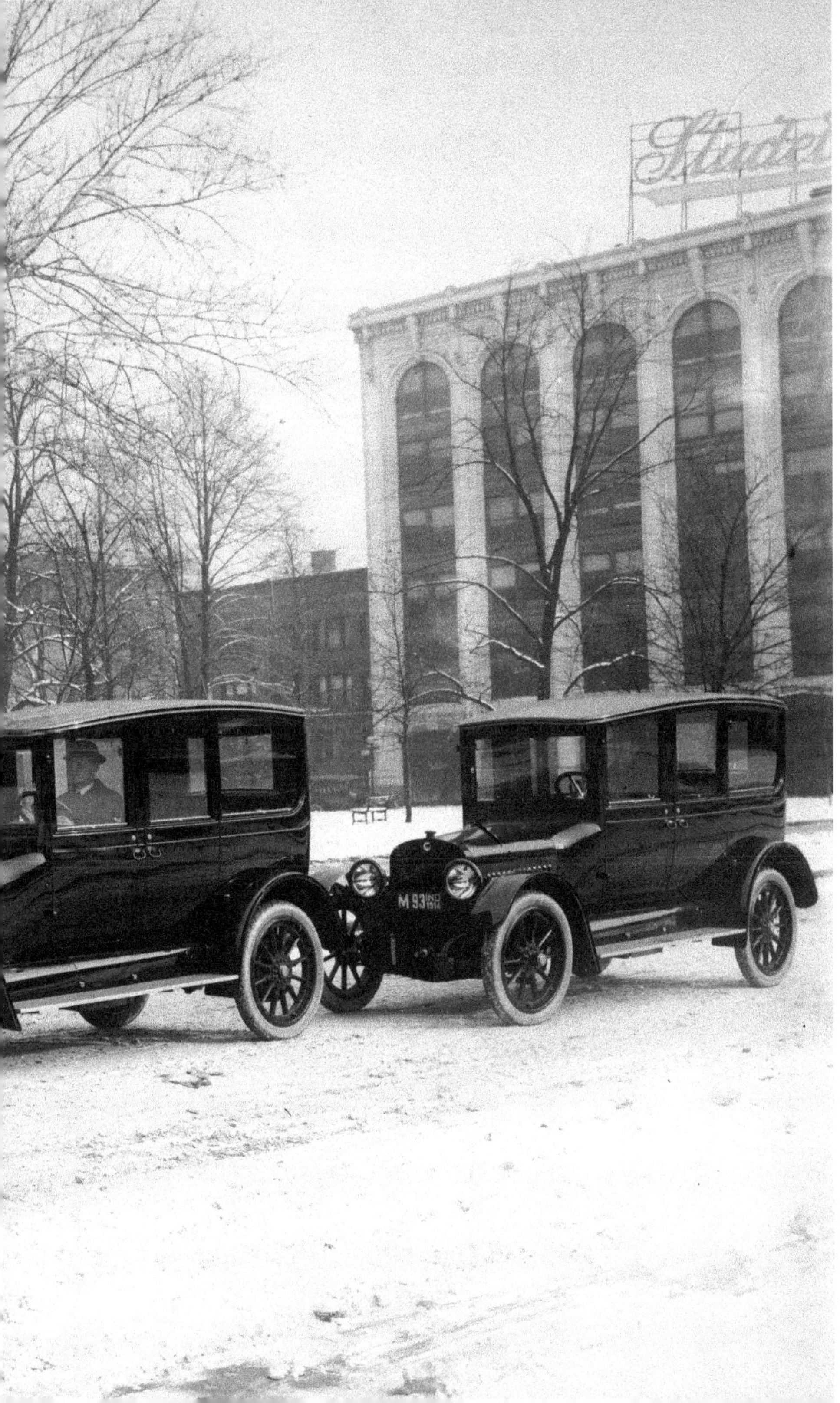

A Flanner and Buchanan hearse leads a funeral procession along the south side of University Park, 1914. Flanner and Buchanan, one of the city's leading funeral homes, dates to 1881, when Frank Flanner opened a mortuary on Illinois Street. The business adopted its current name six years later when Charles Buchanan, Flanner's brother-in-law, joined the firm. Today the Buchanan family continues to operate the business, which includes several facilities in Indianapolis and its suburbs.

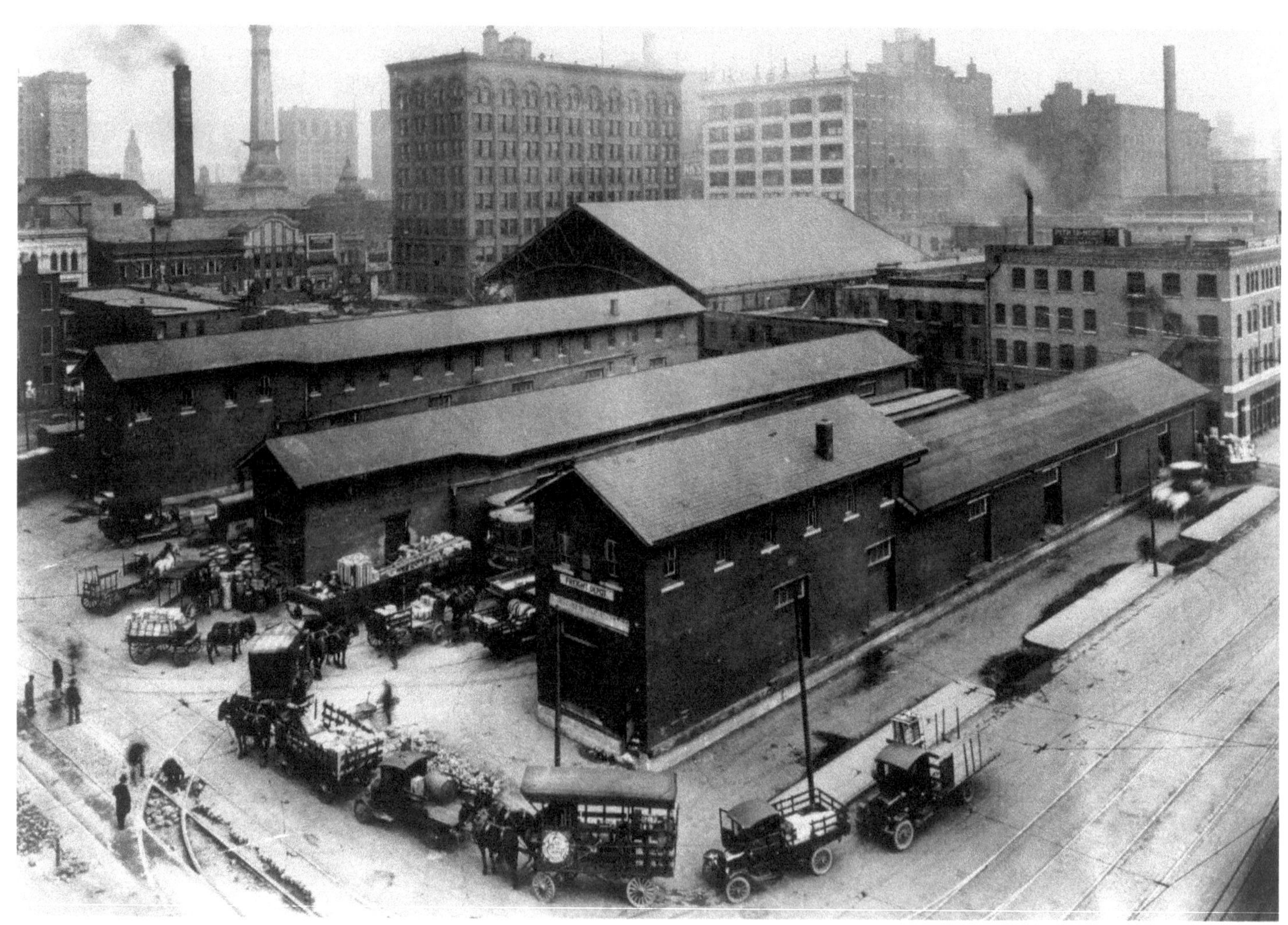

The Indianapolis Traction Terminal's freight houses, circa 1916. These buildings stood on the northwest section of the terminal complex, near the corner of Capitol Avenue and Ohio Street. By 1916 an average of seventy-one cars of freight left the terminal each day.

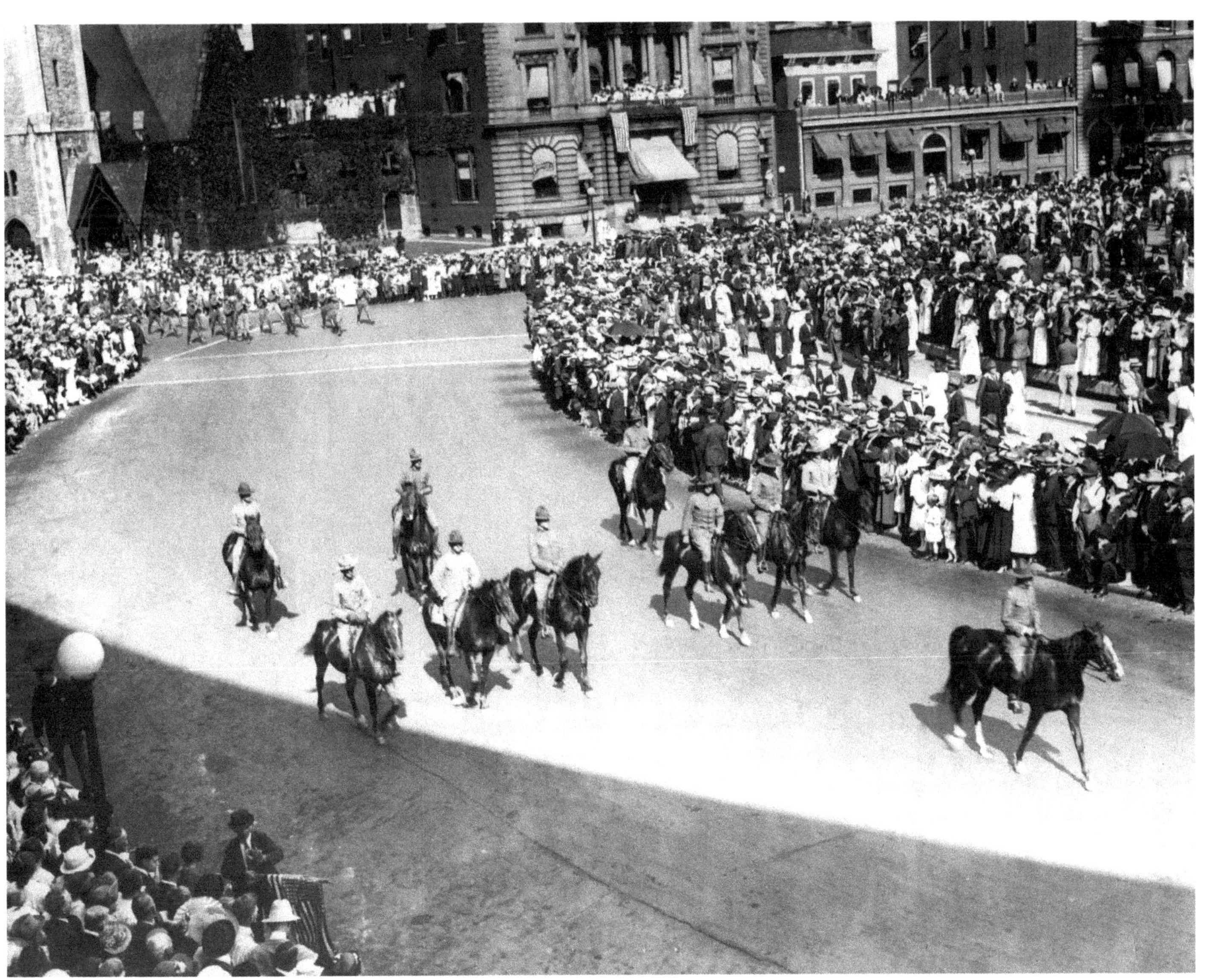

Col. Robert Tyndall leads the Rainbow Division in a parade around Monument Circle, 1917. The division was preparing to depart for World War I. In 1941 Tyndall retired as a major general after forty-four years in the army; he then served as Indianapolis mayor from 1943 to 1947.

Sending off the troops during World War I. This photo was probably taken at Union Station in 1917.

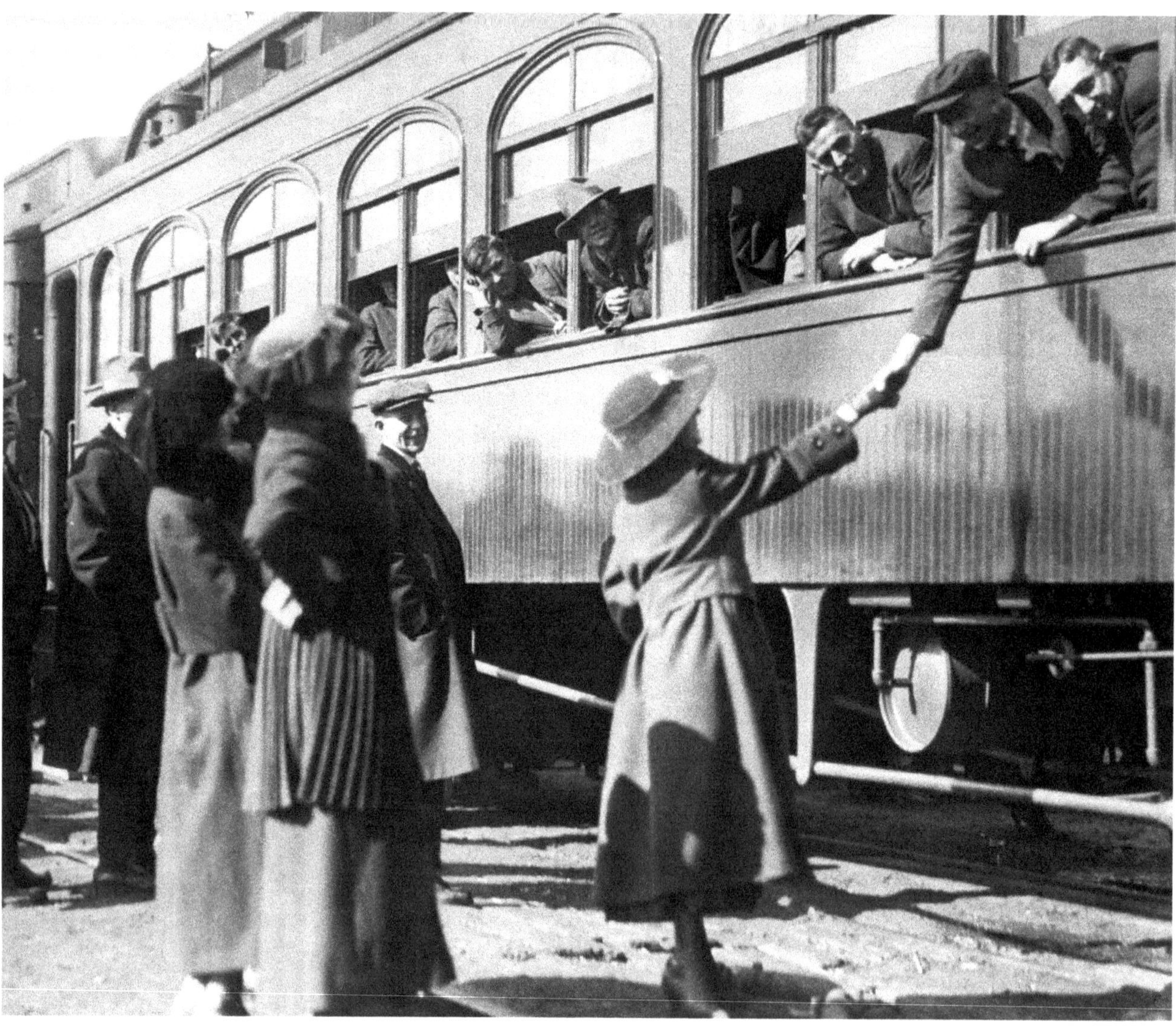

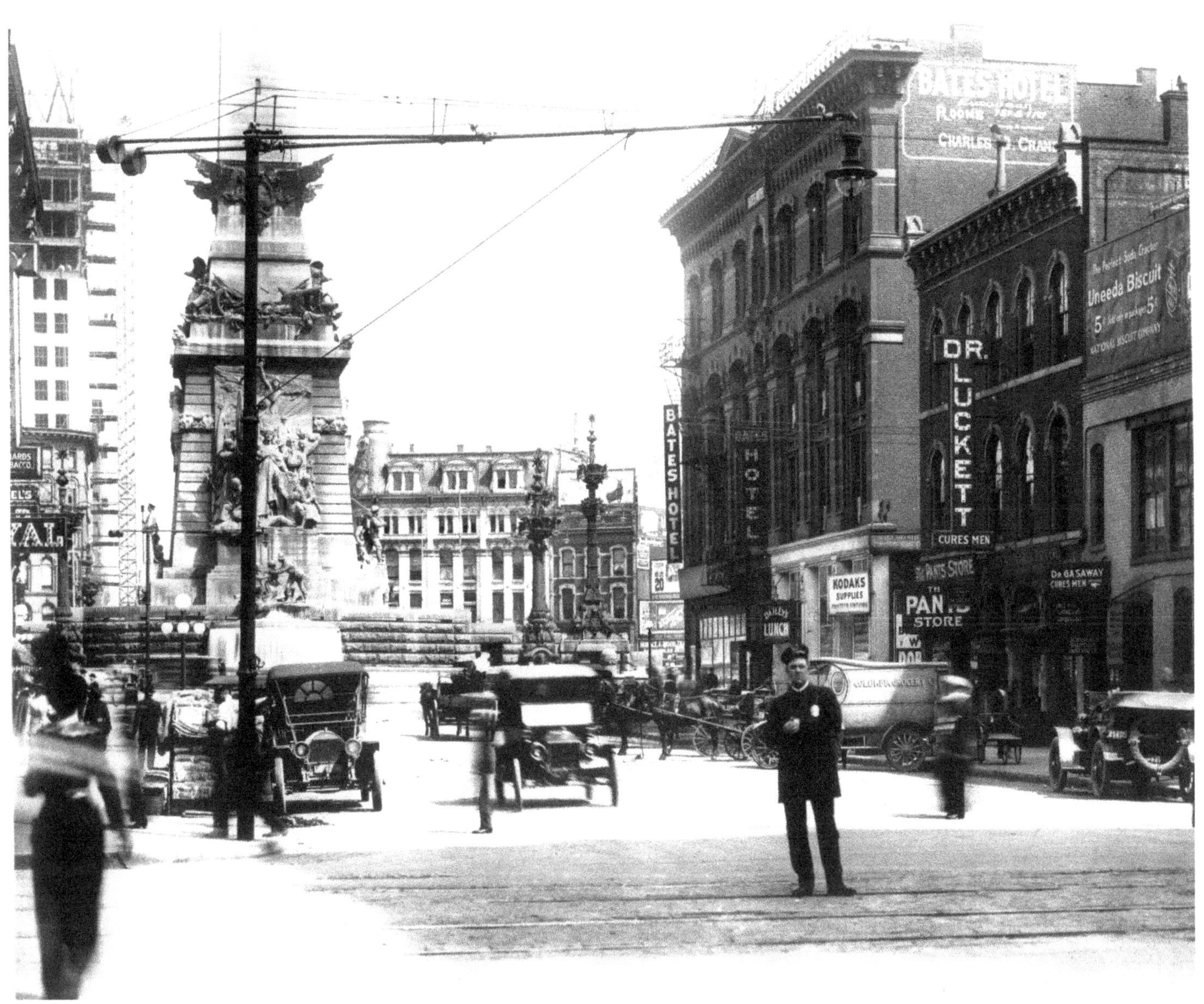

A view of Market Street, looking east toward Monument Circle, circa 1918.

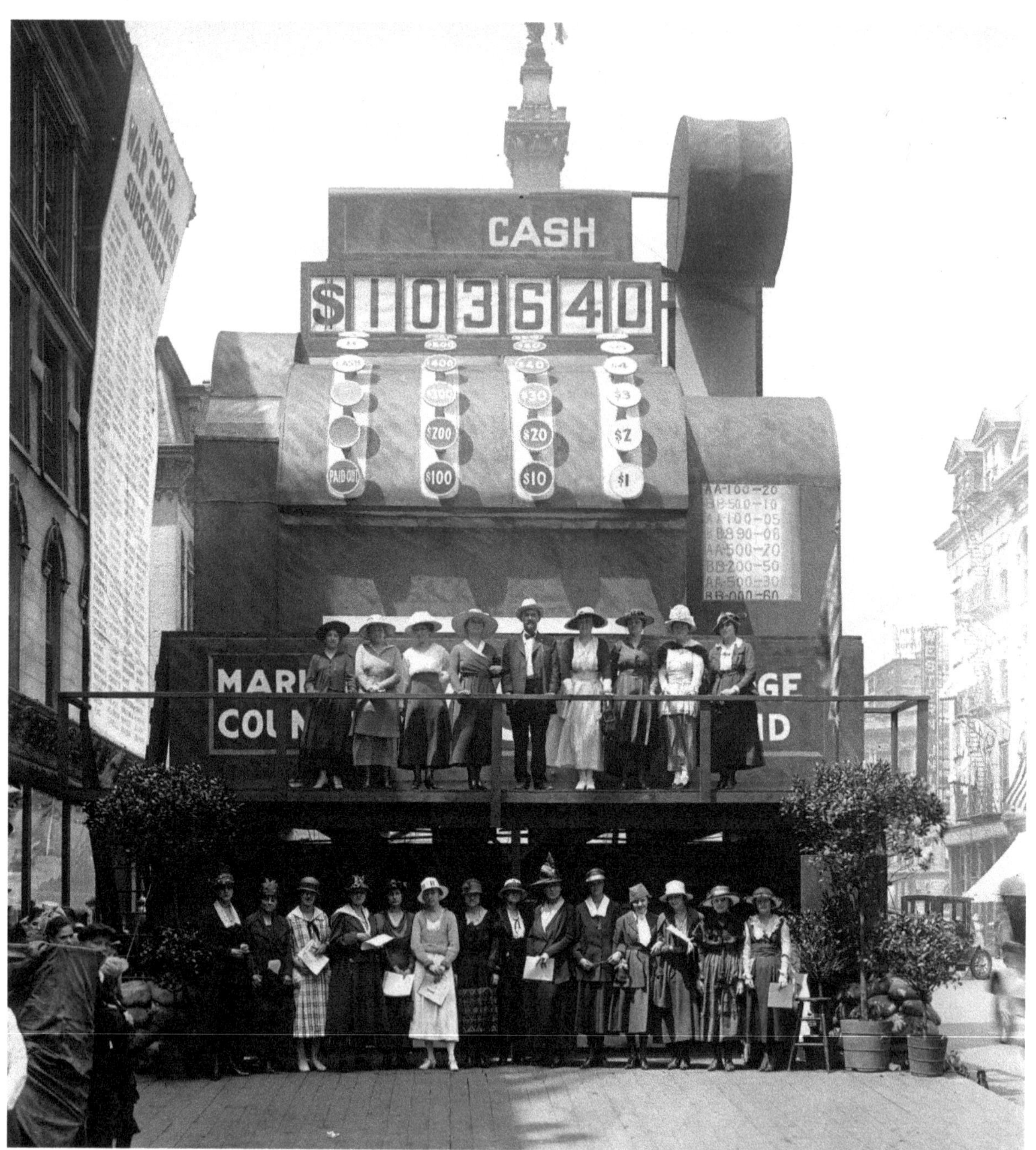

A giant cash register on Monument Circle, 1918. Organizers used this gimmick to track donations to the Marion County War Savings Subscribers Pledge Fund during World War I.

Indianapolis-area children work in a World War I victory garden.

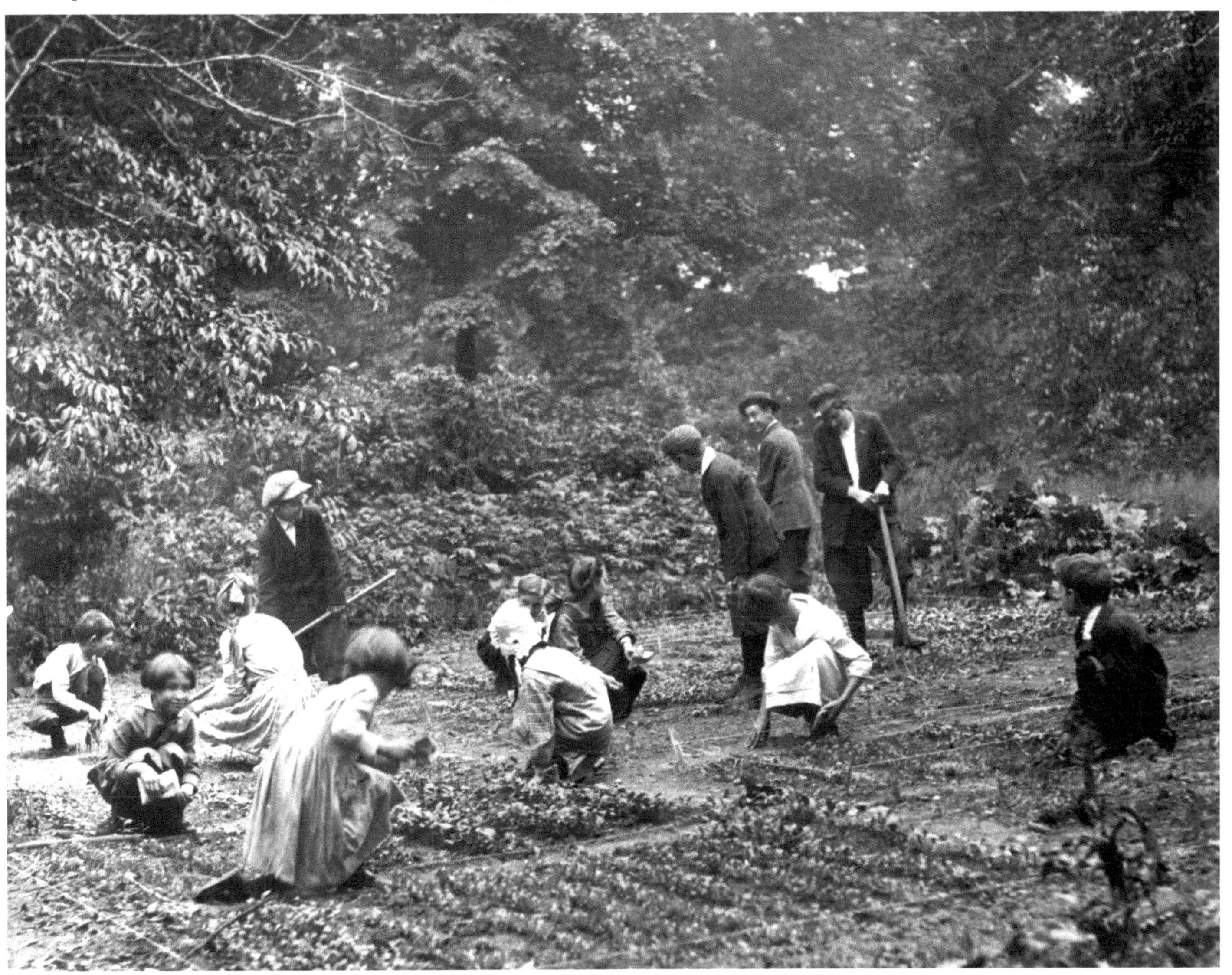

Young Charlene Keller of Indianapolis shows her patriotism during World War I, circa 1918.

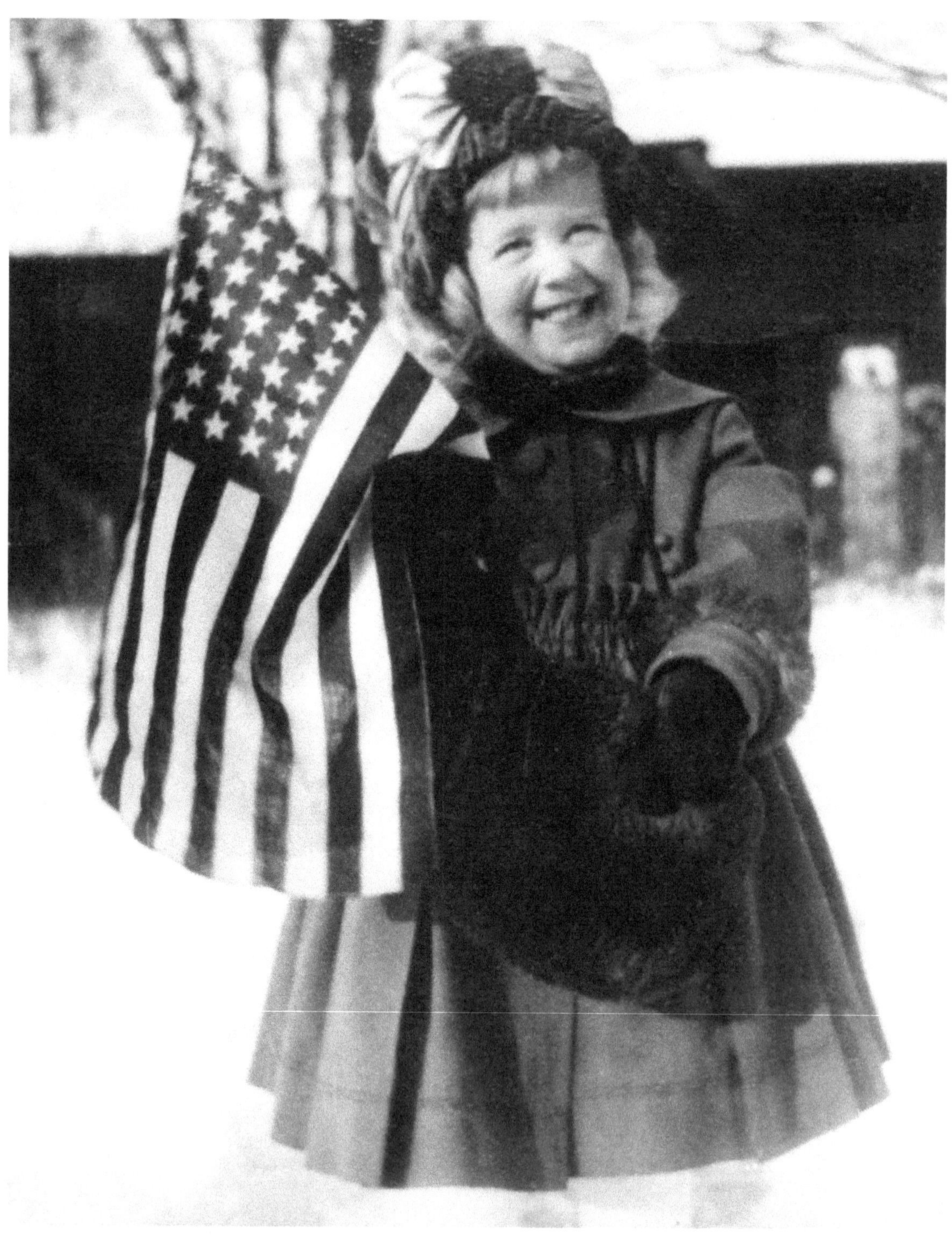

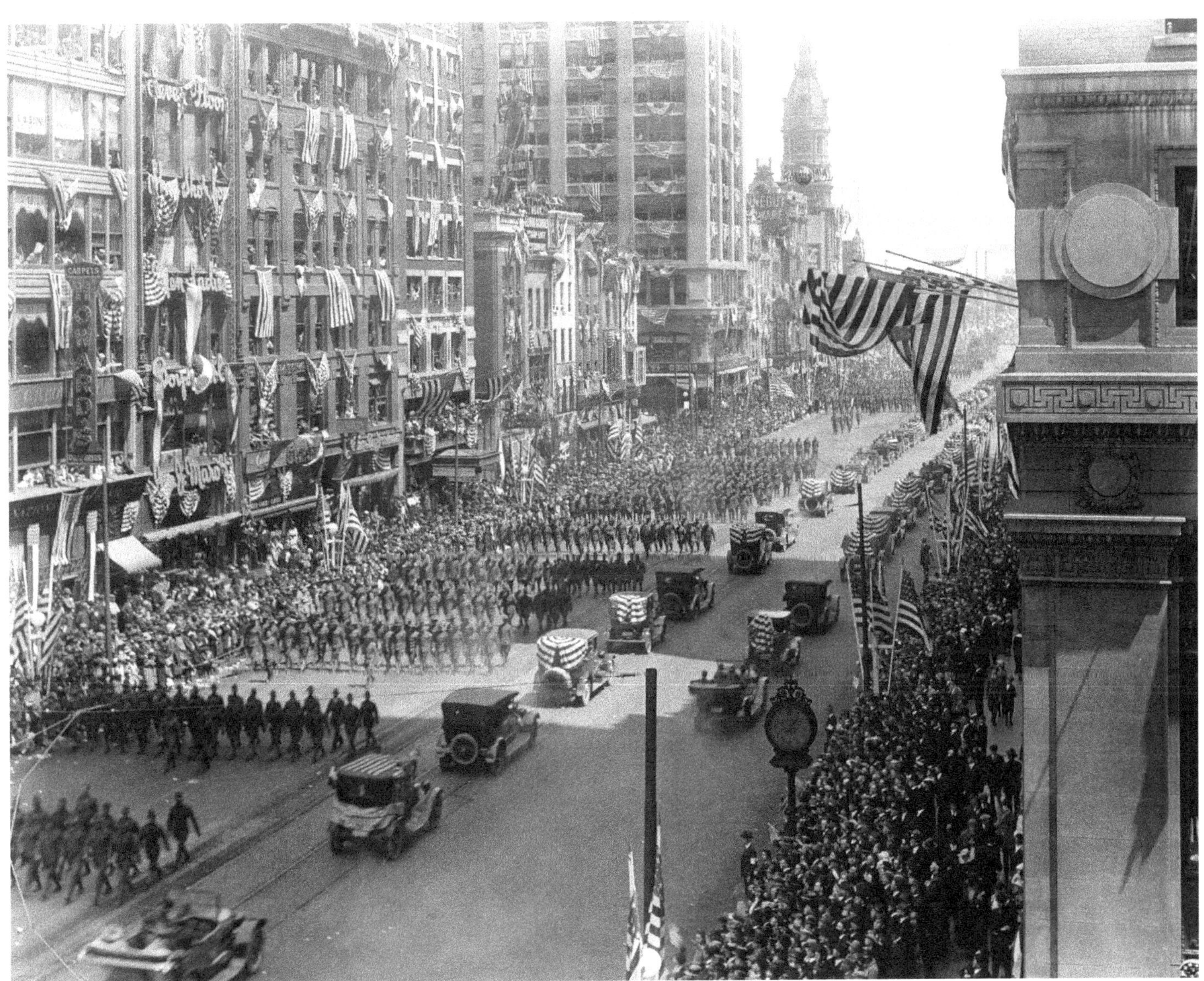

World War I veterans march east along Washington Street during a homecoming parade, May 7, 1919. According to the caption on the photo, the automobiles were carrying wounded soldiers.

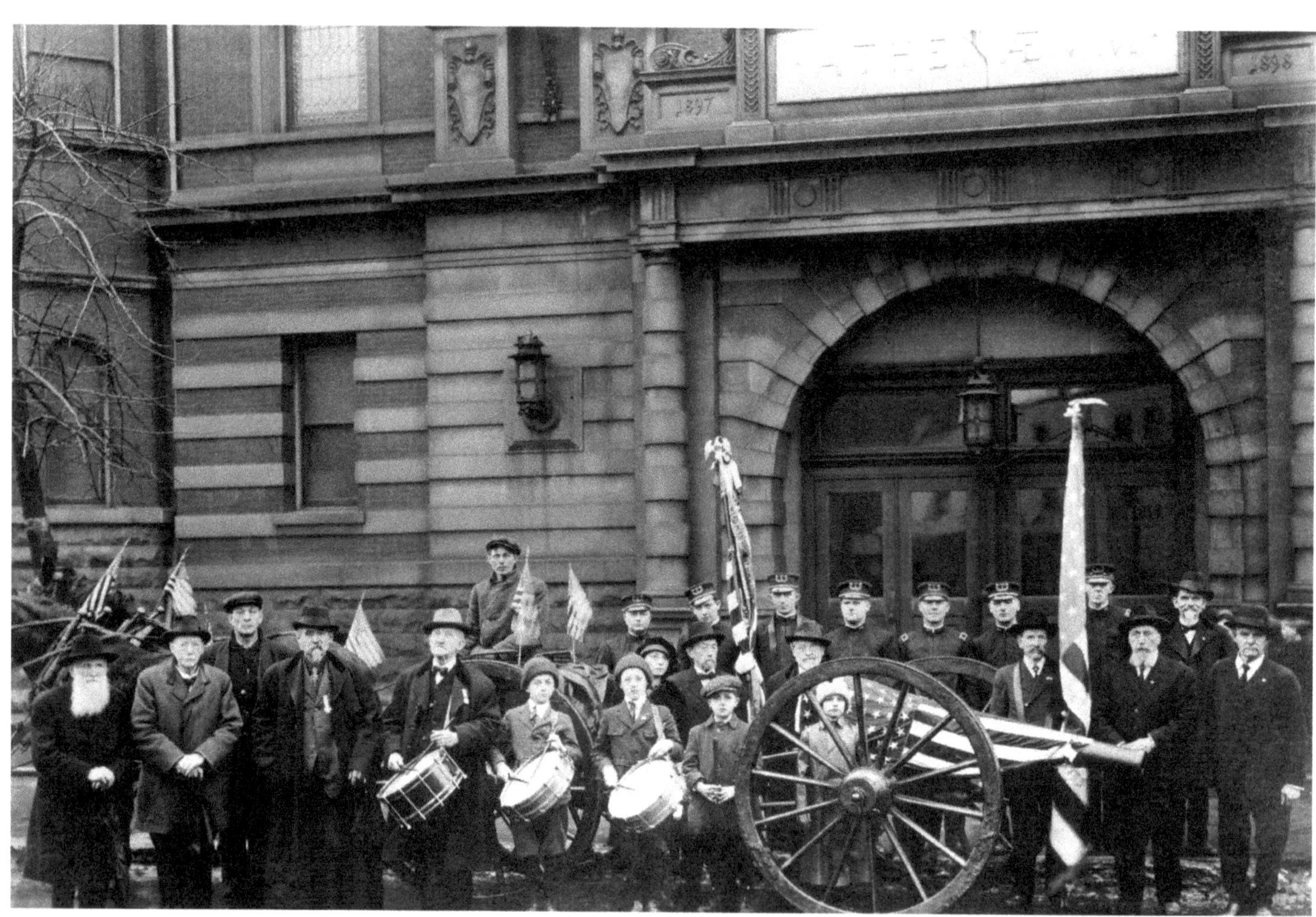

German-American veterans gather in front of the Athenaeum, probably during World War I. The Athenaeum was built in the 1890's as a German cultural and social center. Designed by Indianapolis architects Vonnegut and Bohn (Bernard Vonnegut was the grandfather of renowned author Kurt Vonnegut), it housed meeting rooms, a restaurant, an auditorium, a gymnasium, a bowling alley, and a beer garden. It was originally called Das Deutsche Haus but was renamed the Athenaeum as a result of anti-German sentiments during World War I. Today it still functions as an important community center, and its beer garden continues to draw crowds on summer nights.

A parade on Monument Circle, most likely honoring World War I soldiers.

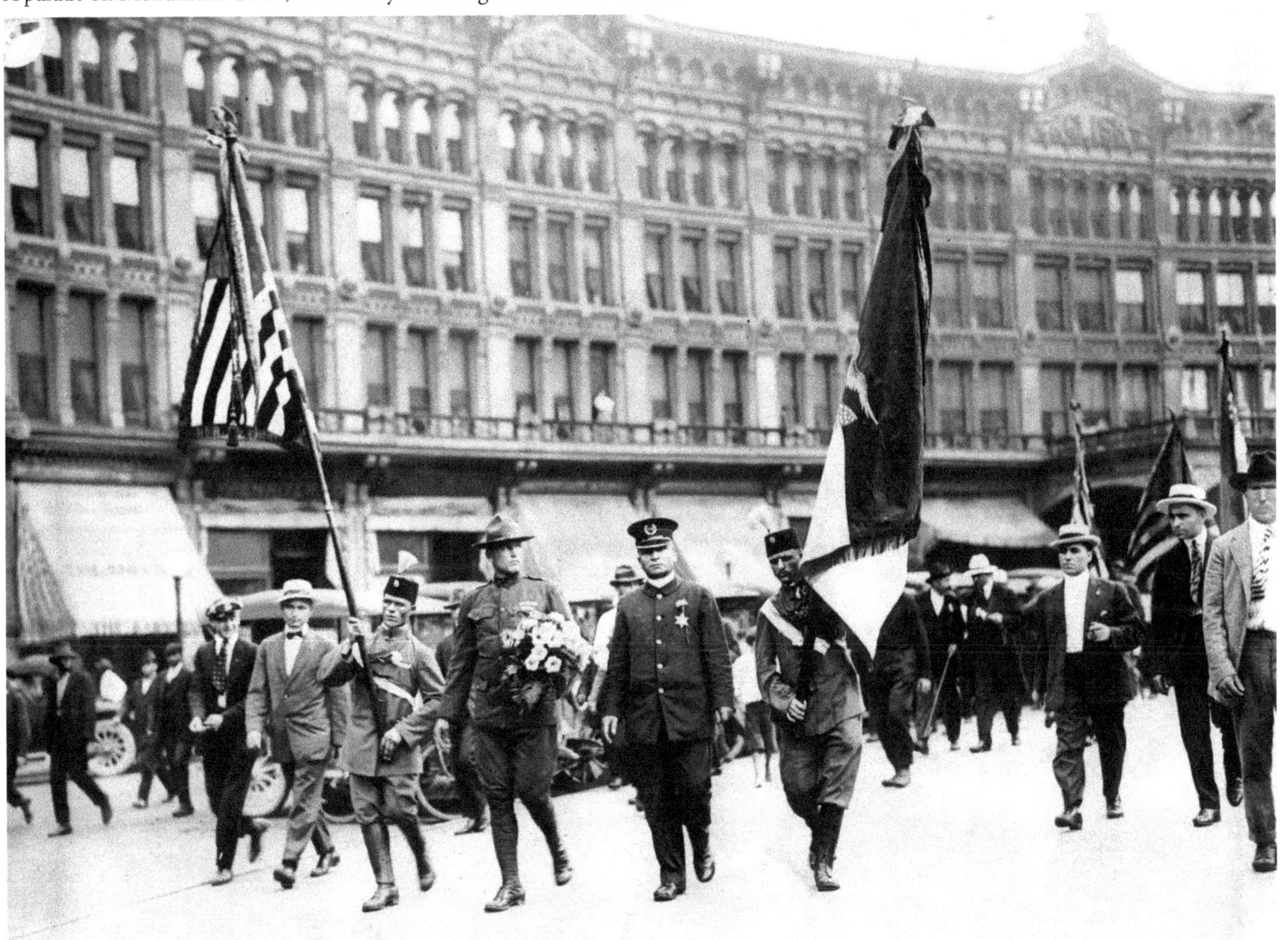

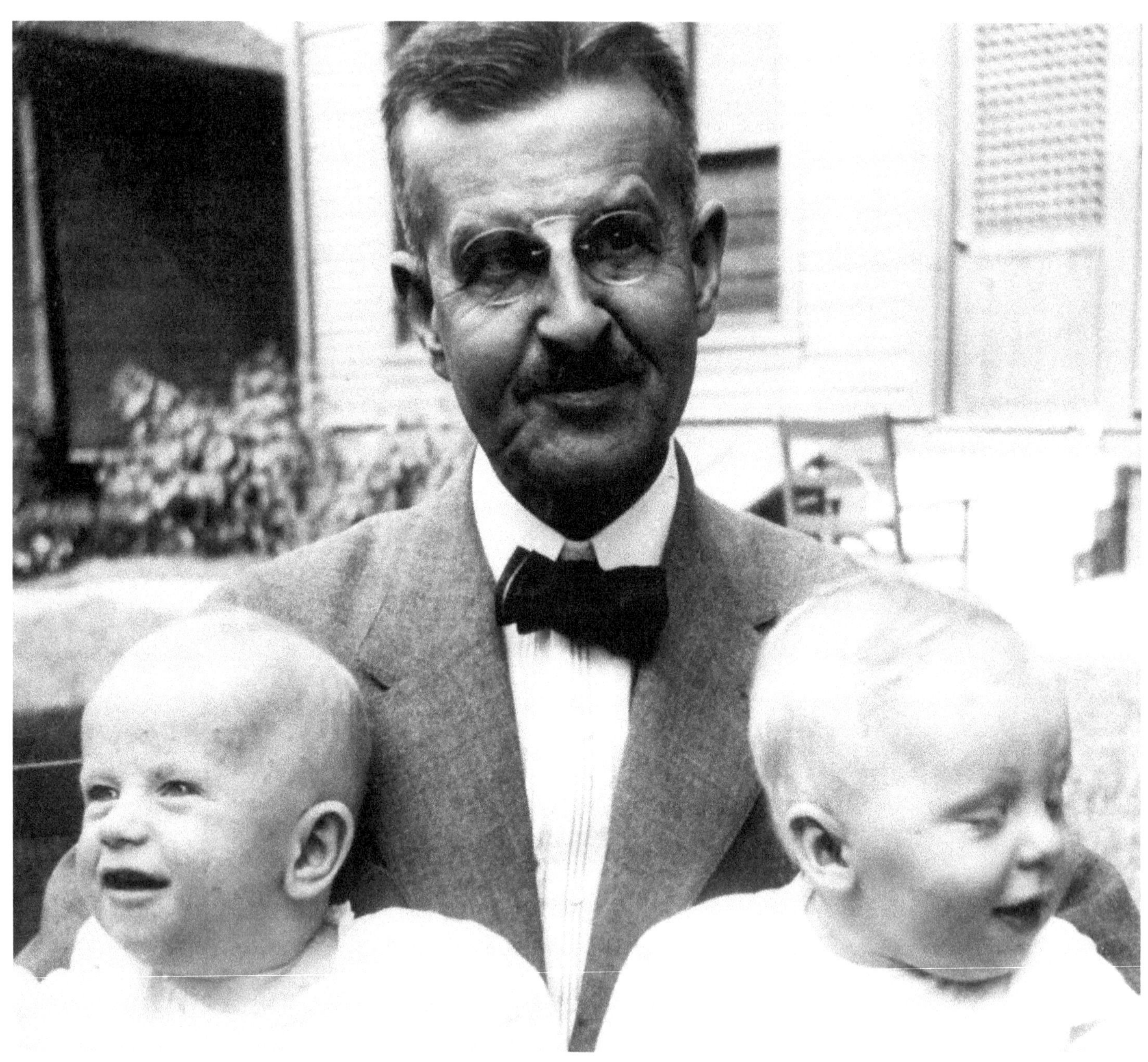

Indianapolis storeowner Frank Geiger holds grandchildren Paul Buchanan and Enos Pray, 1918.

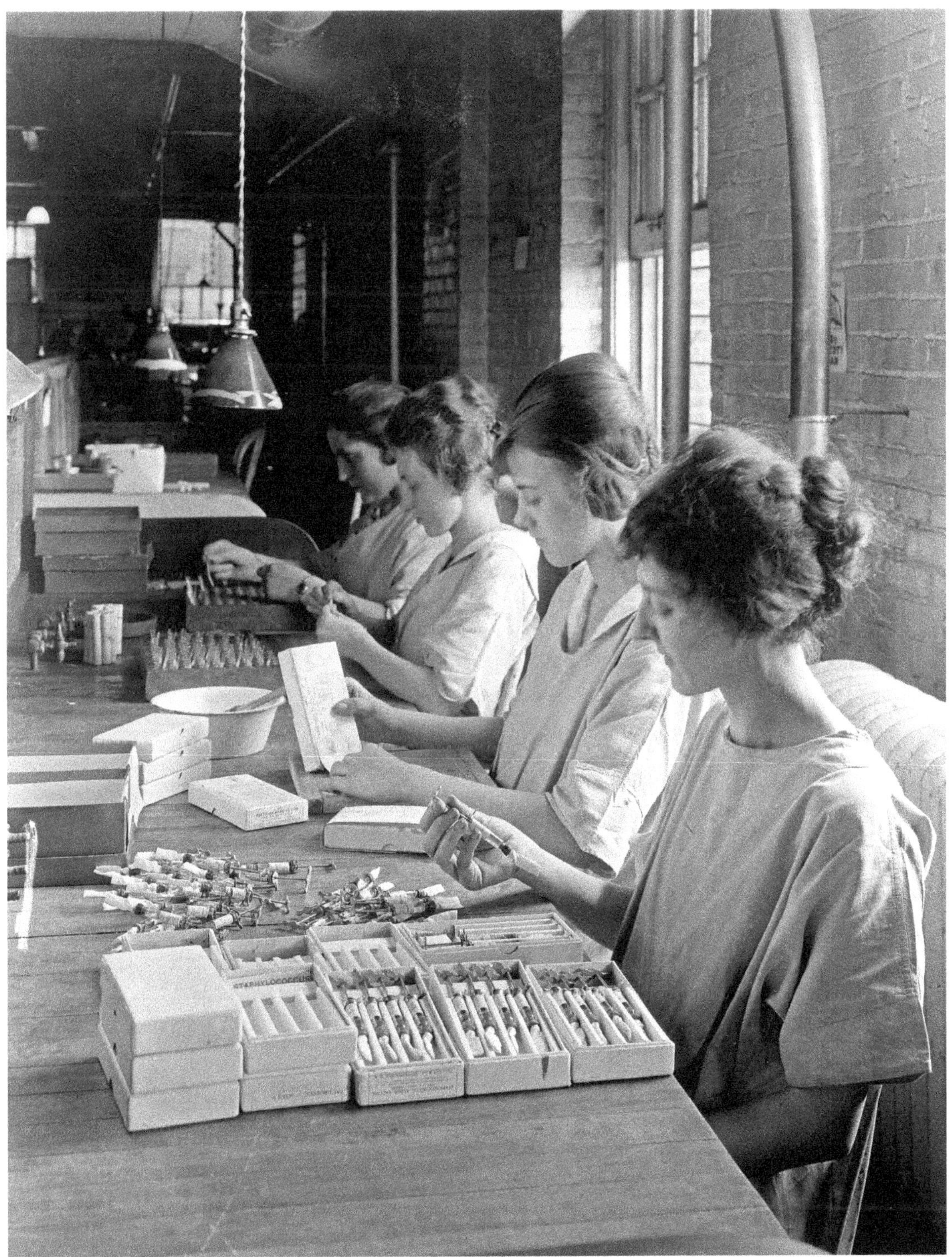

Young women package vaccine at Eli Lilly and Company, 1919. Col. Eli Lilly founded the pharmaceutical company in a small building on Pearl Street in 1876. Still headquartered in its hometown of Indianapolis, Lilly has grown into an international corporation with more than 42,000 employees worldwide.

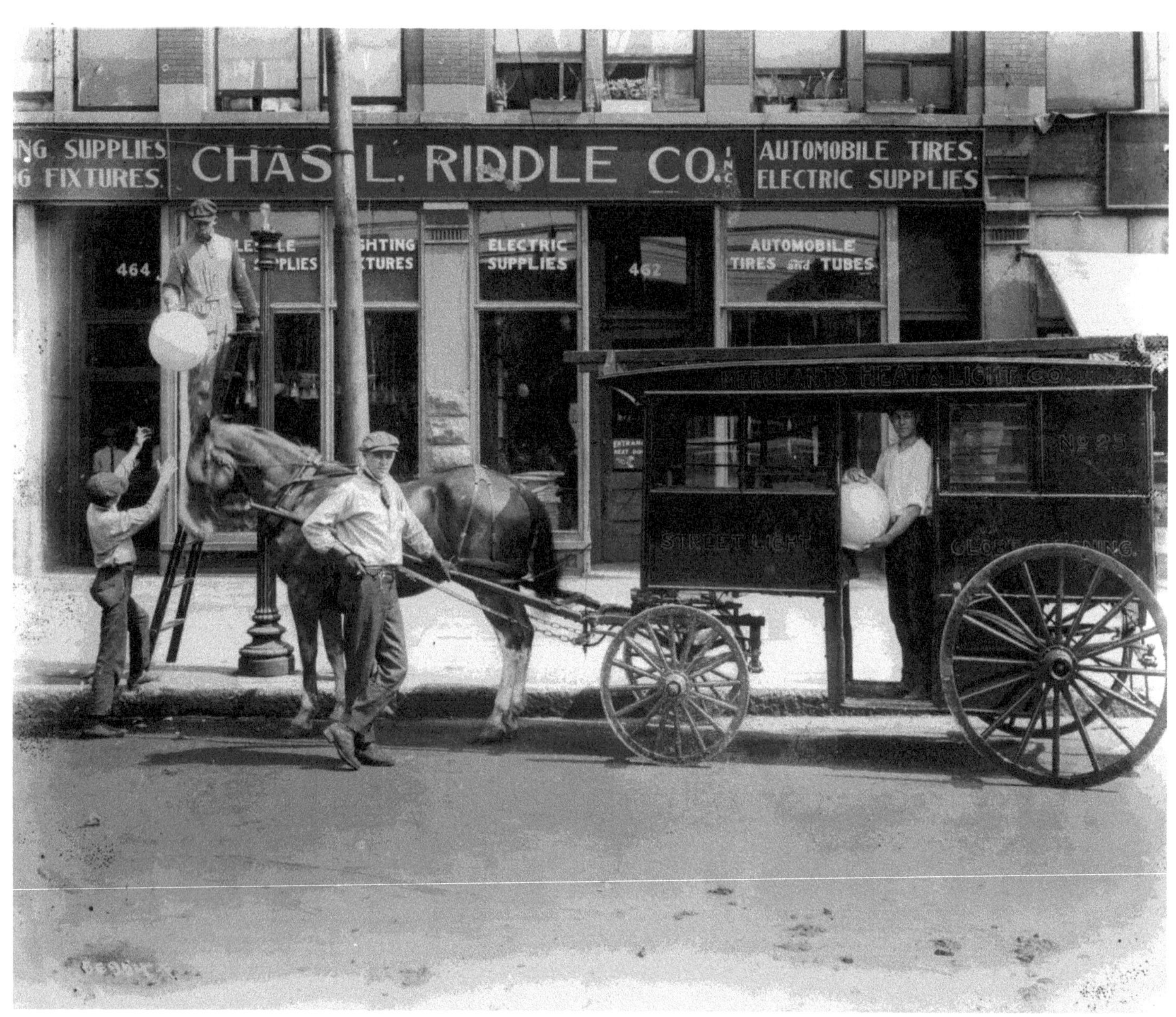

Workers clean streetlights in front of the Charles L. Riddle Company on West Washington Street, 1919. A note on the image indicates that "this simple job needed three men, a boy, a horse, and a wagon."

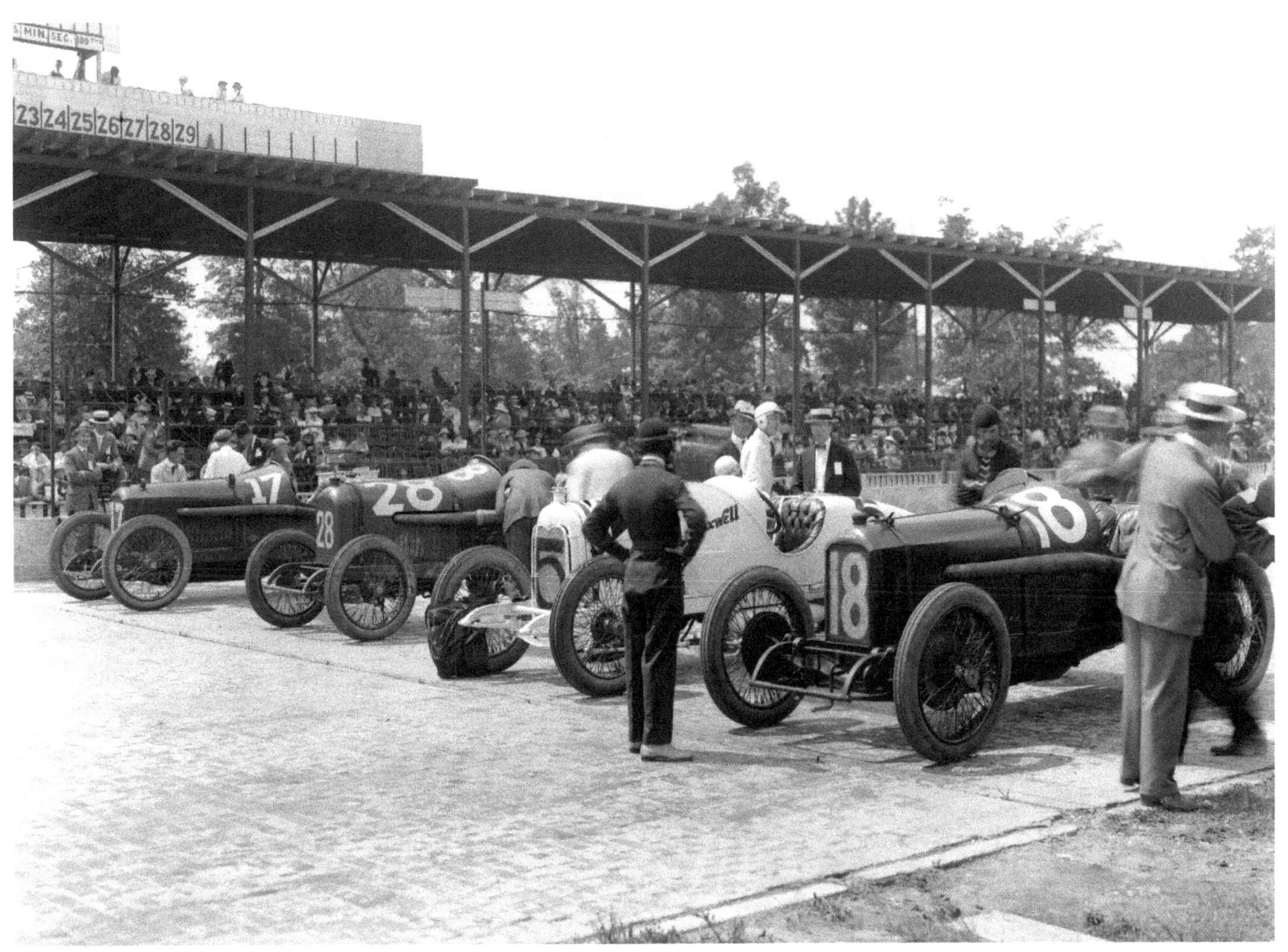

The front-row starters at the 1919 Indianapolis 500. The speedway's owners cancelled the event in 1917 and 1918 because of World War I, so fans were especially eager to see the start of the race that year.

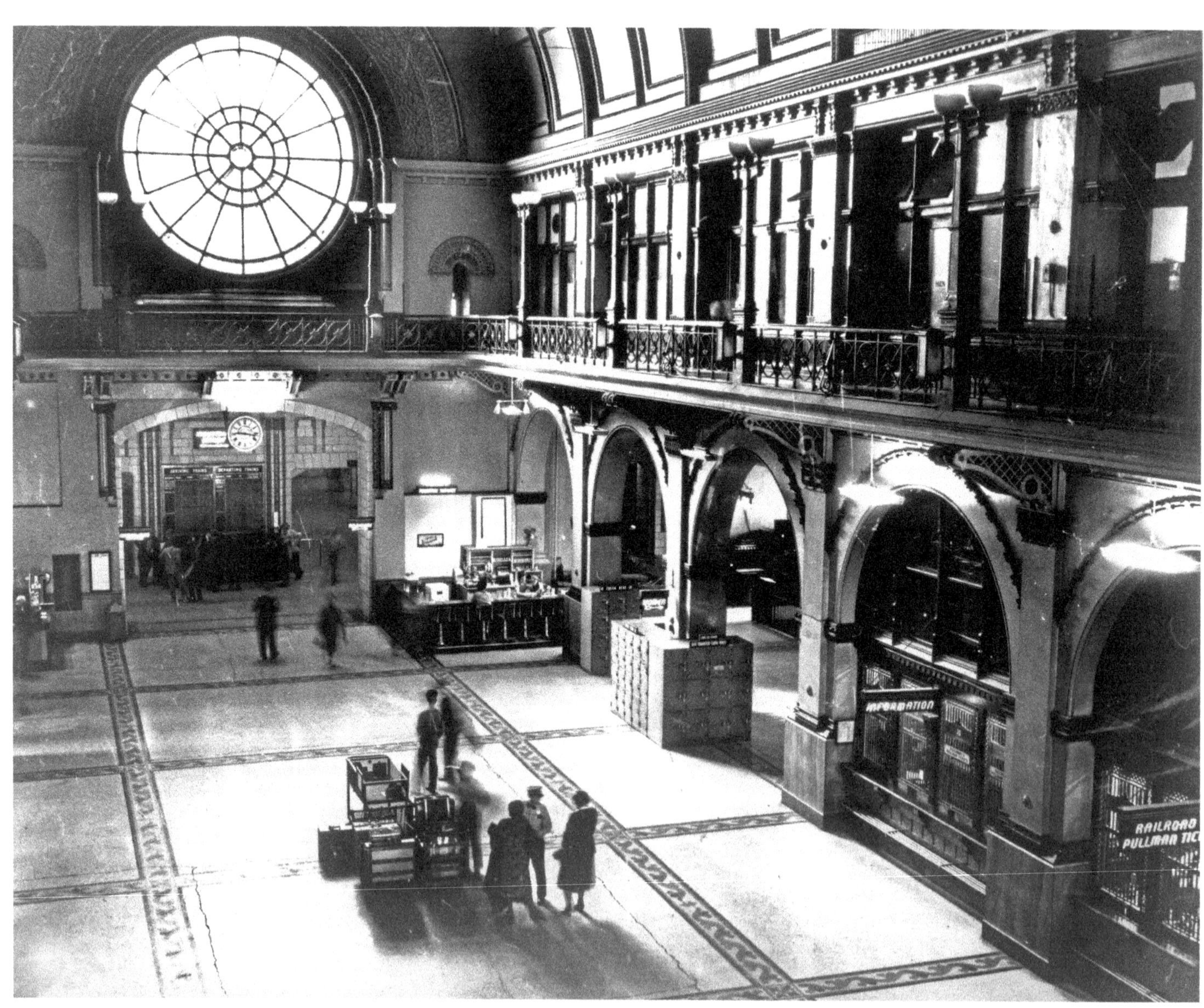

The interior of Union Station, circa 1920's. Light streams through the station's elegant stained-glass windows as porters load bags and prepare to guide passengers through the arched doorway to the elevated tracks.

Hard Hearts, Hard Times 1920–1939

In the early 1920's many Hoosiers were troubled by change. For the first time in history, the U.S. census bureau reported that more Americans lived in the city than on farms. The country's economy was now solidly based upon manufacturing, and for some it brought a sense of loss. A number of Indianapolis residents, forced to punch a factory clock, longed to return to the family homestead. The Indianapolis economy prospered, but large out-of-state conglomerates began controlling more and more of the local manufacturing interests, adding to Hoosiers' sense of loss.

Cultural changes contributed to the anxiety. Mass marketing and advertising brought new products and ideas into the nation's homes, and for those Americans who were more comfortable with restrictive Victorian morals, many of the trends were too open and permissive. Indianapolis citizens responded in part with increased nativism. Many joined the Ku Klux Klan, and the Klan dominated city and state politics until a murder conviction brought down its leader in 1925.

More troubles came with the stock market crash of October 1929. Almost instantly the economic gains of the 1920's were gone. Manufacturing, which had been driving the economy, sputtered to a standstill, and by early 1930 the Indianapolis unemployment rate had already risen to more than 9 percent. The depression continued to grow, with the worst years coming in 1932 and 1933. In the three years after the crash, Indianapolis's manufacturing workforce declined by nearly half, from around 59,000 to 30,000. Unemployment peaked in 1933 at 37 percent. Businesses closed (including the venerable automobile manufacturers Marmon and Stutz), families went on public relief, and a shantytown sprang up along the banks of the White River.

Despite the hard times, however, Indianapolis endured. Immediate help came with the inauguration of Franklin D. Roosevelt as president in 1933 and the adoption of the first New Deal programs. Residents found work with the Civilian Conservation Corps or with public works projects, including the construction of Howe High School, the naval armory, Lockefield Gardens, and the new state fairgrounds coliseum. Employment began to rise. In 1935 about 19 percent of Marion County residents were on public relief, but by 1936 the figure had dropped to 6 percent. Some historians point out that the depression began worsening again in the late 1930's and that the New Deal programs were failing, but by that time the suffering was nearly over. War loomed and while it would bring its own pain and sacrifice, it ended the Great Depression for good.

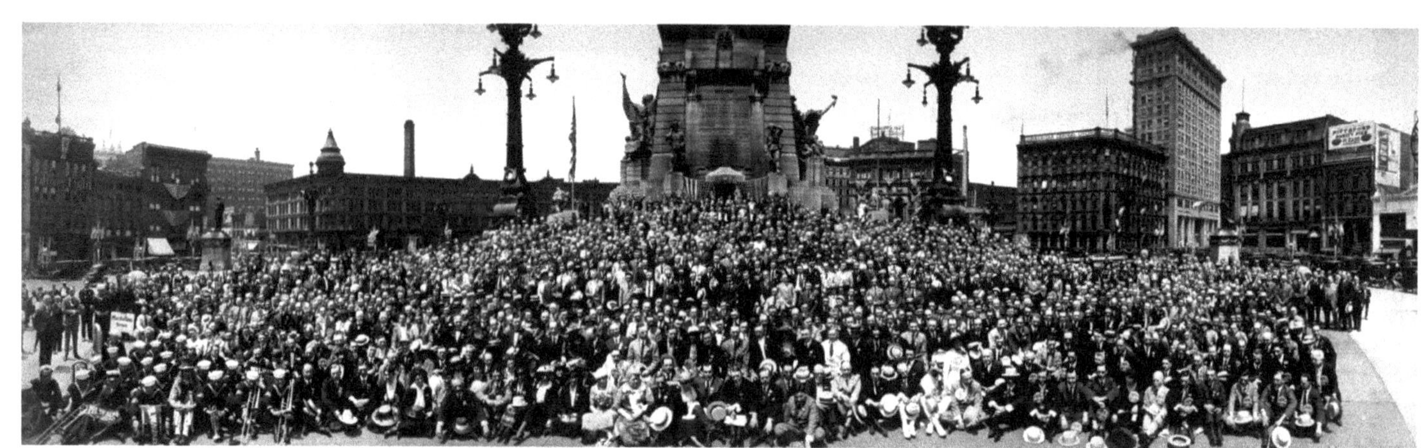

The Associated Advertising Clubs of the World on the south steps of the Soldiers and Sailors Monument, 1920. Over the years many groups have gathered for photos at this spot.

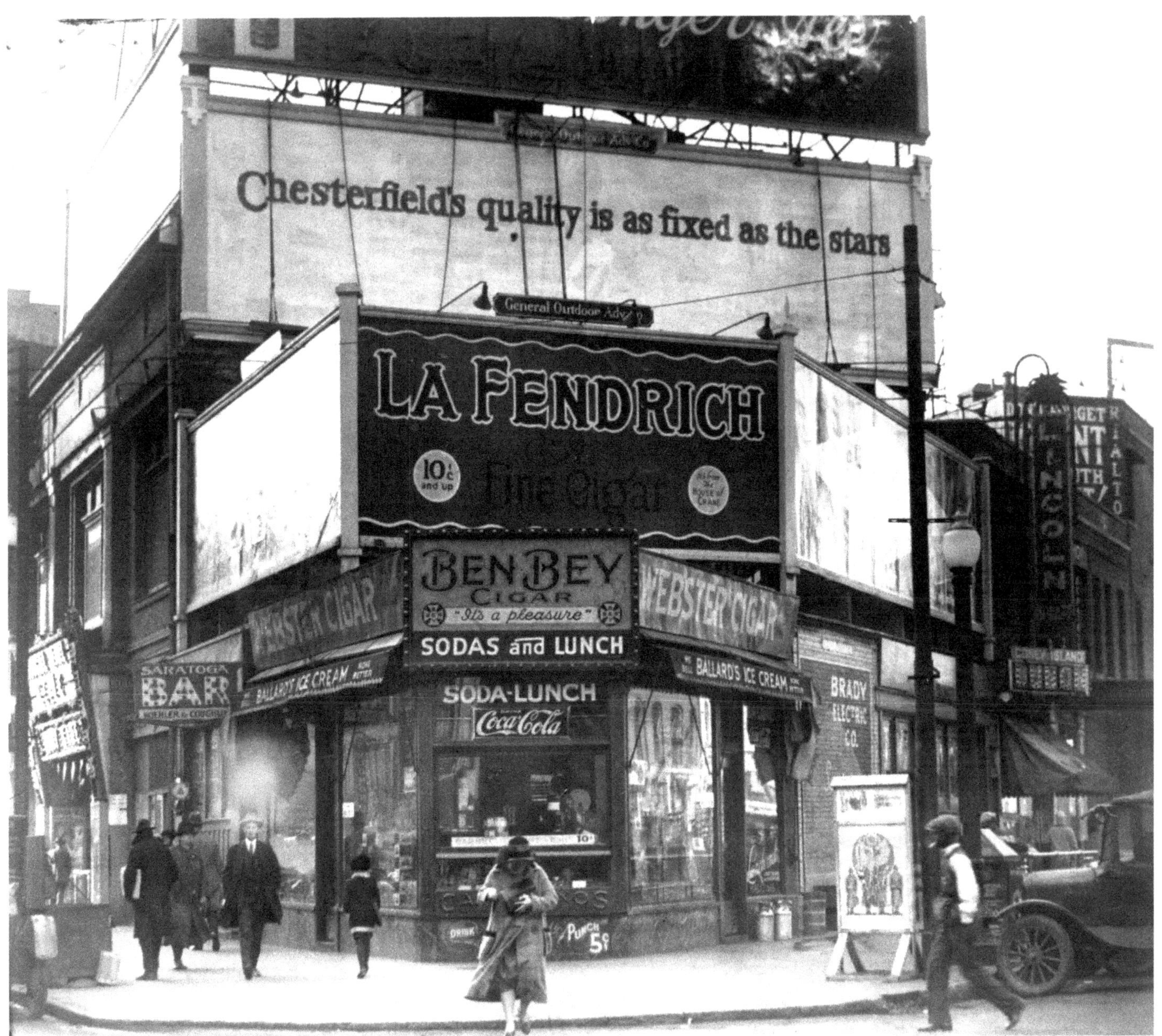

The intersection of Illinois Street and Kentucky Avenue, circa 1920's. The Fendrich Cigar Company of Evansville, Indiana, manufactured the cigar prominently advertised on the billboard.

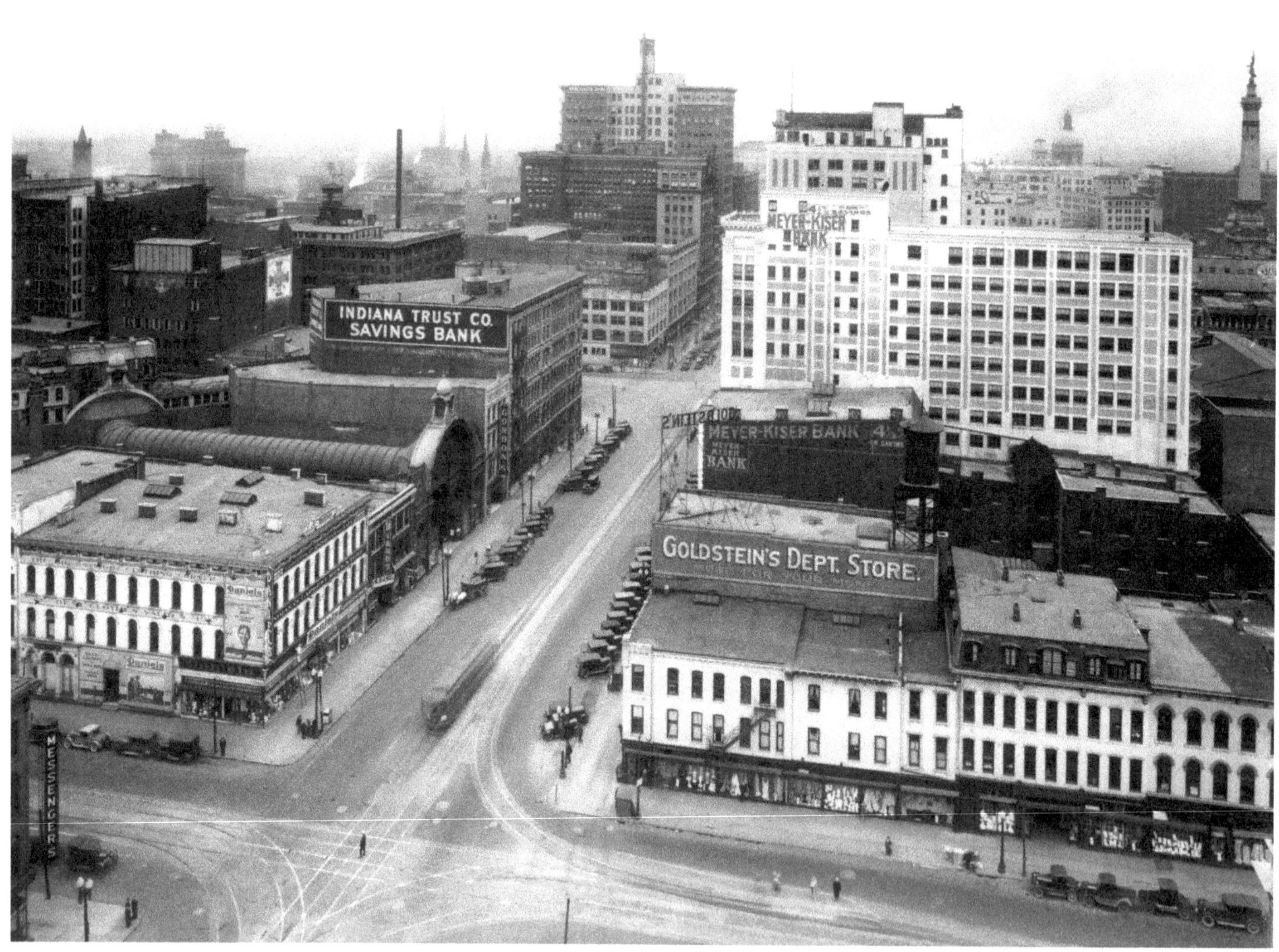

An aerial view of Washington Street looking west, circa 1920's. The barrel-roofed building is the Pembroke Arcade, which ran between Washington Street and Virginia Avenue and housed small shops. It opened in the mid-1890's and was razed in 1943.

Workers at L. S. Ayres and Company, circa 1920's. The windows in the back offer a view of Washington Street.

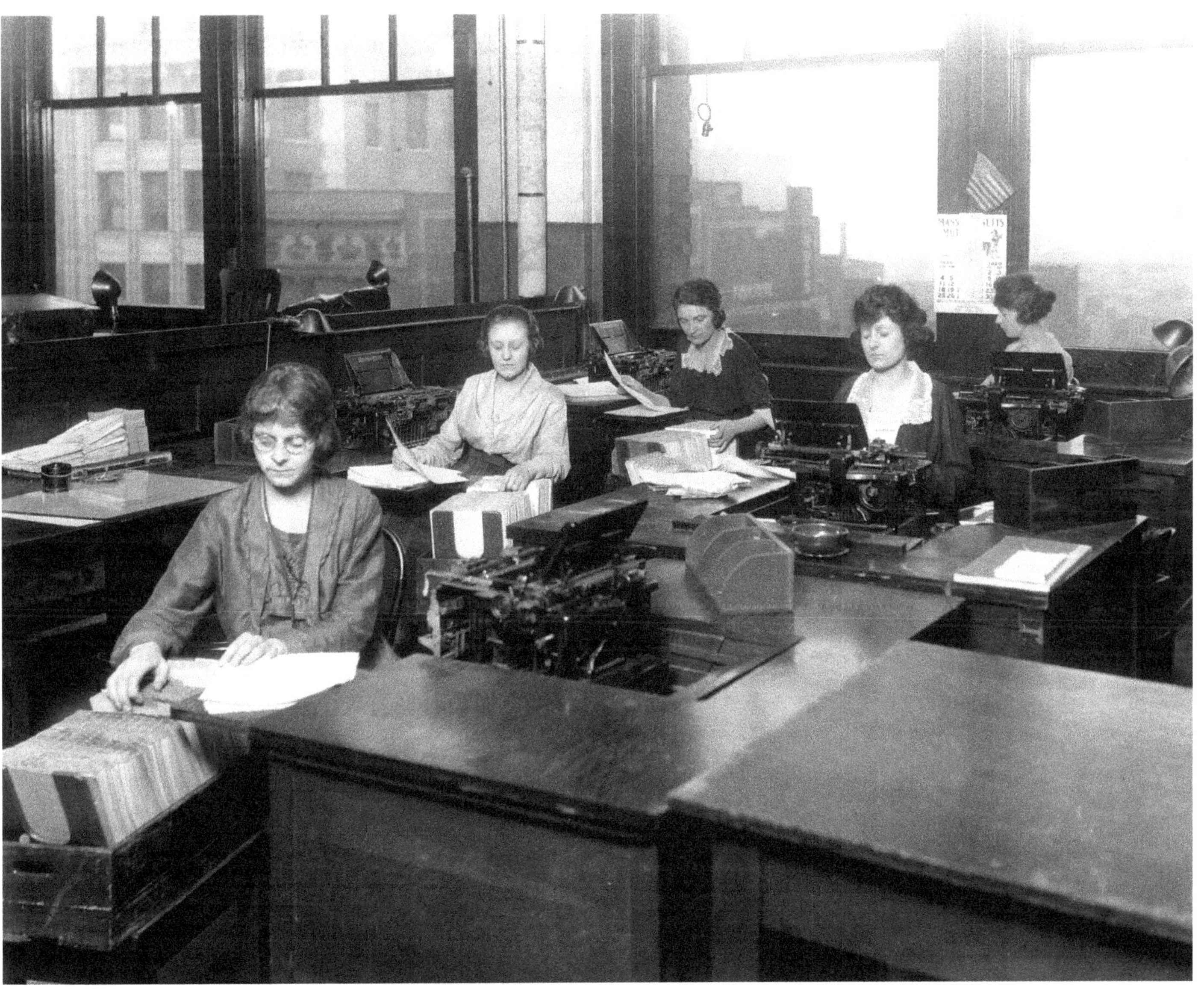

The Majestic building, circa 1920's. The ten-story Majestic is often billed as Indianapolis's first skyscraper. Constructed of carved limestone over a steel skeleton, it opened in 1896 and was the city's tallest building for more than fifteen years. It still stands at the northeast corner of Pennsylvania and Maryland Streets, although it has been stripped of its cornice and balconies.

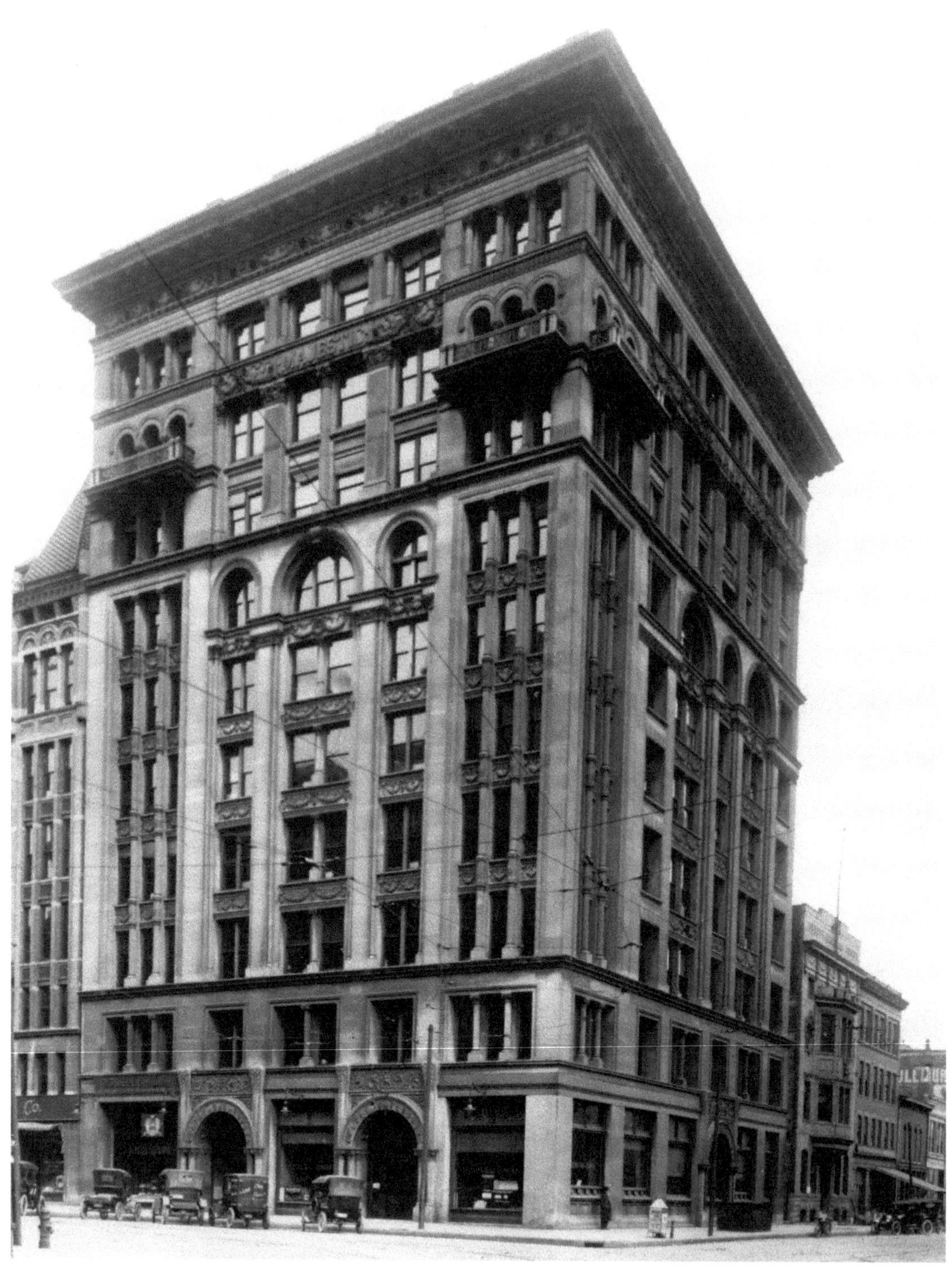

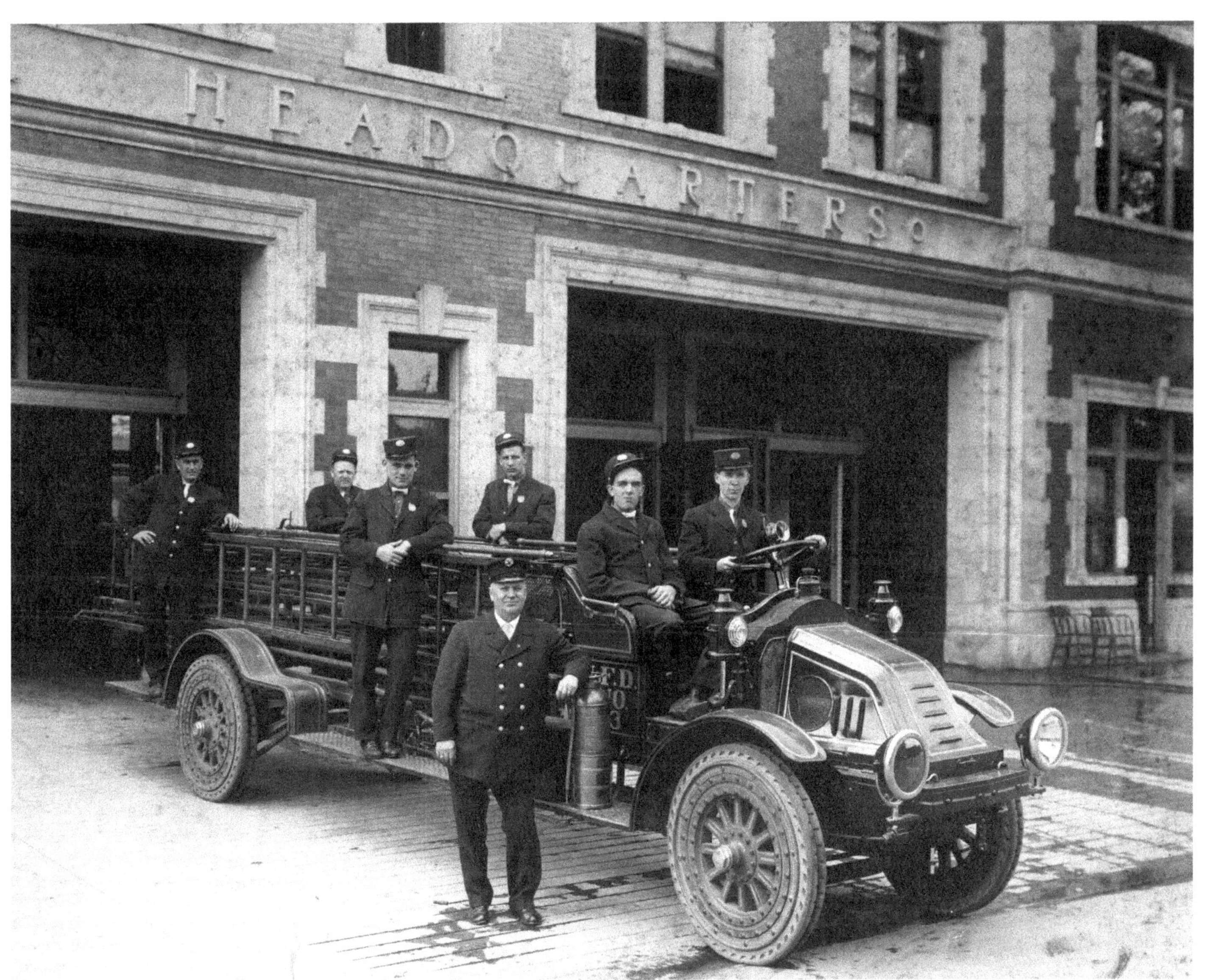

Indianapolis firefighters proudly show off their engine, circa 1920's. This photo was taken outside the fire headquarters, which was located on the southeast corner of New York and Alabama Streets.

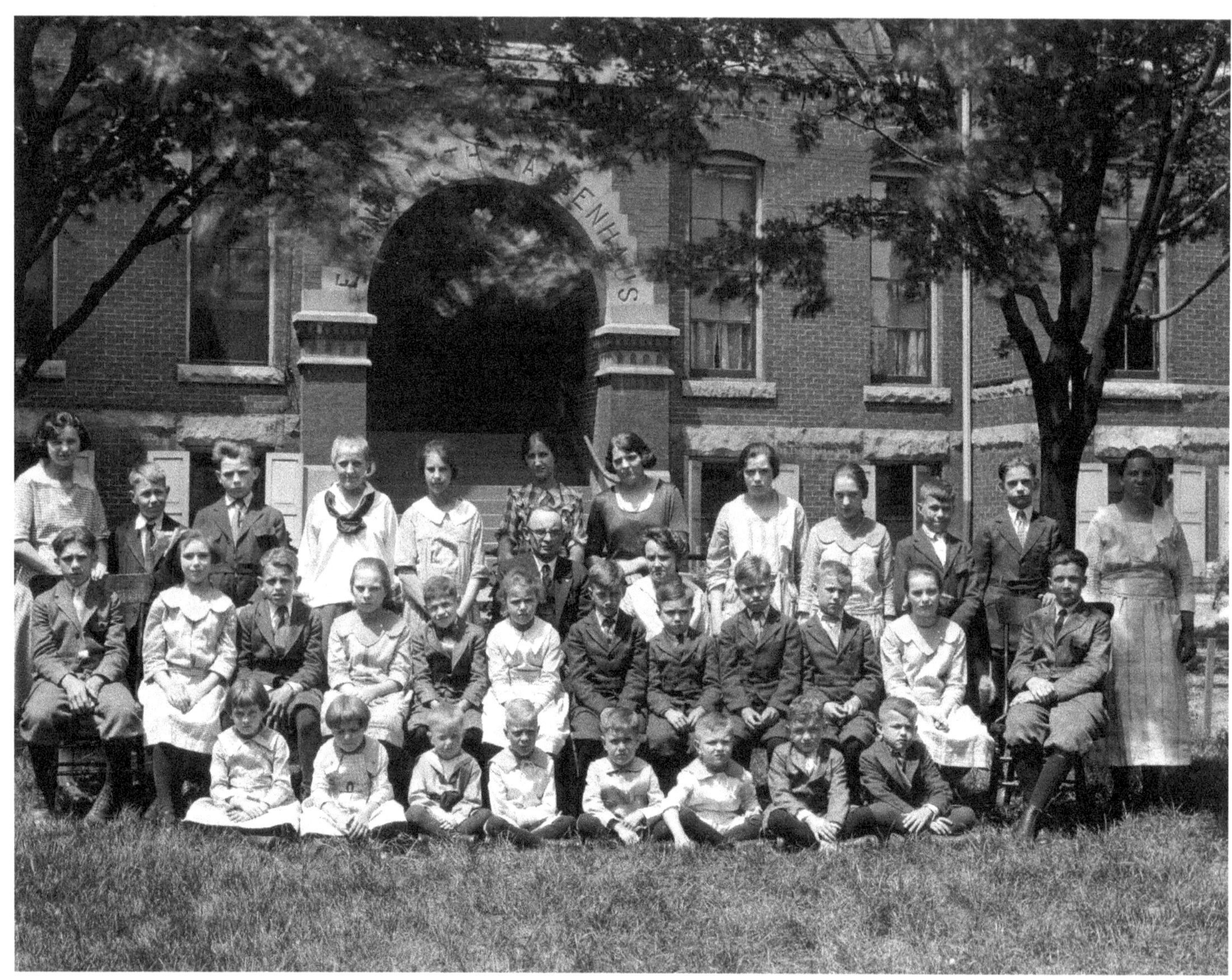

Young wards of the Evangelical Lutheran Orphans' Home, circa 1920's. The orphanage was founded in 1883 and a decade later moved into a new east-side home at Washington and LaSalle Streets. In 1956 it relocated again to Sixteenth Street and Ritter Avenue. Its mission has evolved over the years; today it is known as Lutherwood and serves as a residential treatment center for children who are recovering from the effects of abuse, neglect, or abandonment.

Children play on the grounds of the Evangelical Lutheran Orphans' Home, circa 1920's.

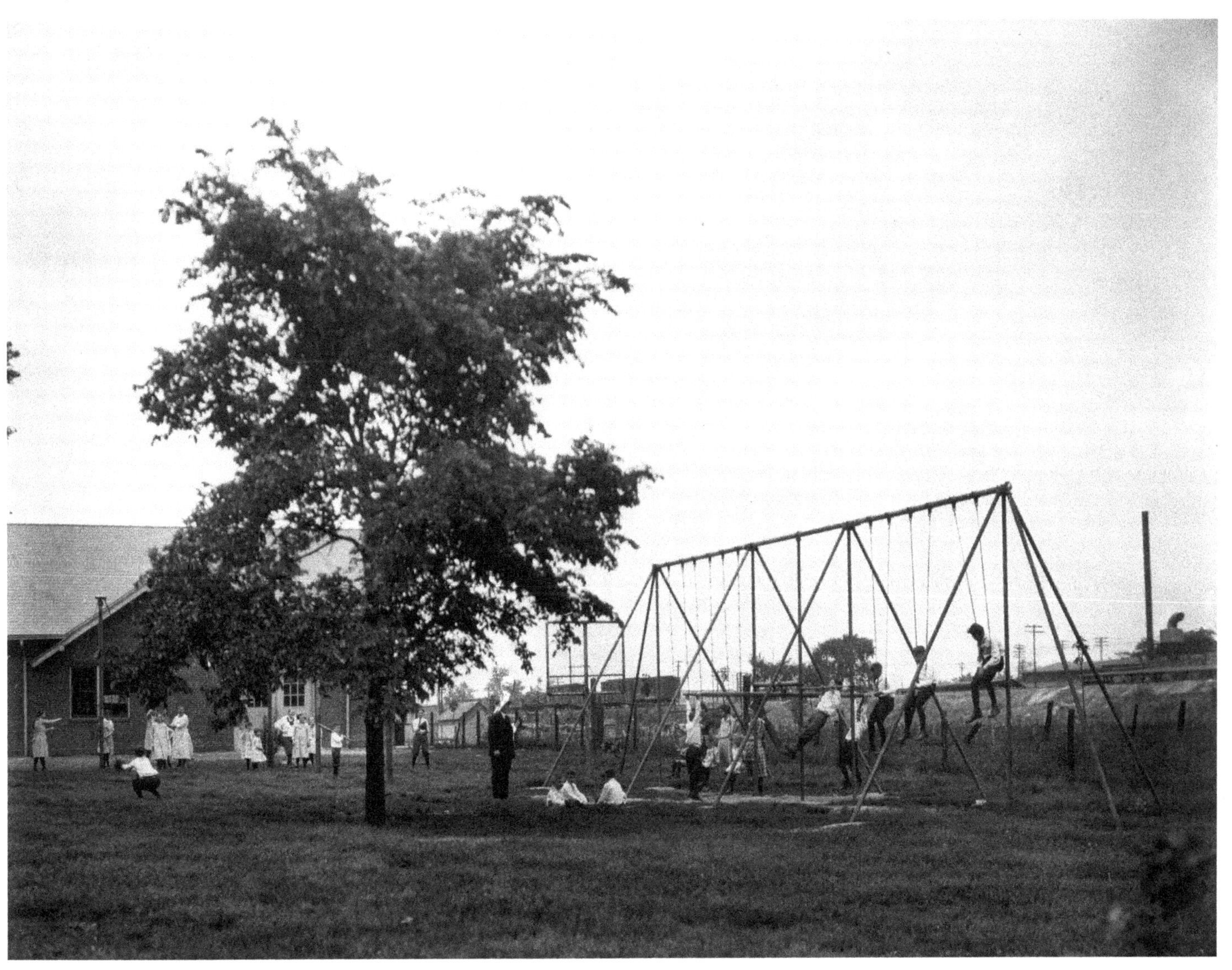

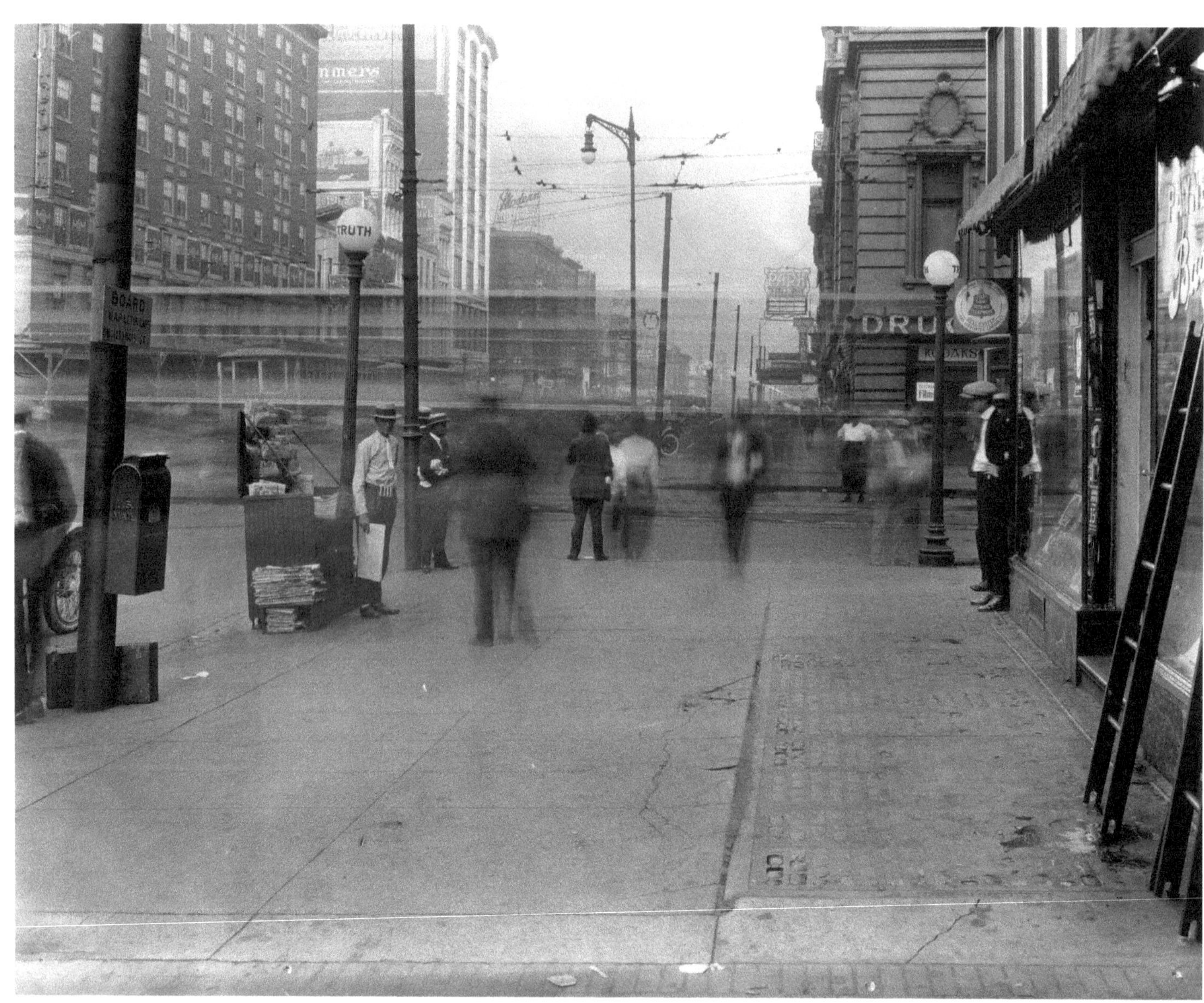

Washington Street looking west at Illinois Street, 1921. Two of the city's most prominent hotels stood at this corner and are seen in this picture. At right in the background is the Claypool Hotel, and across the street from it is the Lincoln Hotel.

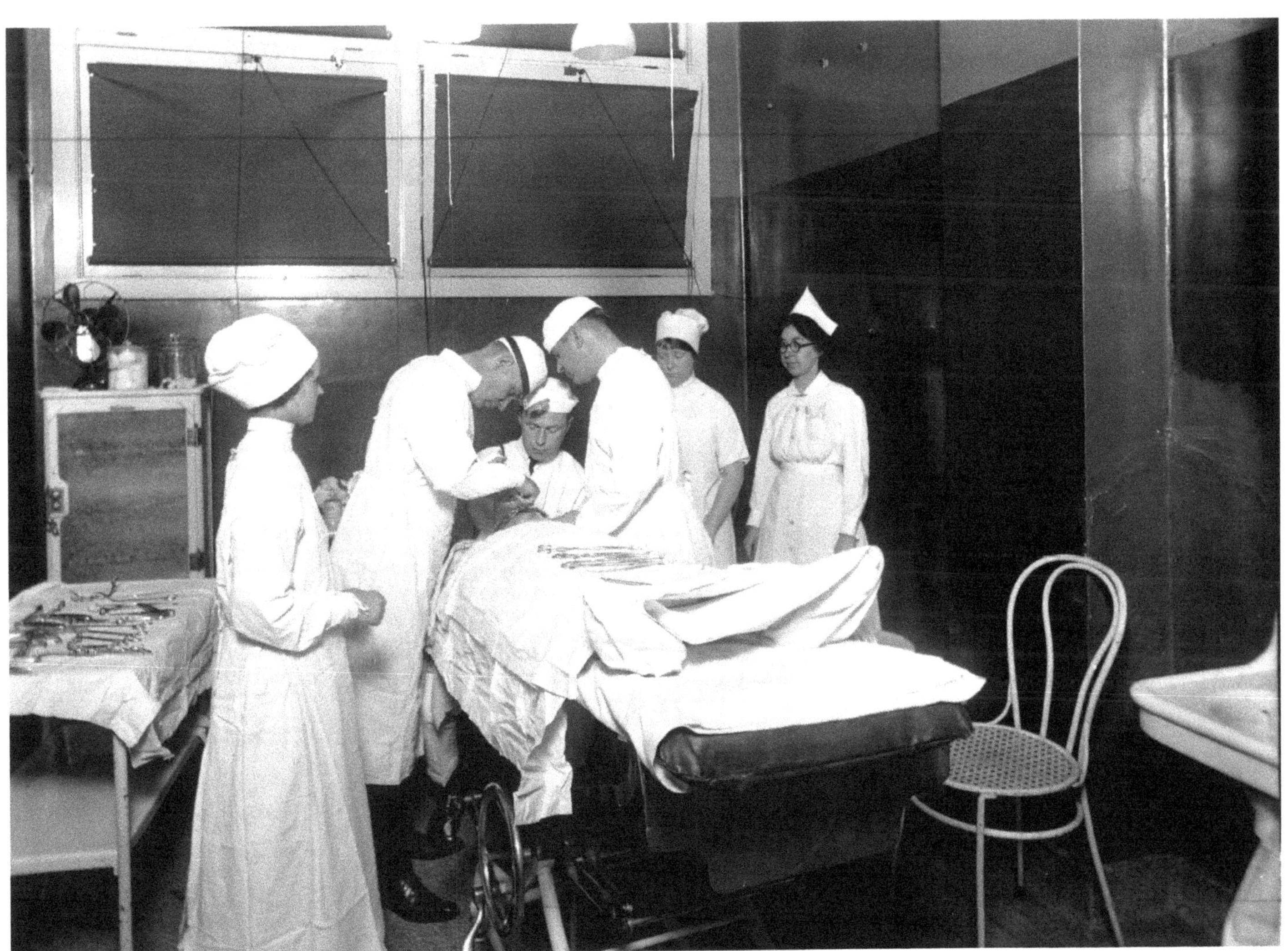

An operation at the Indiana University School of Medicine, 1923. Indiana University began offering medical courses at the main Bloomington campus in 1903, with clinical training conducted in Indianapolis. Five years later all medical schools in the state merged with the Indiana University program to form the IU School of Medicine. The school taught courses and conducted research at Indianapolis-area hospitals, including City Hospital.

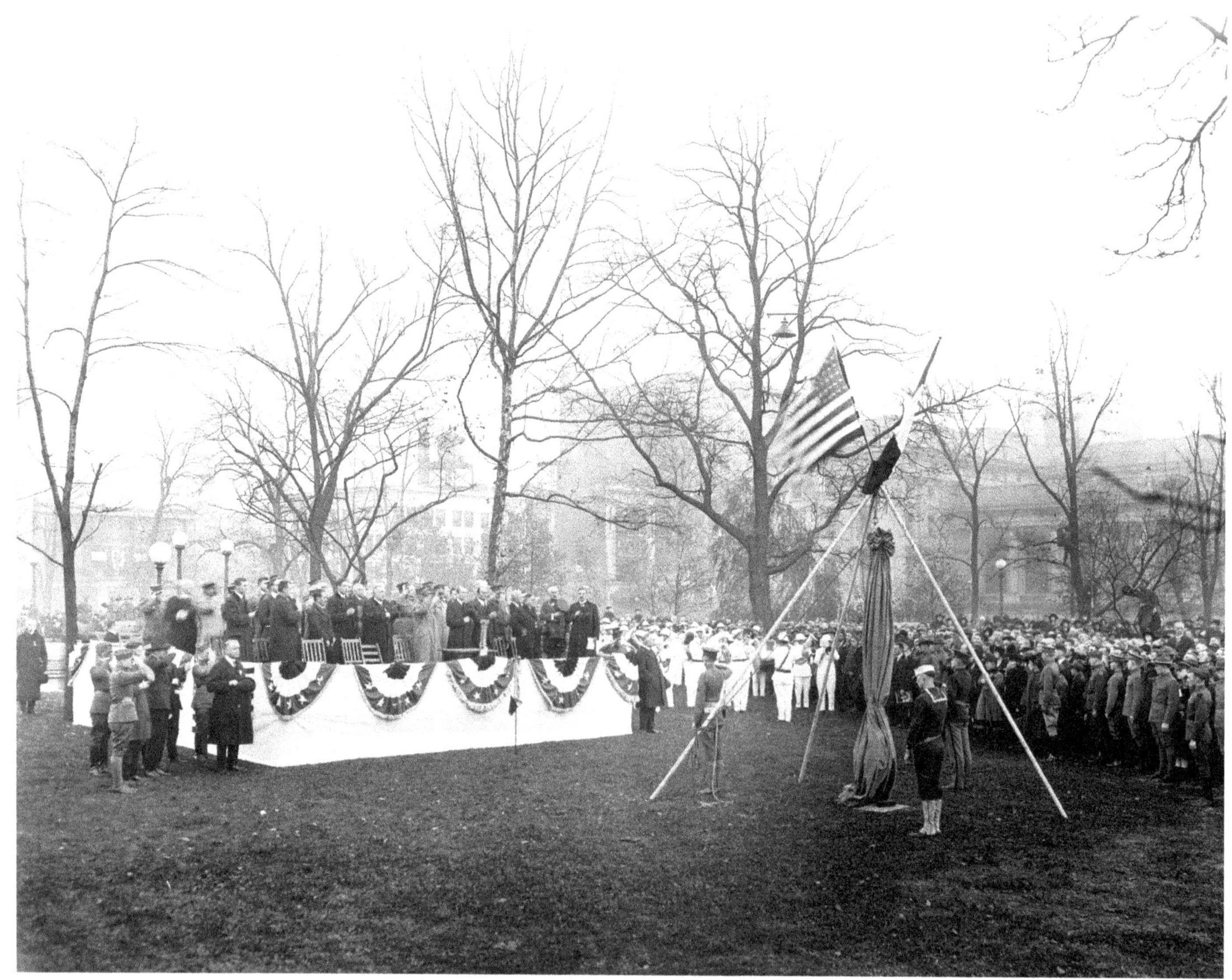

Marshal Foch lays a ceremonial cornerstone for the Indiana World War Memorial during his visit to Indianapolis, November 4, 1921. After World War I the state of Indiana began planning a memorial and plaza to honor veterans of the Great War. Design work began in 1921, and when Foch was in the city he dedicated the stone, which was salvaged from a bridge that spanned the Marne River. The dedication was merely symbolic. Actual construction of the memorial didn't begin until 1927, and at that time Gen. John J. Pershing, leader of the American Expeditionary Force in World War I, laid the actual cornerstone.

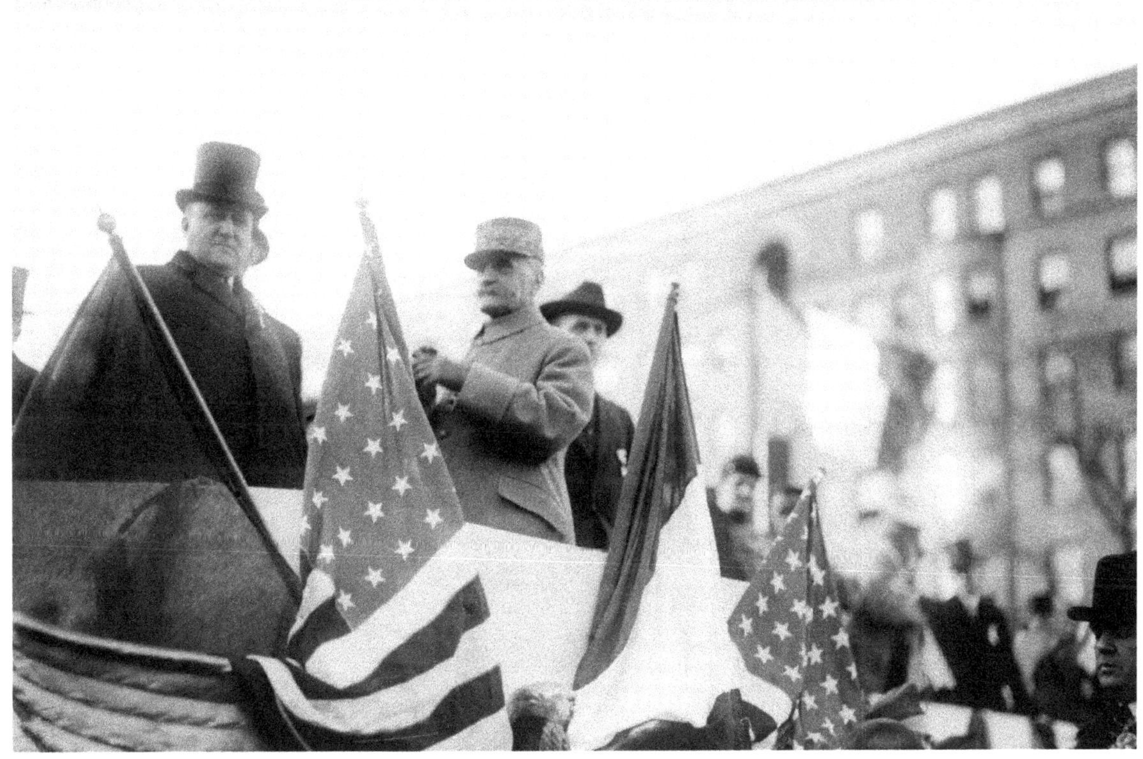

Marshal Foch Day, November 4, 1921. Ferdinand Foch, marshal of France and commander in chief of the Allied armies in World War I, toured the United States in late 1921. His stop in Indianapolis featured a parade, and he is seen here with Indiana governor Warren T. McCray (at left) on the review stand.

The Franklin Press Printers building, circa 1920's. In the late nineteenth century, industry began invading the heart of Indianapolis, dislocating residences and small businesses. This printing plant, located at 225 N. New Jersey St., illustrates the concept well.

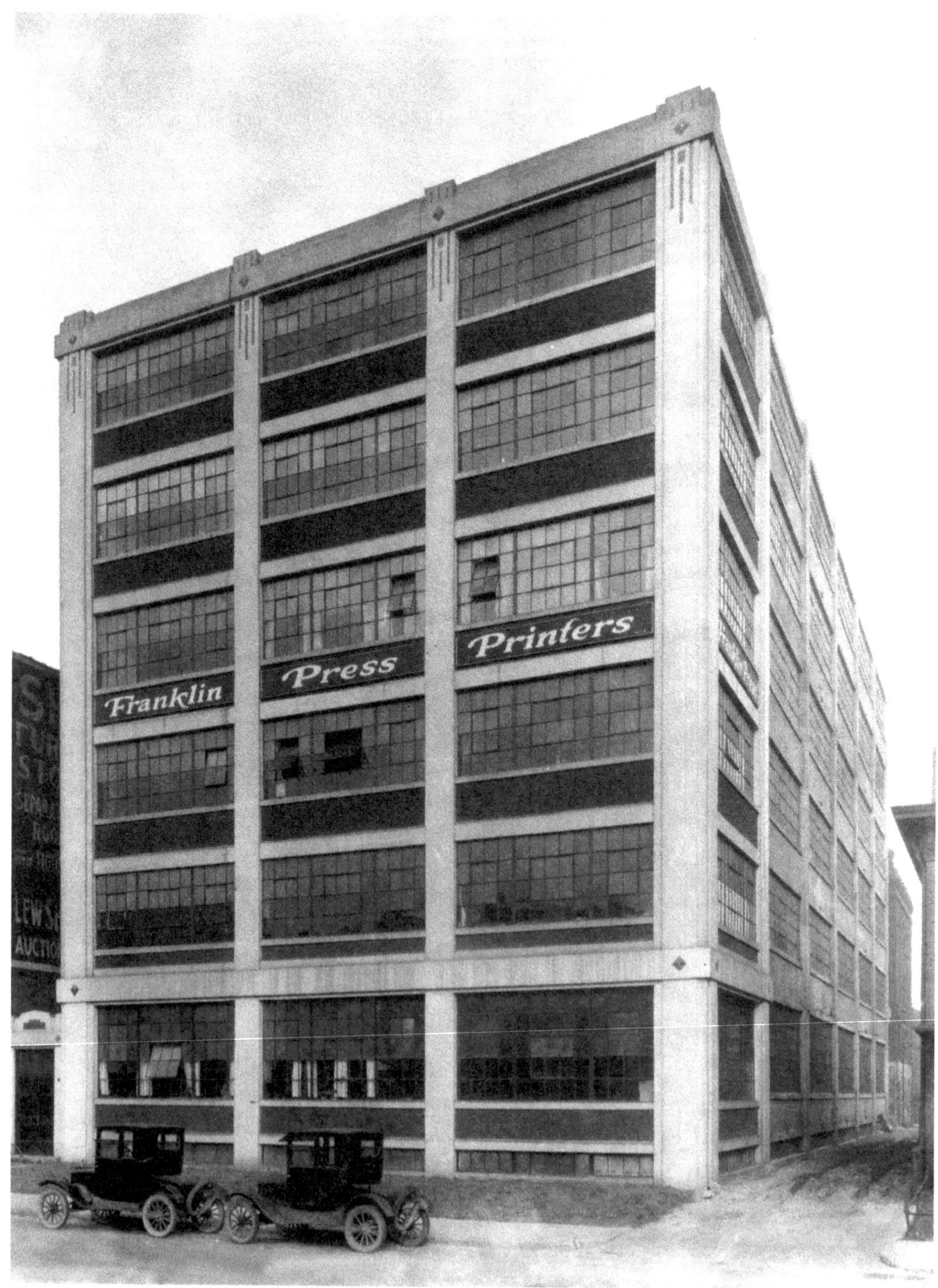

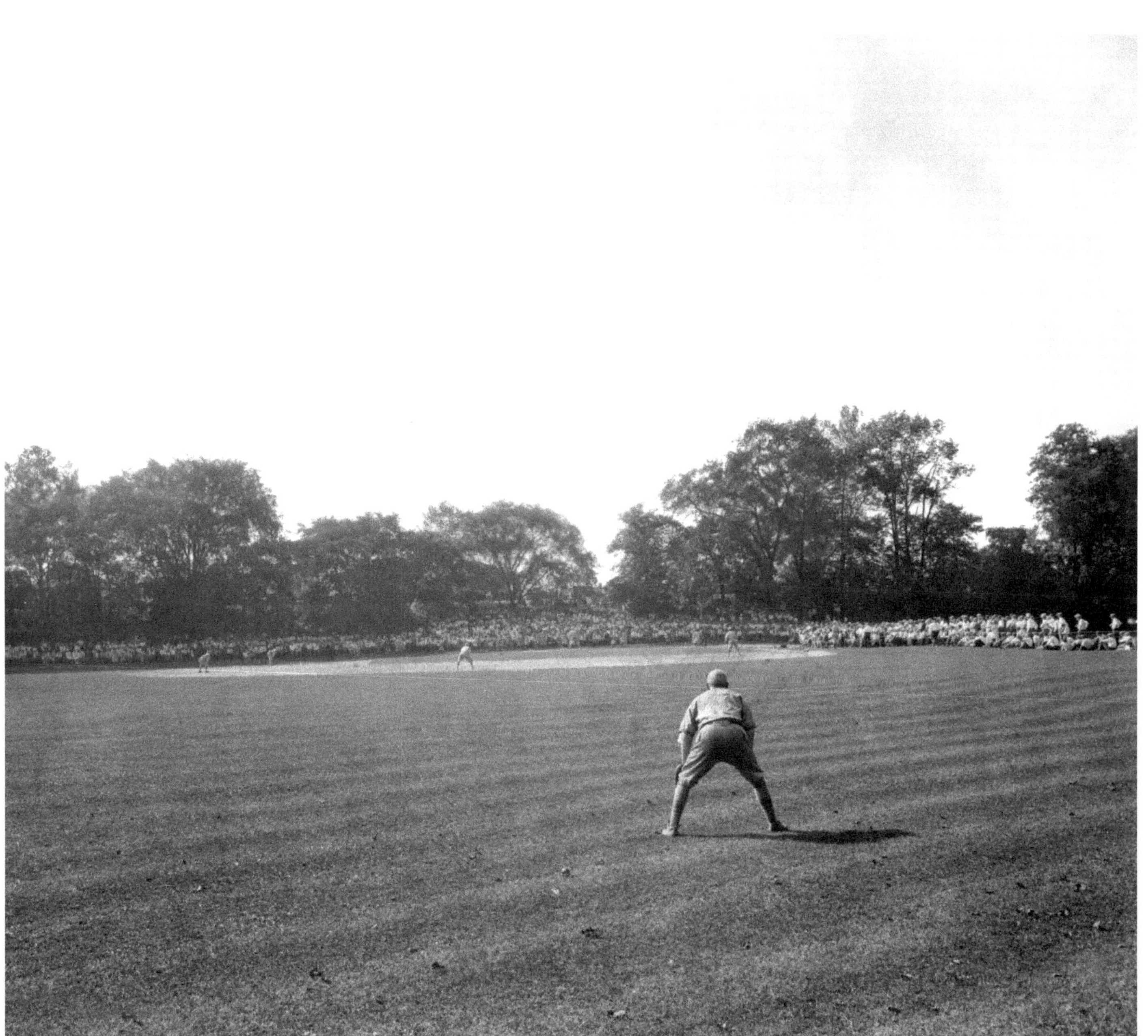

A baseball game in Brookside Park, circa 1920's. This east-side greenspace was one of Indianapolis's earliest; the city bought the land in the 1890's.

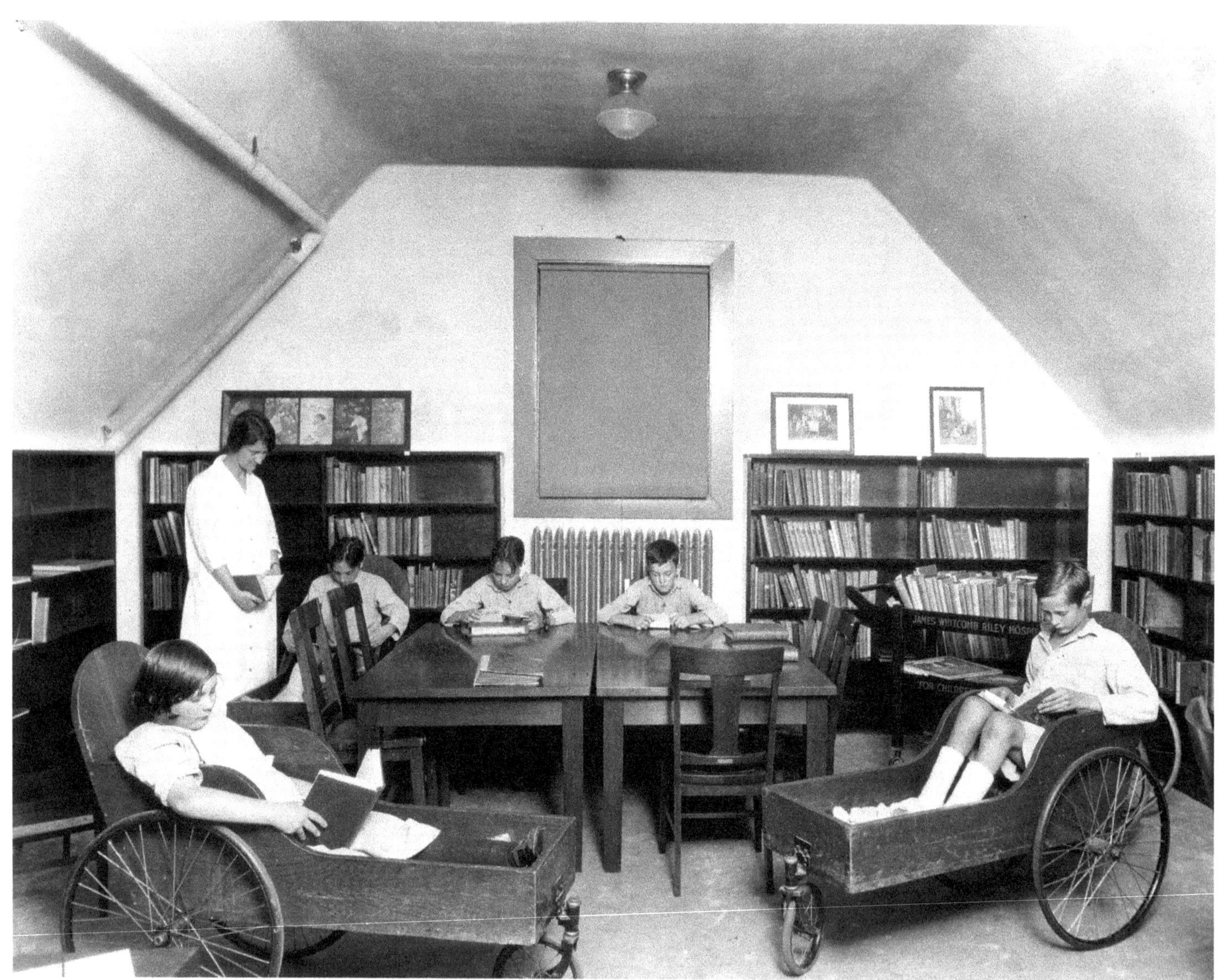

Young patients relax in the library at the James Whitcomb Riley Hospital for Children, circa late 1920's. The hospital opened in fall 1924 as a tribute to Riley, the beloved Hoosier poet. It continues to serve Indiana children today and is renowned for its quality care.

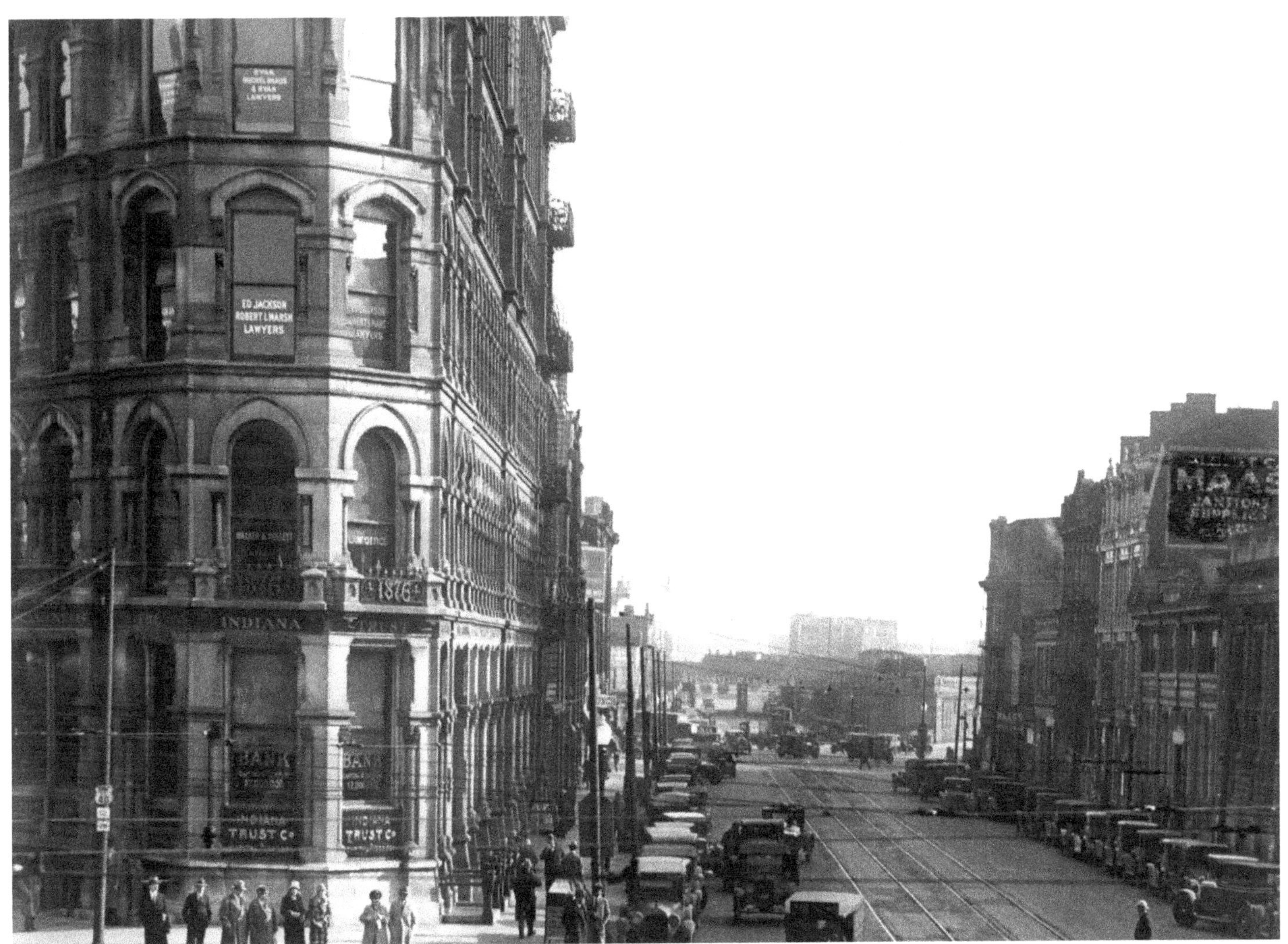

Virginia Avenue looking southeast from Washington Street, circa 1920's. The ornate flatiron building on the left is the Indiana Trust Company building (also known as the Vance block), long ago demolished.

Enjoying a ride (the four-legged kind) at the Indiana state fairgrounds, 1927.

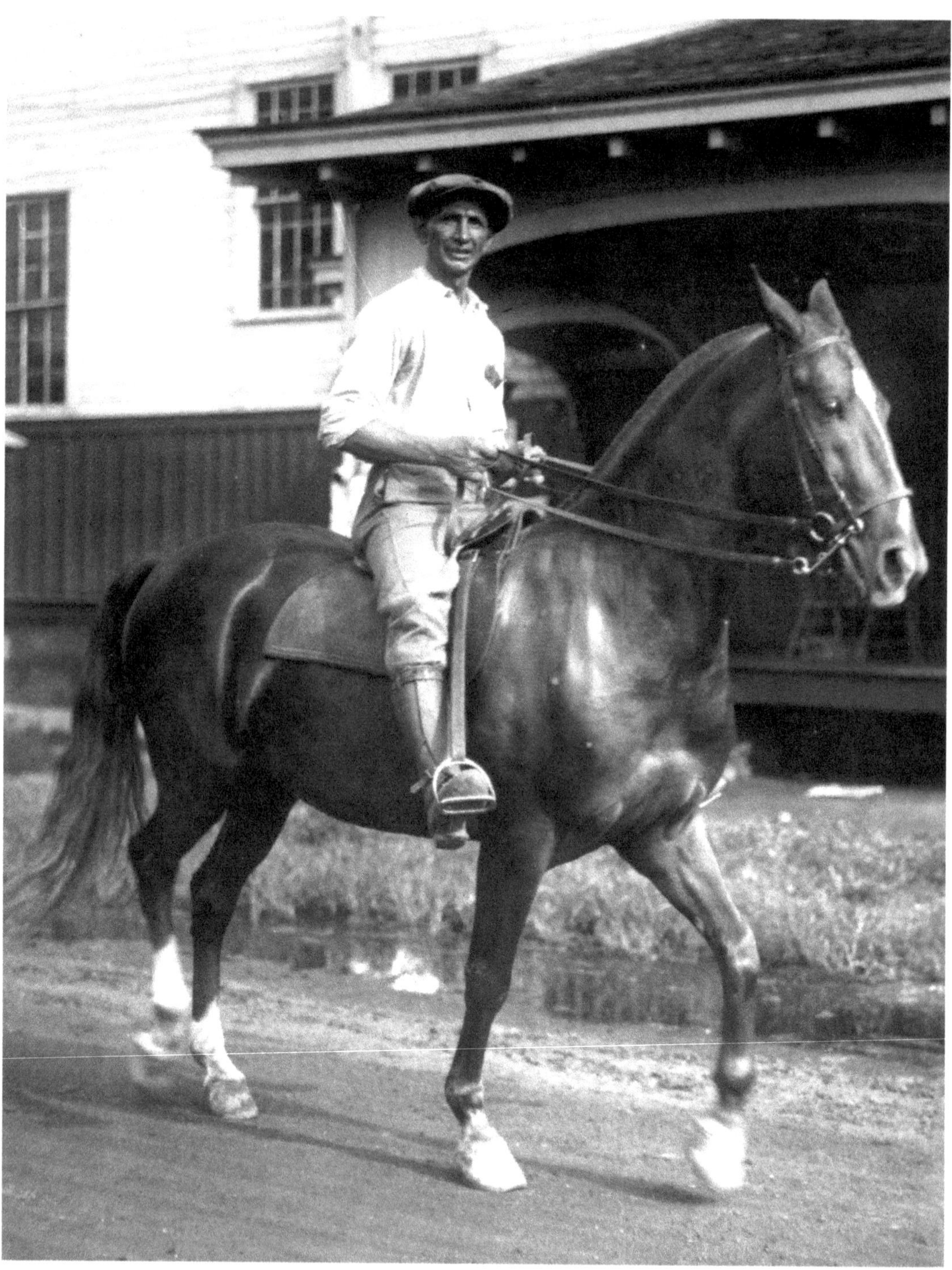

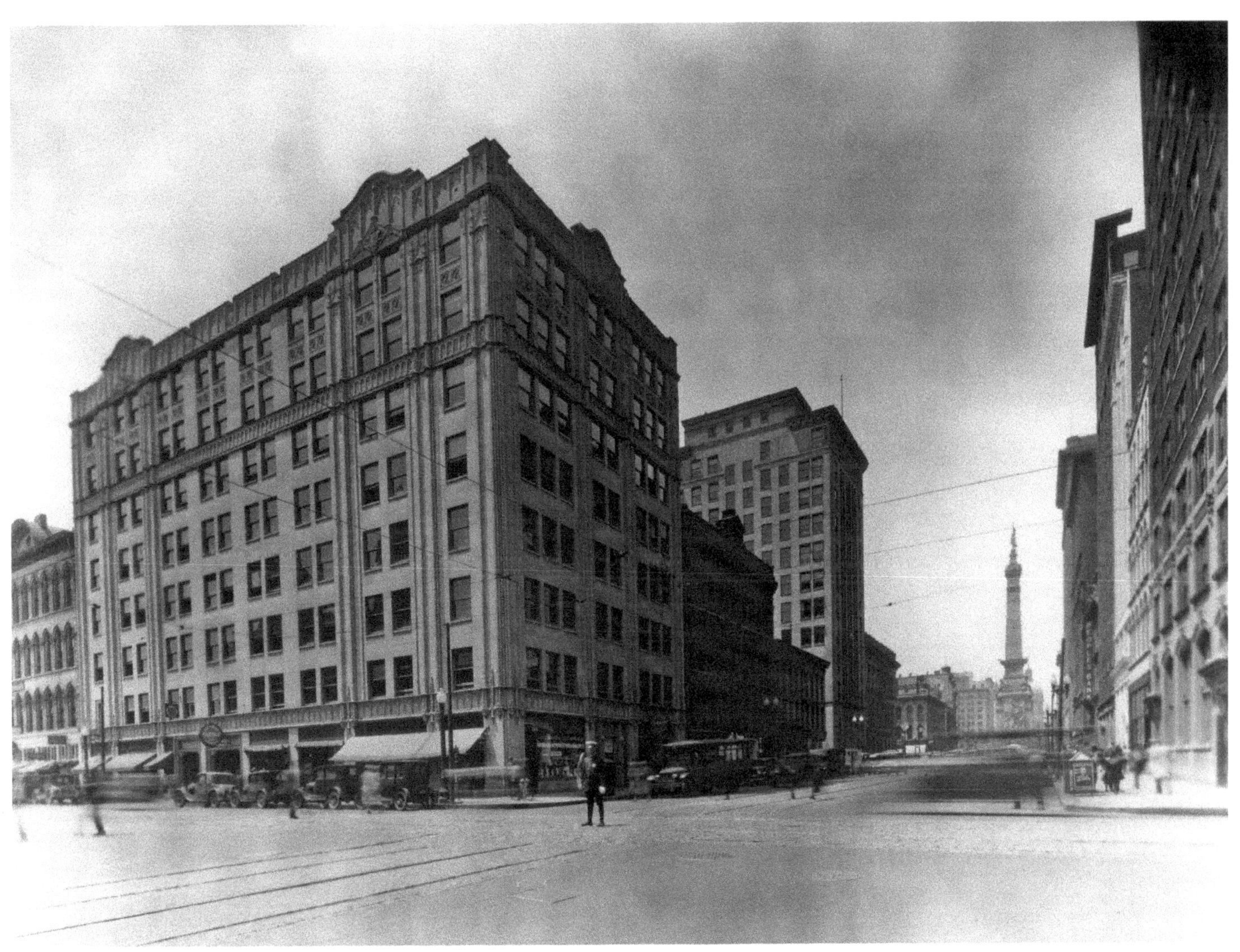

The Union Title building, 1928. This structure still stands on the southwest corner of Market and Delaware Streets.

Tornado destruction on Indianapolis's east side, 1927. On May 18 a tornado swept through the heart of the city, killing two boys and injuring nearly two hundred other residents. This view shows part of a sixteen-block area east of downtown that received the majority of the damage.

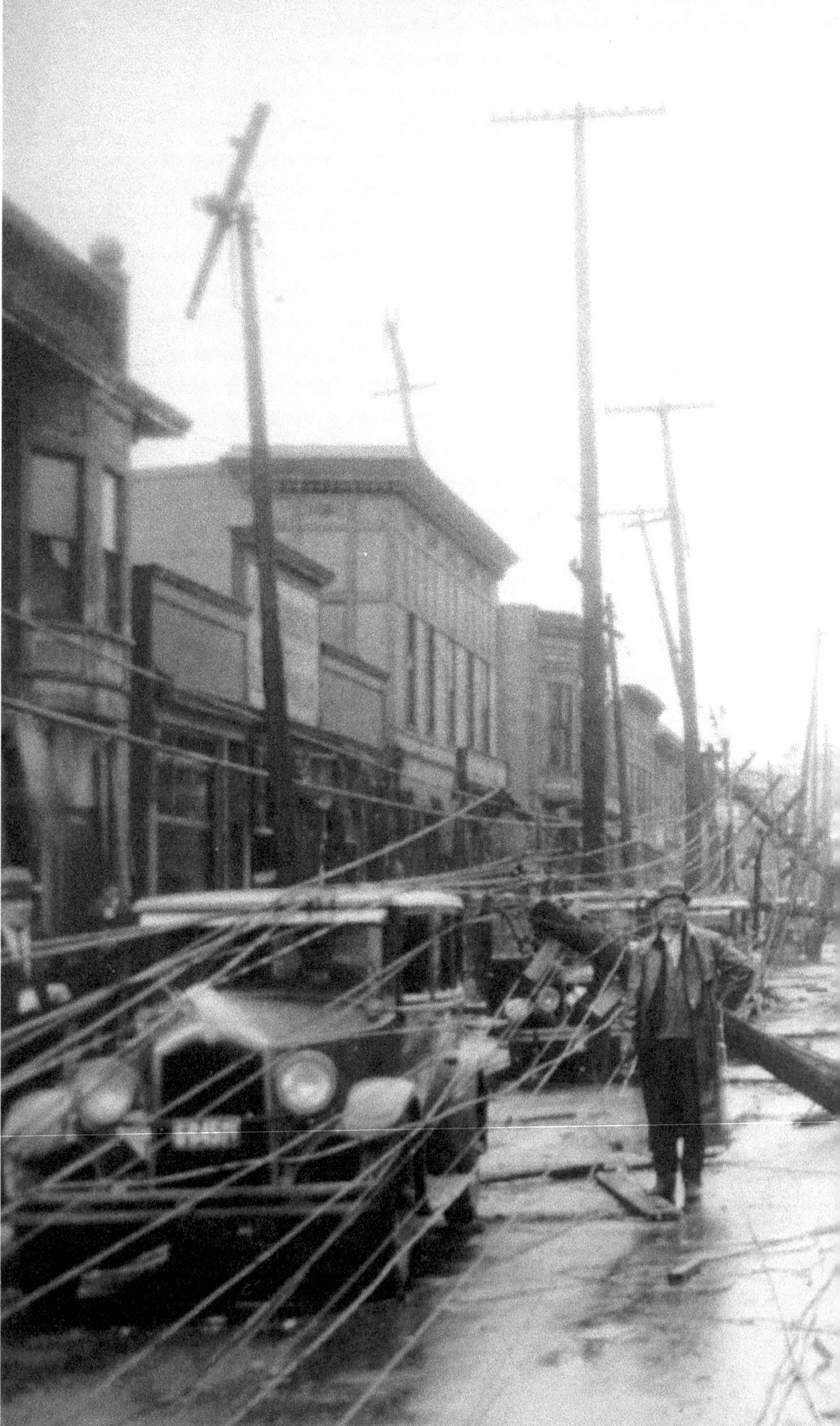

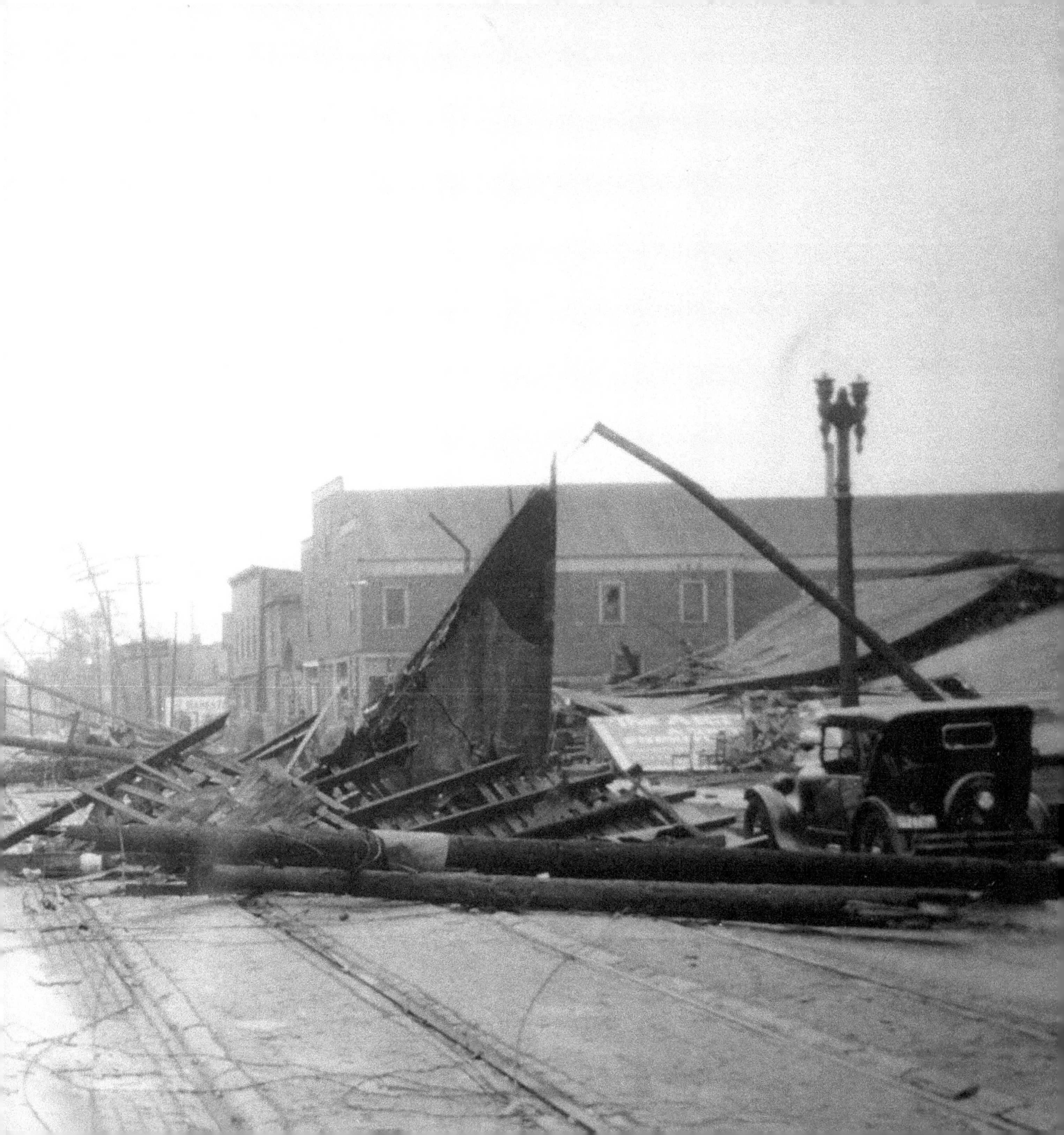

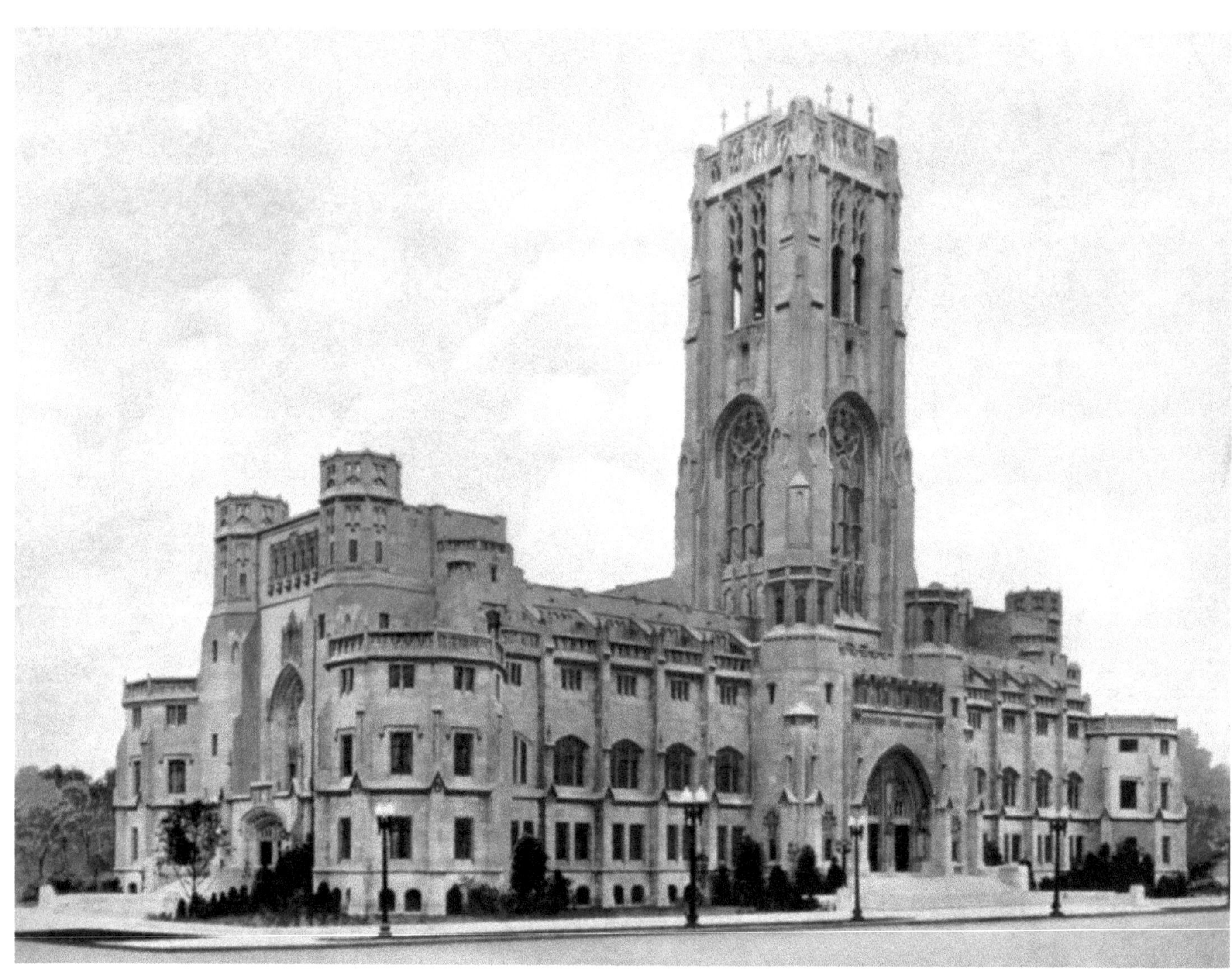

The Scottish Rite Cathedral. Located at Meridian and North Streets, the cathedral is the home of the Scottish Rite Valley of Indiana, a Masonic order. Member George F. Schreiber designed it and laid it out in multiples of thirty-three feet, representing the number of years in Christ's life. The tower holds fifty-four bells and is one of the largest carillons in the world. The cathedral opened in 1929.

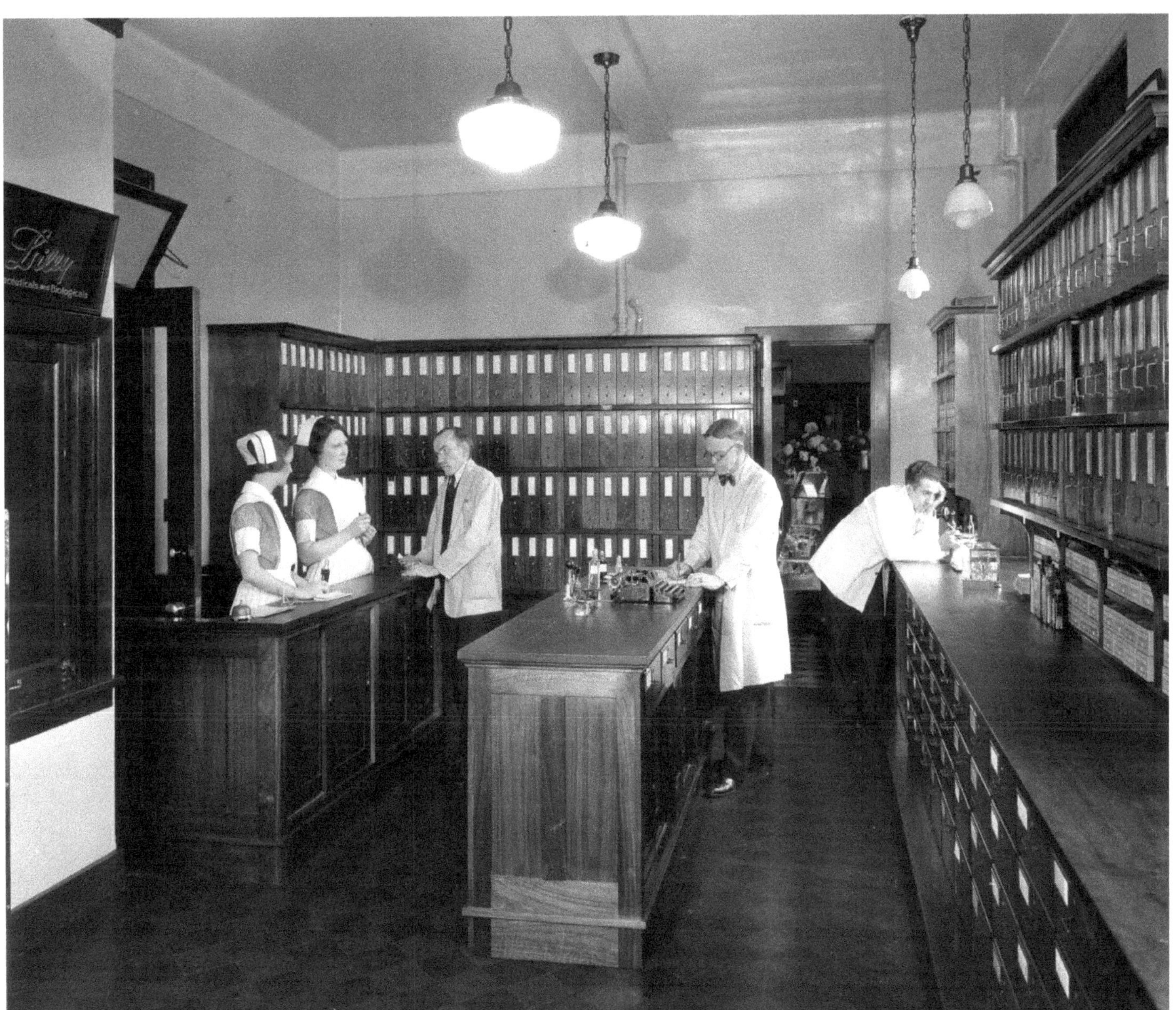

The Methodist Hospital pharmacy, 1931. Methodist Hospital opened in April 1908 at its current location on Capitol Avenue north of Sixteenth Street. Over the years it has been on the leading edge of medical research—working with Indianapolis pharmaceutical firm Eli Lilly and Company in the 1920s to test the use of insulin, for example, and in 1982 becoming the first private hospital in the world to perform a heart transplant. Today the hospital is part of Clarian Health Partners and is noted for its programs in cancer treatment; digestive disorders; ear, nose, and throat conditions; kidney disease; orthopedics; and urology.

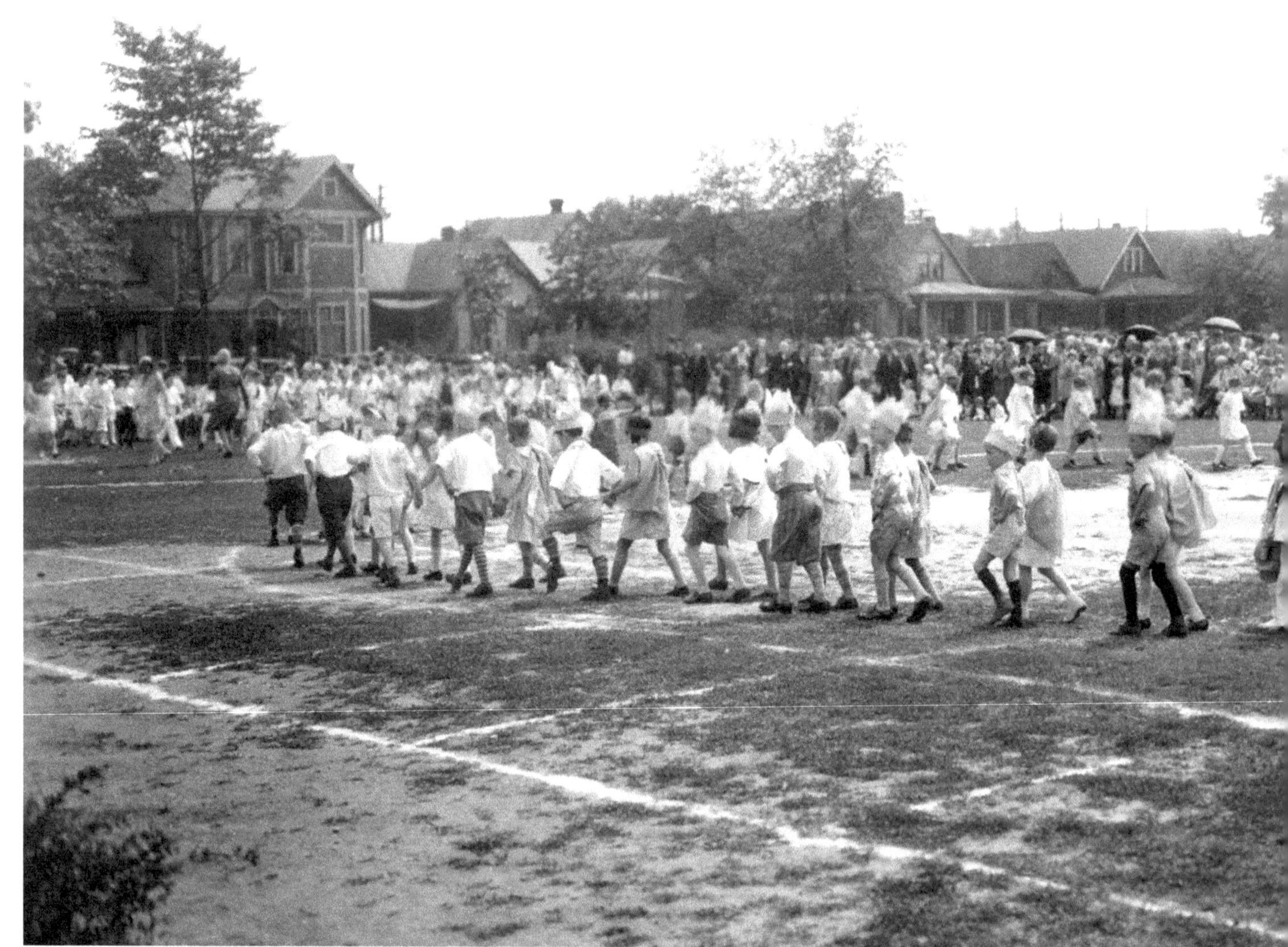

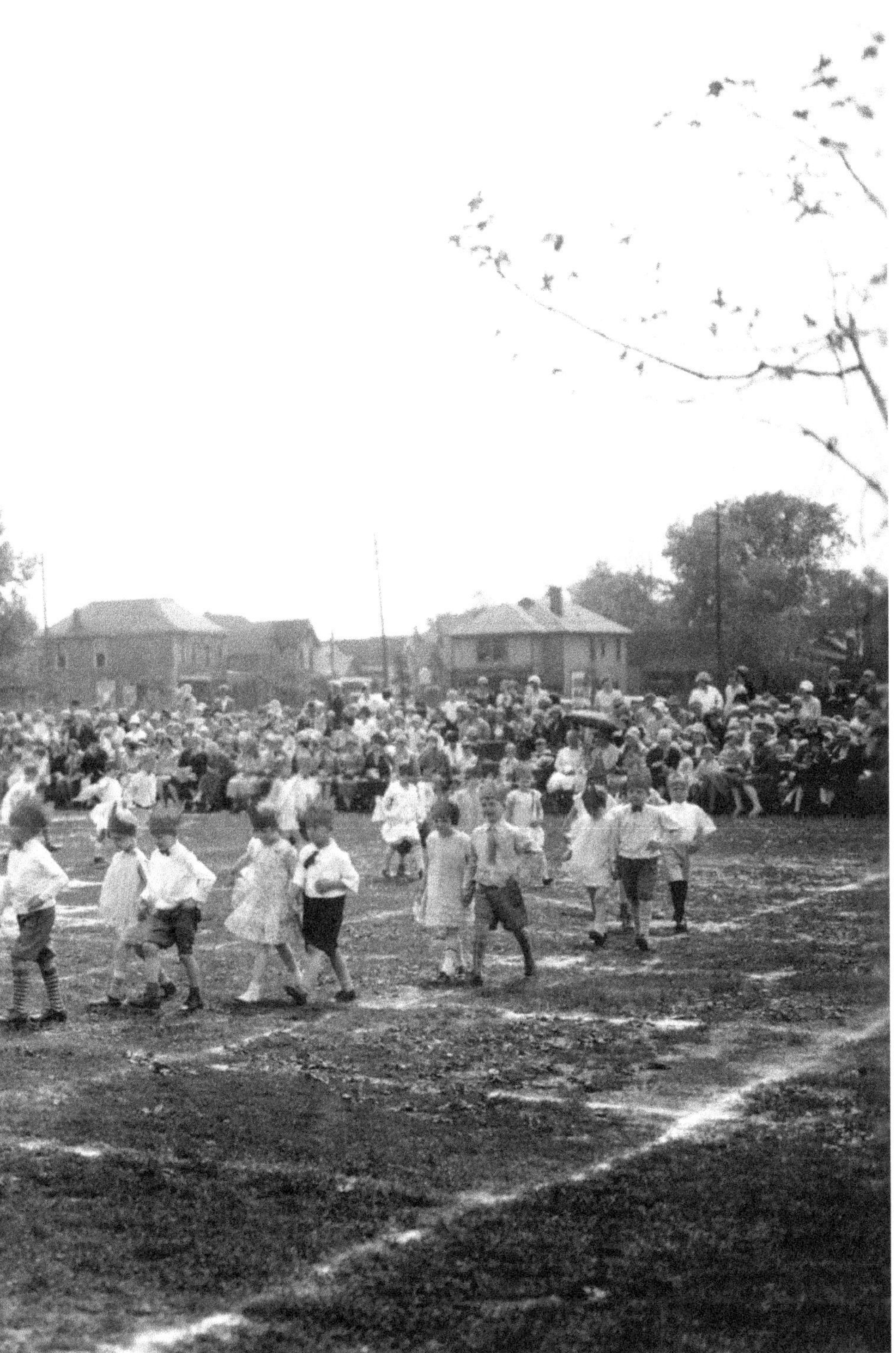

Children parade in a large circle at Finch Park on the city's southeast side, 1929. Upon her death in 1923, Alice Finch bequeathed $10,000 to Indianapolis's parks department, and in honor of her and her family the city opened Finch Park at State and Spann Avenues. In the late 1980's Indianapolis Public Schools swapped land with the parks department and built a new School No. 39 on the site of the old Finch Park. The parks department then opened a new Finch Park two blocks south on State Avenue.

The Public Savings building, 1929. This building stood next to the Union Title building on the south side of Market Street between Pennsylvania and Delaware Streets. A parking garage now occupies the site.

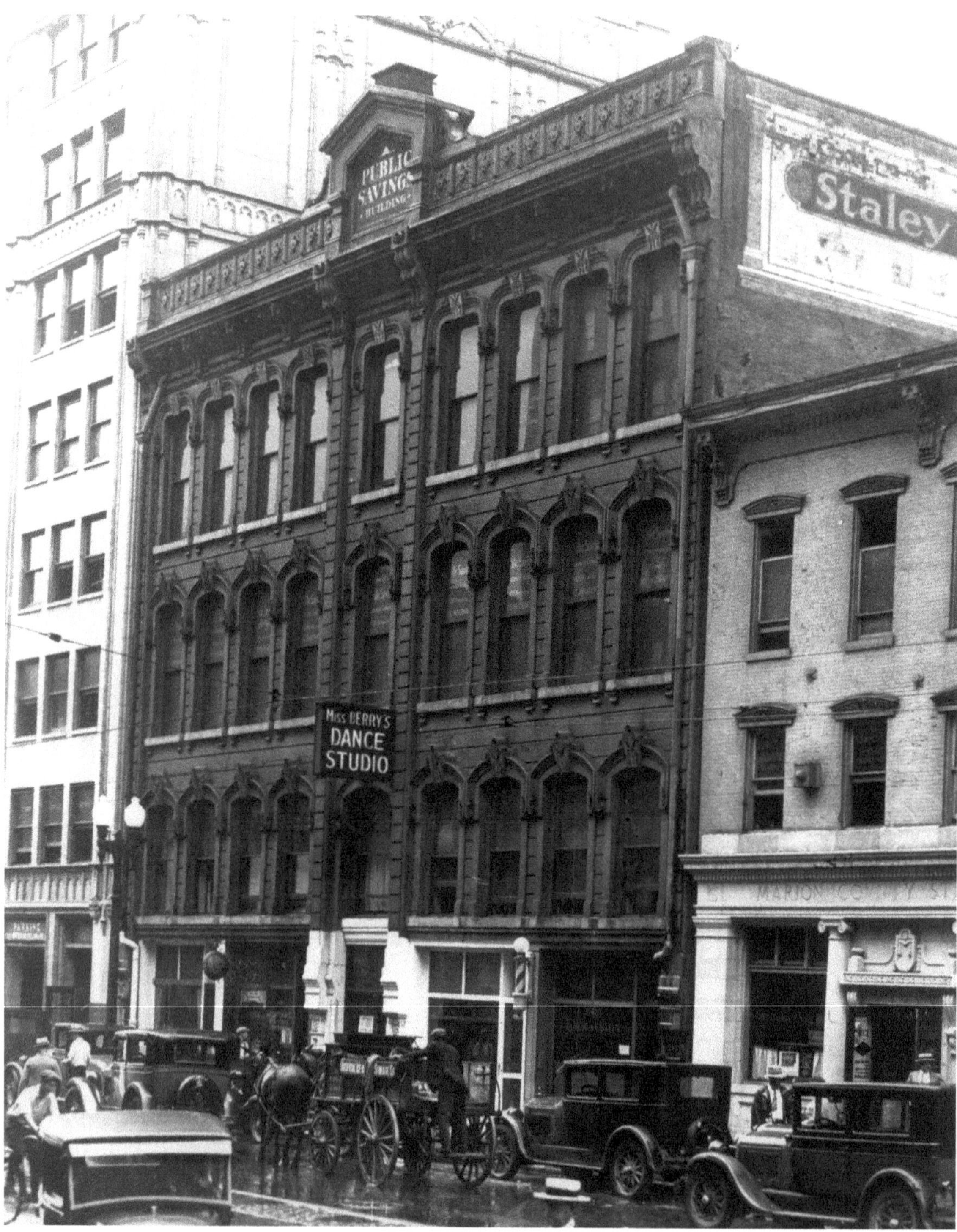

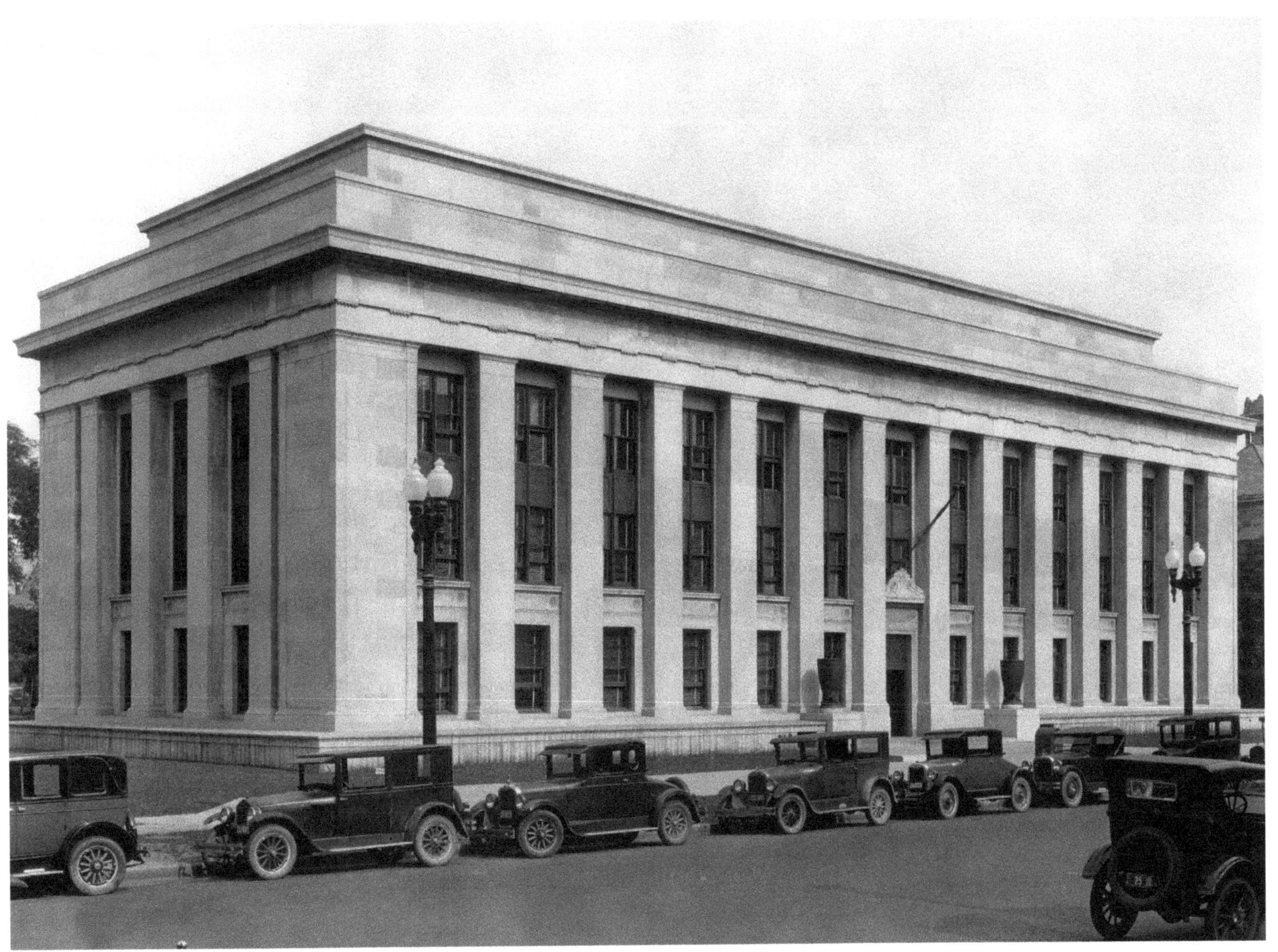

The American Legion headquarters, 1930. Organizers founded the Legion in 1919 to lobby for veterans' affairs and to promote patriotism. That same year they chose Indianapolis as the site for the Legion's national headquarters. Construction of the original headquarters building, located on the southeast corner of Meridian and St. Clair Streets, began in 1925.

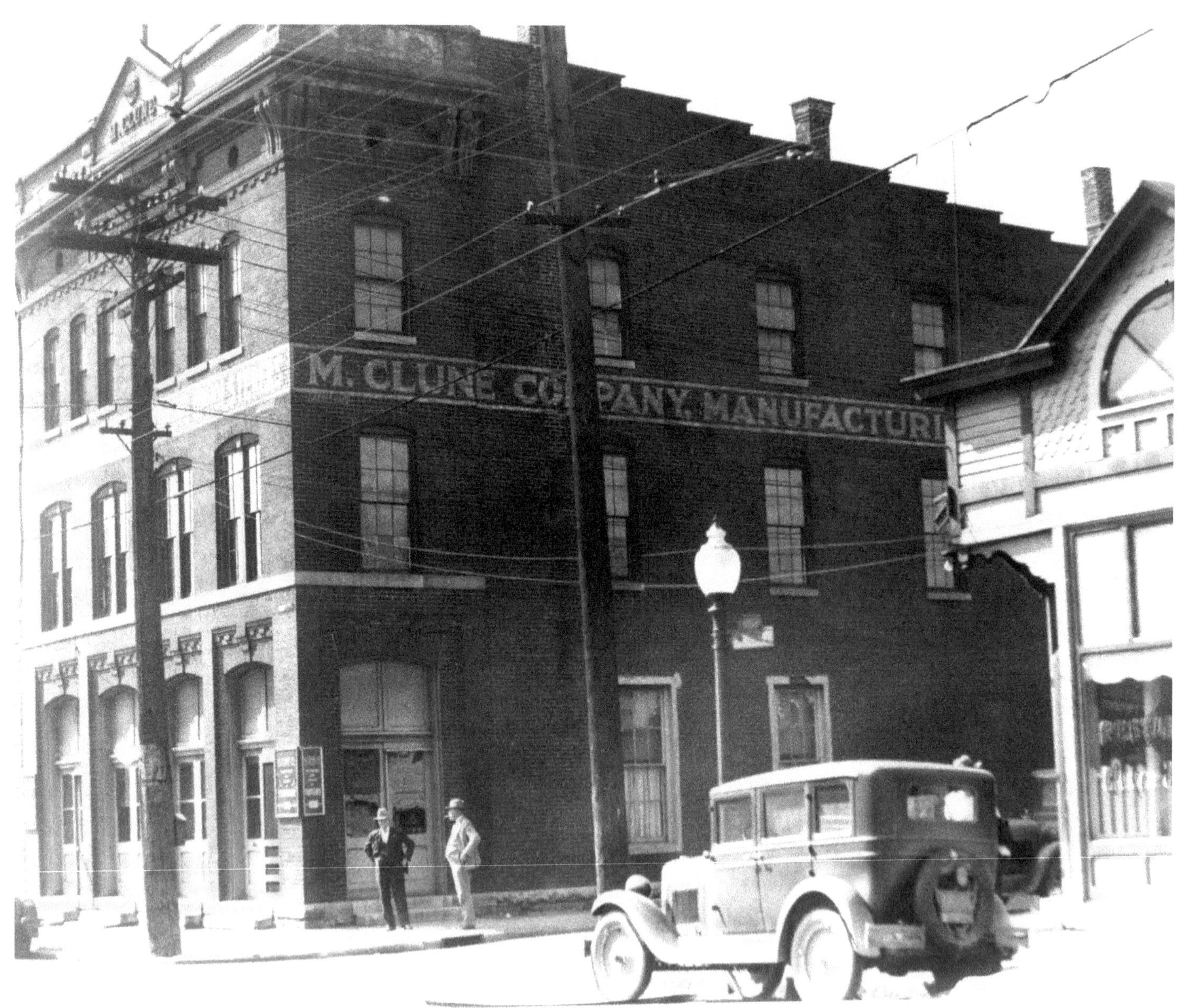

The M. Clune Company, 1932. The company manufactured furniture in the 1400 block of South Meridian Street.

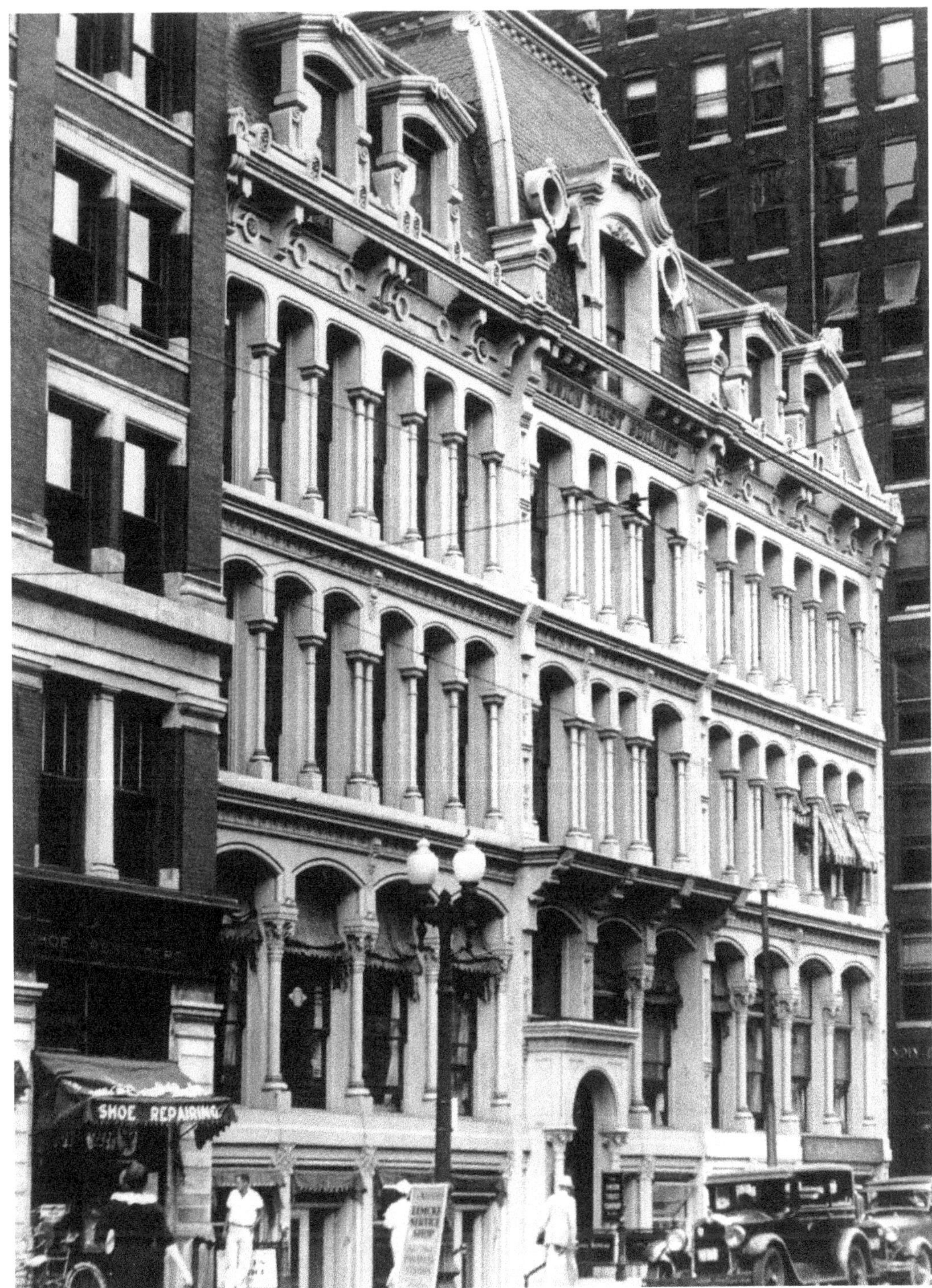

The Union Trust Bank, 1933. The Second Empire-style building that housed the bank was originally known as the Wright block. It stood near the northeast corner of Pennsylvania and Market streets and once housed the law offices of Benjamin Harrison, who served as U.S. president from 1889 to 1893.

A night view of Illinois Street, looking north from Union Station, circa early 1930's. The neon signs of many hotels light the scene.

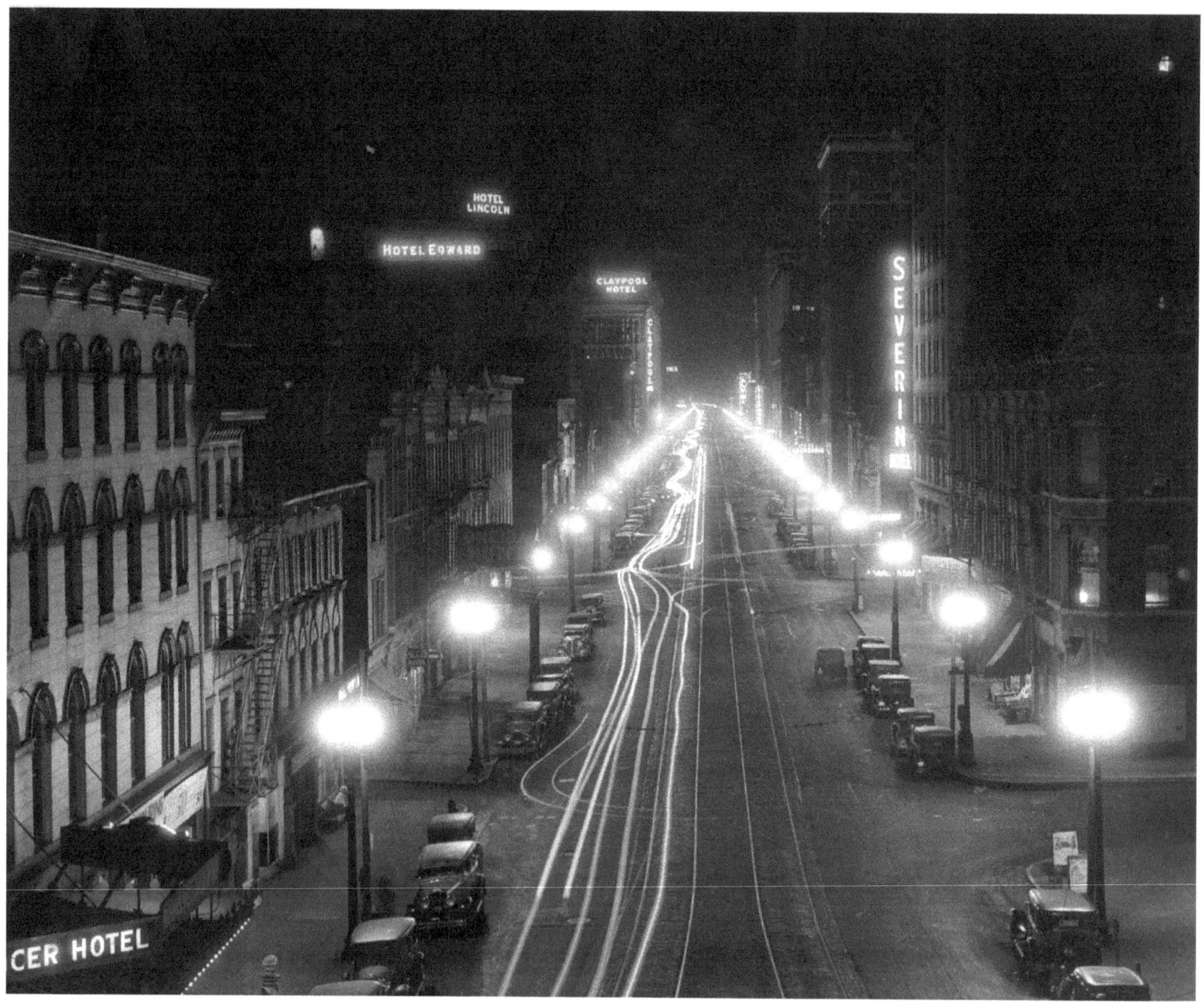

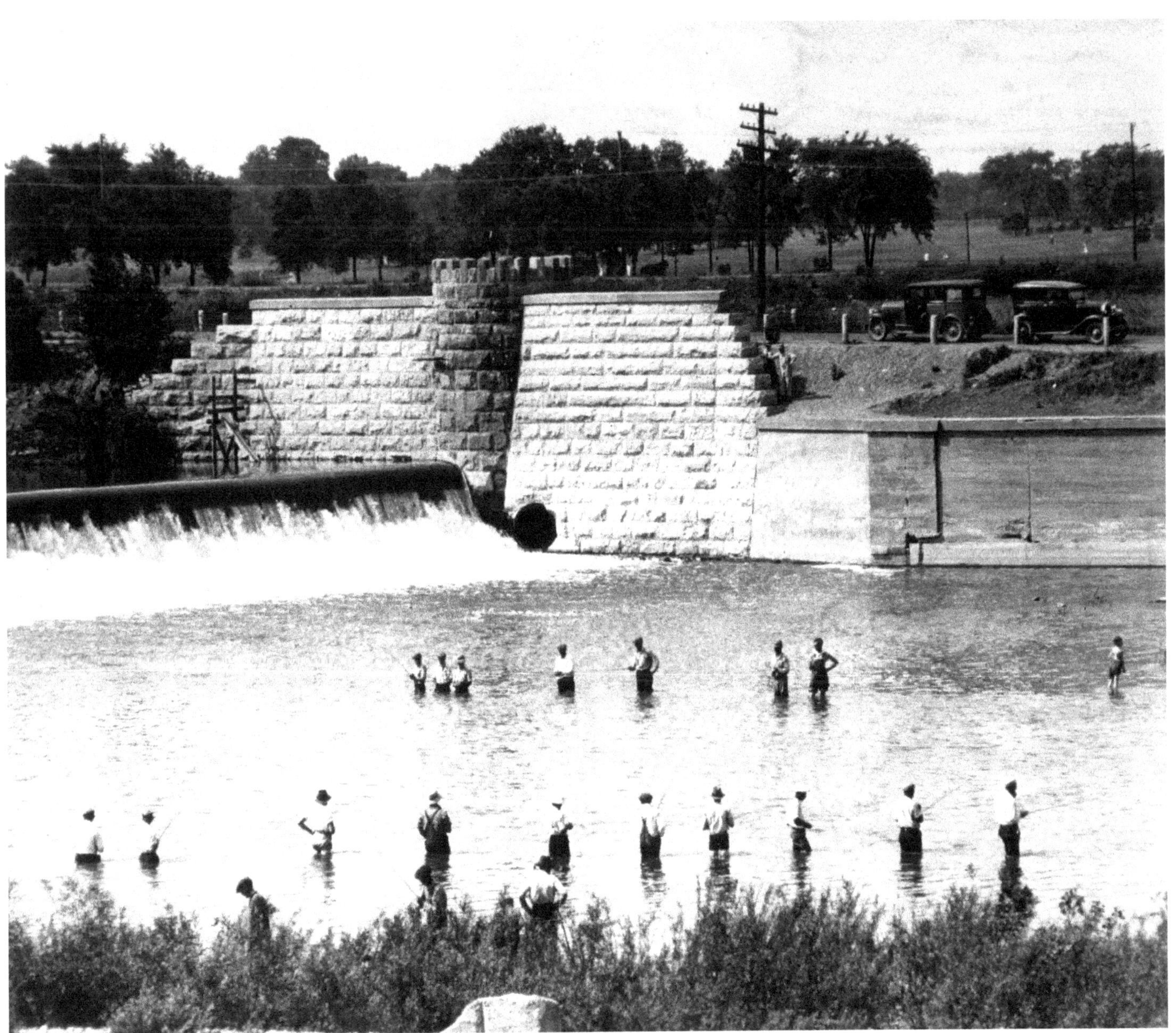

The Emrichsville dam, 1933. The dam is located on the White River near Sixteenth Street. Nearby stood the Emrichsville bridge, which featured a stone archway and tower as well as ornate carvings.

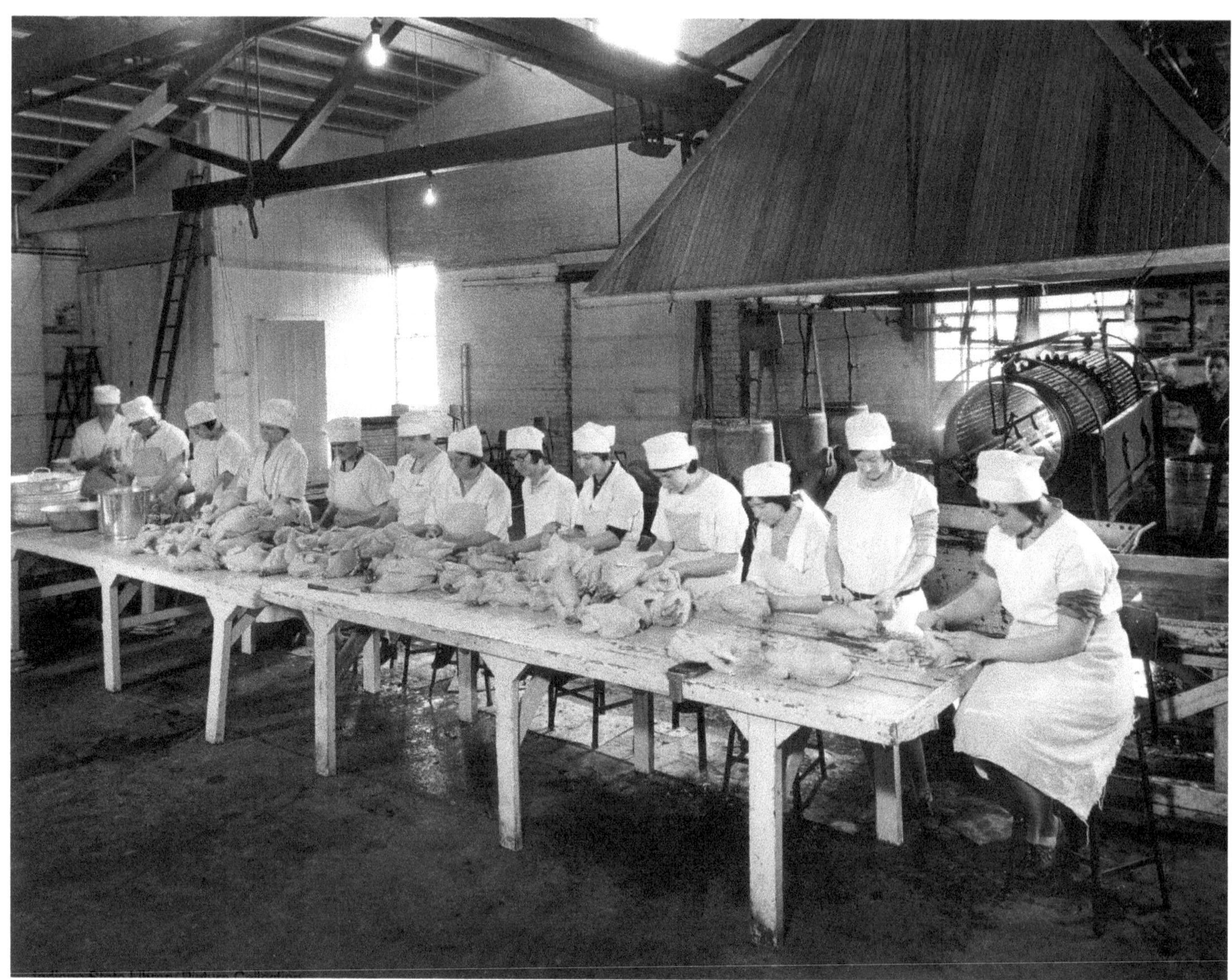

Workers at the Columbia Conserve Company, circa 1930's. Columbia was a canning factory on Indianapolis's southeast side. In 1917, under the guidance of its president, William Powers Hapgood, it underwent an experiment in worker democracy. Hapgood transferred ownership to the employees and gave them the opportunity to make management decisions via a workers' council. They also shared in the profits. The company received international attention for its efforts, but it went bankrupt in the early 1940's and was dissolved.

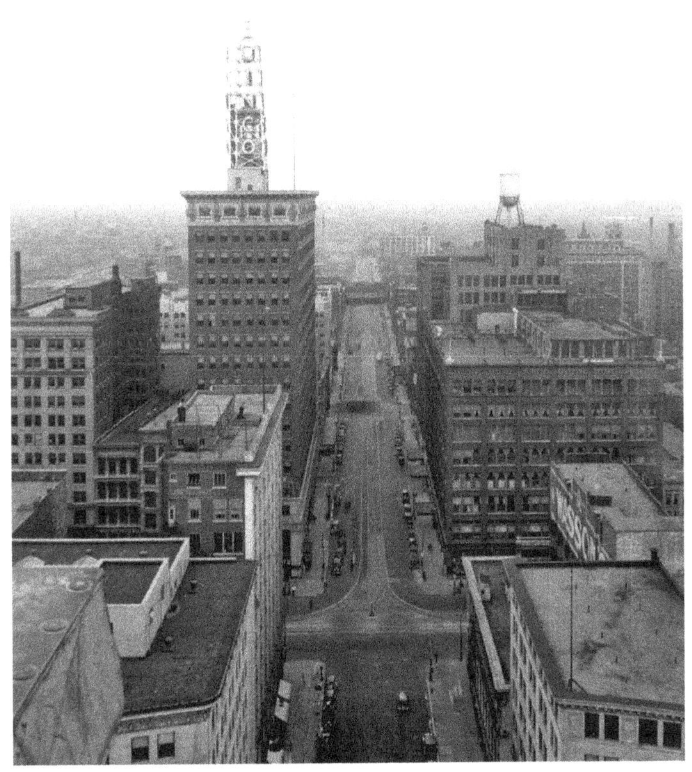

A view of South Meridian Street from the Soldiers and Sailors Monument, 1933.

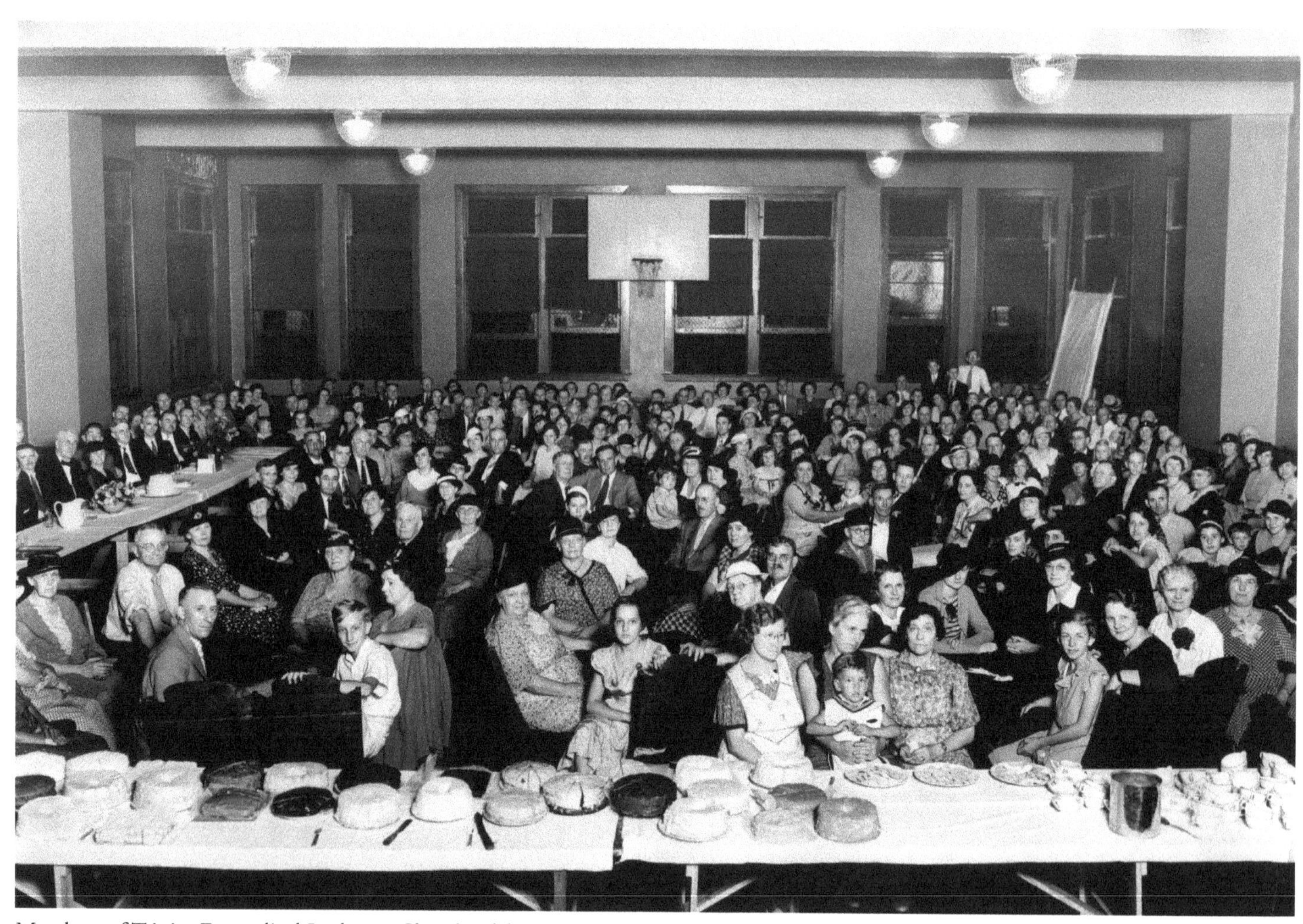

Members of Trinity Evangelical Lutheran Church celebrate twenty-five years of service by Rev. J. W. Matthias, September 18, 1935. The celebratory dinner took place at the church's school building, located at Market and Arsenal Streets on the city's east side. The church's sanctuary was located at Ohio and East Streets.

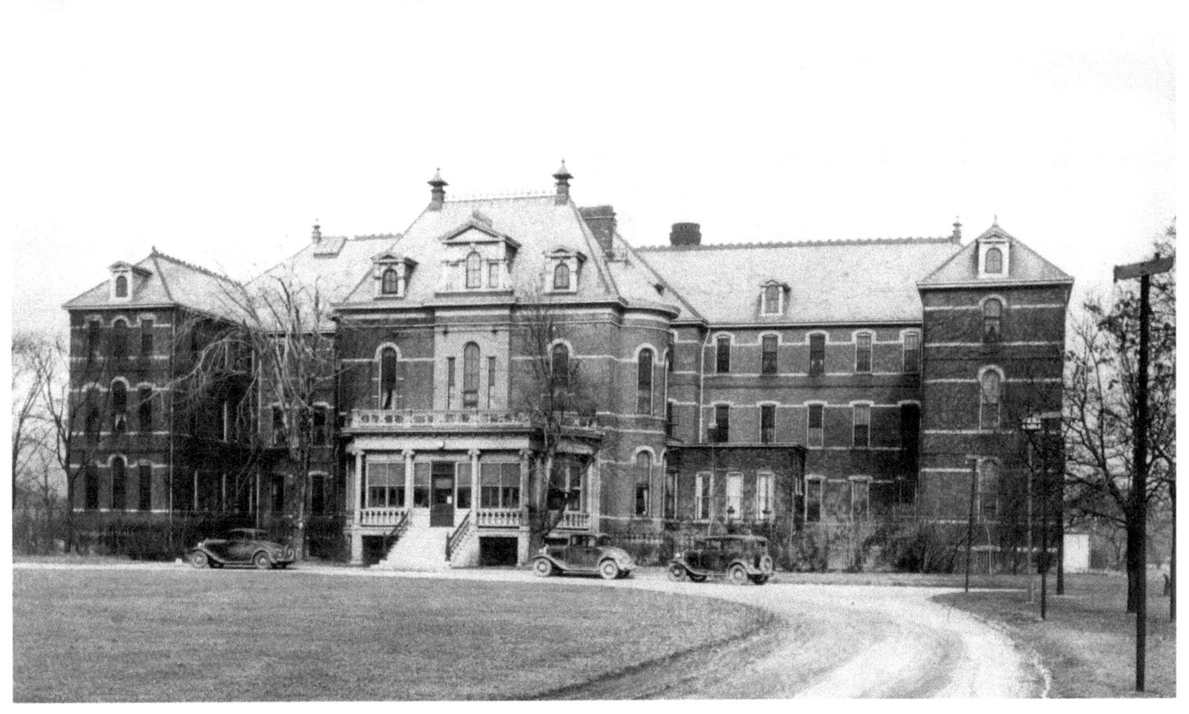

The Indiana Women's Prison, 1935. The prison opened on the east side of Indianapolis in October 1873. Some histories report that it was the first prison built in the United States to house female criminals.

The Raymond Street bridge over the White River, 1936. Raymond Street is a major east-west thoroughfare along the city's south side.

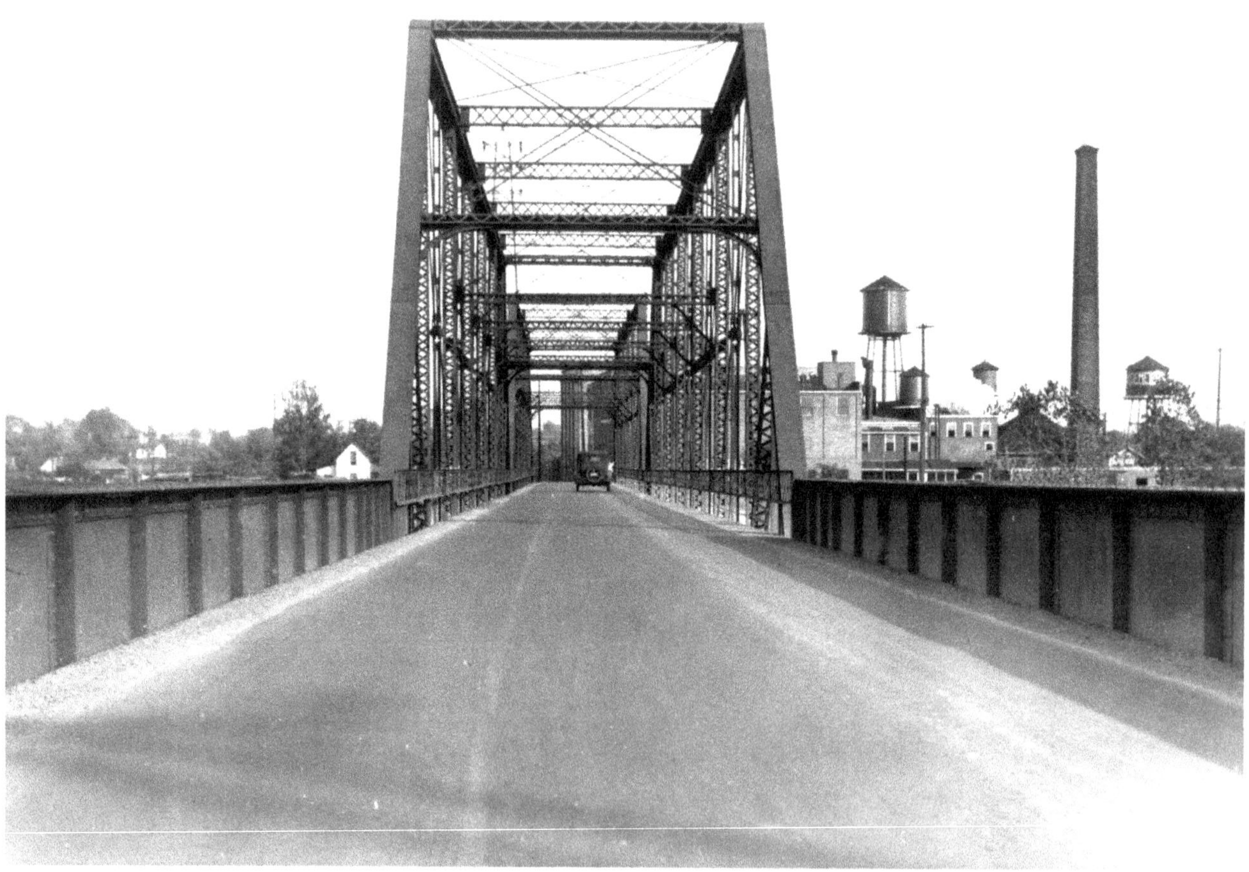

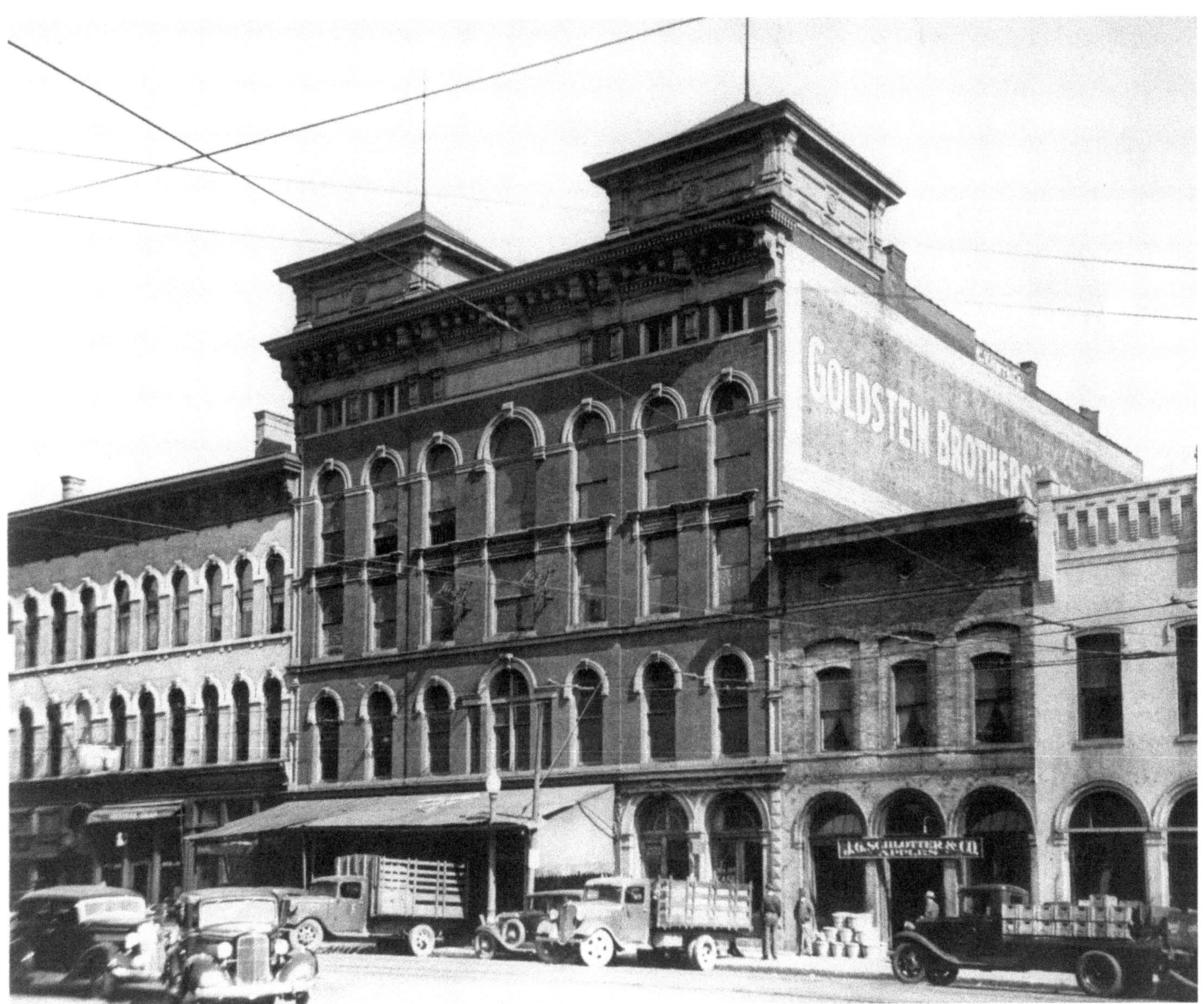

Germania Hall around the time of its demolition in early 1936. The hall was located on South Delaware Street, between Washington and Maryland Streets. It was part of Commission Row, an area along Delaware, Alabama, and Maryland Streets known for its produce firms. Germania Hall hosted many social events for Indianapolis's sizeable German community, including New Year's Eve dances, card games, and German operettas. It had a dining room and meeting rooms and was a convenient gathering place for singing societies and groups such as the Butcher Ladies' Union.

The Railroadmen's Federal Savings and Loan Association building, 1937. The savings and loan was located on Virginia Avenue, near its intersection with Washington and Pennsylvania Streets.

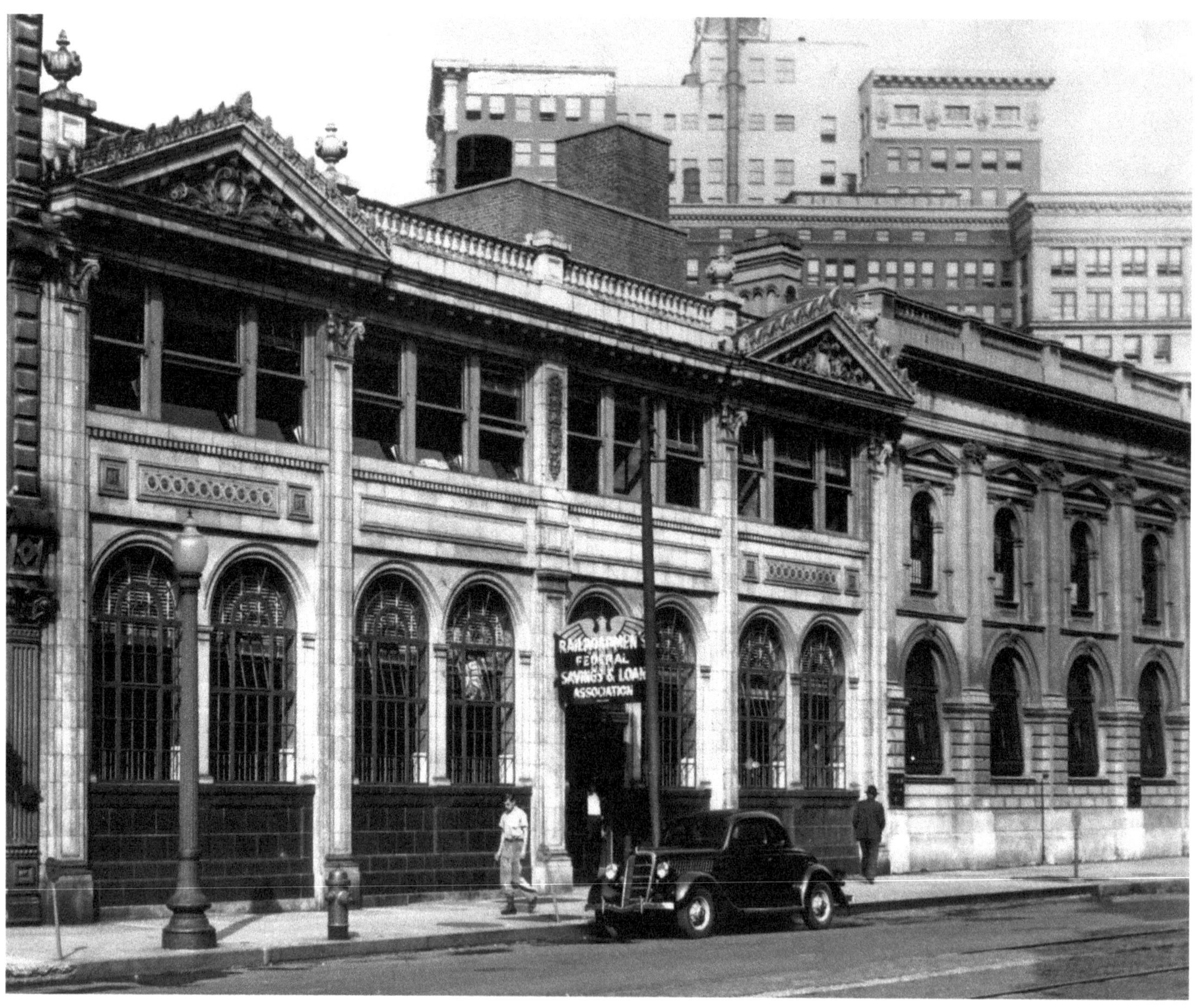

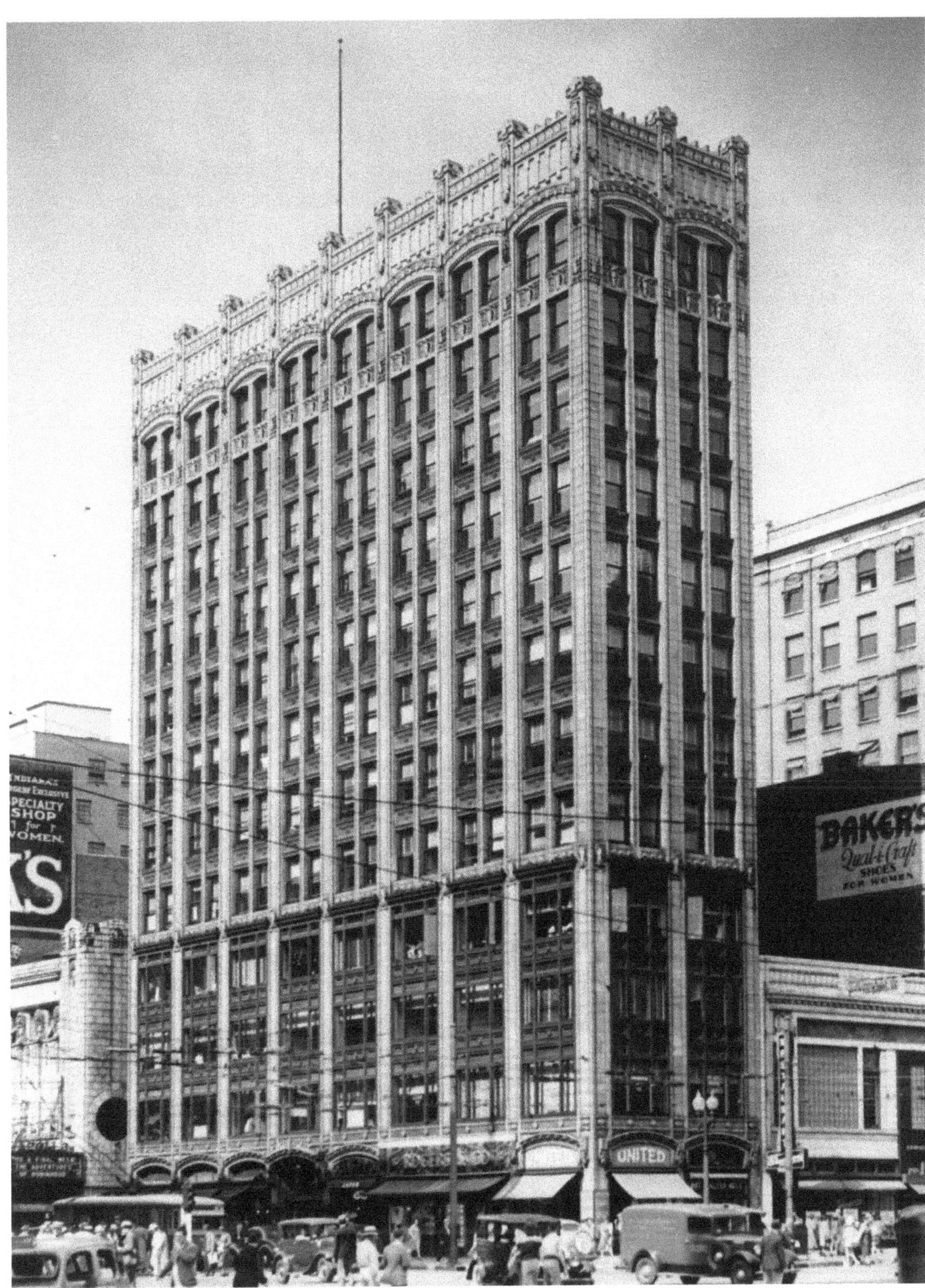

The Roosevelt building, 1938. This narrow skyscraper—designed in the early 1920's by the architectural firm of Vonnegut, Bohn, and Mueller—stood on the northeast corner of Washington and Illinois Streets. The city of Indianapolis demolished it in 1990 to make way for part of Circle Centre Mall, but the lot remained vacant for years. A luxury Conrad Hotel finally opened on the site in spring 2006.

Cenotaph Square, 1937. Located in a sunken garden on the north end of the Indiana World War Memorial Plaza, the cenotaph serves as a tribute to Indiana's war dead. Across St. Clair Street stands the Indianapolis Public Library (today known as the Indianapolis-Marion County Public Library), designed by Philadelphia architect Paul Cret and opened in 1917.

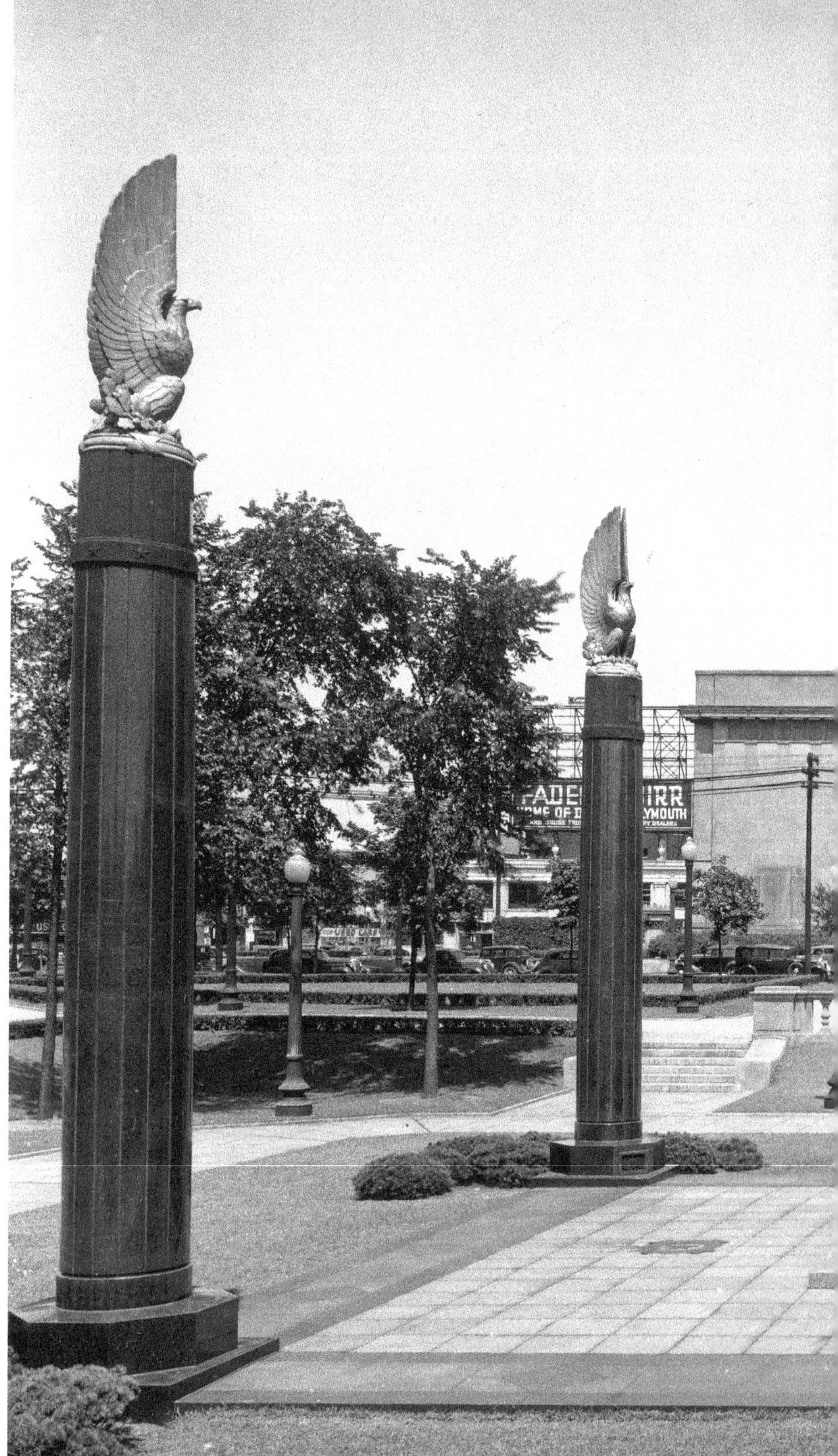

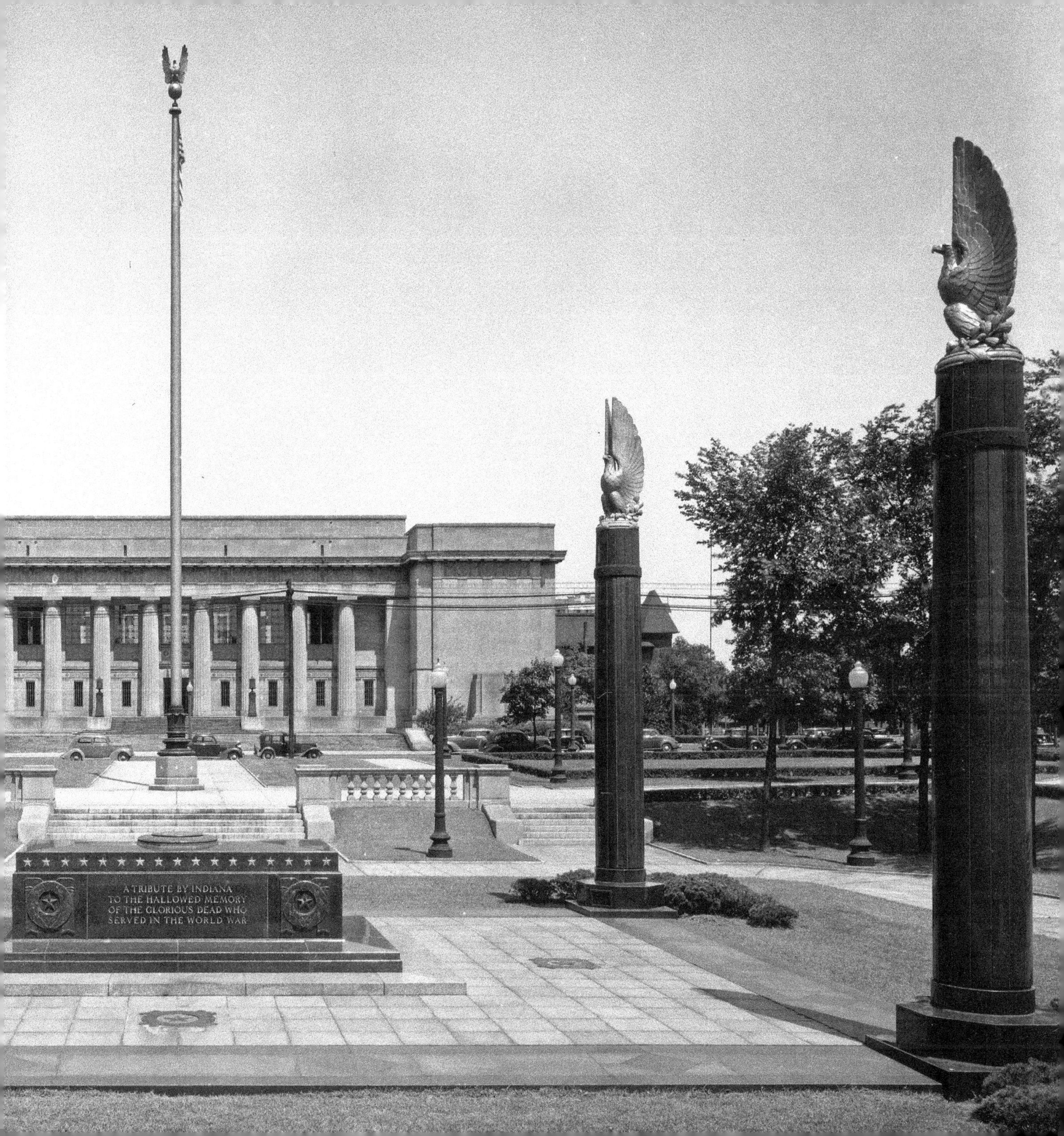
A TRIBUTE BY INDIANA
TO THE HALLOWED MEMORY
OF THE GLORIOUS DEAD WHO
SERVED IN THE WORLD WAR

The tower of the Marion County courthouse soars over East Washington Street, 1936.

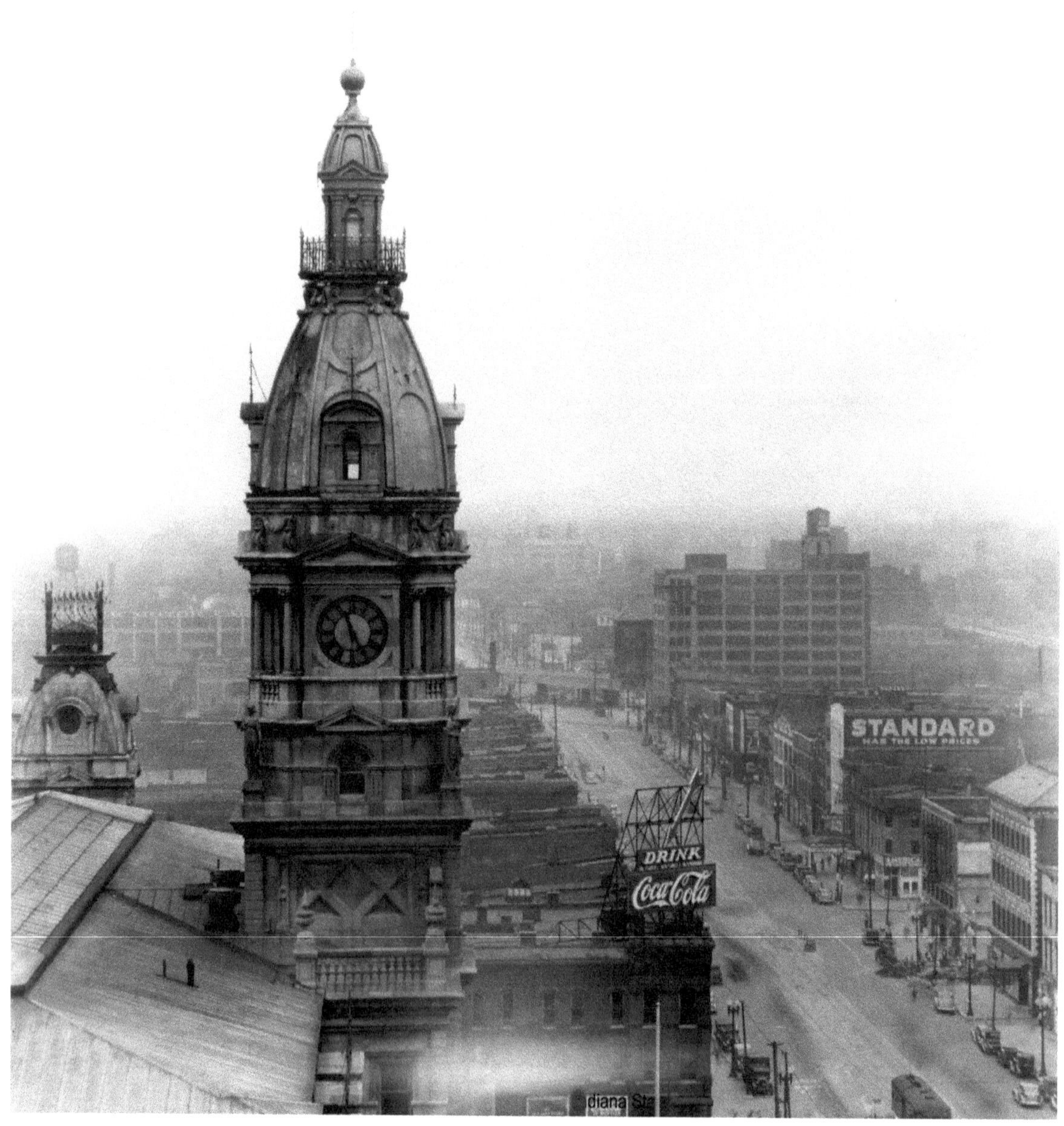

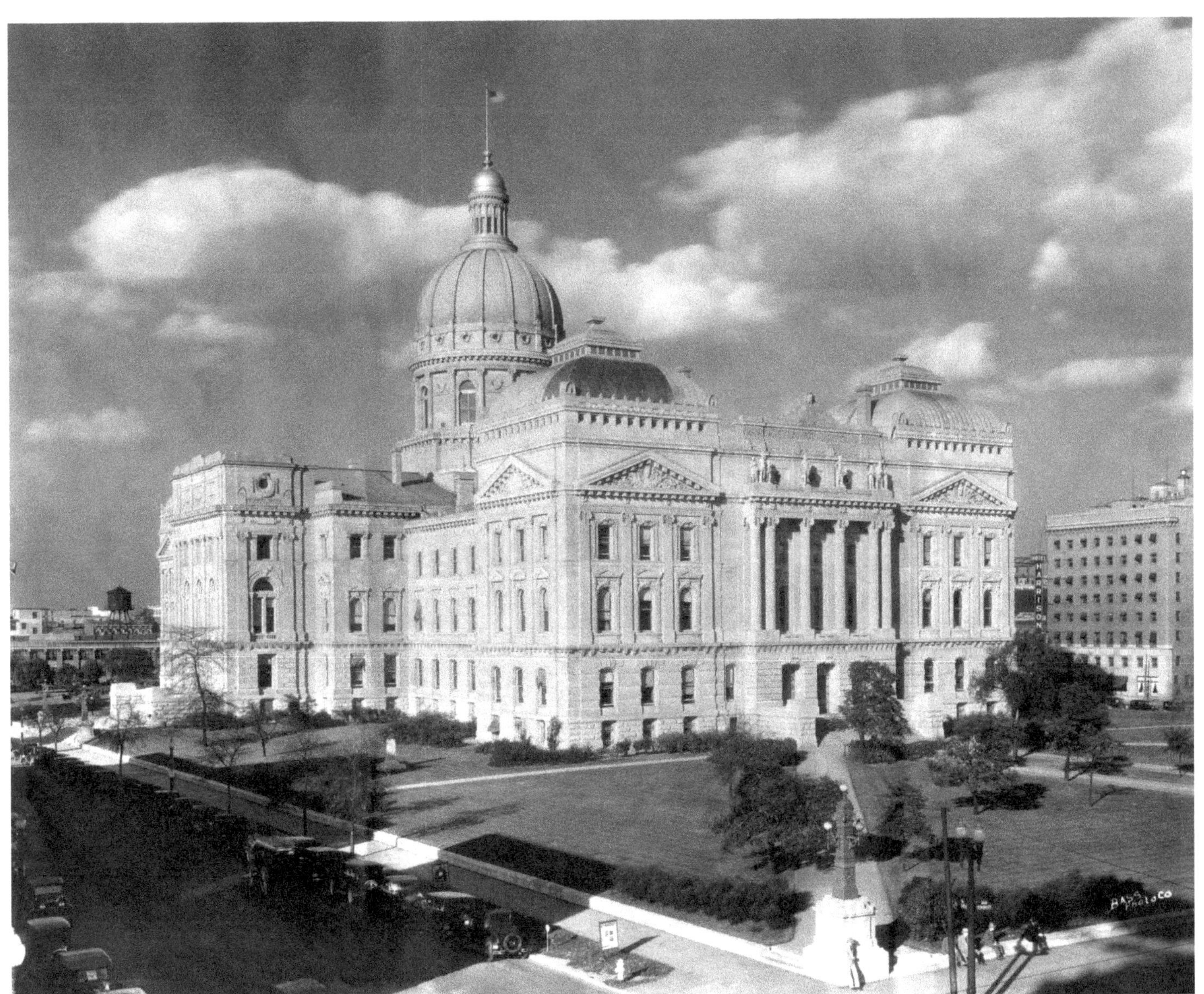

The Indiana state capitol, circa 1930s. Indianapolis officially became Indiana's capital in 1825. This building is the third in the city to serve as the seat of government. It was completed in 1888 and was restored to much of its original splendor in time for its centennial.

Washington Street at night, 1958. This view looks east from the roof of the Lincoln Hotel.

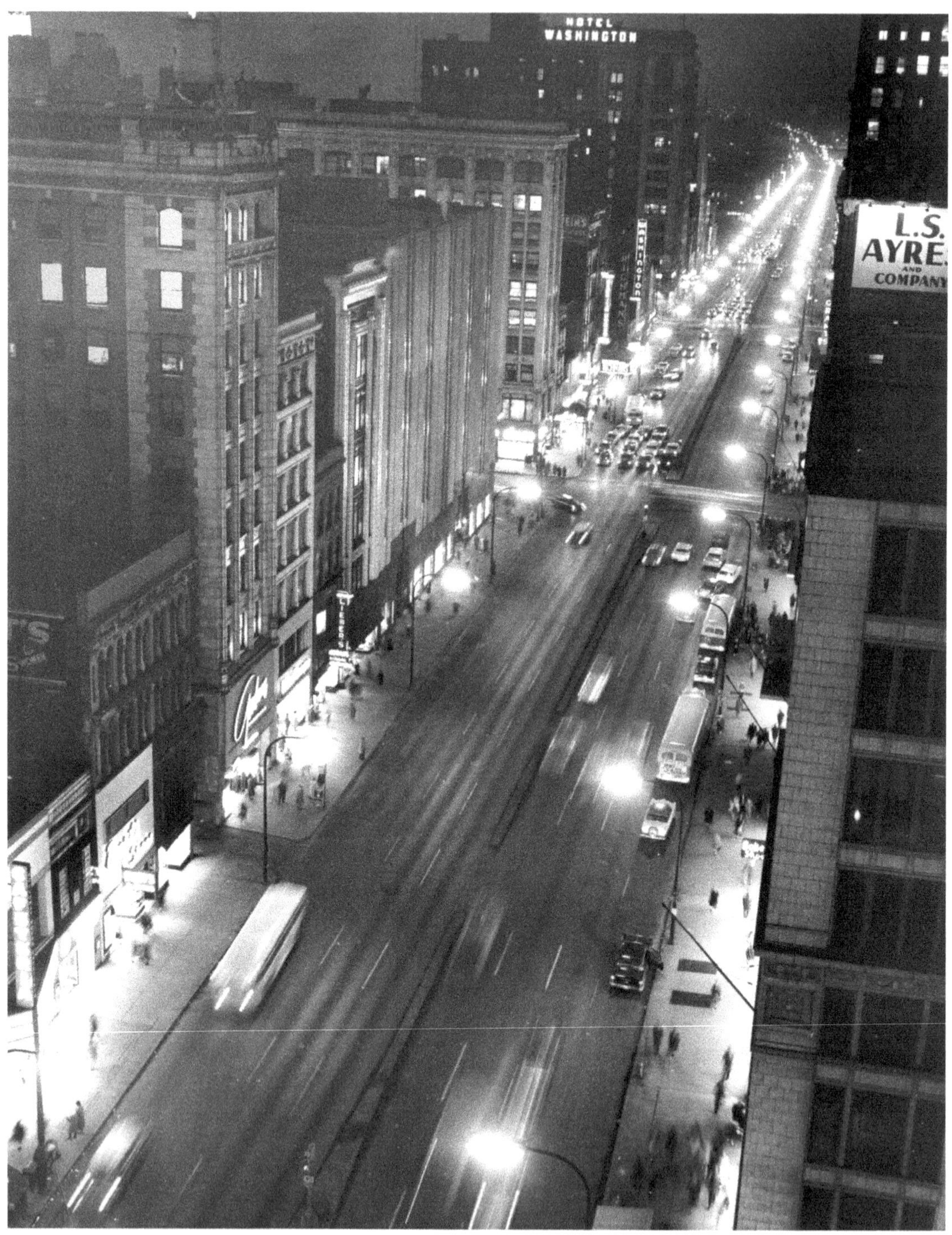

THE CITY AT A CROSSROADS 1940–1969

Although it was the capital of an isolationist state, Indianapolis responded to World War II with fervor. Men went off to battle, and in their absence women picked up hammers and blowtorches at factories such as Allison (producer of aircraft engines) and Curtiss-Wright (maker of propellers). Defense spending drove the Indianapolis economy out of the depression, and the city made the nation's top ten for wartime production.

With peace at hand, Americans were eager for a lifestyle they hadn't known for a decade and a half. Years of depression and war had worn on them, and they wanted material comfort. For an increasing number of Indianapolis residents, that life took place in the suburbs outside the old city limits.

One group to benefit from postwar changes was Indianapolis's African American community. The Crispus Attucks basketball team of 1955 was a dazzling example. Attucks, the city's all-black high school, won the state championship that year, the first Indianapolis team to do so. In a basketball-crazed city, this accomplishment held meaning. Some resented it, to be sure, but for many others it sparked the beginnings of racial tolerance and integration. As the years progressed and the city grew outward, blacks were finally able to settle outside their segregated neighborhoods along Indiana Avenue.

As Indianapolis moved into the 1960's, local leaders became increasingly concerned about the rapid decline of the downtown and surrounding neighborhoods. There had been no significant investment in the central city since the 1920's, and it was a telling sign that for nearly fifty years the tallest building in Indianapolis was the Merchants National Bank, completed in 1913. To help combat the situation, community leaders established Unigov, which merged city and county functions on January 1, 1970. Unigov expanded the city limits to include nearly all of Marion County and brought in much-needed tax revenues. In the ensuing years, Indianapolis focused on redeveloping its downtown, making it an attractive place for residents and visitors alike. In the 1970's, leaders focused on making the city an amateur sports capital, and over the next several years new arenas and sporting venues sprouted around town. Ideas for a downtown mall and urban state park also bore fruit, amenities that now contribute significantly to Indianapolis's quality of life.

Today Indianapolis enjoys much commercial and residential redevelopment in the heart of the city. It still faces challenges, including a struggling public school system, declining neighborhoods on the fringes of downtown, and the loss of old-line manufacturing jobs. But throughout its history the city and its residents have always faced and overcome adversity, a precedent that heralds promise for Indianapolis in the twenty-first century.

The Merchants National Bank, 1940. Daniel Burnham's Chicago architectural firm designed this building, which stands on the southeast corner of Washington and Meridian Streets. It was the tallest building in Indianapolis for nearly fifty years, from the time it opened in 1913 until the dedication of the city-county building in 1962. Merchants merged with National City Bank in 1992 and later moved from the building. Today the law firm Barnes and Thornburg owns it and occupies most of the space. The opulent lobby, which still retains many original features, is now home to a bookstore.

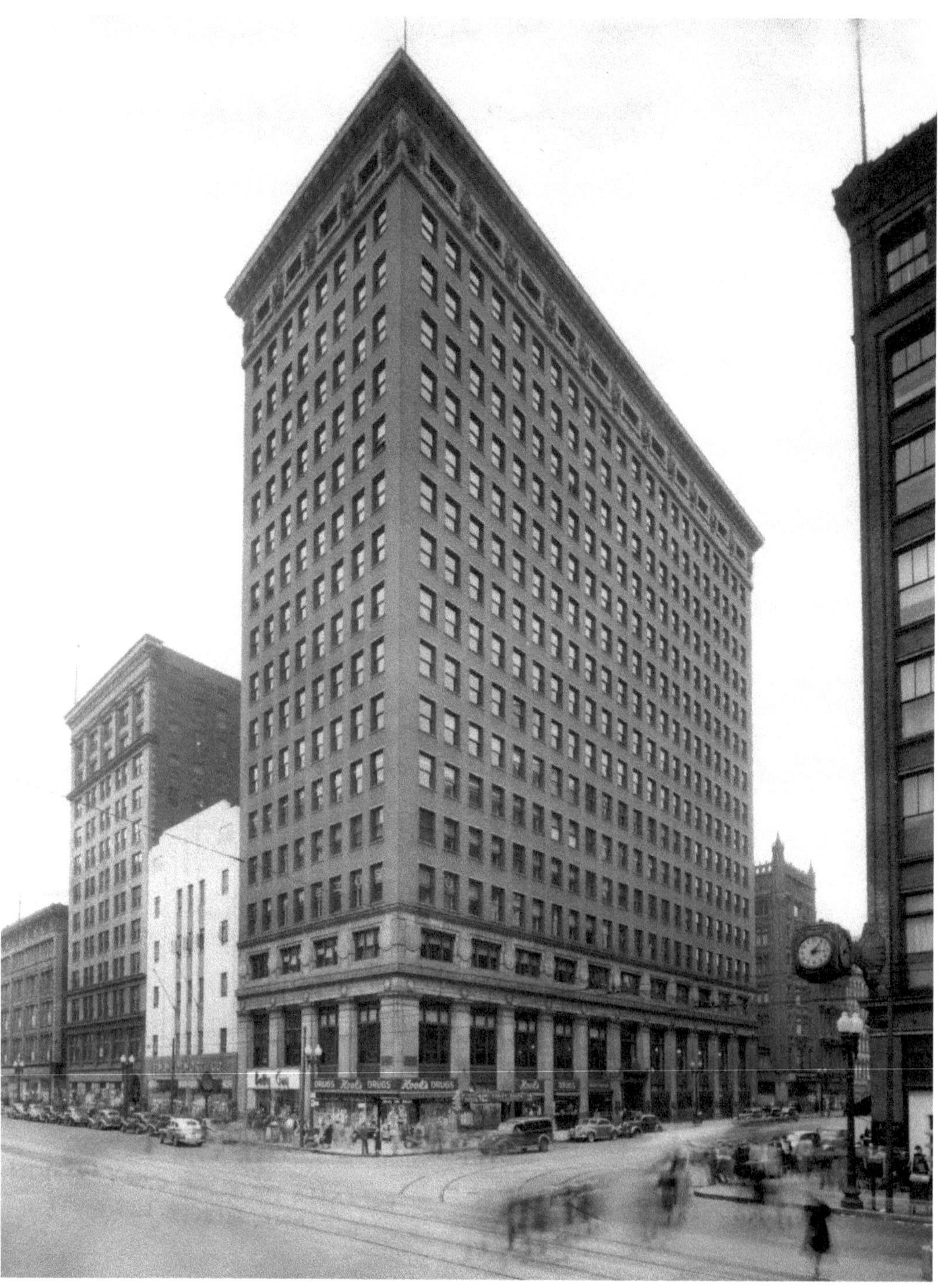

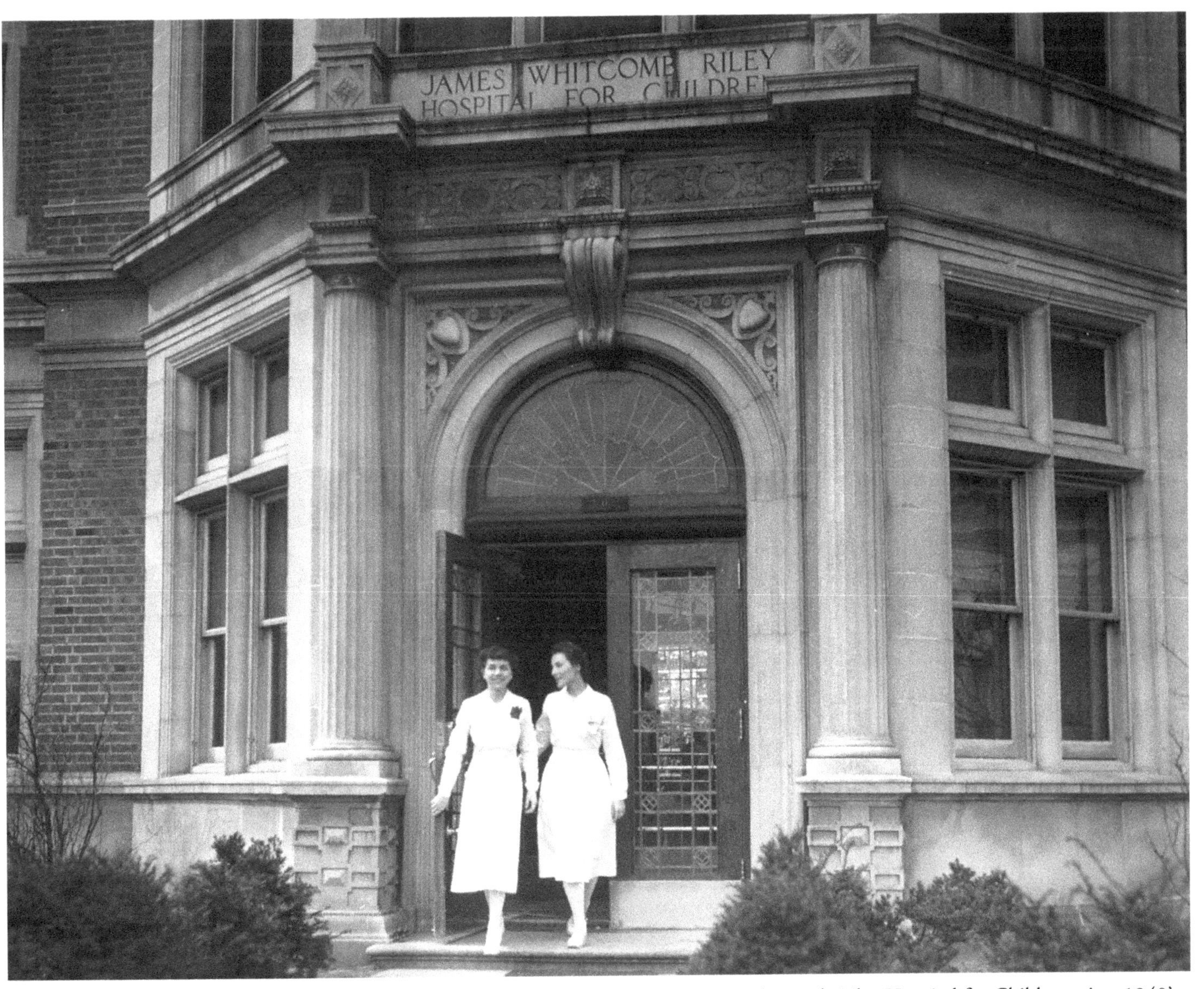

Nurses leave the James Whitcomb Riley Hospital for Children, circa 1940's. Many of the hospital's staff members received training at the nearby Indiana University School of Nursing.

Farmers participate in a horse-pulling contest at the 1941 Indiana State Fair.

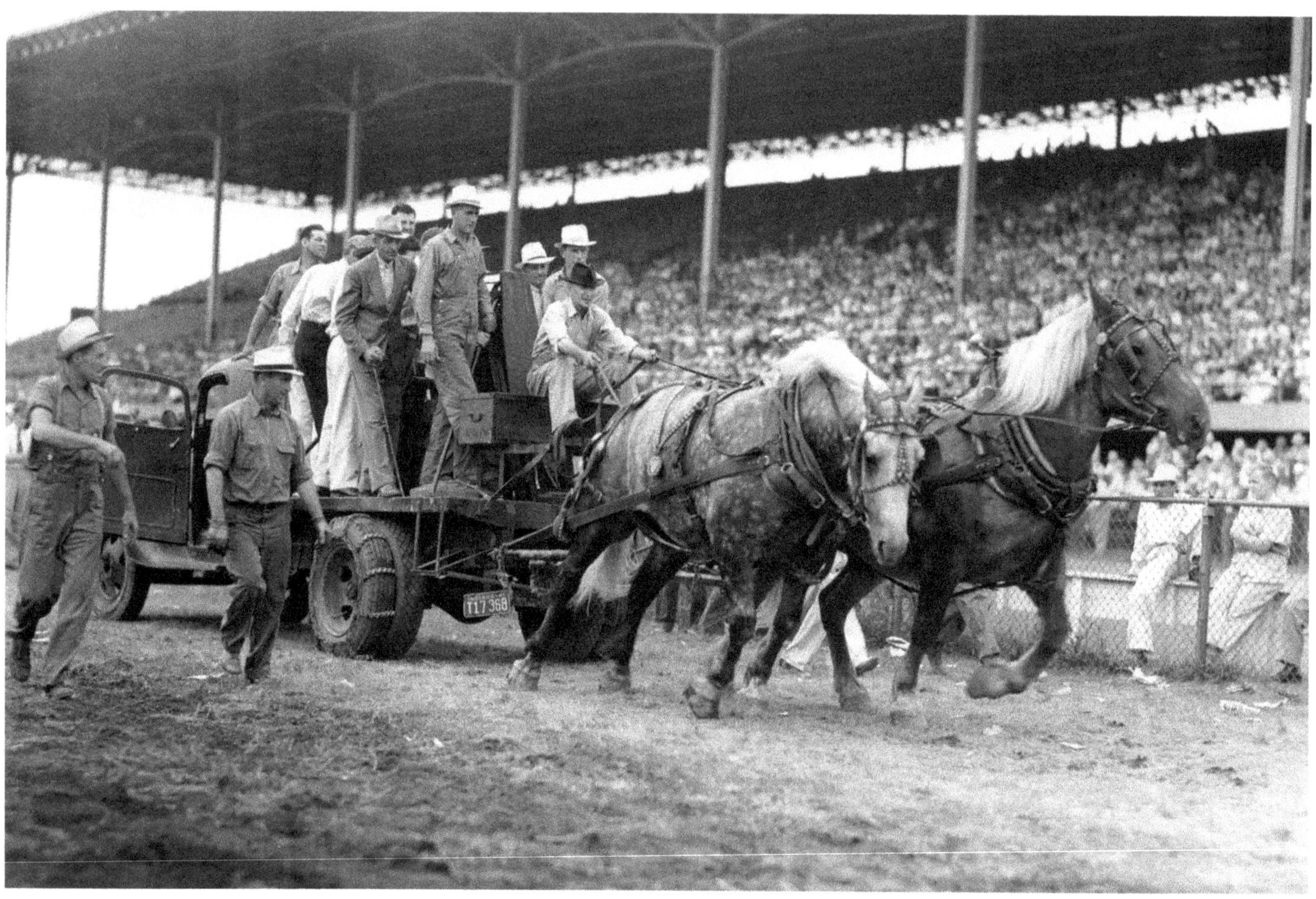

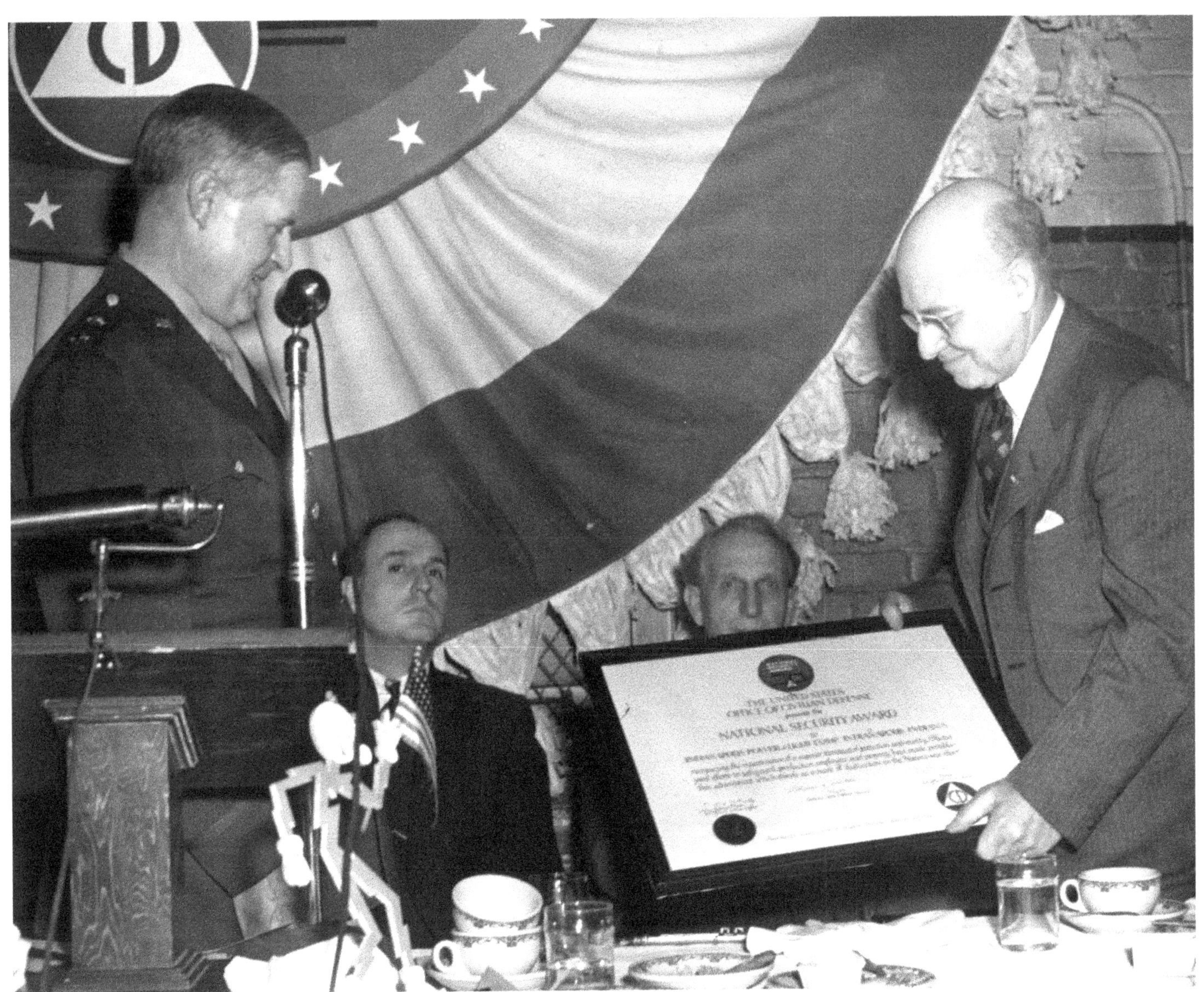

Maj. Gen. Ulysses S. Grant III, representing the United States Office of Civilian Defense, presents a National Security Award to H. T. Pritchard, president of the Indianapolis Power and Light Company, March 22, 1944. IPL received the award for its efforts to protect its employees and facilities from fire, sabotage, air raids, and accidents during World War II.

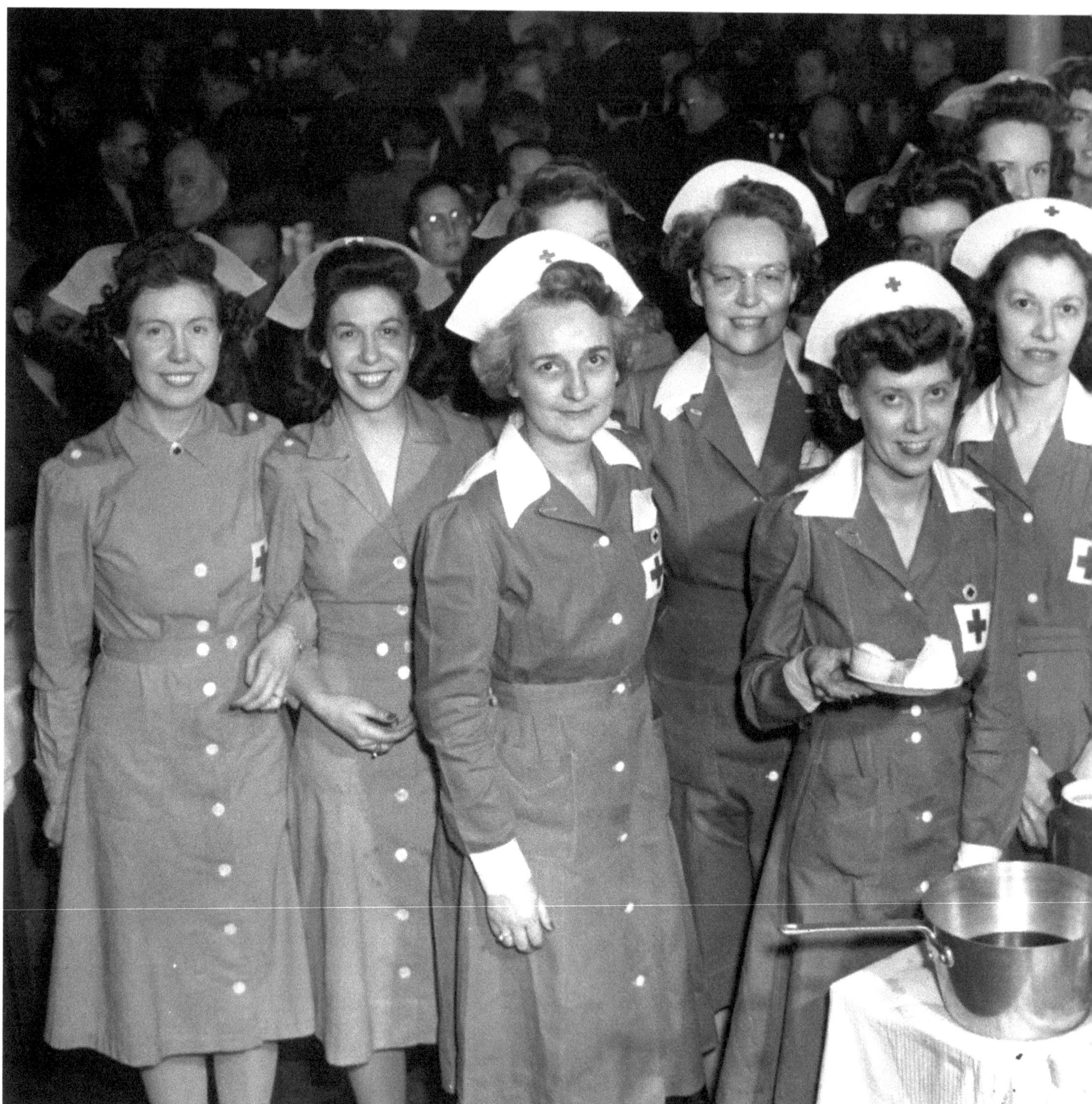

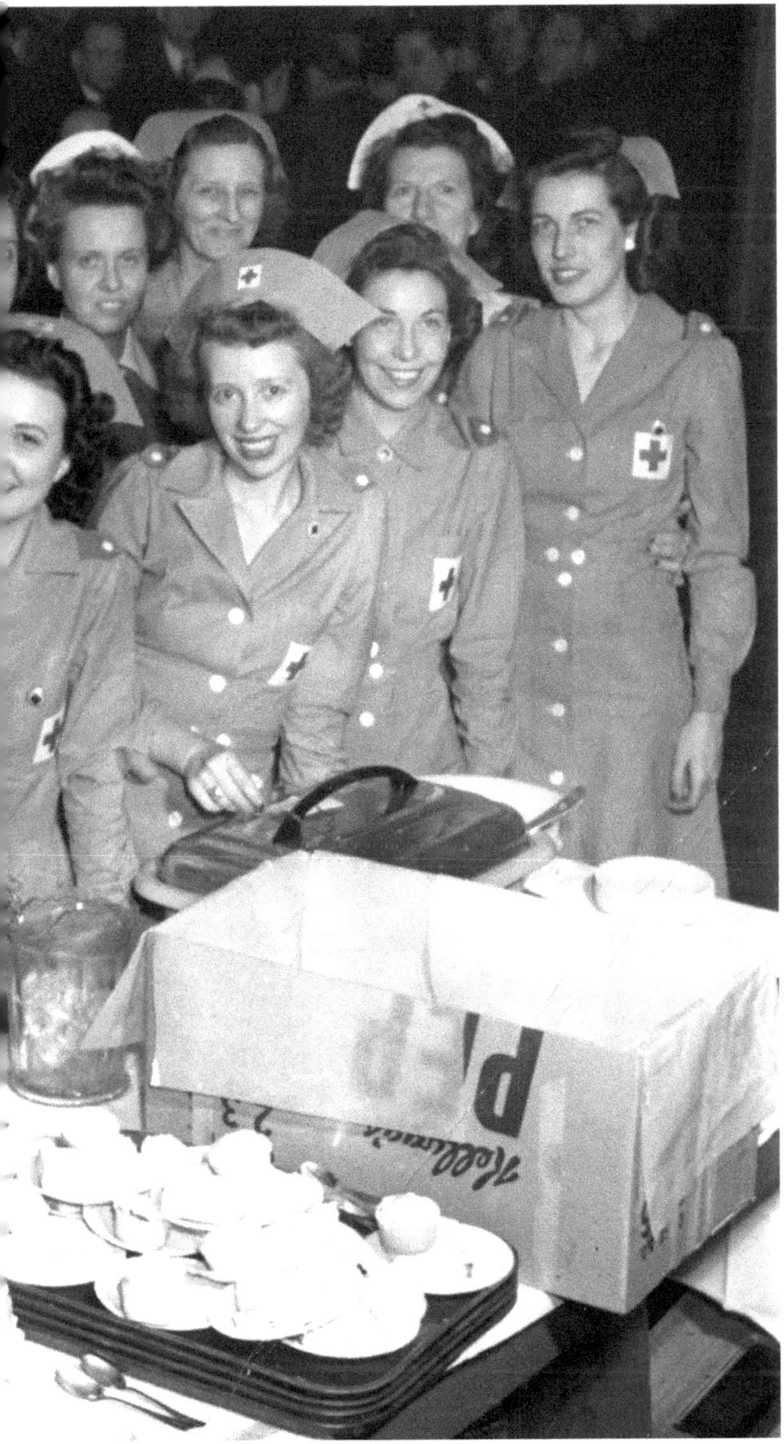

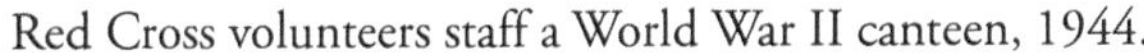

Red Cross volunteers staff a World War II canteen, 1944.

A parade on Monument Circle. Judging from the size of the crowd, the military uniforms, and the large amount of confetti, this was likely a veterans' parade, perhaps one to welcome home soldiers after World War II.

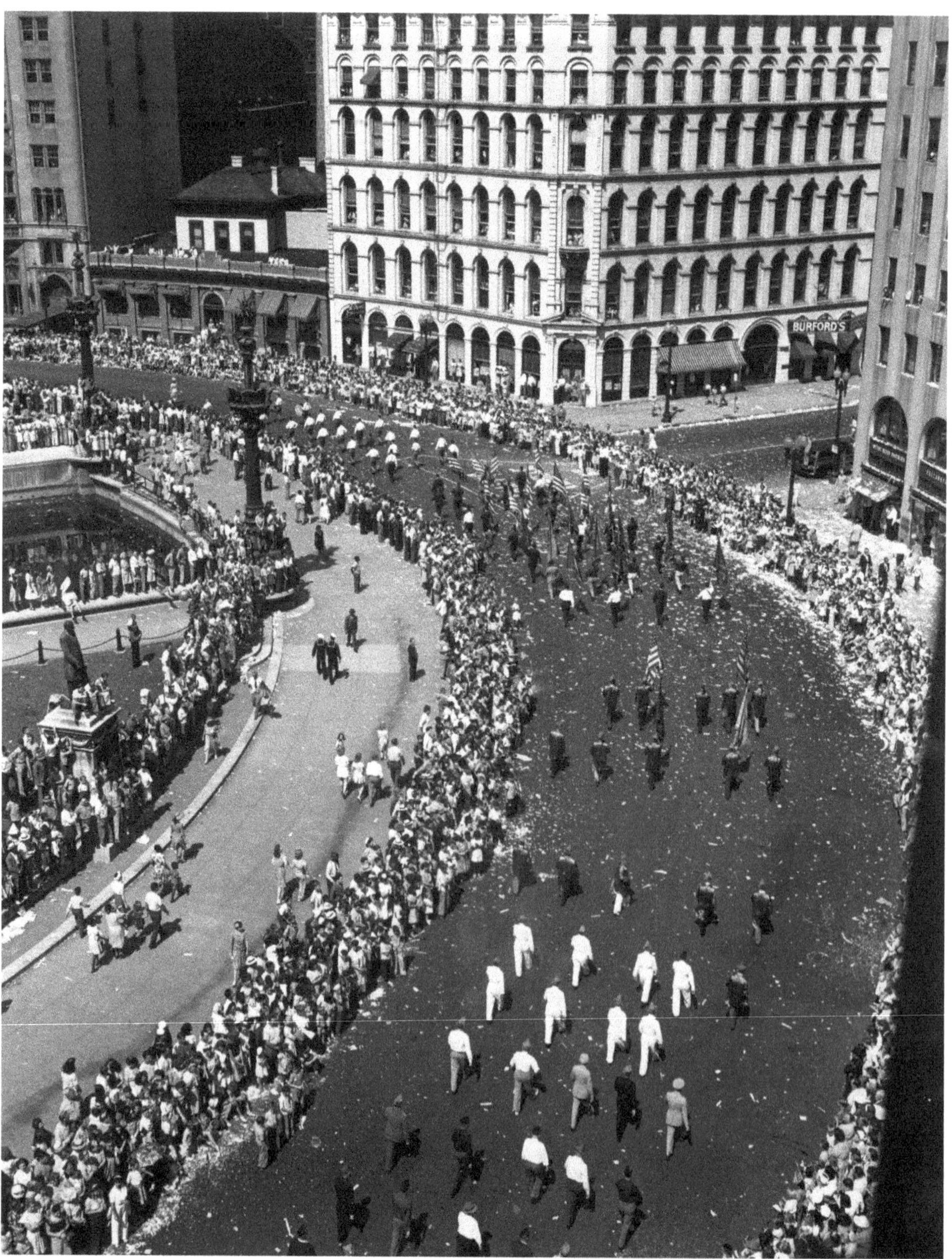

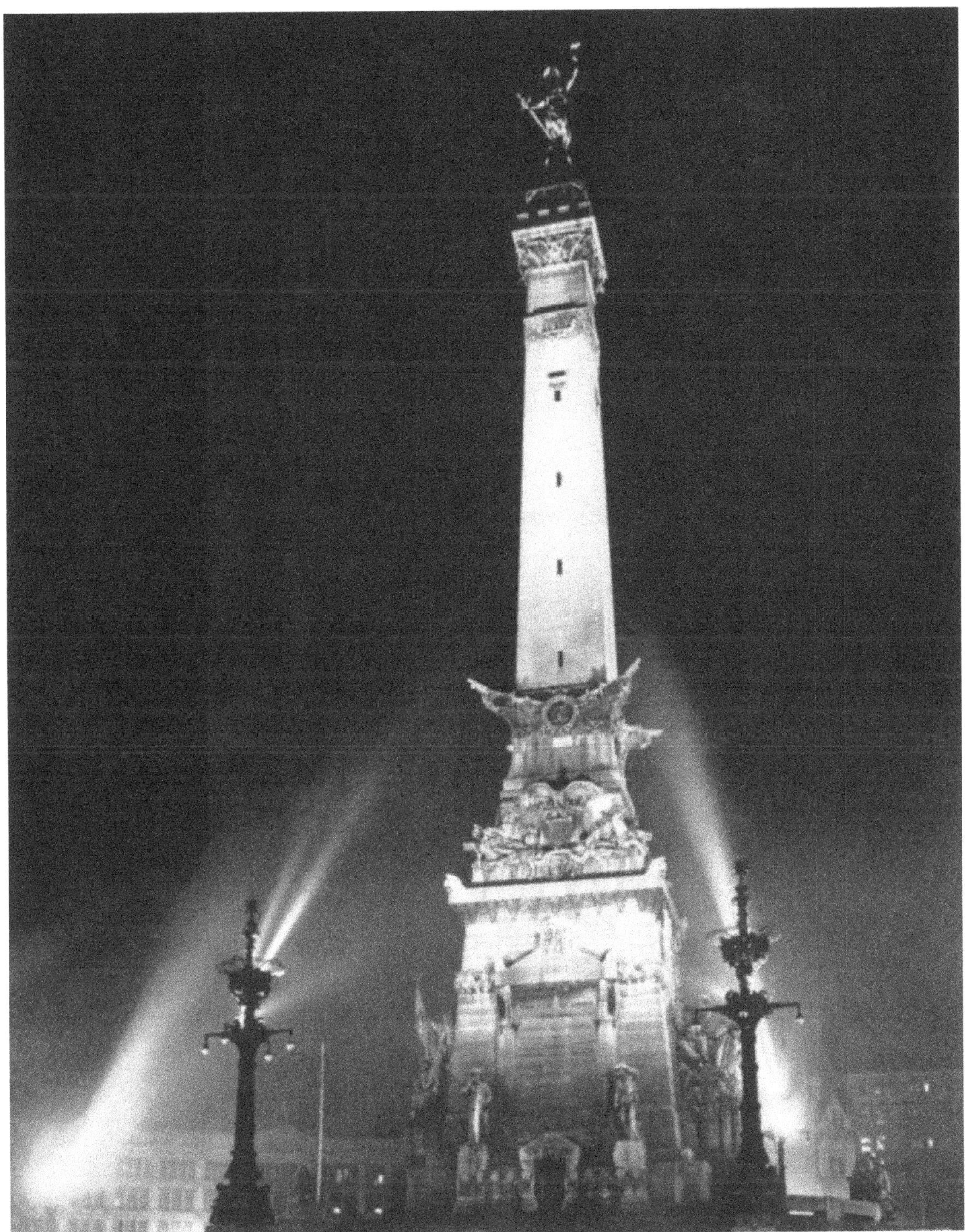

The Soldiers and Sailors Monument at night. The English Hotel can be seen in the background of this photo, which means it was taken sometime before the hotel's demolition in 1949.

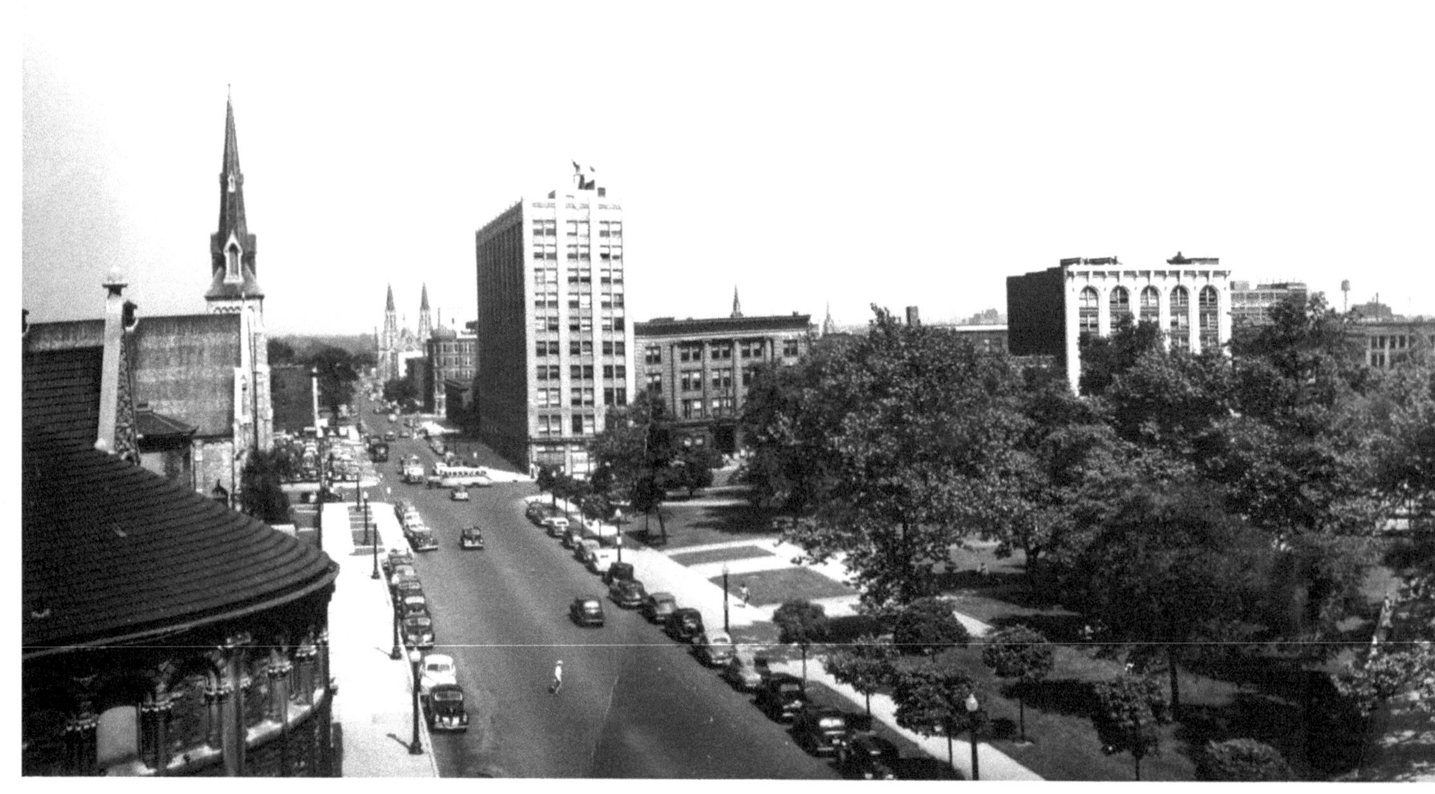

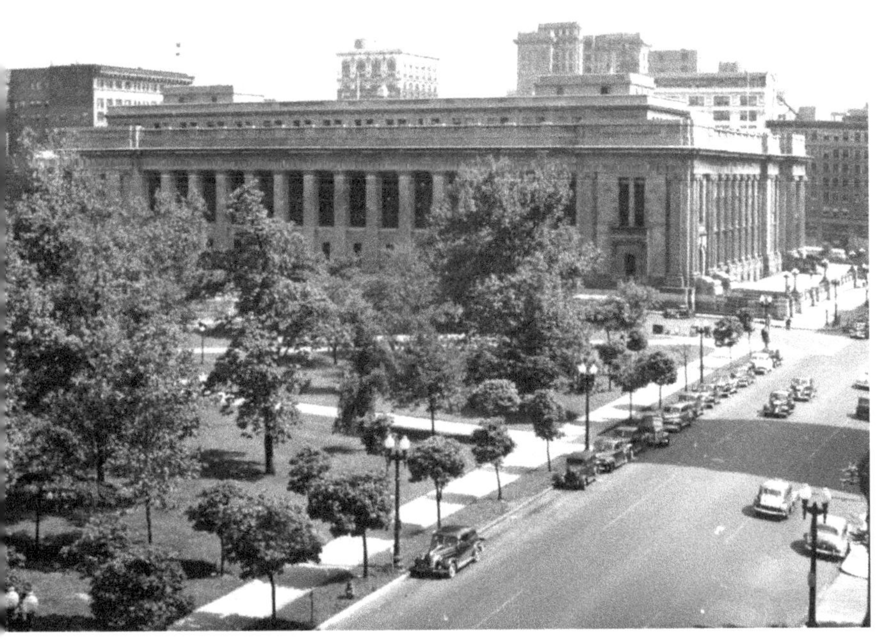

A view of University Park from the Blacherne apartment building, June 9, 1947. When Alexander Ralston laid out Indianapolis, he created University Square (as it was originally known) with the understanding that it would become the site of a state university. None ever opened there, but the land did house the Marion County Seminary from 1833 to 1853 and Indianapolis's first high school from 1853 to 1858. Troops drilled on the ground during the Civil War, and in 1876 the city opened it as a park. Today University Park is noted for its statuary and the Depew Fountain, which serves as its centerpiece.

A high school band parades up North Meridian Street in honor of the Indiana State Fair's centennial, August 29, 1952. Thirty-eight more Indiana high school bands joined the procession, held on the fair's opening day, while 70,000 spectators cheered from the sidelines.

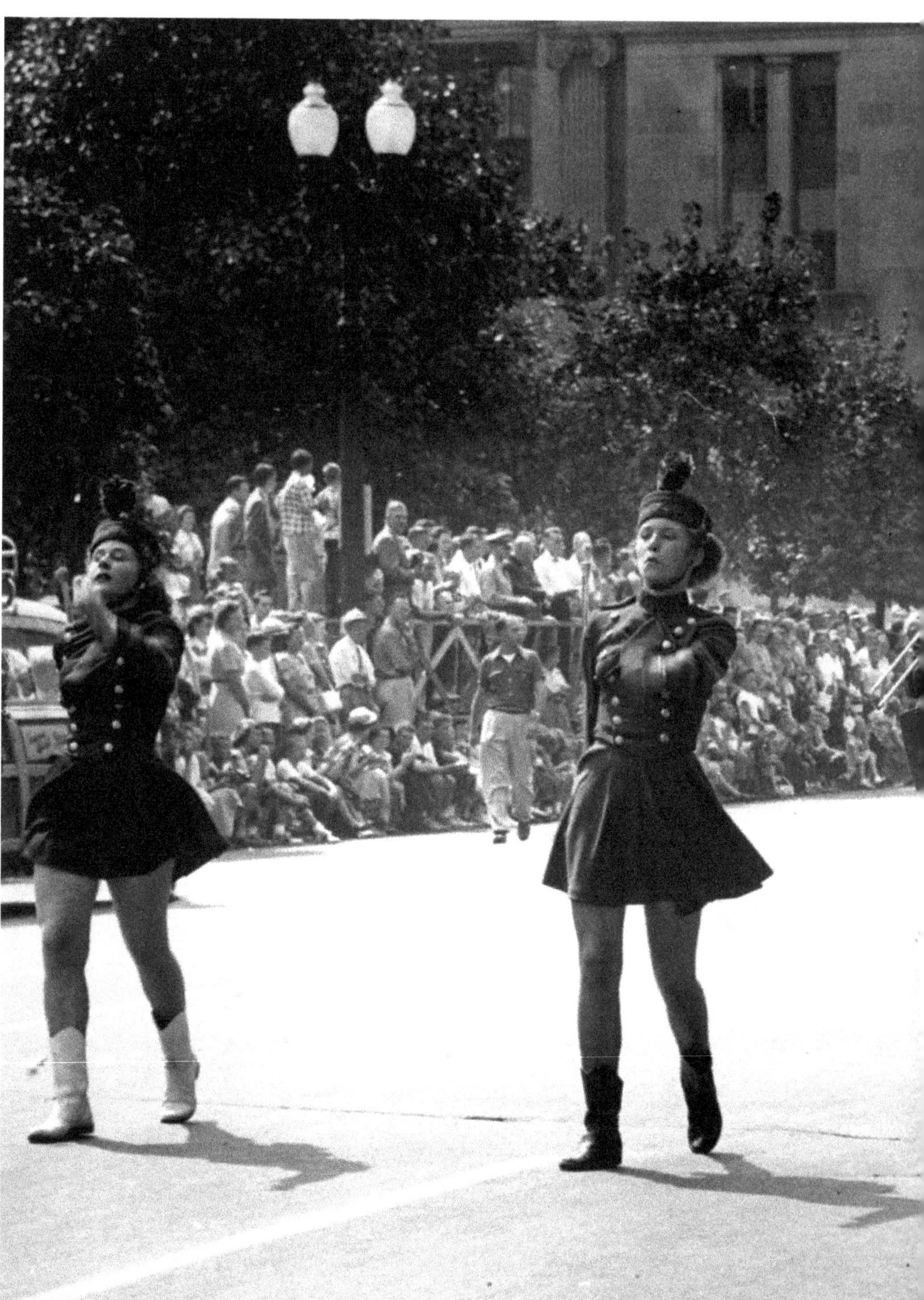

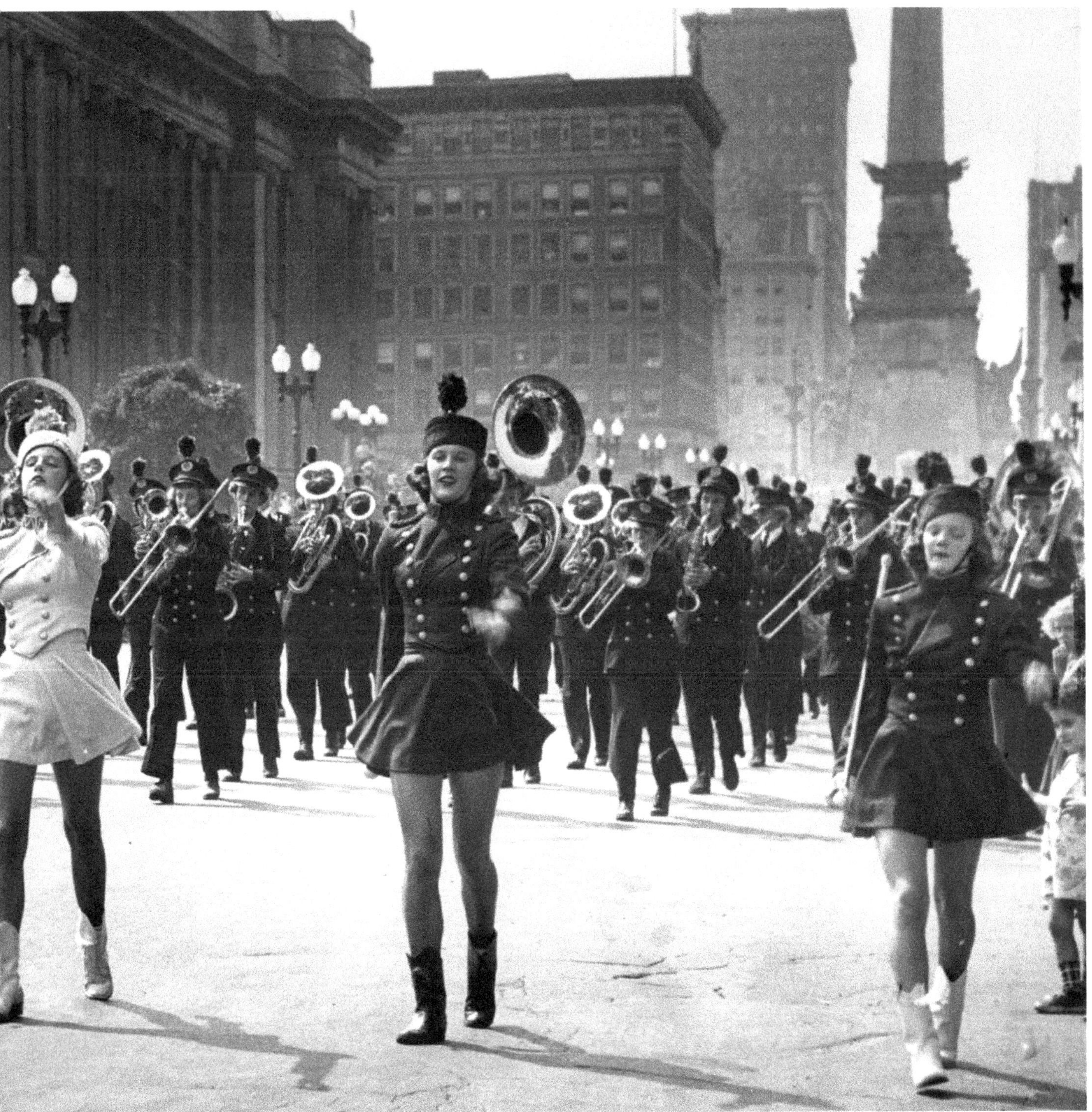

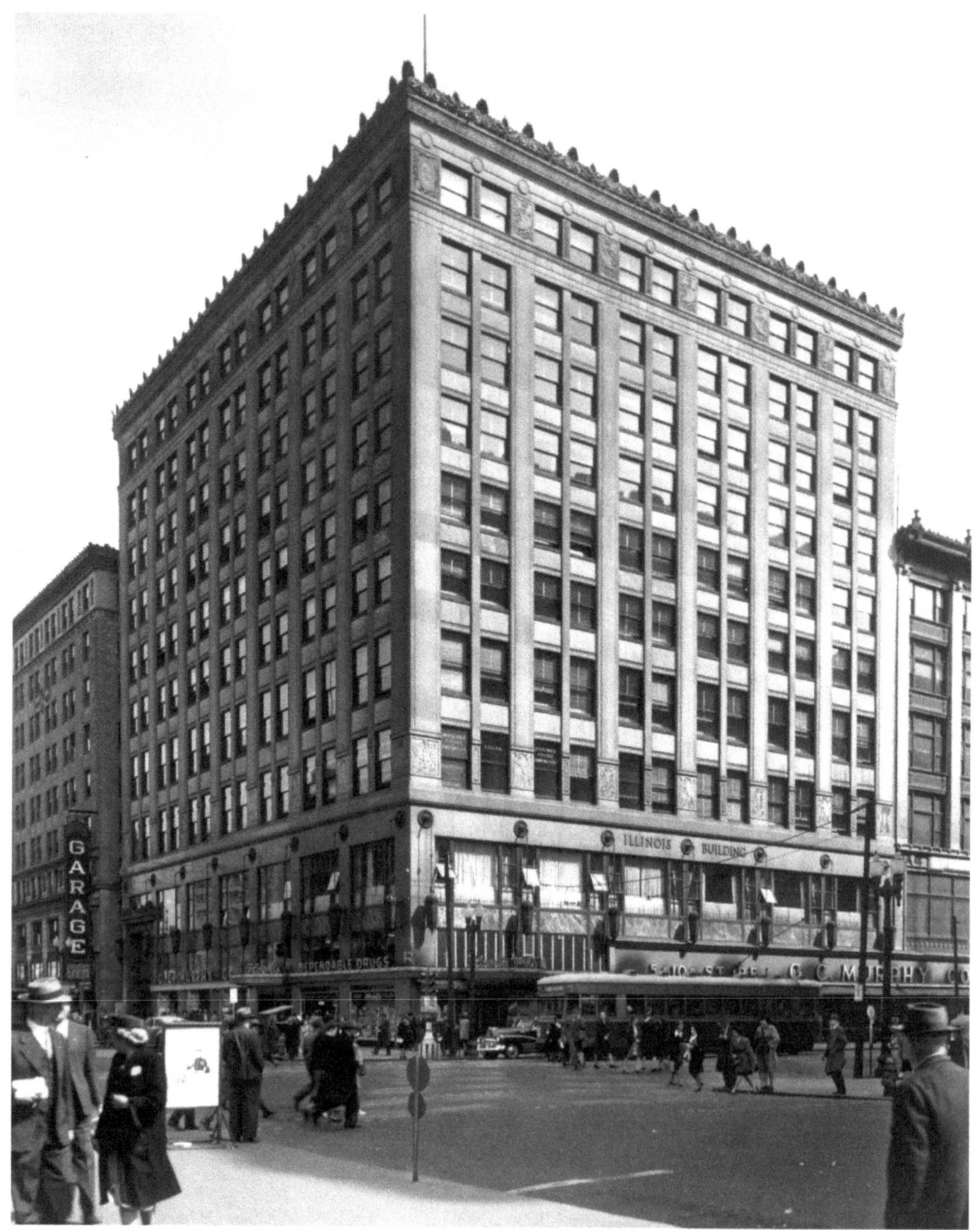

The Illinois building, 1947. Leading Indianapolis architects Rubush and Hunter designed this ten-story edifice, which opened in 1925 on the southeast corner of Market and Illinois Streets. Though structurally sound, it sits vacant today, and some suggest its owner, locally based HDG Mansur, may demolish it to make way for a high-rise condo tower. The Historic Landmarks Foundation of Indiana has named the Illinois building one of its ten most-endangered landmarks for 2006.

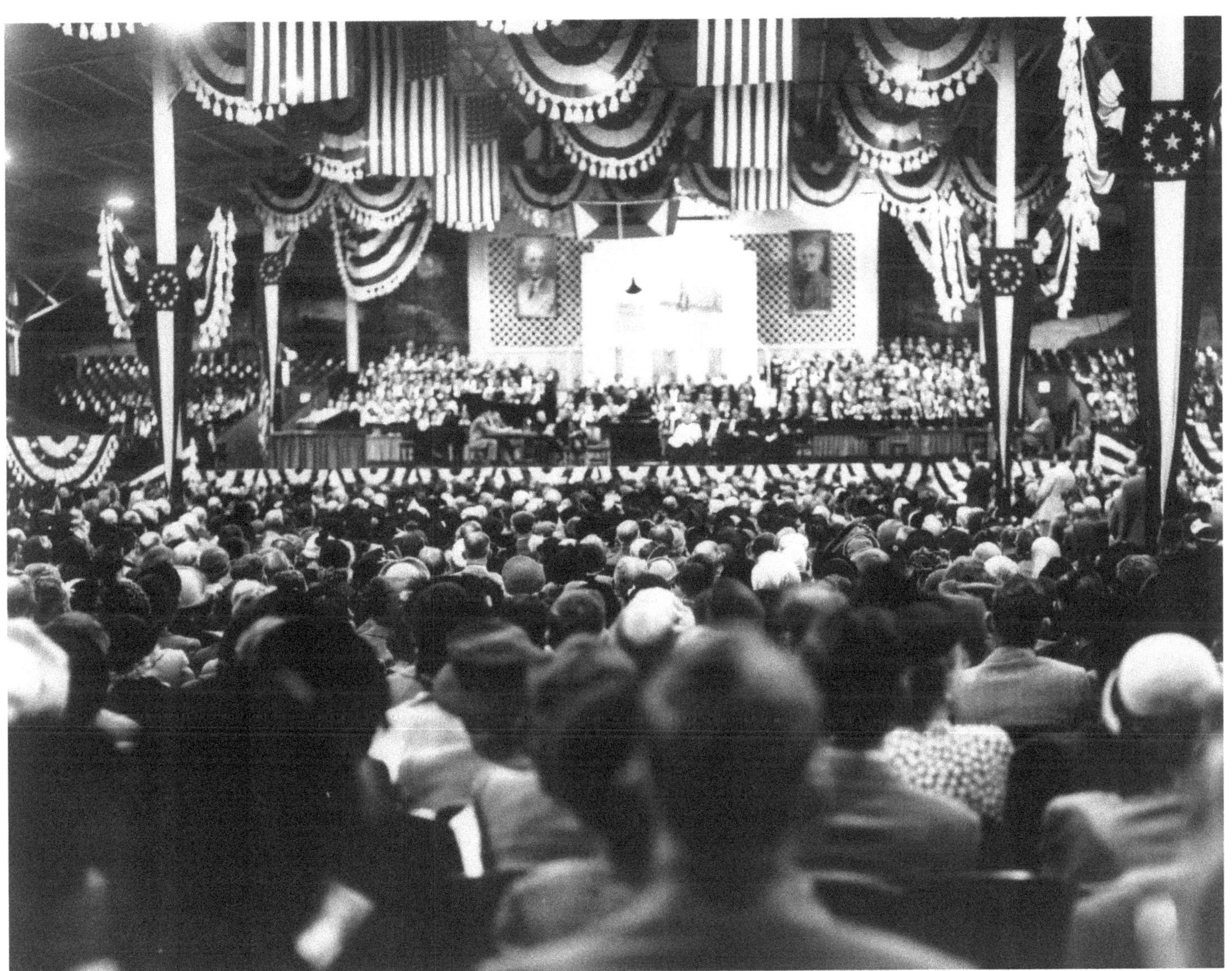

Church Federation Reformation Day services at the Cadle Tabernacle, October 29, 1950. Cadle Tabernacle stood on the northwest corner of Ohio and New Jersey Streets from the early 1920's to the late 1960's. E. Howard Cadle built it for the promotion of Christianity. In the 1930's he broadcast a popular evangelical radio program, the *Nation's Family Prayer Period*, from the site, and over the years well-known preachers such as Aimee Semple McPherson and Billy Sunday preached there. In addition to religious activities, the tabernacle hosted cultural and civic convocations.

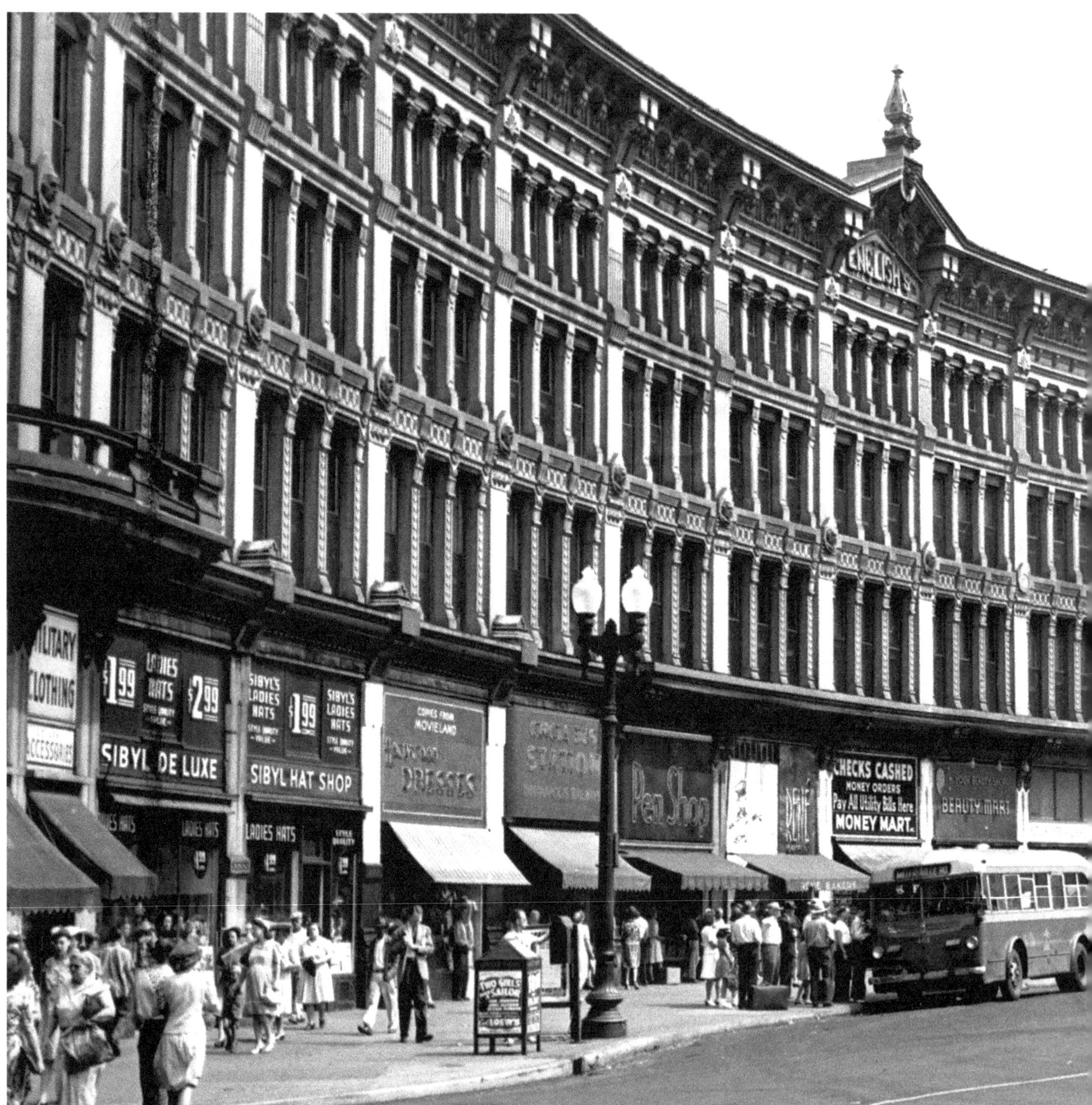
ENGLISH'S
CLOTHING
ACCESSORIES
$1.99
LADIES HATS
$2.99
SIBYL DE LUXE
SIBYL'S LADIES HATS
$1.99
SIBYL'S LADIES HATS
SIBYL HAT SHOP
LADIES HATS
LADIES HATS
COPIES FROM MOVIELAND
DRESSES
Pen Shop
CHECKS CASHED
MONEY ORDERS
Pay All Utility Bills Here
MONEY MART
BEAUTY MART

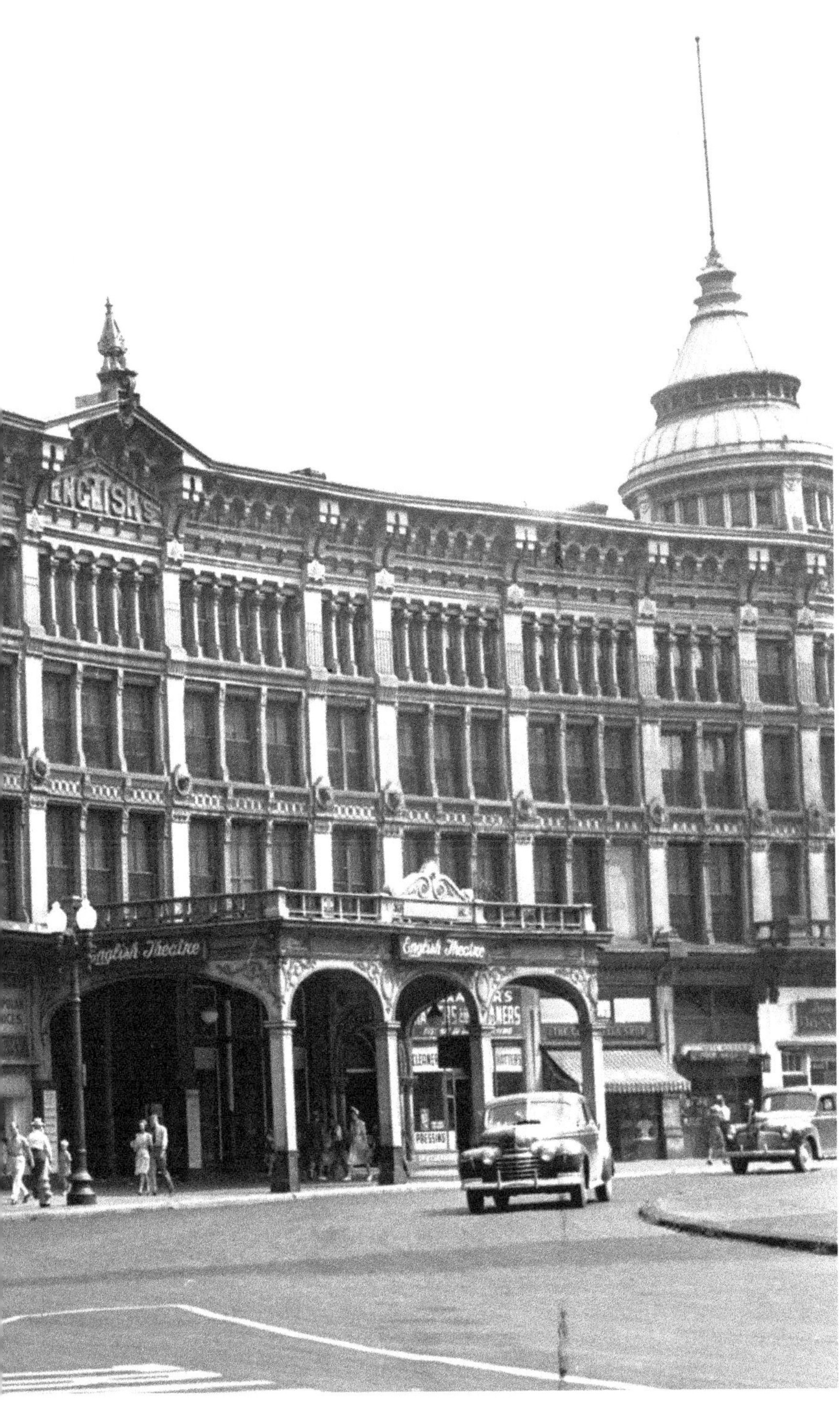

The English Hotel and Opera House, circa 1948. Prominent Indianapolis businessman (and Democratic vice-presidential nominee) William H. English opened a theater on the northwest quadrant of Monument Circle in 1880. Modeled after New York's Grand Opera House, it drew the leading performers of the day. Four years later English built a hotel onto the theater, and his son added another hotel section in 1896. For many years the hotel was one of the most fashionable in the city, but years took their toll, and by the mid-twentieth century both it and the theater were in disrepair. Wrecking crews demolished the English in early 1949.

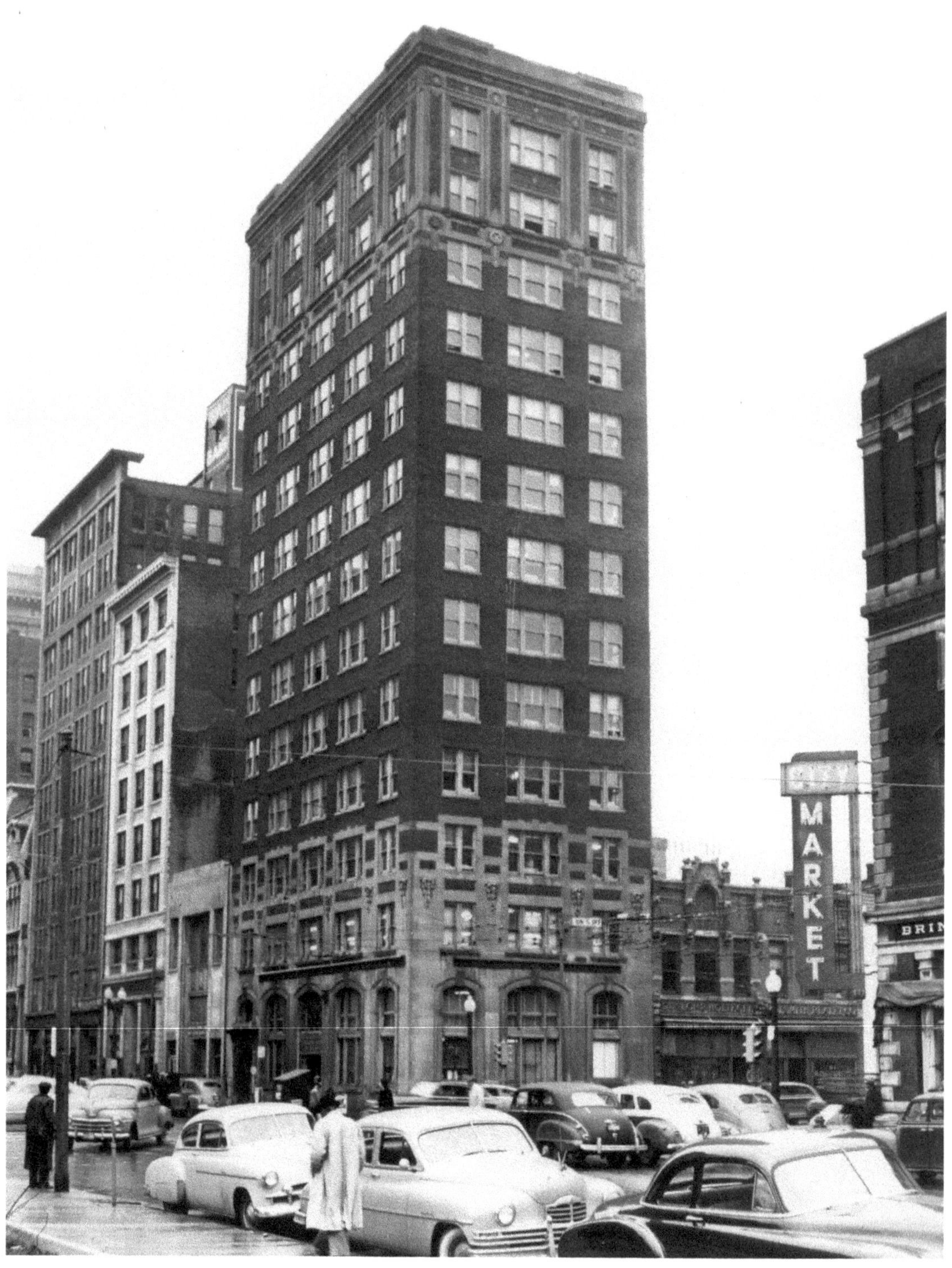

The Inland building, 1950. This building, originally a bank, stands on the northwest corner of Market and Delaware Streets.

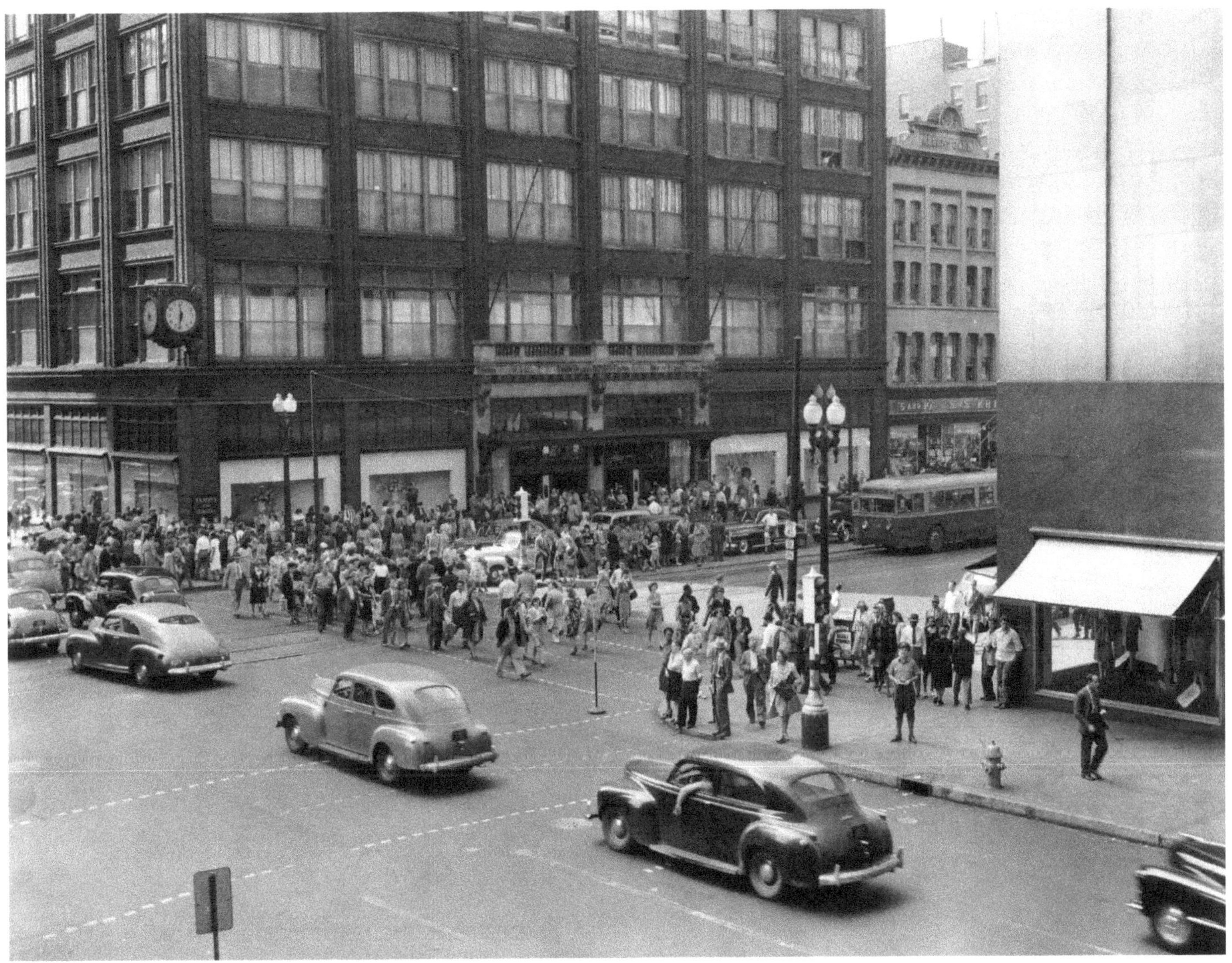

The intersection of Washington and Meridian Streets, early 1950's. This view shows the "Crossroads of America," and in it is seen two of Indianapolis's competing department stores. On the right is H. P. Wasson and Company, which operated on or near the corner from 1883 until 1979. Across the street and dominating this photo is L. S. Ayres and Company, the city's most prominent retail establishment. Ayres opened this building in 1905 and remained here until early 1992, when its out-of-town owner, the May Company, decided to close the downtown store. Parisian department store now operates out of the building, which is part of Circle Centre Mall. Federated Department Stores acquired the May Company in 2005 and in late 2006 will rebrand all remaining suburban Ayres stores as Macy's, obliterating the proud Ayres name from Indianapolis's retail landscape.

The northwest quadrant of Monument Circle in the 1950's. Developers tore down the English Hotel and Opera House to make way for this building, which housed J. C. Penney and F. W. Woolworth stores. Though many over the years have lamented the loss of the English, famed architect Frank Lloyd Wright praised the Penney building during a 1950's visit, saying it was one of the best examples of architecture in the city.

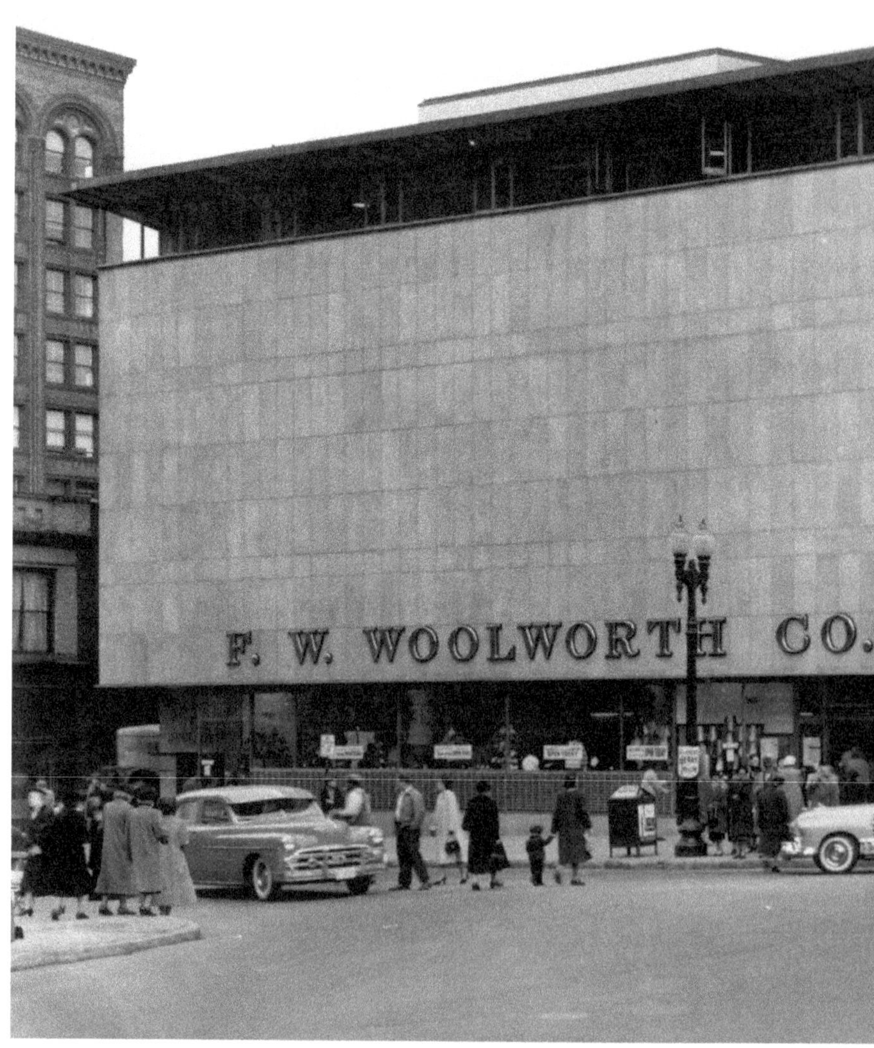

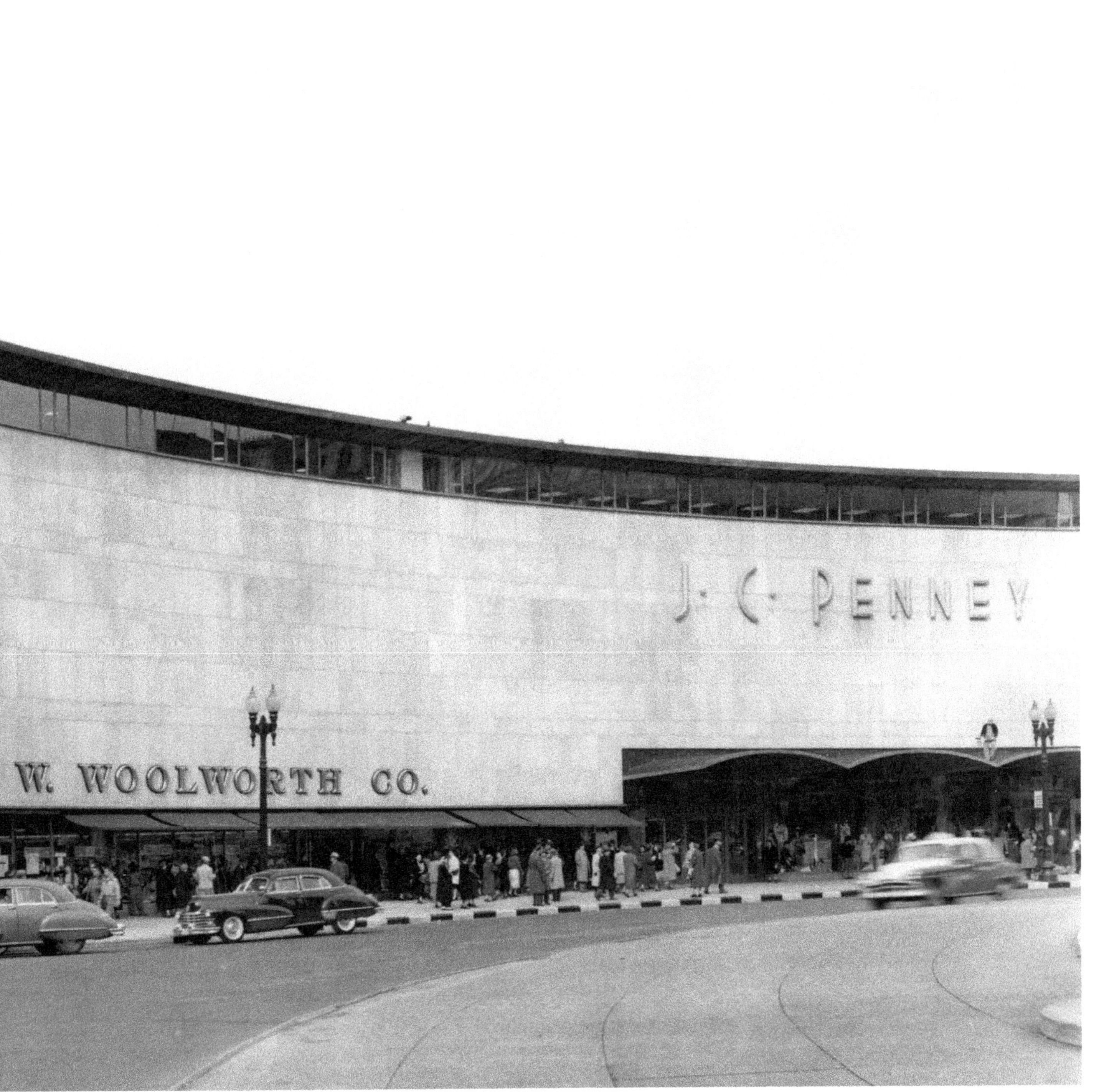
J. C. PENNEY
W. WOOLWORTH CO.

Workers assemble telephones at Western Electric on Indianapolis's east side, circa 1950's. Located on Shadeland Avenue, the Western Electric plant was the world's largest telephone factory. It covered forty acres and at one time employed some 8,000 people. After thirty-five years of operation, the plant closed in 1985, the result of changing technology and declining business.

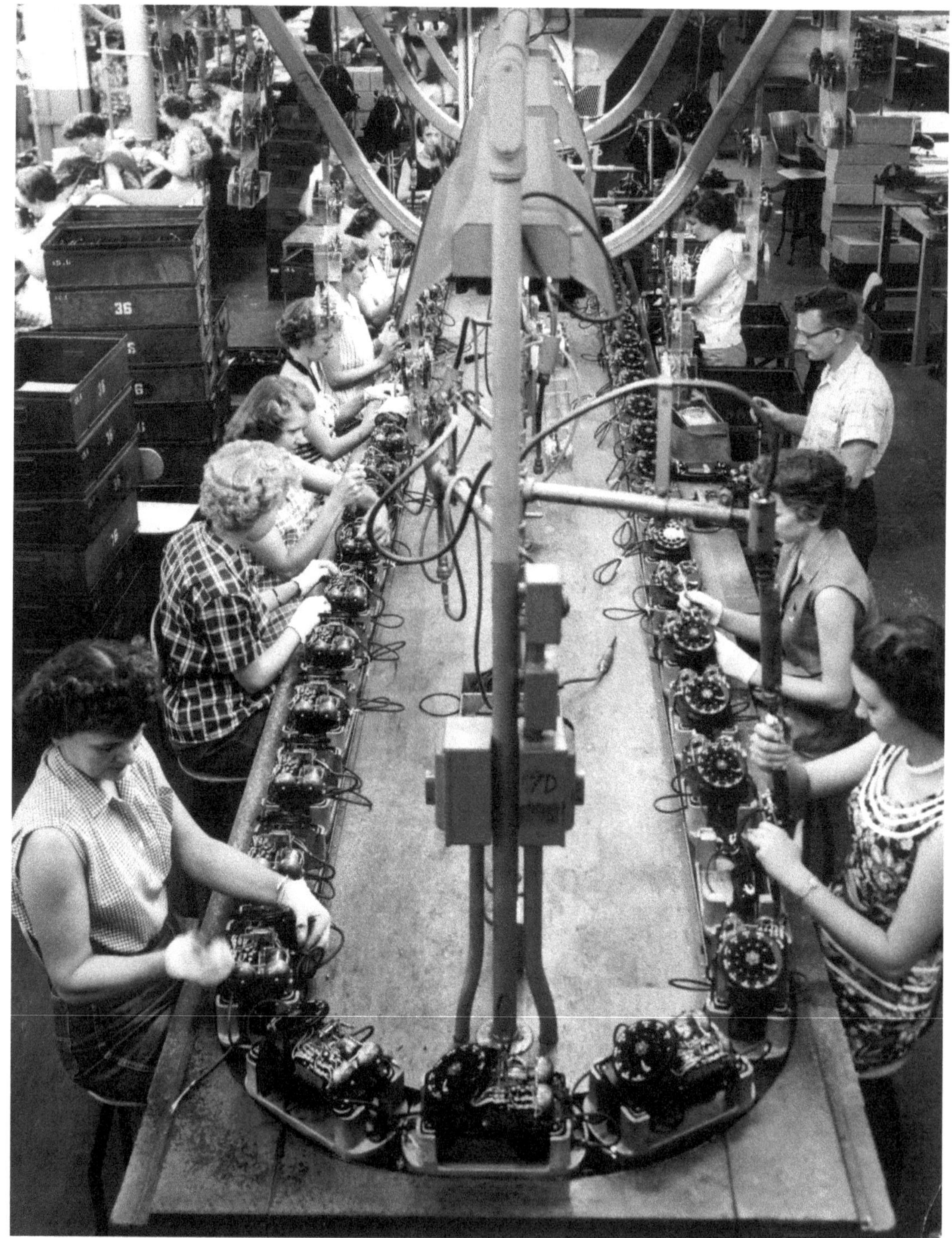

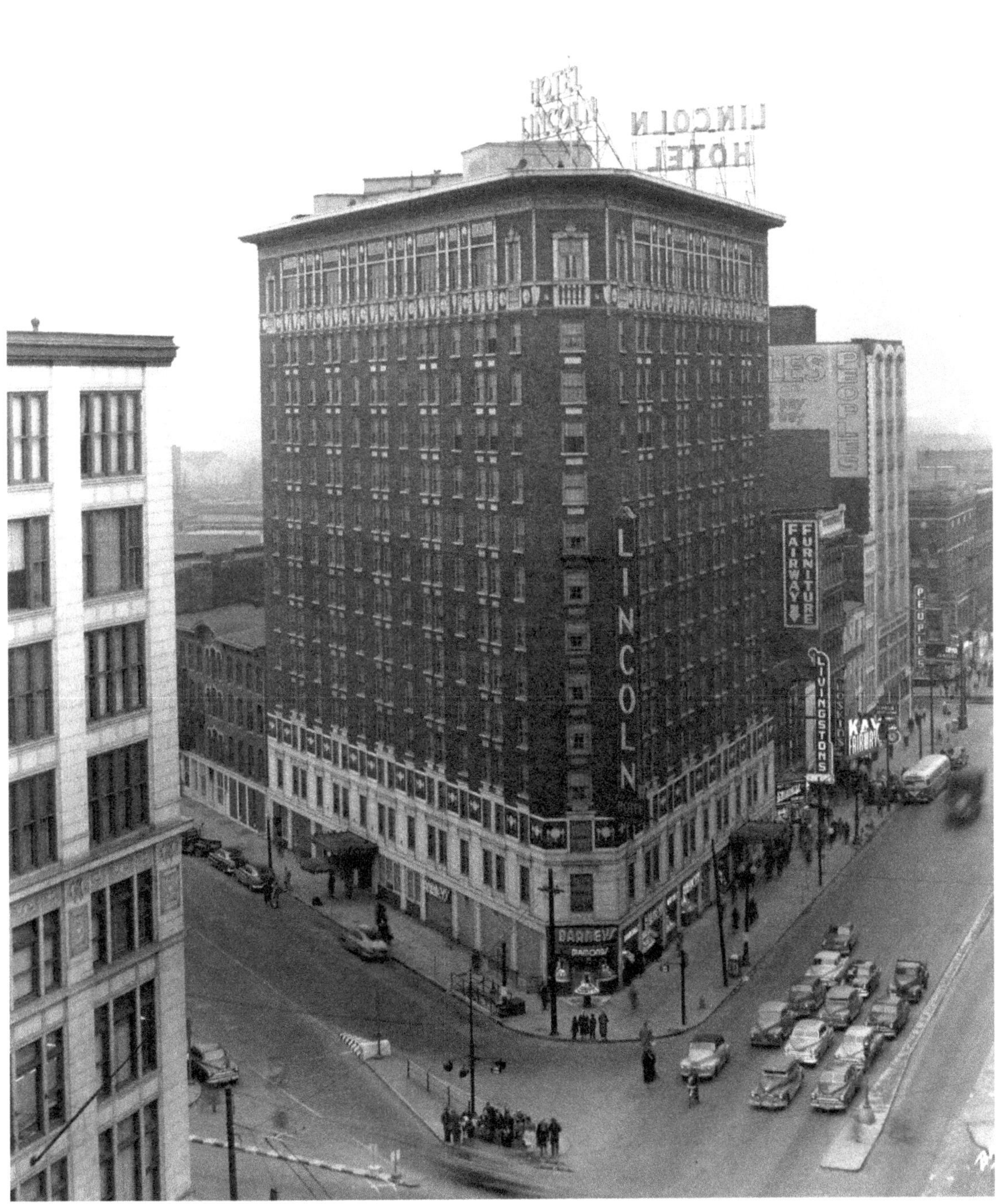

The Lincoln Hotel, circa 1950's. This fourteen-story flatiron hostelry stood at the corner of Washington Street, Illinois Street, and Kentucky Avenue. The entire intersection is now gone. At one time all four of Indianapolis's angling avenues ran to within one block of the circle, but in the early 1970's city leaders began allowing developers to cut them off and build over them, destroying the beauty and symmetry of Indianapolis's original plan. The Lincoln Hotel was a victim of this, felled by a wrecking ball in 1973 to make way for the Merchants Plaza.

The Circle Tower, 1957. Opened in 1930 on the east side of Monument Circle, the Circle Tower is one of Indianapolis's finest examples of Art Deco architecture. It features Egyptian motifs at its entrances, black marble and bronze in the lobby, and Italian terrazzo floors in the offices. Architects Rubush and Hunter set the upper floors back from one another, becoming the first in the city to employ this style.

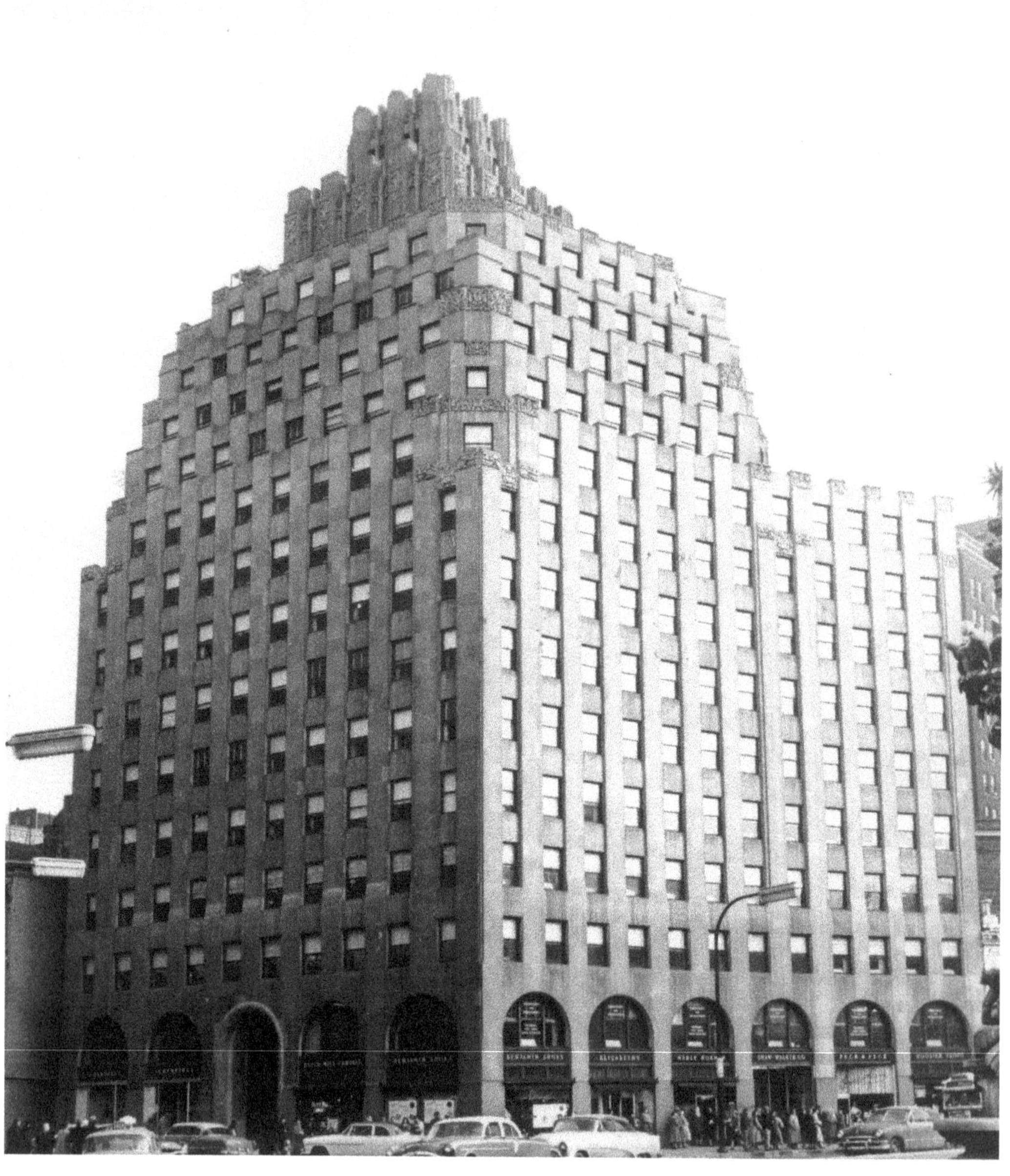

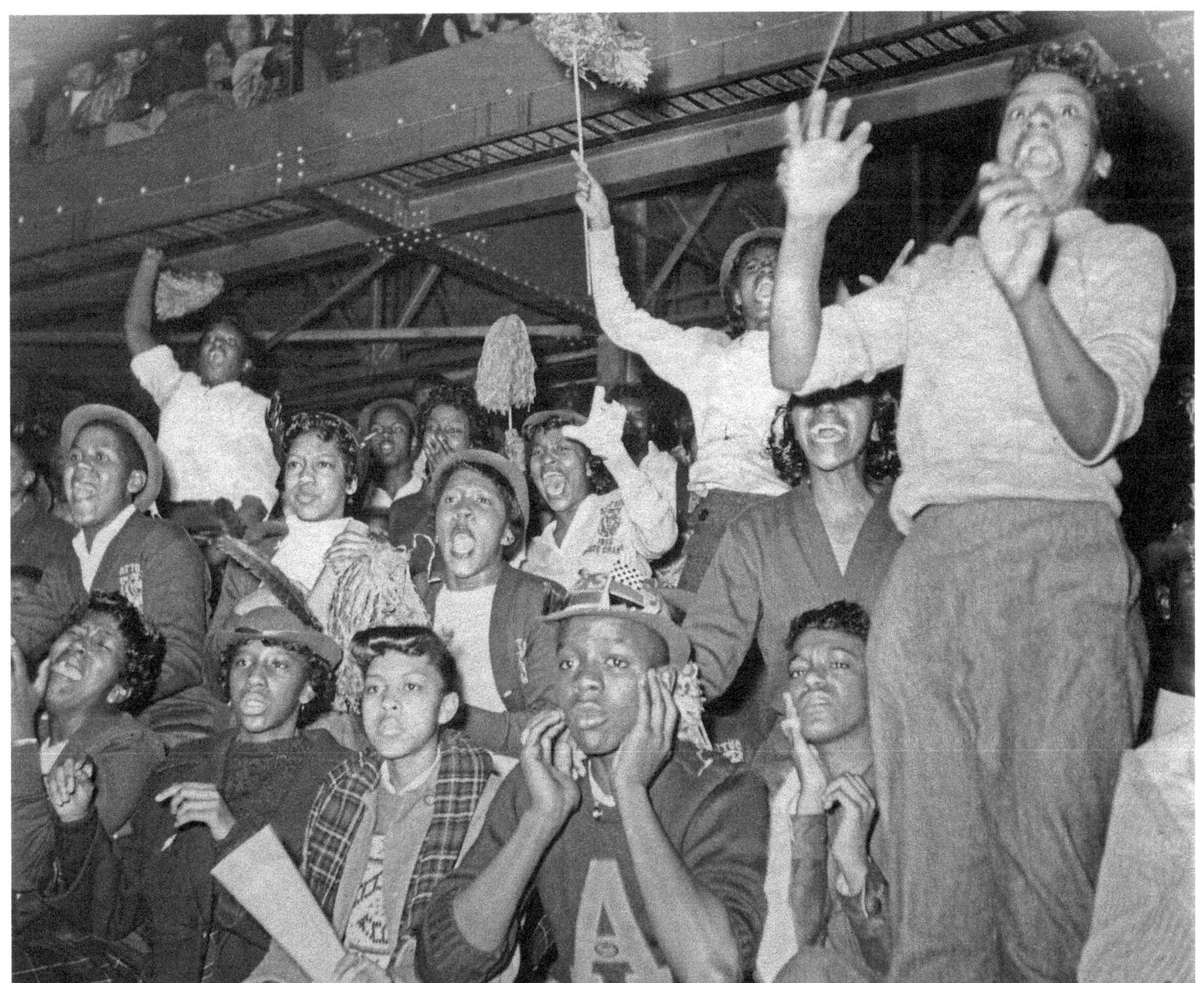

Fans cheer during a Crispus Attucks High School basketball game, 1958. The Indianapolis public school board opened Attucks in 1927 in order to segregate the city's African-American high school students. Even though it received few resources, Attucks had some of the best teachers in Indianapolis, and its students benefited from a quality education. In the 1950's its basketball team was a powerhouse, winning the state championship in 1955, 1956, and 1959. Though Attucks converted to a junior high in 1986, the school board plans to reopen it as a high school, with a curriculum focusing on medical sciences.

Gen. Dwight D. Eisenhower campaigns in Indianapolis, 1952. In this photo Eisenhower parades along Indiana Avenue, in the heart of the city's African-American community. Eisenhower defeated Adlai Stevenson to win the presidency that November.

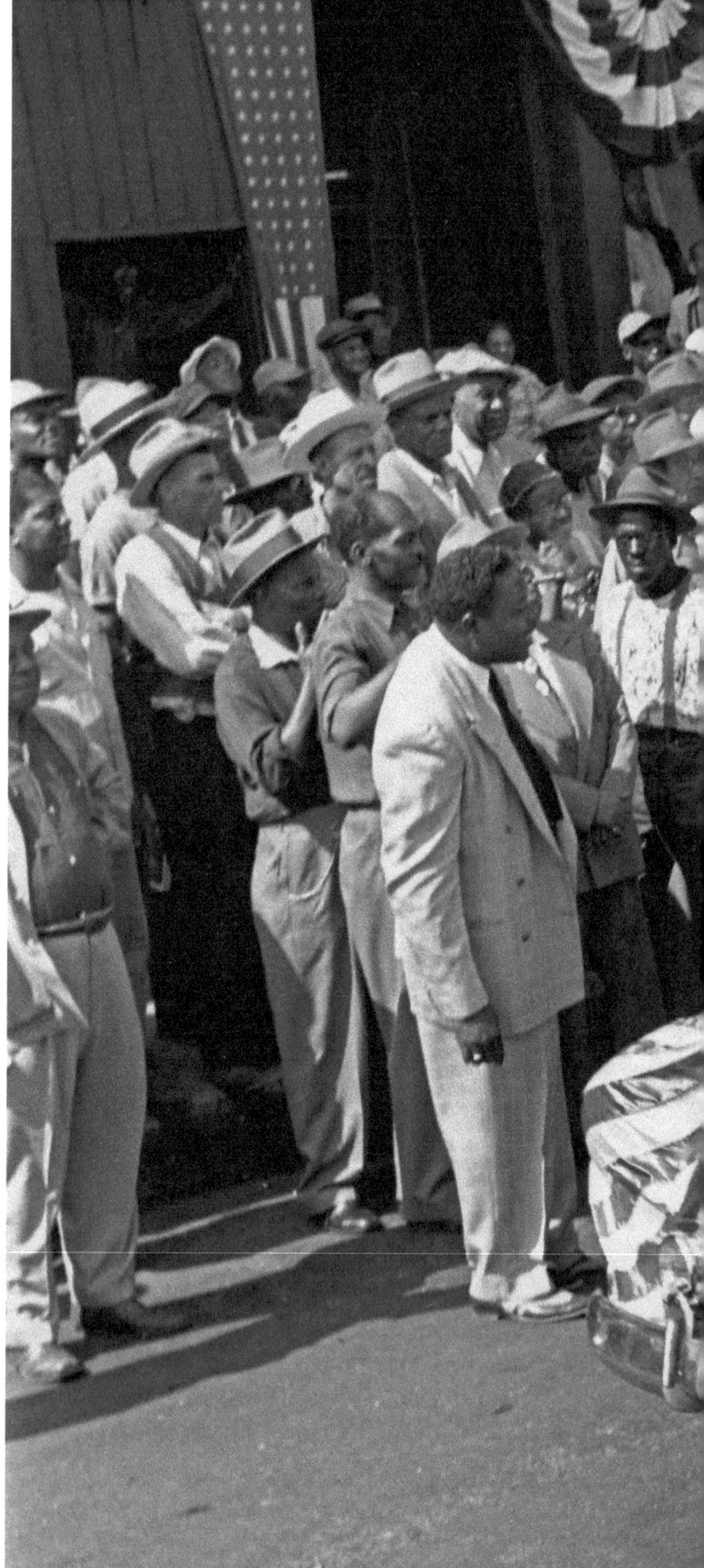

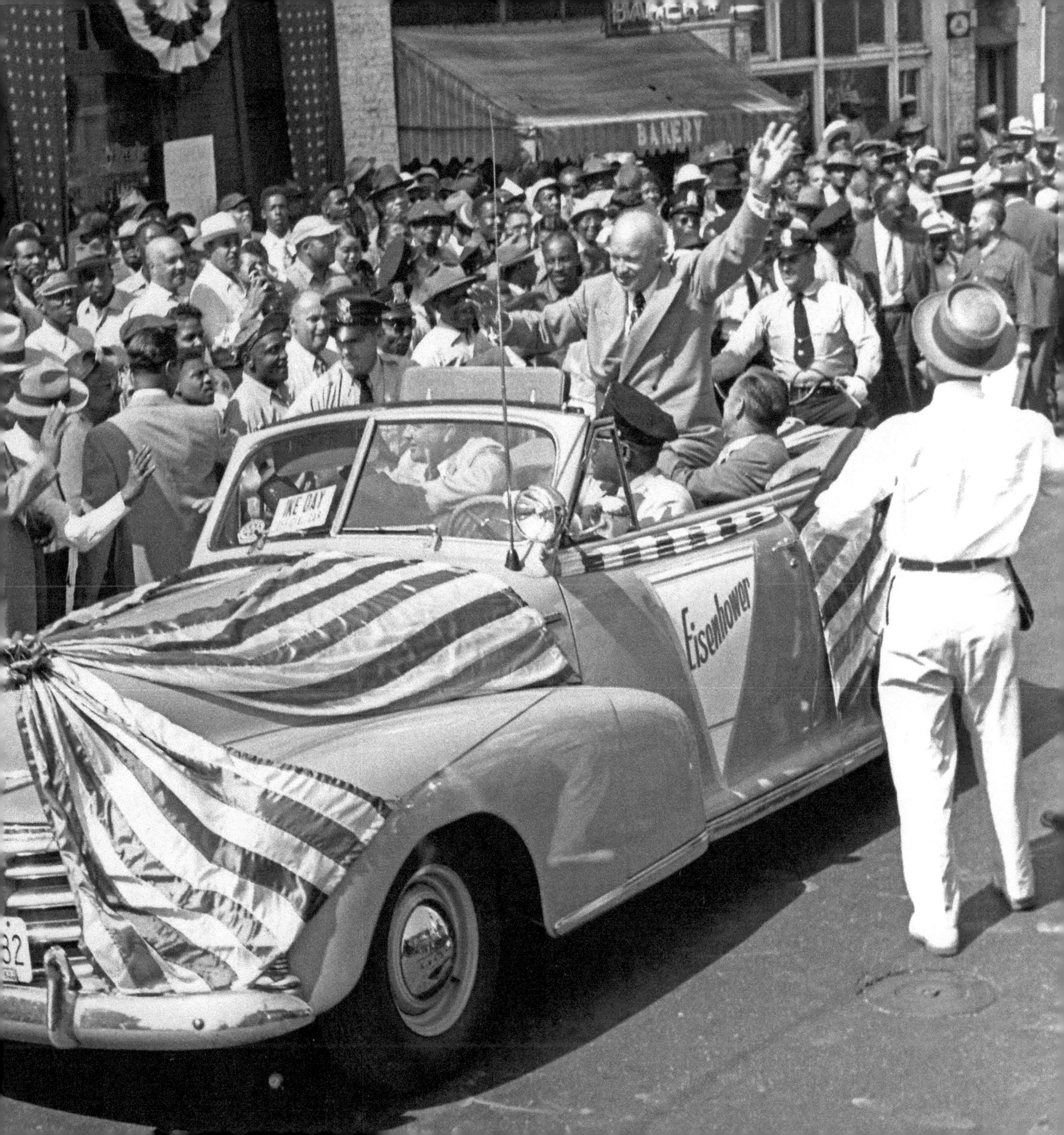
BAKERY
IKE DAY
Eisenhower

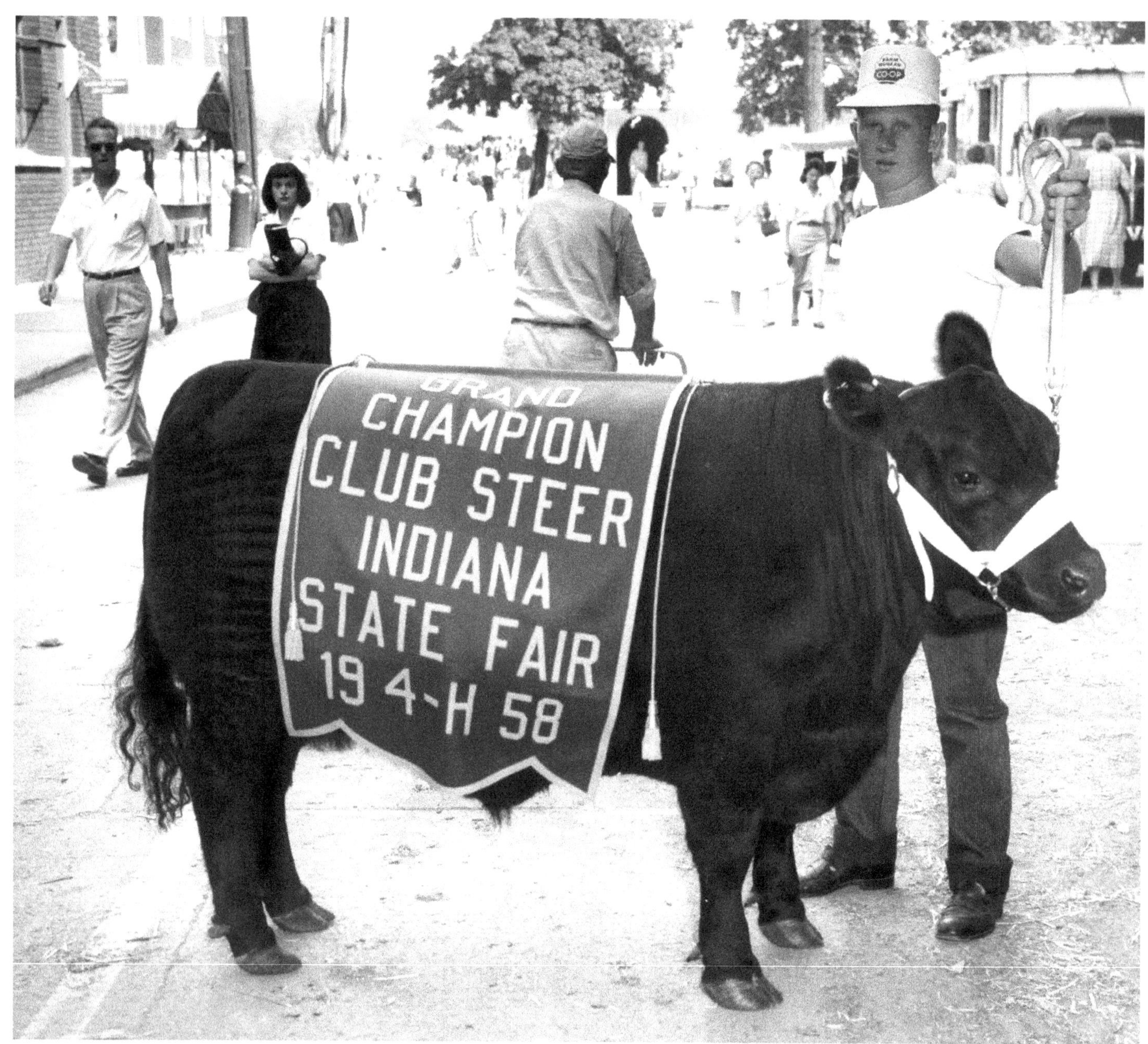

A 4-H member shows off his grand-champion club steer at the Indiana State Fair, 1958.

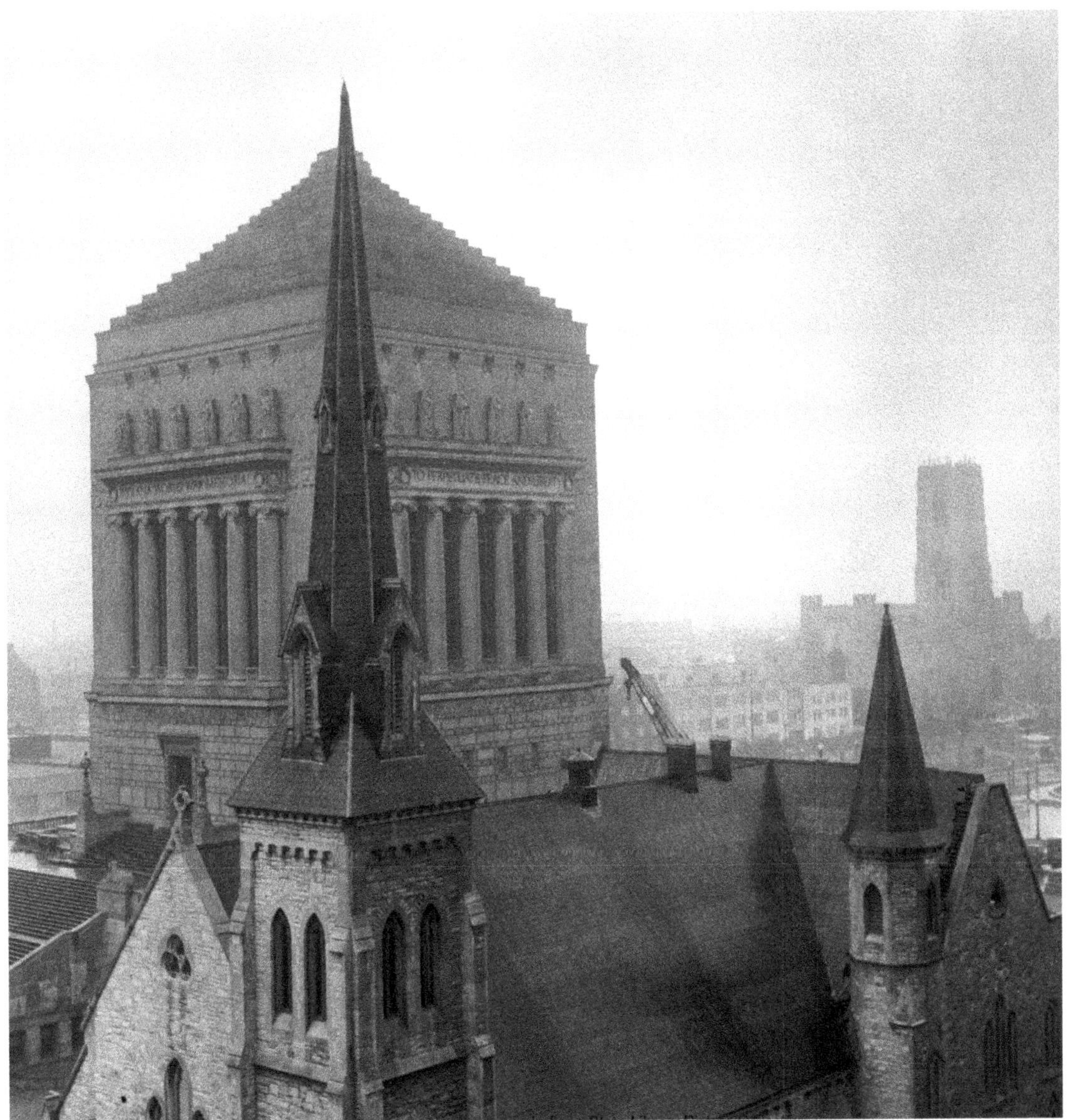

Second Presbyterian Church and the Indiana World War Memorial, 1960. Second Presbyterian, one of the city's oldest and most prominent churches, was founded in 1838. In the years after the Civil War it moved to the northwest corner of Vermont and Pennsylvania Streets, in the neo-Gothic structure seen here. When construction on the war memorial began in 1926, most of the buildings on the block were demolished. Only Second Presbyterian and nearby First Baptist remained, and the memorial hovered over them for decades. Eventually the churches moved as well, and in 1960, presumably shortly after this photo was taken, they were torn down. Second Presbyterian now occupies a large French Gothic building in the 7700 block of North Meridian Street.

The Meridian Street bridge over Fall Creek, 1960. In the early 1900's the city began building concrete bridges over Fall Creek, which resulted in rapid growth on the north side. The Meridian Street bridge was the most lavish. It was designed after the Victor Emmanuel II bridge over the Tiber River in Rome and today retains many of its original decorative features. The Marott Hotel stands in the background of this photo.

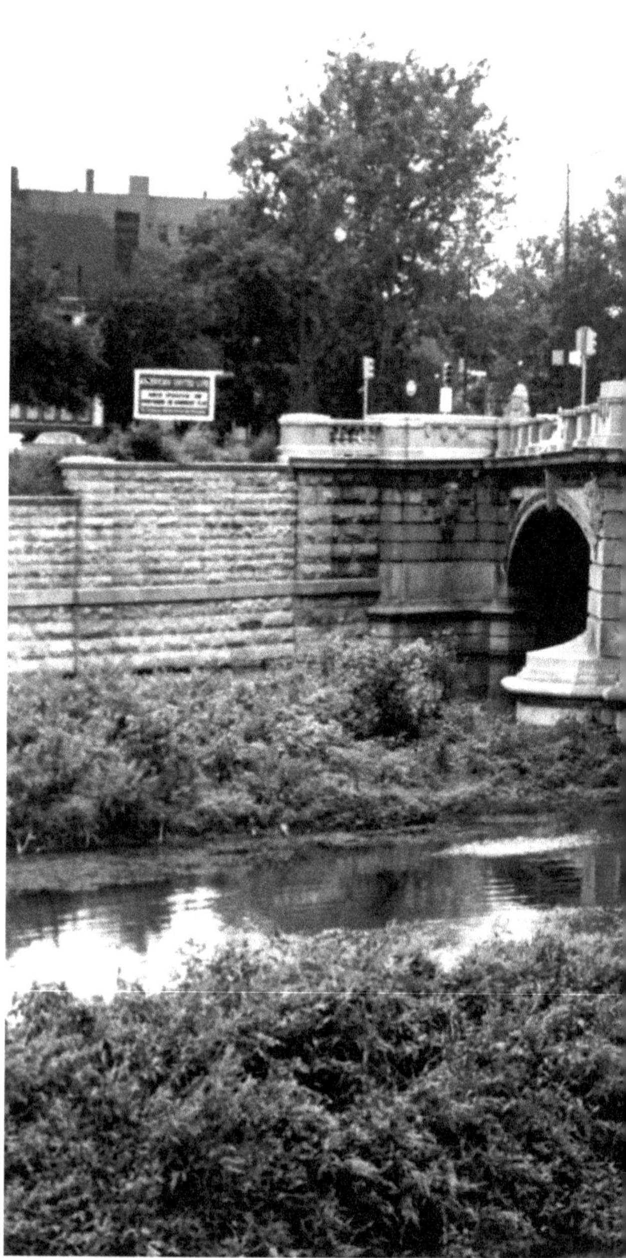

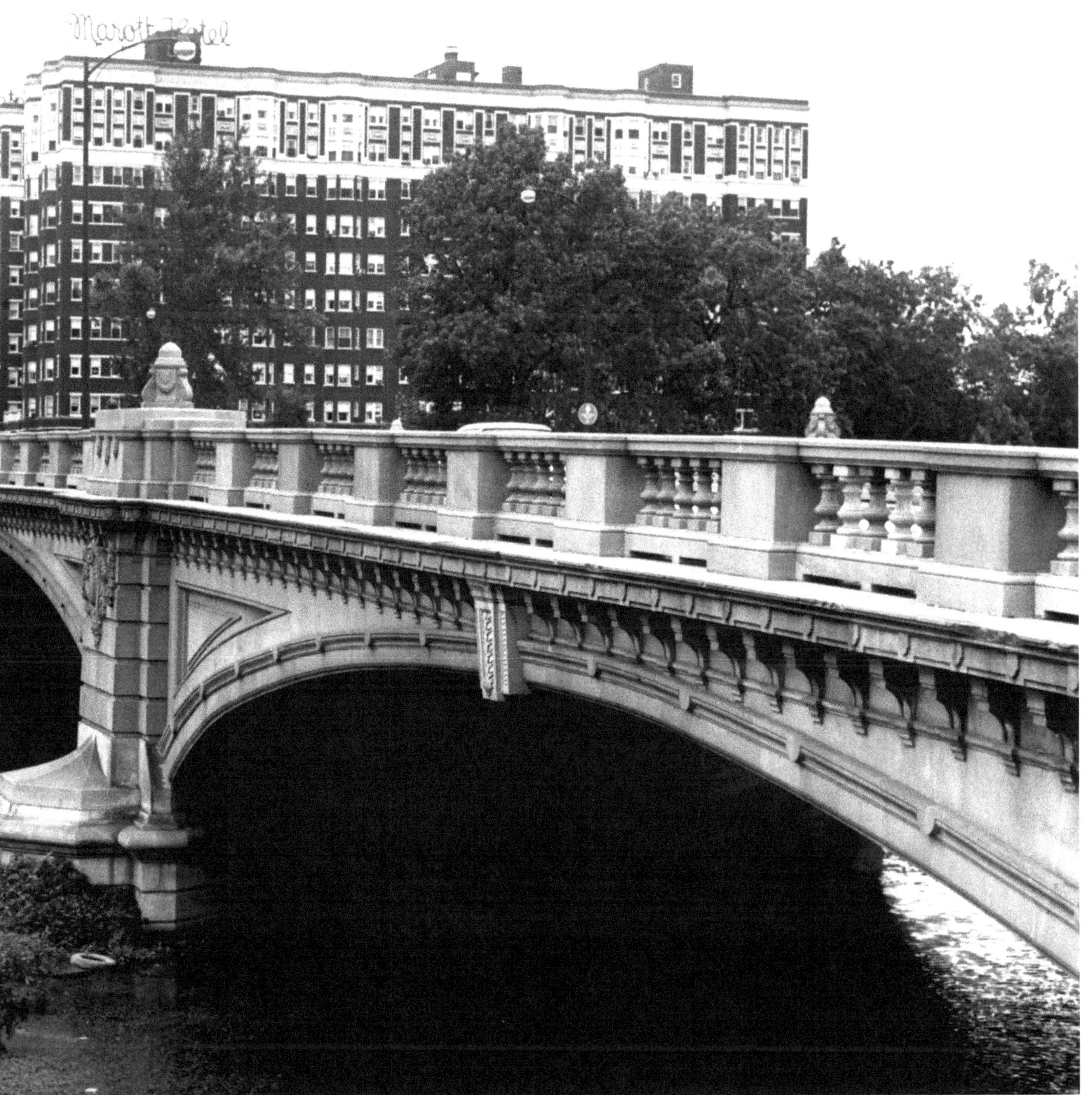
Marott Hotel

A priest and acolytes lead worship at Christ Church Cathedral, circa 1960's.

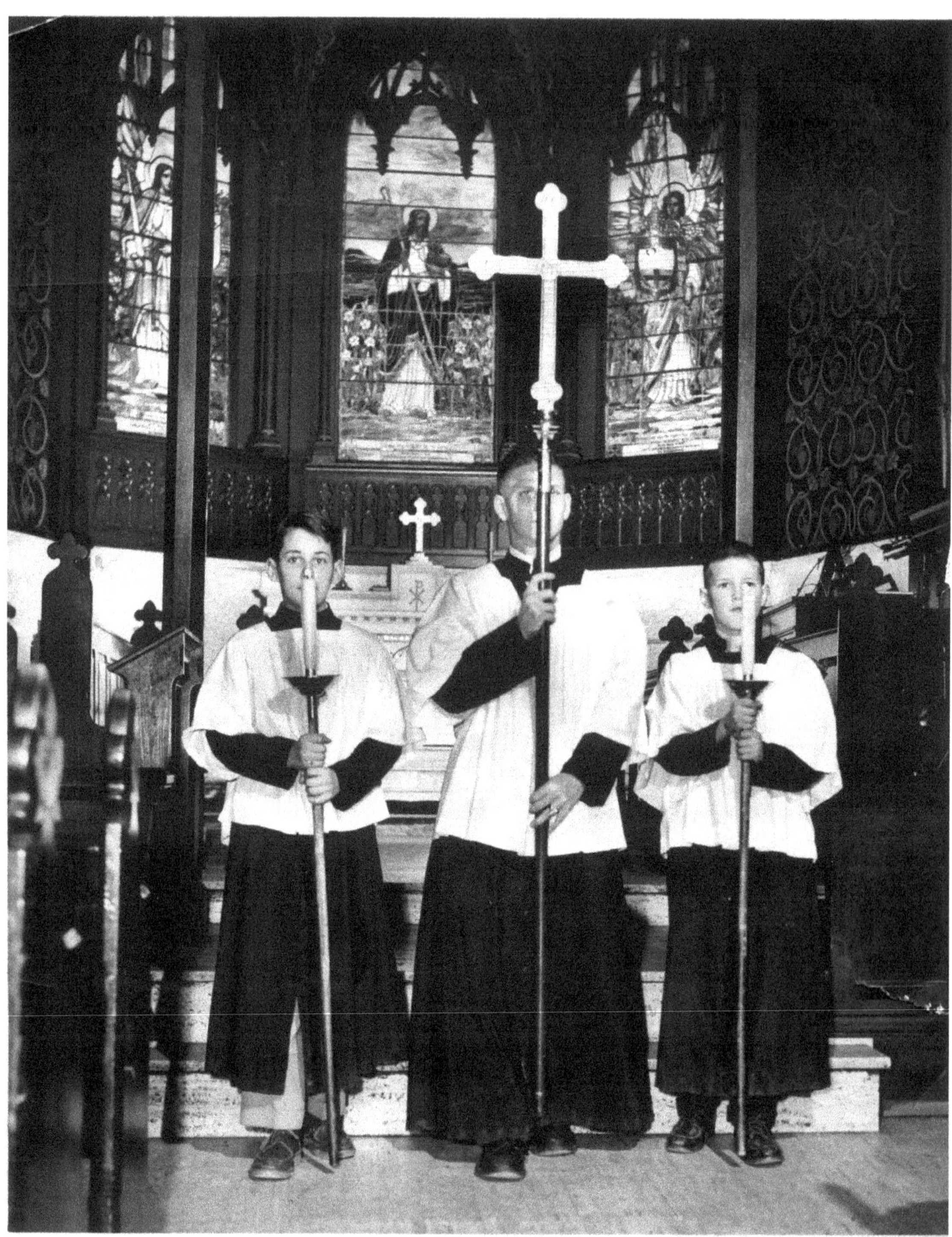

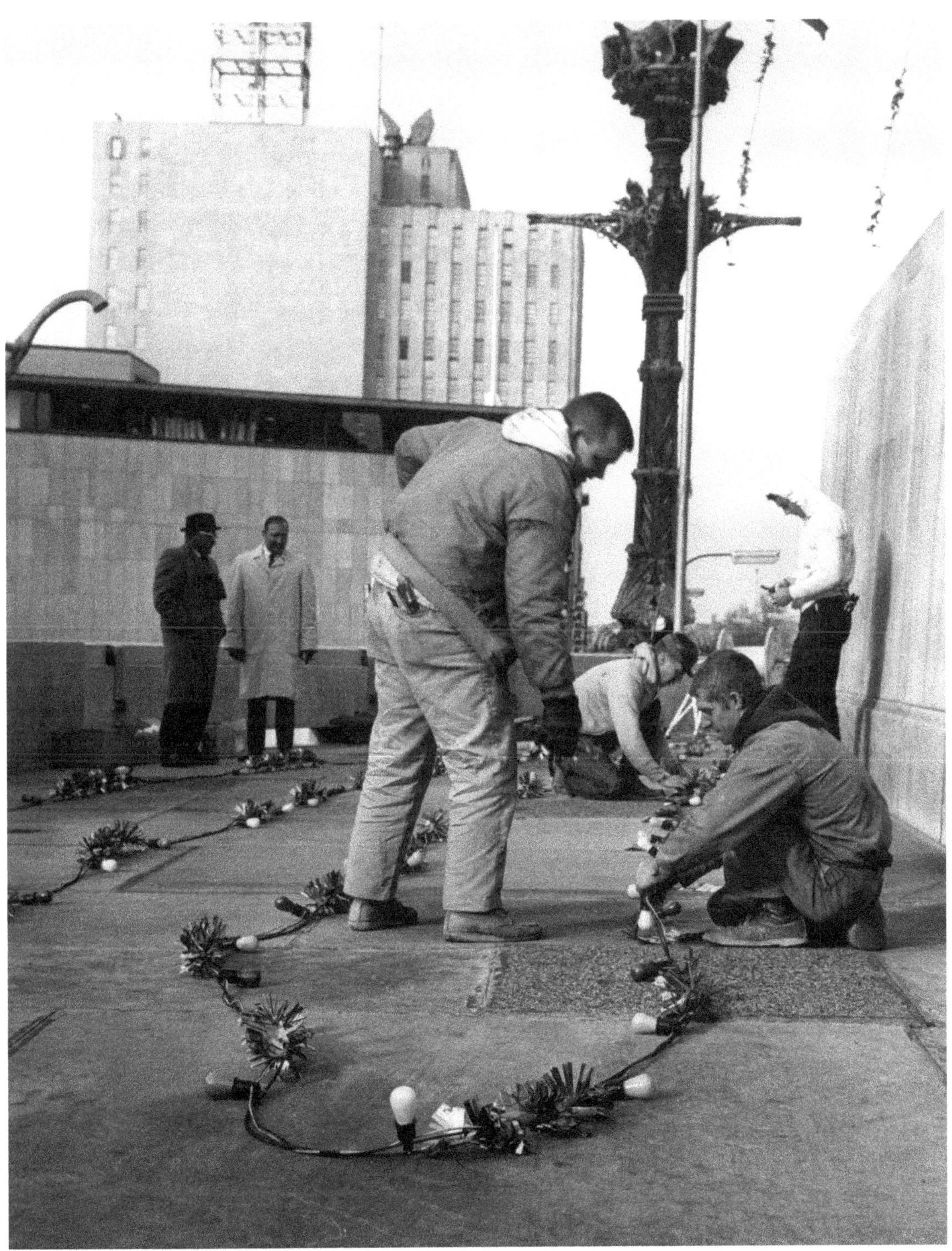

Workers prepare to string lights on the Soldiers and Sailors Monument, 1964. The city has decorated the monument with strands of lights since 1962, and each year the lighting ceremony, which takes place the day after Thanksgiving, draws tens of thousands of spectators.

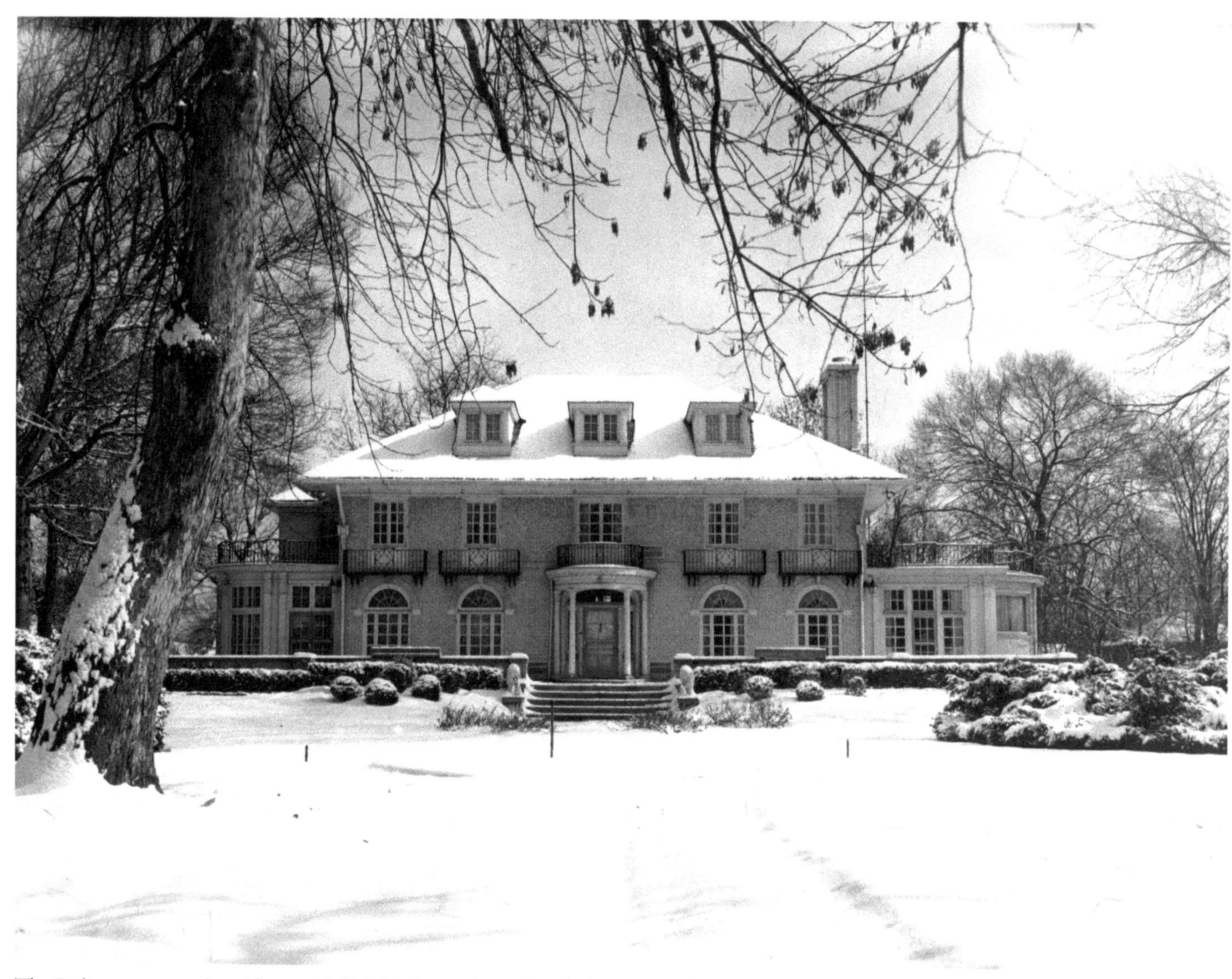

The Indiana governor's residence, 1963. This house, located at 4343 N. Meridian St., served as the fourth governor's residence from 1945 to 1973. William N. Thompson, head of the Stutz Motor Car Company, had it built in 1920. In the early 1970's the state decided that the house was too small to accommodate the governor's family and allow for entertaining, so it bought another home, located a few blocks north near Meridian and Forty-sixth Street.

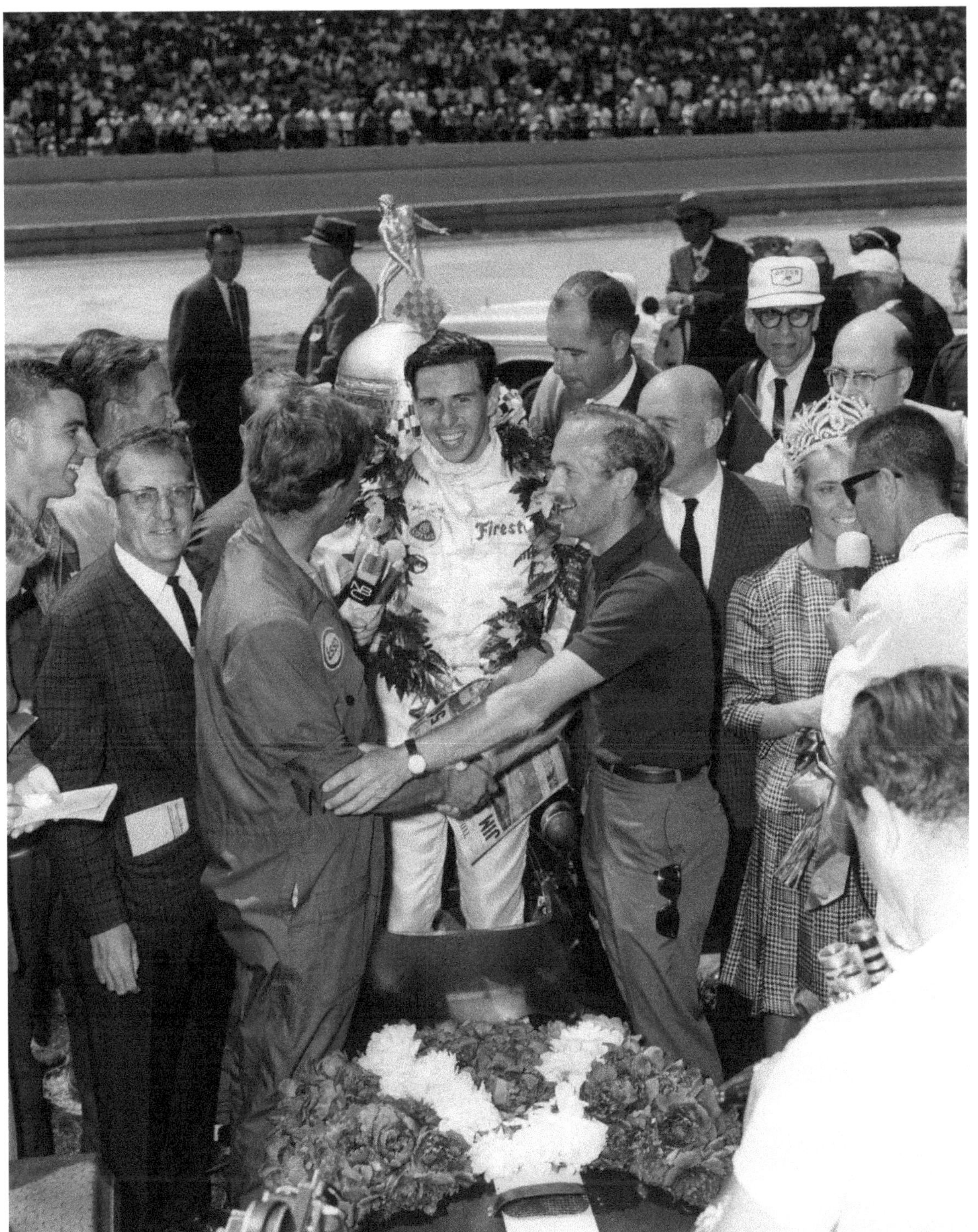

Jim Clark celebrates victory at the 1965 Indianapolis 500. Clark, a Scotsman, dominated the event, leading 190 of the 200 laps and sustaining a 150-mile-per-hour average. He died three years later at a Formula 2 race in Germany.

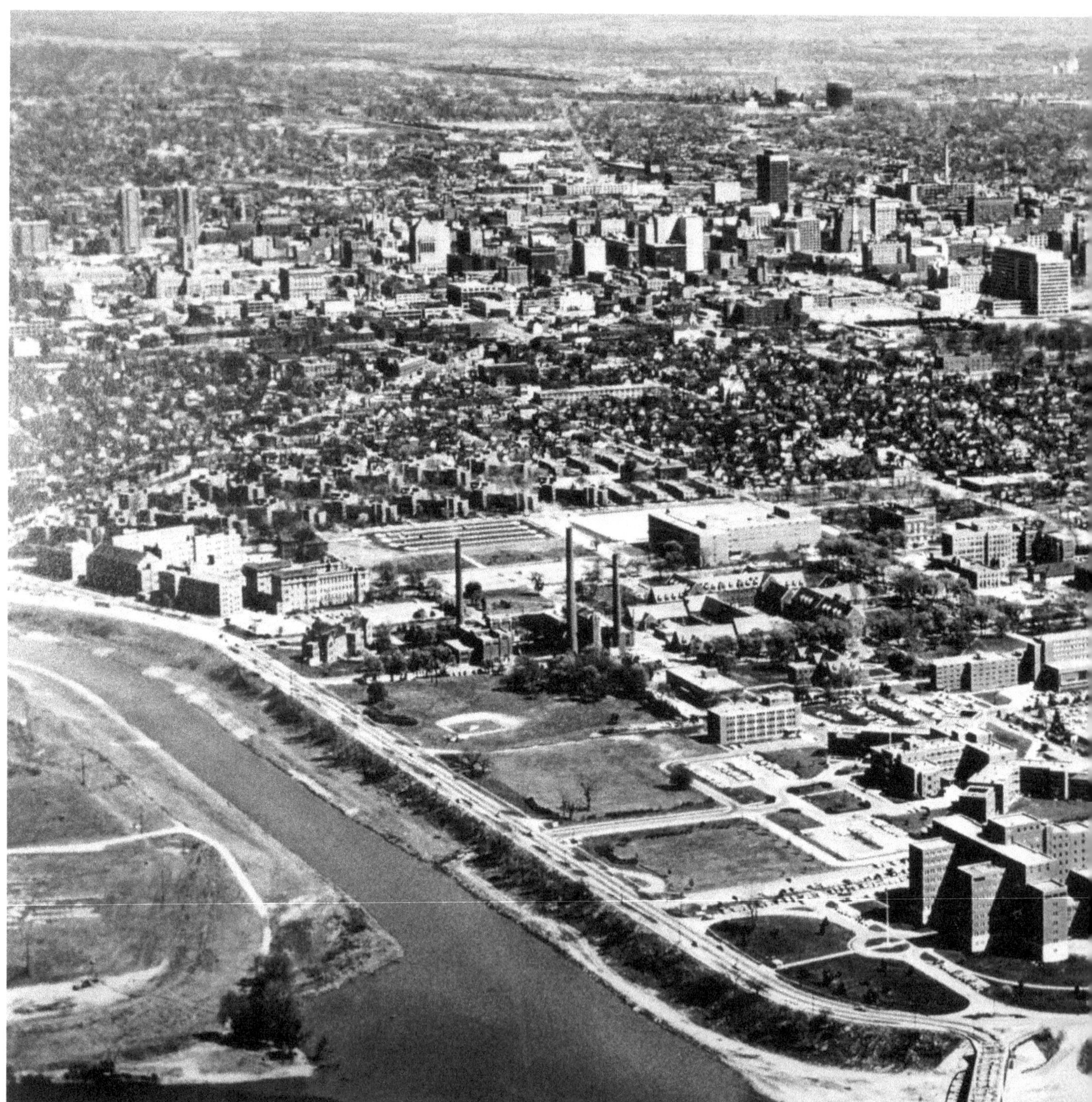

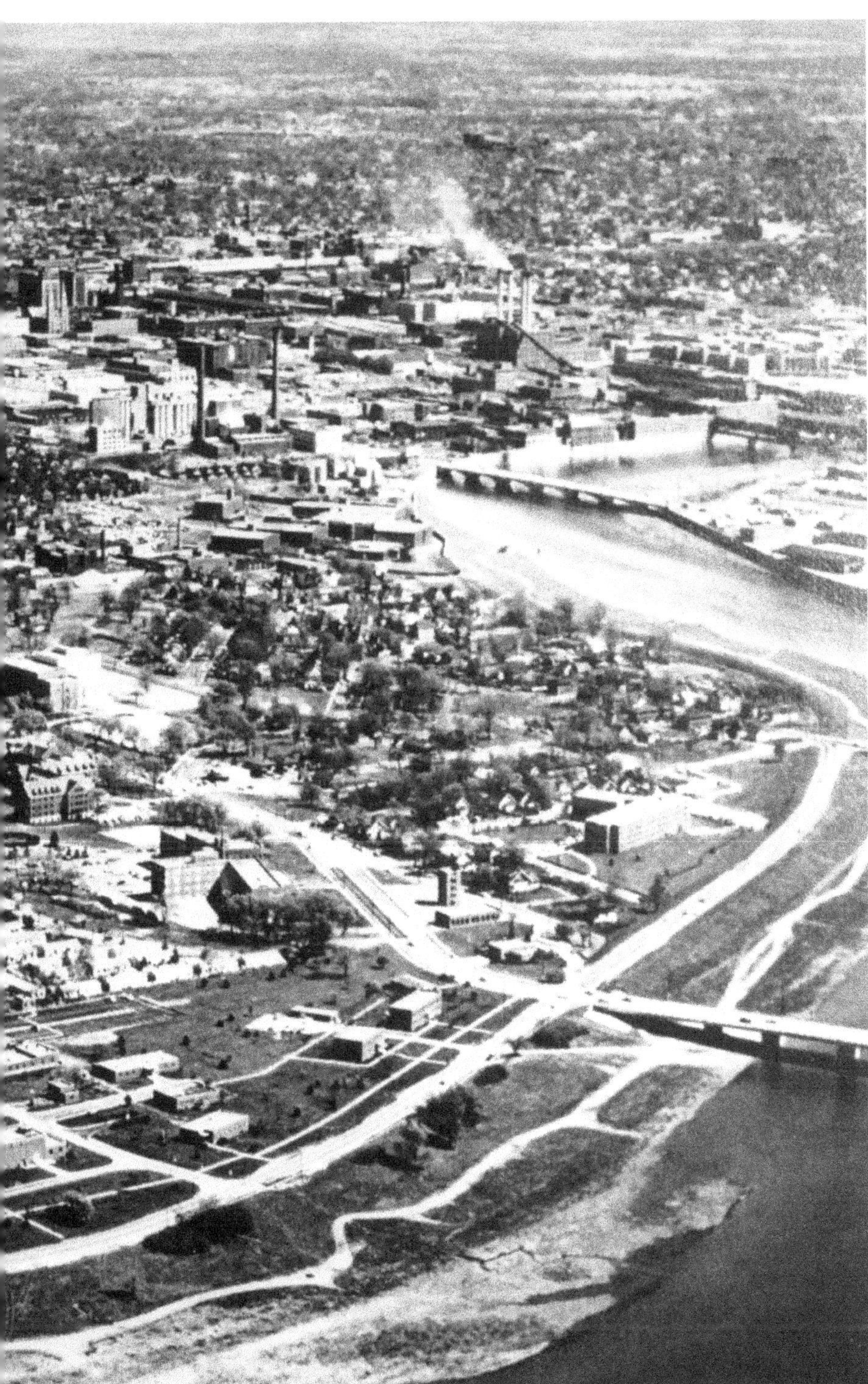

An aerial view of the Indiana University Medical Center and downtown Indianapolis, 1960's. Much of the land surrounding the medical center has been developed for the campus of Indiana University-Purdue University Indianapolis, which was created when the Indianapolis branches of the two universities merged in 1969.

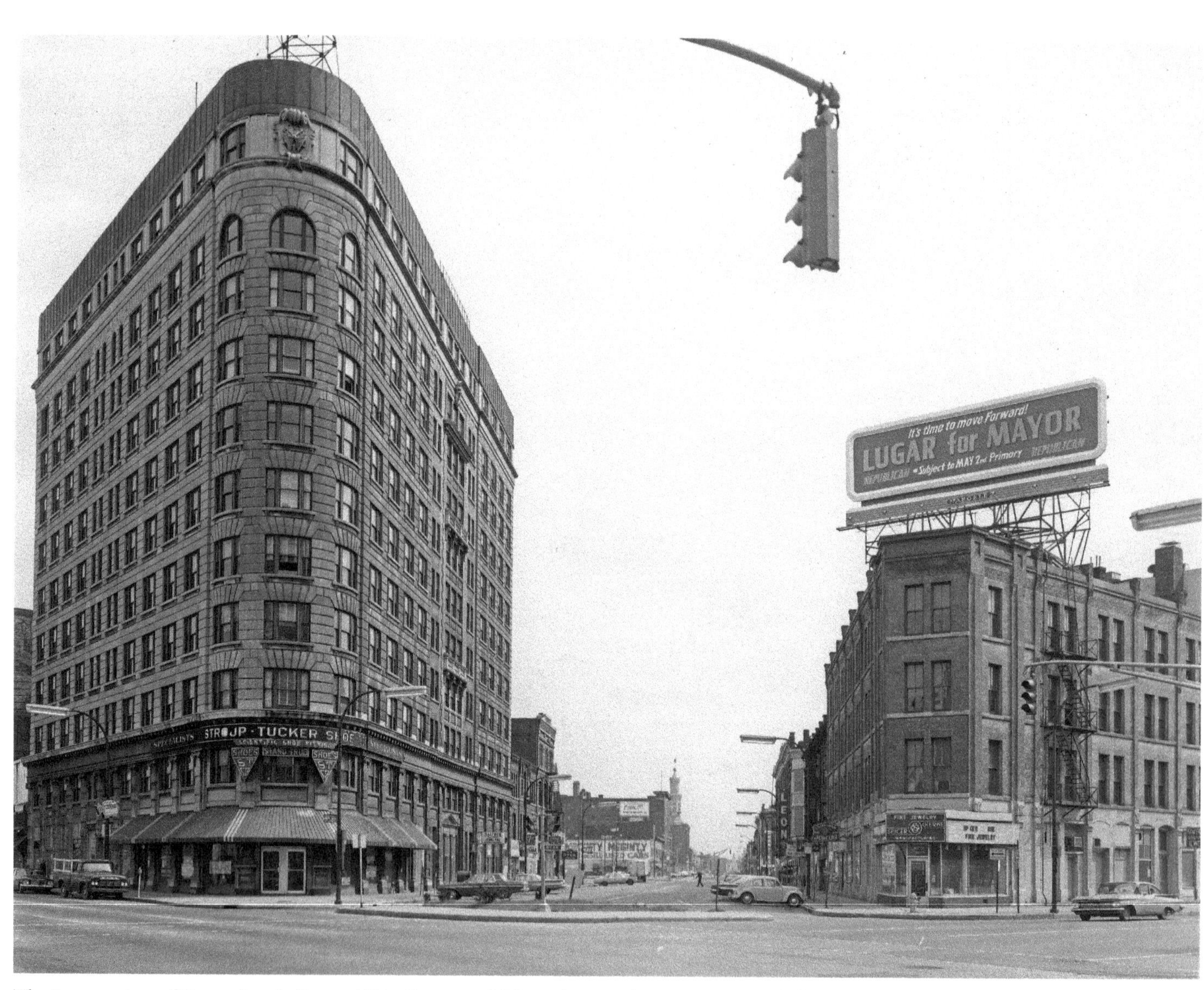

The intersection of Pennsylvania Street, Ohio Street, and Massachusetts Avenue, 1967. At left is the Knights of Pythias building, in its day one of Indianapolis's finest examples of flatiron architecture. It and the other buildings in the foreground were demolished soon after this photograph was taken in order to make way for the Indiana National Bank (today the Regions Bank.)

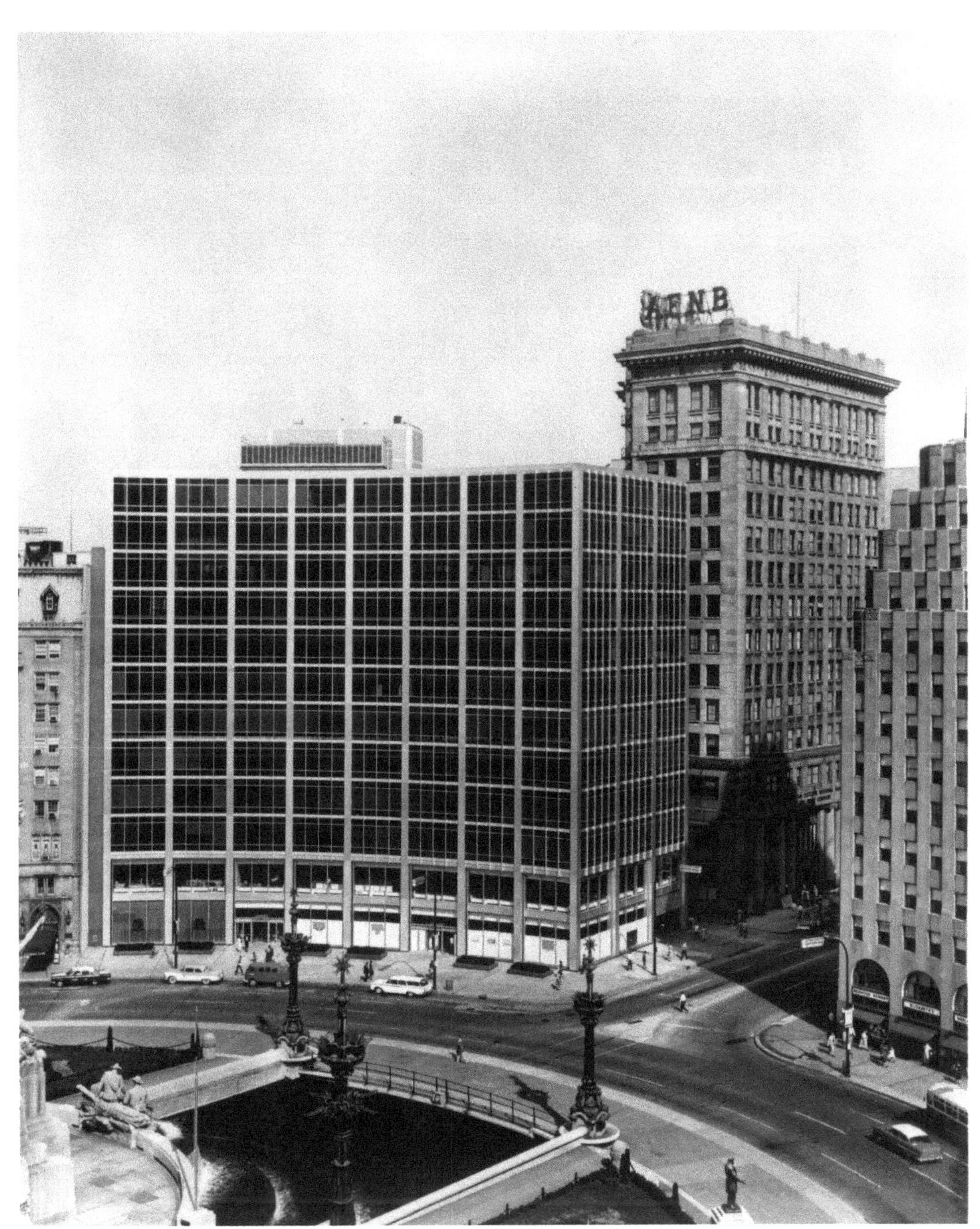

The American Fletcher National Bank and Trust Company, 1968. Chicago architects Skidmore, Owings and Merrill designed this Monument Circle building, the first curtainwall structure in Indianapolis, for the Fidelity Bank and Trust Company. By the time the building opened in 1959, however, Fidelity had merged with American Fletcher National Bank, and the structure served as an addition to the main AFNB headquarters, seen here just to the east on the northwest corner of Pennsylvania and Market Streets.

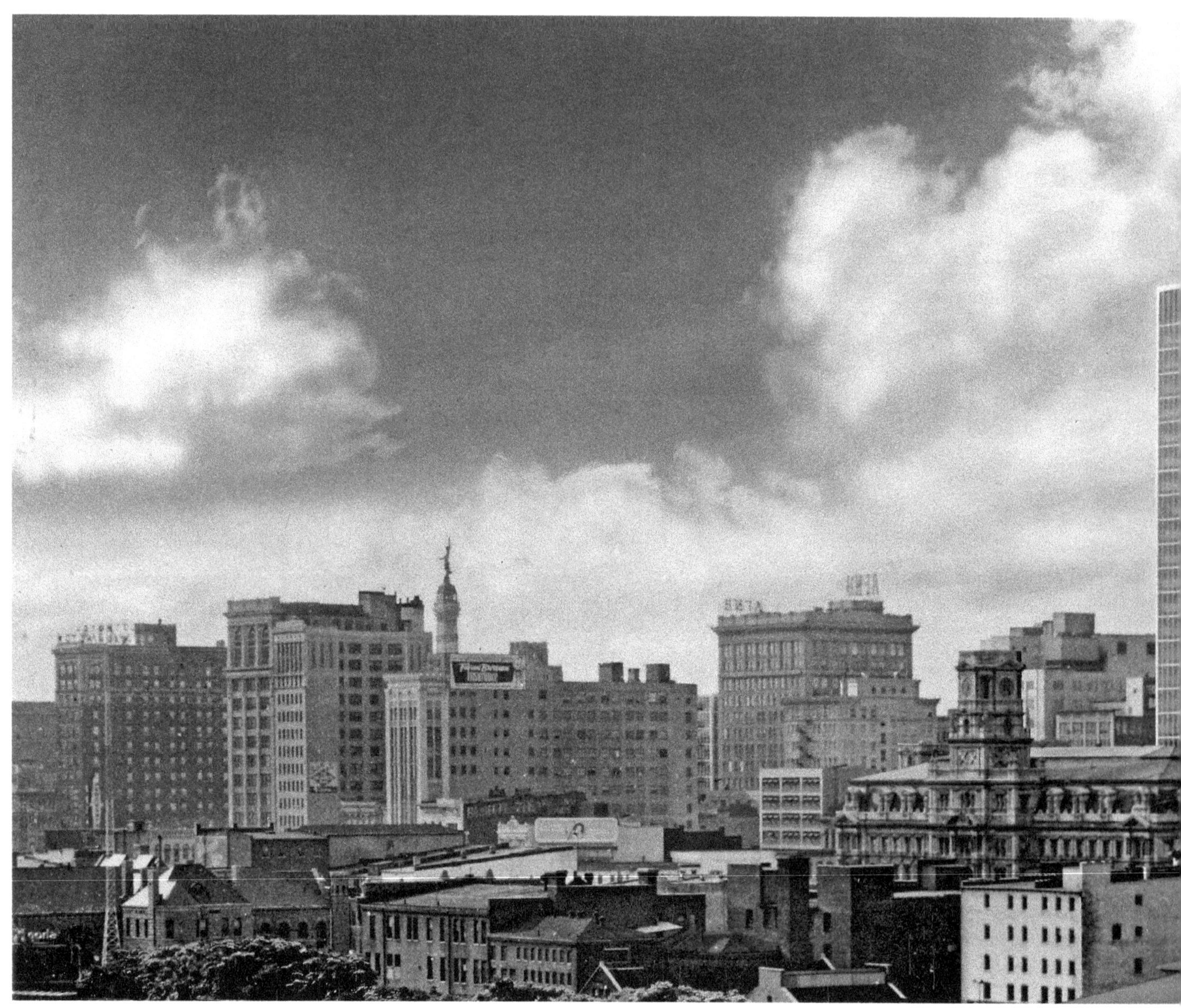

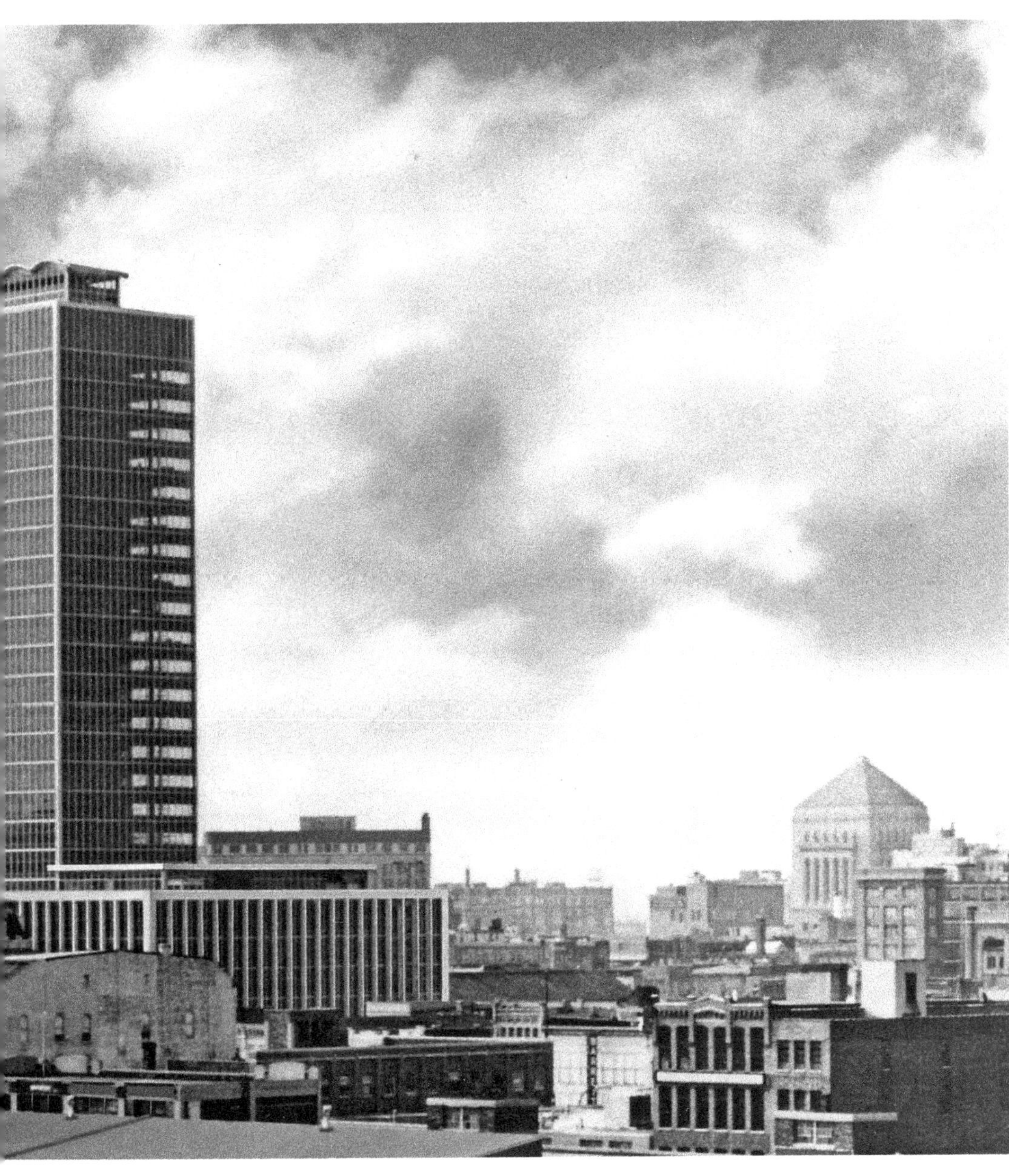

The city-county building under construction, circa 1961. At twenty-eight stories, the structure dominated the skyline of Indianapolis when it was completed in 1962. Despite its stature, however, architectural critics soundly derided it, and many residents lamented the fact that such an undistinguished building had replaced the elegant Marion County courthouse (still seen in this image).

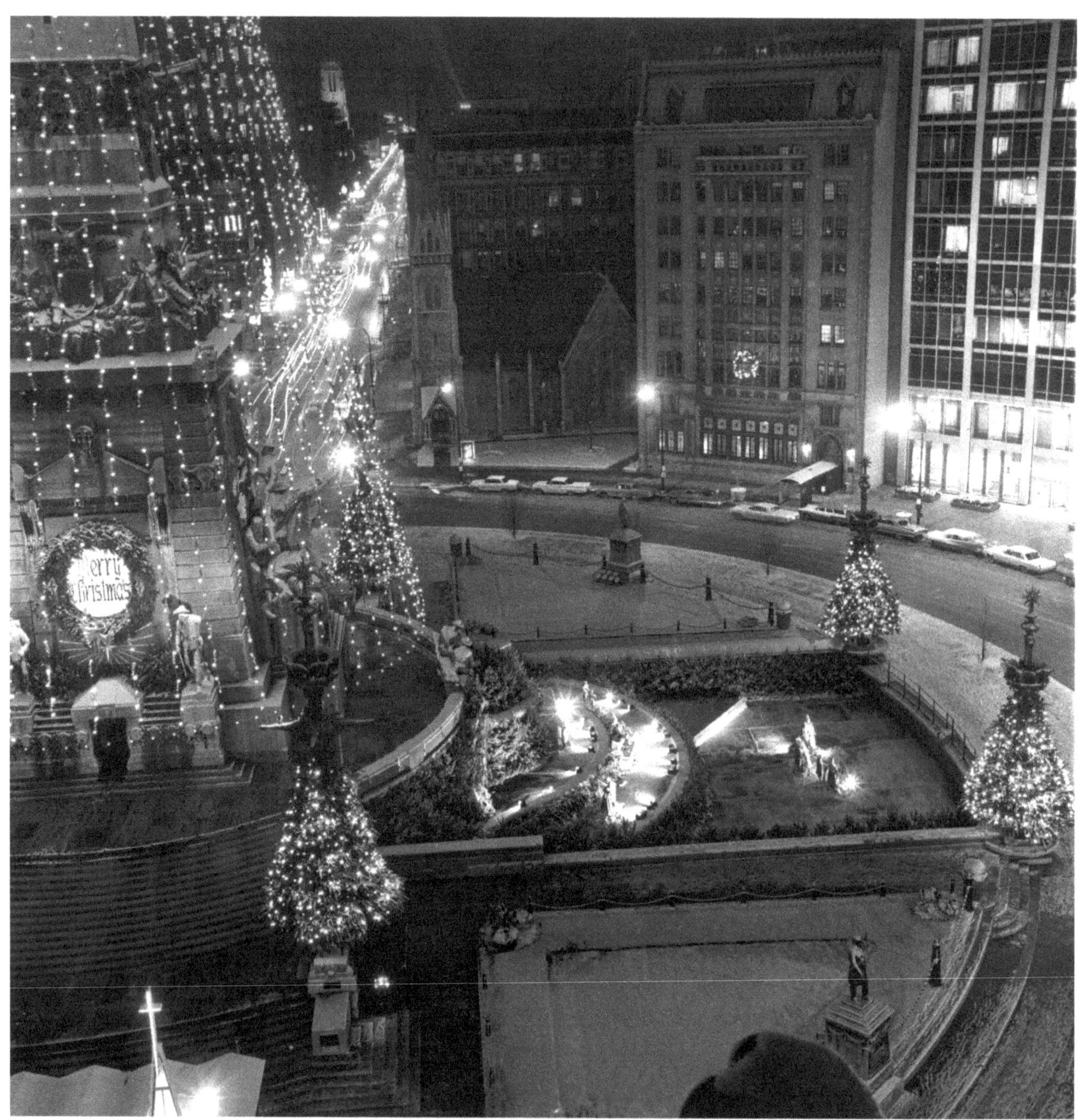

Christmas lights on the Circle Monument, circa 1960's. The monument's caretakers used to freeze water in the fountains and allow ice skating during the holidays, but that practice ended when they discovered it was damaging the structure.

Notes on the Photographs

These notes, listed by page number, attempt to include all aspects known of the photographs. Each of the photographs is identified by the page number, photograph's title or description, photographer and collection, archive and call or box number when applicable, as provided by the source. Although every attempt was made to collect all available data, in some cases complete data was unavailable due to the age and condition of some of the photographs and records.

II **Noon Hour at an Indianapolis Meat Packing House, Aug. 1908**
Library of Congress Prints and Photographs Division
Hine, Lewis Wickes, 1874-1940, photographer Call # Lot 7483, v. 1, no. 0100 [P&P]
Reproduction # LC-DIG-nclc-04461

VI **Washington Street Corner Looking East from Pennsylvania Street**
Indiana Historical Society
P130: Bass Photo Collection
PO130–P–Box1–Folder3–69863-F

X **A Street in Indianapolis**
Manuscript Section, Indiana State Library
Marion Co.–Indianapolis–Streets–?

2 **Entrance to Camp Morton, Indianapolis, 1964**
Manuscript Section, Indiana State Library
Marion Co.–Indianapolis–Camp Morton

3 **Indiana State House Draped for Lincoln's Funeral, 1865**
Manuscript Section, Indiana State Library
Marion Co.–Indianapolis–State House (old)

4 **Old Wooden Bridge over White River Probably Built Sometime in 1930s**
Manuscript Section, Indiana State Library
Marion Co.–Indianapolis–Bridges

5 **Fish Market Where Keilh's + Attached Hotel Theatre is—in existence in 1872, Grand Hotel + Theatre opened by Dixon +Talbott**
Manuscript Section, Indiana State Library
Marion Co.–Indianapolis–Businesses

6 **Nordyke and Marmon Co., 1886 or 1887**
Manuscript Section, Indiana State Library
Marion Co.–Indianapolis–Businesses

7 **Children's Ward in 1887, State Board of Health?**
Manuscript Section, Indiana State Library
Marion Co.–Indianapolis–Hospitals

8 **Early Picture of Indianapolis Public Library**
Manuscript Section, Indiana State Library
Marion Co.–Indianapolis–Libraries

9 **Dedication of Cornerstone of Soldiers and Sailors Monument, ca. 1889**
Manuscript Section, Indiana State Library
Marion Co.–Indianapolis–Soldiers and Sailors Monument

10 **L.G. Twente Upholstering Shop "Photo Taken in 1889—Shop Located on Ft. Wayne Avenue Just North of 10th St."**
Manuscript Section, Indiana State Library
Marion Co.–Indianapolis–Stores

11 **36,000 lb Stone for Soldiers Monument Hauled by C. E. Shover, Indianapolis, Ind.**
Manuscript Section, Indiana State Library
Marion Co.–Indianapolis–Soldiers and Sailors Monument

12 **McCarty St. About 1890**
Manuscript Section, Indiana State Library
Marion Co.–Indianapolis–Streets–M

13 **Virginia Avenue Looking Northwest from Shelby Street, 1886-1888**
Manuscript Section, Indiana State Library
Marion Co.–Indianapolis–Streets–V

14 **Soldiers and Sailors Monument During onstruction, ca. 1890s**
Manuscript Section, Indiana State Library
Marion Co.–Indianapolis–Circle

15 DENISON HOTEL EXTERIOR IMAGE FROM INDIANAPOLIS ILLUSTRATED/ERNEST P. BICKEN II
Manuscript Section, Indiana State Library
Marion Co.–Indianapolis–Hotels

16 ODD FELLOWS BLDG. CORNER OF PENN. + WASH (N.E.) SITE OF PRESENT IOOF BLDG.
Manuscript Section, Indiana State Library
Marion Co.–Indianapolis–Bridges

17 LOOKING NORTH ON MERIDIAN ST. FROM SOUTH OF WASHINGTON ST. EARLY 1890S. MERCHANTS NAT'L BANK ON SW CORNER OF WASH. AND MERIDIAN—NOW L. S. AYERS
Manuscript Section, Indiana State Library
Marion Co.–Indianapolis–Soldiers and Sailors Monument

18 M. P. GRADY SALOON
Manuscript Section, Indiana State Library
Marion Co.–Indianapolis–Buildings–G

19 BOWEN-MERRILL CO., 9-11 W. WASHINGTON, CA. 1898
Manuscript Section, Indiana State Library
Marion Co.–Indianapolis–Buildings–Misc.

20 GRAND HOTEL, MARYLAND AND ILLINOIS, EARLY 1890S
Manuscript Section, Indiana State Library
Marion Co.–Indianapolis–Hotels

21 SECOND PRESBYTERIAN CHURCH WHERE HENRY WARD BEECHER PREACHED
Manuscript Section, Indiana State Library
Marion Co.–Indianapolis–Schools

22 BUSY EAST WASHINGTON STREET CORNER
Indiana Historical Society
P130: Bass Photo Collection
PO130–P–Box 63–Folder 7–211646–F

24 INDIANA INSTITUTION FOR EDUCATING THE DEAF AND DUMB PARADE
Manuscript Section, Indiana State Library
Marion Co.–Indianapolis–School for the Deaf

25 A HOME IN INDIANAPOLIS AROUND THE TURN OF THE CENTURY
Manuscript Section, Indiana State Library
Marion Co.–Indianapolis–Homes

26 MERIDIAN STREET LOOKING SOUTH TOWARD MONUMENT CIRCLE
Manuscript Section, Indiana State Library
Marion Co.–Indianapolis–Streets–Meridian

27 DEACONESS HOSPITAL
Manuscript Section, Indiana State Library
Marion Co.–Indianapolis–Hospitals

28 LOOKING NORTHEAST FROM COURT HOUSE
Manuscript Section, Indiana State Library
Marion Co.–Indianapolis–Aerial Views

30 CARNIVAL ARCH, 1903
Manuscript Section, Indiana State Library
Marion Co.–Indianapolis–Circle

32 ARMORY OF BATTERY A. INDIANAPOLIS
Manuscript Section, Indiana State Library
Marion Co.–Indianapolis–Buildings–A

33 UNIVERSITY PARK, MAN & WOMAN IN BUGGY
Manuscript Section, Indiana State Library
Marion Co.–Indianapolis–Parks

34 INDIANAPOLIS UNION STATION AND VICINITY, JACKSON PLACE
Manuscript Section, Indiana State Library
Marion Co.–Indianapolis–Stations

35 BROAD RIPPLE PARK–2 WOMEN SLEDDING
Manuscript Section, Indiana State Library
Marion Co.–Indianapolis–Parks

36 STREETCAR, 7/31/1890
Manuscript Section, Indiana State Library
Marion Co.–Indianapolis–Streets–M-Z

37 STATE LIFE BUILDING, INDIANAPOLIS
Manuscript Section, Indiana State Library
Marion Co.–Indianapolis–Buildings–S

38 MICKLEYVILLE GENERAL STORE
Manuscript Section, Indiana State Library
Marion Co.–Indianapolis–Mickleyville

39 MICKLEYVILLE GROCERY, JACOB A. MIDLEY AND FAMILY
Manuscript Section, Indiana State Library
Marion Co.–Indianapolis–Mickleyville

40 COMMERCIAL CLUB BLDG.
Manuscript Section, Indiana State Library
Marion Co.–Indianapolis–Buildings–C

41 ENTERPRISE THEATRE
Manuscript Section, Indiana State Library
Marion Co.–Indianapolis–Theatres

42 COLLEGE AVENUE
Manuscript Section, Indiana State Library
Marion Co.–Indianapolis–Streets–C

43 TOMLINSON HALL AND MARKET PLACE FROM NUSSBAUM POSTCARD COLLECTION
Manuscript Section, Indiana State Library
Marion Co.–Indianapolis–Buildings–T

44 NORDYKE AND MARMON CO. INTERIOR OF OFFICE
Manuscript Section, Indiana State Library
Marion Co.–Indianapolis–Businesses

45 UNION STATION AND STREETCAR TUNNEL
Indiana Historical Society
P130: Bass Photo Collection
PO130–69–5–91484–F

46 **Butler College, 1904 (Bass #3074)**
Indiana Historical Society
P130: Bass Photo Collection
folder497–doc10.jpg

47 **Cozy Buffet Indianapolis Jan 5-07**
Manuscript Section, Indiana State Library
Marion Co.–Indianapolis–Buildings–Misc.

48 **N. Meridian St. from Top of Monument**
Manuscript Section, Indiana State Library
Marion Co.–Indianapolis–Aerial Views

49 **A Little "Shaver," Indianapolis Newsboy**
Library of Congress Prints and Photographs Division
Hine, Lewis Wickes, 1874-1940, photographer
Call # Lot 7480, v. 1, no. 0105 [P&P]
Reproduction # LC-DIG-nclc-03216

50 **Washington Street Looking East From Illinois**
Indiana Historical Society
P130: Bass Photo Collection
PO130–P–Box60–Folder8–66244-F

52 **Inter-Urban Terminal**
Manuscript Section, Indiana State Library
Marion Co.–Indianapolis–Transportation

53 **Traction Terminal Bldg.**
Manuscript Section, Indiana State Library
Marion Co.–Indianapolis–Buildings–T

54 **Ancient Accepted Scottish Rite Golden Jubilee Banquet**
Library of Congress Prints and Photographs Division
Bretzman, C.F., 1866-1934
Call # Events No. 74 [P&P]
Reproduction # LC-USZC4-8080

56 **Building in Indianapolis**
Manuscript Section, Indiana State Library
Marion Co.–Indianapolis–Buildings–Misc.

57 **Lombard Building on Washington Street**
Manuscript Section, Indiana State Library
Marion Co.–Indianapolis–Buildings–L

58 **L. S. Ayres Tea Room**
Manuscript Section, Indiana State Library
Marion Co.–Indianapolis–Stores

59 **Blocks, Wm. H. Early 1900s**
Manuscript Section, Indiana State Library
Marion Co.–Indianapolis–Stores

60 **Hiawatha's Farewell**
Library of Congress Prints and Photographs Division
Card # pan1993003081/PP

61 **The Old Grand Opera House**
Manuscript Section, Indiana State Library
Marion Co.–Indianapolis–Buildings–G

62 **Dance Class, 1907-8**
Manuscript Section, Indiana State Library
Marion Co.–Indianapolis–Schools

63 **Monument Circle Market + West Segments**
Manuscript Section, Indiana State Library
Marion Co.–Indianapolis–Circle

64 **Old Court House–NW Corner of E. Wash and Alabama**
Manuscript Section, Indiana State Library
Marion Co.–Indianapolis–Buildings–C

65 **Fruit Venders, Indianapolis Market, Aug. 1908**
Library of Congress Prints and Photographs Division
Hine, Lewis Wickes, 1874-1940, photographer
Call # Lot 7480, v. 1, no. 0084 [P&P]
Reproduction # LC-DIG-nclc-03212

66 **Indianapolis Market, Aug, 1908**
Library of Congress Prints and Photographs Division
Hine, Lewis Wickes, 1874-1940, photographer
Call # Lot 7480, v. 1, no. 0097 [P&P]
Reproduction # LC-DIG-nclc-03213

68 **Indianapolis Moments After Start of First Dash Race in 1909 Meet**
Manuscript Section, Indiana State Library
Marion Co.–Indianapolis–Speedway

69 **Greel's Shoe-Shining Parlor, Indianapolis**
Library of Congress Prints and Photographs Division
Hine, Lewis Wickes, 1874-1940, photographer
Call # Lot 7480, v. 1, no. 0050 [P&P]
Reproduction # LC-DIG-nclc-03204

70 **Indianapolis Newsboys Waiting for Baseball Edition**
Library of Congress Prints and Photographs Division
Hine, Lewis Wickes, 1874-1940, photographer
Call # Lot 7480, v. 1, no. 01137 [P&P]
Reproduction # LC-DIG-nclc-03221

72 **8th Grade Graduation Class of 1910**
Manuscript Section, Indiana State Library
Marion Co.–Indianapolis–Schools

73 **Masonic Temple**
Manuscript Section, Indiana State Library
Marion Co.–Indianapolis–Buildings–M

74 **Noon Hour at an Indianapolis Cannery, Aug. 1908**
Library of Congress Prints and Photographs Division
Hine, Lewis Wickes, 1874-1940, photographer
Call # Lot 7476, v. 1, no. 0130 [P&P]
Reproduction # LC-DIG-nclc-00744

76 Postal Telegraph Messenger, Indianapolis
Library of Congress Prints and Photographs Division
Hine, Lewis Wickes, 1874-1940, photographer
Call # Lot 7480, v. 1, no. 0116 [P&P]
Reproduction # LC-DIG-nclc-03223

77 Kindergarten Class–Probably at the American Settlement on W. Maryland
Manuscript Section, Indiana State Library
Marion Co.–Indianapolis–Schools

78 Moore Grocery Co., Illinois & Ohio
Manuscript Section, Indiana State Library
Marion Co.–Indianapolis–Stores

79 Monument Circle Street Scenes About 1904-7
Manuscript Section, Indiana State Library
Marion Co.–Indianapolis–Circle

80 Indianapolis Candy
Manuscript Section, Indiana State Library
Marion Co.–Indianapolis–Stores

81 Board of Trade, 1912
Manuscript Section, Indiana State Library
Marion Co.–Indianapolis–Buildings–T

82 G & J Tire Co., circa 1910s
Manuscript Section, Indiana State Library
Marion Co.–Indianapolis–Bridges

83 Market House. Stands Around Courthouse
Manuscript Section, Indiana State Library
Marion Co.–Indianapolis–Markets

84 Crowds at Indianapolis Speedway
Library of Congress Prints and Photographs Division
George Grantham Bain Collection
Call # LC-B2-2041-14 [P&P]
Reproduction # LC-DIG-ggbain-08274

86 Dynamite Defendants Leave Federal Building Indianapolis
Library of Congress Prints and Photographs Division
George Grantham Bain Collection
Call # LC-B2-2538-3 [P&P]
Reproduction # LC-DIG-ggbain-11740

87 Jules Goux 1913 Winner, Indianapolis 500
Manuscript Section, Indiana State Library
Marion Co.–Indianapolis–Speedway

88 Judge Parker Speaking - Indianapolis
Library of Congress Prints and Photographs Division
George Grantham Bain Collection
Call # LC-B2-2431-16 [P&P]
Reproduction # LC-DIG-ggbain-10691

90 Wagner Flagging Joe Dawson - Indianapolis
Library of Congress Prints and Photographs Division
George Grantham Bain Collection
Call # LC-B2-2494-13 [P&P]
Reproduction # LC-DIG-ggbain-11279

92 1913 Flood - Scene of Tracks and Engines on Belt R.R.
Manuscript Section, Indiana State Library
Marion Co.–Indianapolis–Floods

93 1913 Flood. Scene on West Morris St.
Manuscript Section, Indiana State Library
Marion Co.–Indianapolis–Floods

94 Robert W. Long Hospital (Indianapolis) Indiana University
Manuscript Section, Indiana State Library
Marion Co.–Indianapolis–Hospitals

95 L. S. Ayers & Co., Sept. 1916
Manuscript Section, Indiana State Library
Marion Co.–Indianapolis–Businesses

96 Early Period Hearse and Funeral Procession
Buchanan Group
Flanner and Buchanan Funeral Centers

98 Indianapolis Traction Terminal and Bldg.
Manuscript Section, Indiana State Library
Marion Co.–Indianapolis–Transportation

99 Col. Robert H. Tyndall Heads a Parade in Downtown Indianapolis
Manuscript Section, Indiana State Library
Marion Co.–Indianapolis–WWI

100 Men on Train with People Sending Them Off
Manuscript Section, Indiana State Library
World War I

101 Looking East on Market Toward Circle
Manuscript Section, Indiana State Library
Marion Co.–Indianapolis–Streets–Market

102 World War I- Big Cash Register
Manuscript Section, Indiana State Library
Marion Co.–Indianapolis–World War I

103 Victory Garden, Children Working in Gardens During 1st World War
Manuscript Section, Indiana State Library
Marion Co.–Indianapolis–Bridges

104 Young Charlene Keller
Buchanan Group

105 Marching and Countermarching on Washington St
Manuscript Section, Indiana State Library
Marion Co.–Indianapolis–World War I

106 Athenaeum (Previously Known as Das Deutsche House) German American Veterans
Manuscript Section, Indiana State Library
Marion Co.–Indianapolis–Buildings–A

107 Parade on Monument Circle, circa 1910s
Manuscript Section, Indiana State Library
Marion Co.–Indianapolis–Circle

108 Frank Geiger with Grandchildren
Buchanan Group

109 Eli Lilly & Co., Interior, 1919
Indiana Historical Society
P130: Bass Photo Collection
folder210–doc7.jpg

110 Cleaning Streetlights, 1919
Indianapolis Power and Light

111 First Row-Start of 500 Mile Race, 1919
Manuscript Section, Indiana State Library
Marion Co.–Indianapolis–Speedway

112 Union Station Grand Hall w/ Wheel Window
Indiana Historical Society
P130: Bass Photo Collection
PO130–69–7–330094

114 Associated Advertising Clubs of the World
Library of Congress Prints and Photographs Division
Card # pan1993001276/PP

115 First State Bank of Indiana, Erected in 1840
Manuscript Section, Indiana State Library
Marion Co.–Indianapolis–Banks

116 Looking West on Washington from Delaware
Manuscript Section, Indiana State Library
Marion Co.–Indianapolis–Aerial Views

117 L. S. Ayres and Co. Office with Women Working
Manuscript Section, Indiana State Library
Marion Co.–Indianapolis–Stores

118 Majestic Building N.E. Corner of Penn. and Maryland
Manuscript Section, Indiana State Library
Marion Co.–Indianapolis–Buildings–M

119 Indianapolis Fire Department Headquarters
Manuscript Section, Indiana State Library
Q–Marion Co.–Indianapolis–Fire Stations

120 Lutheran Orphans Home, Indianapolis
Manuscript Section, Indiana State Library
Marion Co.–Indianapolis–Orphanages

121 Lutheran Orphans Home, Indianapolis
Manuscript Section, Indiana State Library
Marion Co.–Indianapolis–Orphanages

122 North Side of Washington Street and East of Illinois Street, July 13, 1921
Manuscript Section, Indiana State Library
Marion Co.–Indianapolis–Streets–Misc. A-L

123 Indiana University, An Operation, 1923
Manuscript Section, Indiana State Library
Marion Co.–Indianapolis–Libraries

124 Laying the Cornerstone for the National Memorial American Legion Building
Manuscript Section, Indiana State Library
Marion Co.–Indianapolis–Foch Day

125 Marshal Foch Day, Nov. 4, 1921, Indianapolis (Reviewing Stand)
Manuscript Section, Indiana State Library
Marion Co.–Indianapolis–Foch Day

126 Franklin Press Printers, 1920s
Manuscript Section, Indiana State Library
Marion Co.–Indianapolis–Buildings–F

127 Brookside Park During a Baseball Game
Manuscript Section, Indiana State Library
Marion Co.–Indianapolis–Bridges

128 James Whitcomb Riley Hospital Library
Manuscript Section, Indiana State Library
Marion Co.–Indianapolis–Libraries

129 Looking Down Virginia Ave. from Pennsylvania + Washington
Manuscript Section, Indiana State Library
Marion Co.–Indianapolis–Banks

130 Man on Horse at the Indiana State Fair
Manuscript Section, Indiana State Library
Marion Co.–Indianapolis–State Fair

131 Union Title Building, 5-17-1928
Manuscript Section, Indiana State Library
Marion Co.–Indianapolis–Buildings–U

132 Tornado Destruction, 1927
Indianapolis Power and Light

134 Scottish Rite Cathedral, Indianapolis
Manuscript Section, Indiana State Library
Marion Co.–Indianapolis–Buildings–S

135 Methodist Hospital Pharmacy, October 29, 1931
Manuscript Section, Indiana State Library
Marion Co.–Indianapolis–Hospitals

136 Finch Park, June 5, 1929
Manuscript Section, Indiana State Library
Marion Co.–Indianapolis–Parks

138 Public Savings Building, 7-9-1929
Manuscript Section, Indiana State Library
Marion Co.–Indianapolis–Buildings–P

139 American Legion Headquarters, 3-5-1930
Manuscript Section, Indiana State Library
Marion Co.–Indianapolis–Buildings–A

140 M. Clune Furniture Factory, 11-3-1932
Manuscript Section, Indiana State Library
Marion Co.–Indianapolis–Industries

141 Union Trust Bank, 1933
Manuscript Section, Indiana State Library
Marion Co.–Indianapolis–Banks

142 Illinois St. at Night from Union Station
Manuscript Section, Indiana State Library
Marion Co.–Indianapolis–Streets–I

143 Emerichsville Dam, 6-14-1933
Manuscript Section, Indiana State Library
Marion Co.–Indianapolis–Bridges

144 Columbia Conserve Company? Poultry Company
Manuscript Section, Indiana State Library
Marion Co.–Indianapolis–Industries

145 South from Top of Monument-Indianapolis
Manuscript Section, Indiana State Library
Marion Co.–Indianapolis–Aerial Views

146 Trinity Evangelical Lutheran Church, Ohio and East Street
Manuscript Section, Indiana State Library
Marion Co.–Indianapolis–Churches

147 Indiana Womens' Prison, Jan. 1935, Indianapolis, Indiana
Manuscript Section, Indiana State Library
Prisons–Women

148 Raymond Street Bridge, 10-19-1936
Manuscript Section, Indiana State Library
Marion Co.–Indianapolis–Bridges

149 Germania Hall
Manuscript Section, Indiana State Library
Marion Co.–Indianapolis–Buildings–G

150 Railroadmen's Federal Savings, Loan Building
Manuscript Section, Indiana State Library
Marion Co.–Indianapolis–Banks

151 Roosevelt Building, Ill., Washington Sts., 6-9-1938
Manuscript Section, Indiana State Library
Marion Co.–Indianapolis–Buildings–R

152 Central Branch of the Indianapolis Public Library
Indiana Historical Society
P130: Bass Photo Collection
PO130–Box39–Folder1–238558-F

154 Marion County Courthouse
Manuscript Section, Indiana State Library
Marion Co.–Indianapolis–Buildings–C

155 Indiana State House from Senate and Washington Streets
Manuscript Section, Indiana State Library
Marion Co.–Indianapolis–State House

156 E. Washington Off of Roof of Lincoln Hotel, 2/8/58
Manuscript Section, Indiana State Library
Marion Co.–Indianapolis–Streets–Washington

158 Merchants National (S.E. Corner Wash. + Meridian)
Manuscript Section, Indiana State Library
Marion Co.–Indianapolis–Banks

159 James Whitcomb Riley Hospital for Children
Manuscript Section, Indiana State Library
Marion Co.–Indianapolis–Hospitals

160 Indiana State Fair Horse Pull
Manuscript Section, Indiana State Library
Marion Co.–Indianapolis–State Fair

161 Office of Civilian Defense Giving Award to Indianapolis Power and Light
Manuscript Section, Indiana State Library
Marion Co.–Indianapolis–Businesses

162 Red Cross Canteen, Mar 22, 1944 (World War II)
Manuscript Section, Indiana State Library
World War II

164 Parade on Monument Circle, ca. 1950s
Manuscript Section, Indiana State Library
Marion Co.–Indianapolis–Circle

165 Soldiers and Sailors Monument at Night
Manuscript Section, Indiana State Library
Marion Co.–Indianapolis–Circle

166 June 9, 1947 - View from #60 Blacherne Indianapolis
Manuscript Section, Indiana State Library
Marion Co.–Indianapolis–Aerial Views

168 Fancy Steppers
Manuscript Section, Indiana State Library
Marion Co.–Indianapolis–State Fair

170 Illinois Building, Illinois + Market St., 1947
Manuscript Section, Indiana State Library
Marion Co.–Indianapolis–Buildings–I

171 Church Federation Reformation Day Services Oct. 29, 1950, Cadle Tabernacle
Manuscript Section, Indiana State Library
Marion Co.–Indianapolis–Buildings–C

172 English Hotel on Monument Circle, 1949
Manuscript Section, Indiana State Library
Marion Co.–Indianapolis–Hotels

174 Inland Building, 1950
Manuscript Section, Indiana State Library
Marion Co.–Indianapolis–Buildings–I

175 Meridian at Washington, 1950s
Manuscript Section, Indiana State Library
Marion Co.–Indianapolis–Streets–Meridian

176 N.W. Segment of Circle Showing J.C. Penney and F.W. Woolworth Stores
Manuscript Section, Indiana State Library
Marion Co.–Indianapolis–Circle

178 Women and Men Working on Telephone Factory Assembly Line
Manuscript Section, Indiana State Library
Marion Co.–Indianapolis–Industries

179 Hotel Lincoln
Manuscript Section, Indiana State Library
Marion Co.–Indianapolis–Hotels

180 Circle Tower Building, 1957
Manuscript Section, Indiana State Library
Marion Co.–Indianapolis–Buildings–C

181 Crispus Attucks H.S. Basketball Fans
Indiana Historical Society
P303: Indianapolis Recorder Collection
P303–Box9–Folder4–C7853

182 Ike Takes a Beach Head: Indiana Avenue
Indiana Historical Society
P266: O. James Fox Collection
p266–Box1–18

184 Grand Champion Club Steer, Indiana State Fair 1958
Manuscript Section, Indiana State Library
Marion Co.–Indianapolis–State Fair

185 Old 2d Presbyterian, 14 Jan, 1960, Indiana World War Memorial in Background
Manuscript Section, Indiana State Library
Marion Co.–Indianapolis–Churches

186 Meridian St. Fall Creek Bridge, June 19, 1960 with Marott Hotel in Background
Manuscript Section, Indiana State Library
Marion Co.–Indianapolis–Bridges

188 Christ Church Indianapolis
Manuscript Section, Indiana State Library
Marion Co.–Indianapolis–Churches

189 Hatfield Electric, Bill Southern, Jack Arthur (Monument) Circle, April 1964
Manuscript Section, Indiana State Library
Marion Co.–Indianapolis–Circle

190 1963, Governors Mansion, 4343 N. Meridian St., Indianapolis
Manuscript Section, Indiana State Library
Marion Co.–Indianapolis–Governors Mansion

191 Jim Clark-Winner 1965
Manuscript Section, Indiana State Library
Marion Co.–Indianapolis–Speedway

192 Indiana University Medical Center, Indianapolis Campus
Manuscript Section, Indiana State Library
Marion Co.–Indianapolis–Hospitals

194 Massachusetts Avenue, "Lugar for Mayor" Billboard
Indiana Historical Society
P130: Bass Photo Collection
folder419–doc42.jpg

195 American Fletcher Nat'l Bank + Trust Co., 101 Monument Circle, 1968
Manuscript Section, Indiana State Library
Marion Co.–Indianapolis–Banks

196 Indianapolis Skyline: City-County Building
Indiana Historical Society
P130: Bass Photo Collection
folder88–doc1.jpg

198 Circle Monument in December
Manuscript Section, Indiana State Library
Marion Co.–Indianapolis–Circle

206 James Whitcomb Riley with a Group of Children
Indiana Historical Society
M660: Indianapolis-Marion County Public Library Riley Collection
MO660–Box34–Folder6–003

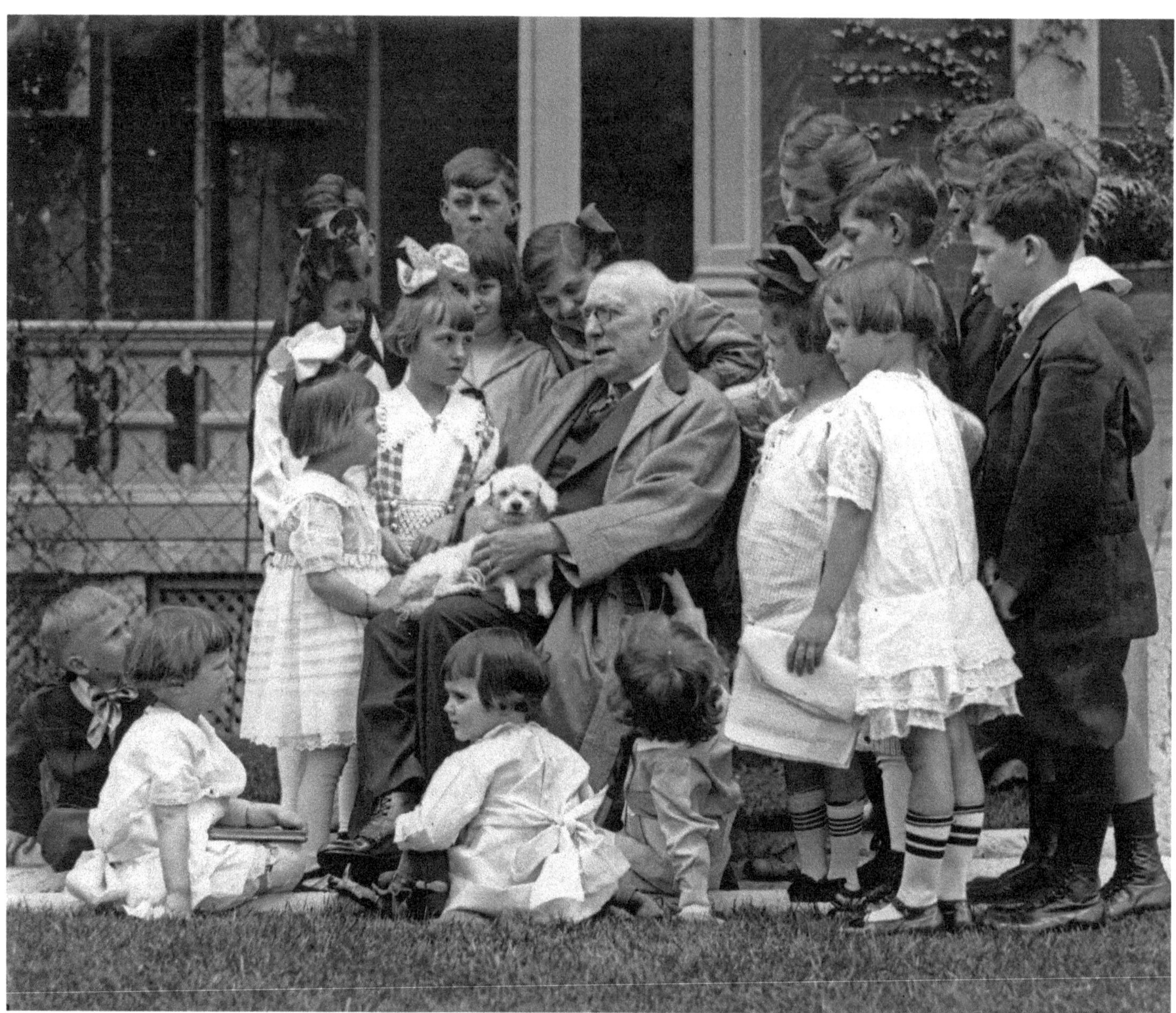

James Whitcomb Riley and children, 1916. Riley, one of the most popular poets in the late-nineteenth and early twentieth centuries, was well known for writing poems in the Hoosier dialect. Children especially loved him and were drawn to many of the characters he created, including Little Orphan Annie and the Raggedy Man. Here they gather around him and his dog Lockerbie on the lawn of his Indianapolis home. The photographer recorded this scene as Riley and the children were being filmed for a movie celebrating Indiana's centennial.

HISTORIC PHOTOS OF INDIANAPOLIS

By the mid nineteenth century, the city of Indianapolis was a vibrant cultural center. Through the Civil War, the early twentieth century, two World Wars, and into the modern era, Indianapolis has continued to grow and prosper by overcoming adversity and maintaining the strong independent culture of its citizens.

This volume, *Historic Photos of Indianapolis,* captures this journey through still photography from the finest archives of local, state, and private collections. From the Civil War, the Depression era, and to the building of a modern metropolis, *Historic Photos of Indianapolis* follows life, government, education, and events throughout the city's history.

The book captures unique and rare scenes through the lens of hundreds of historic photographs. Published in striking black and white, the images communicate historic events and everyday life of two centuries of people building a unique and prosperous city.

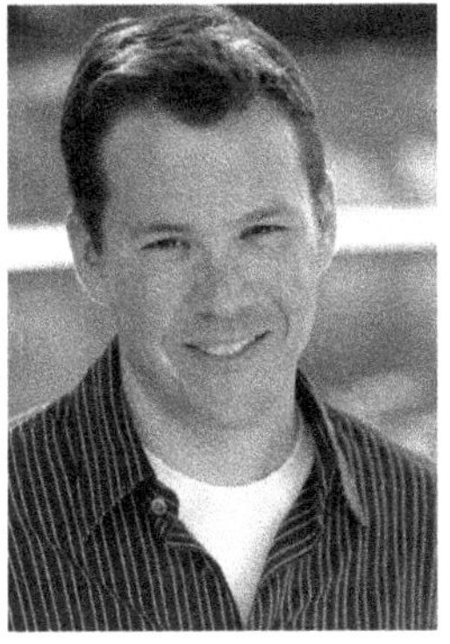

George R. Hanlin worked at the Indiana Historical Society for eleven years, editing award-winning books such as *Indiana in Stereo: Three-Dimensional Views of the Heartland* and *Skirting the Issue: Stories of Indiana's Historical Women Artists.* He also helped produce the Society's illustrated magazine, *Traces of Indiana and Midwestern History.* He studied journalism, Spanish, and history at Indiana University and currently works for FlashPoint, a human-resource consulting firm in Indianapolis. He is a sixth-generation Hoosier, raised in Jay County on a farm his family has owned since 1837.

WWW.TURNERPUBLISHING.COM

www.ingramcontent.com/pod-product-compliance
Lightning Source LLC
LaVergne TN
LVHW060609110826
845154LV00003B/62

9781683369103